Global Comparative Management

To my life partner, Nidia, with love,
and in memory of my parents, Bror and Gunborg Edfelt

Global Comparative Management

A Functional Approach

Ralph B. Edfelt
San Jose State University

Los Angeles • London • New Delhi • Singapore • Washington DC

For information:

SAGE Publications, Inc.
2455 Teller Road
Thousand Oaks, California 91320
E-mail: order@sagepub.com

SAGE Publications India Pvt. Ltd.
B 1/I 1 Mohan Cooperative
    Industrial Area
Mathura Road, New Delhi 110 044
India

SAGE Publications Ltd.
1 Oliver's Yard
55 City Road
London EC1Y 1SP
United Kingdom

SAGE Publications Asia-Pacific Pte. Ltd.
33 Pekin Street #02-01
Far East Square
Singapore 048763

Printed in the United States of America

Library of Congress Cataloging-in-Publication Data

Edfelt, Ralph B.
Global comparative management : a functional approach/Ralph B. Edfelt.
    p. cm.
Includes bibliographical references and index.
ISBN 978-1-4129-4469-4 (cloth)
ISBN 978-1-4129-4470-0 (pbk.)
    1. Comparative management. I. Title.

HD30.55.E34 2009
658—dc22   2008036300

10   11   12   13   14   10   9   8   7   6   5   4   3   2   1

Acquisitions Editor:	Lisa Cuevas Shaw
Editorial Assistant:	MaryAnn Vail
Production Editor:	Carla Freeman
Copy Editor:	Carol Anne Peschke
Typesetter:	C&M Digitals (P) Ltd.
Proofreader:	Wendy Jo Dymond
Indexer:	Jeanne Busemeyer
Cover Designer:	Candice Harman
Marketing Manager:	Jennifer Reed Banando

Contents

Preface

It is impossible to study anything without at least implicitly comparing it with something else. Comparative analysis is a shift away from concentration on a unique organization, country, or culture toward seeking generalization about patterns of relationships in a variety of settings.

—K. J. Fukuda (1988, p. 23)

This book explores management in different national and regional settings. Its premise is that much insight and perspective can be gained from experiences elsewhere, essential for becoming an effective manager, employee, and citizen in a more interdependent world. It offers integrative and interdisciplinary coverage of managerial practice, issues, problems, and context in different countries and regions.

As time passes, few topics are more relevant. Advances in communication and transportation have shrunk the planet. Growth of cross-border trade, travel, information, and investment regularly exceeds that of world output. Consequently, more of us engage regularly with colleagues, partners, suppliers, subordinates, bosses, lenders, regulators, investors, educators, relatives, and others across national boundaries.

Globalization often blurs the distinction between what is local and what is not. For example, the quality control circle, an employee participation practice originating in the United States, was eventually seen as Japanese because of its wider application in Japan. Practices linked early on to large American corporations, such as financial evaluation tools (the DuPont system of financial control), decentralized organization structures (autonomous product and geographic area divisions), and CEO incentive pay, are becoming more common elsewhere. Also, long-held management stereotypes have been eroding. It is no longer so easy to view German managers as more technically oriented or Japanese and Swedish managers as more quality oriented (rather than mass production oriented) than their North American counterparts.

Nonetheless, managerial environment and practice are far from homogeneous. Significant variations in method and style persist in different regional and national settings. For example, North Americans tend to be more individualistic and self-reliant than most peoples. This contributes to more personalized CEO pay packages based on individual performance. Japanese CEOs are more group oriented and egalitarian, and they earn much less. Northern Europeans are more likely to include employees on company boards of directors, a practice far less common elsewhere. In East Asia, interfirm relational business networks help to overcome limitations of enterprise size and breadth. Nordic managers (in Sweden, Finland, Norway, and Denmark) are very collegial in their decision making, whereas their Latin European and Latin American peers tend to be more authoritarian.

Attention to these and other differences can improve our understanding of one another's mind-sets and actions and enhance organizational performance.

Throughout, this text brings significant historical context. On that score, Smith (2007) reminded management educators that "we often neglect to provide a foundation and understanding of the historical context of the times and theories we teach about. . . . In so doing we miss opportunity to think, critically and reflectively, about the past and its implications for the present" (p. 22).

This book draws from many sources, including scholarly books and articles and opinion and insight from practicing managers, consultants, and journalists. It is geared for students and practitioners of management and international business. It can be a stand-alone or complementary text for a course on comparative management or a supplement for management, international management, or global studies courses. In these contexts, it contributes the following:

- Improved interaction with colleagues, supervisors, investors, regulators, lenders, creditors, debtors, and others, in and from diverse settings

- Insight into alternative management styles, techniques, and approaches that could be adopted or adapted elsewhere

- Better understanding of whether, when, where, and why certain methods and style may need adjustment when tried in other settings

- Perspective on macroenvironmental change (e.g., economic, political, cultural) and its influence on management practice and performance

- Perspective on formal management education and how it varies in content and delivery worldwide

Each chapter starts with a succinct economic, political, and cultural overview of each setting. Then follows a look at the personal backgrounds and career paths of prototype CEOs. Attention then turns to the management process (i.e., to the functions of planning, organizing, controlling, and directing), a common framework used in management textbooks.

Chapter 1 looks at the field of management from a conceptual, temporal, and contextual perspective, including the evolution of management thought and theory. For some students, this will be their initial exposure to the subject of management; for others, it will be a useful review (or bring a different perspective). Apart from attending to management theory and terminology, it brings cultural terminology, economic and political typologies, and global macroenvironmental trends.

The other chapters focus on managerial context and practice in different national and regional settings.

Chapter 2 covers the United States, highlighting distinctive features of its macroenvironment and some prevalent patterns, strengths, limitations, and criticisms of American management. Additional points of comparison with other settings surface in other chapters.

Chapter 3 is about Western Europe, including 15 (of now 27) European Union nations plus Norway and Switzerland. It notes some intraregional differences in managerial context, values, behavior, practice, and style. Europe's social democratic traditions have much influenced management and employee relations practices, contributing to more employee involvement in decision making.

Chapter 4 reviews management practice and performance in the former Soviet Union. Although the Soviet era (1917–1990) is now history, the managerial lessons of state socialism apply today in any group (even in capitalist economies) where managerial decisions are made without guidance of markets, including inside work groups, departments, and divisions of private companies and in state-owned enterprises, public agencies, and nonprofit organizations.

Chapter 5 covers the strengths and limitations of employee control (management by democracy), a practice compatible with any social, economic, political, and cultural system. It is sometimes seen as the wave of the future in postindustrial societies becoming ever more oriented toward knowledge work. The chapter includes some historical context, including the national system of self-management prevalent in the former Yugoslavia before its breakup, and in diverse collectives, partnerships, and cooperatives in Europe, North America, and beyond.

Chapters 6 and 7 cover East Asia, which has the only non-Western nations other than oil exporters to have become affluent economies. Chapter 6 encompasses China, Taiwan, Hong Kong, Singapore, and South Korea, highlighting managerial patterns and challenges of South Korean *chaebol* enterprise groups and the network capitalism of private Chinese business at home and abroad. Chapter 7 covers the managerial traits, triumphs, and tribulations of Japan, an economic superpower whose management practices and patterns have been studied extensively for many years. Recent economic stagnation there has been contributing to social and economic change that is influencing managerial change.

Chapter 8 covers Latin America, about which little has been published in the management literature. This region is in transition from traditional family capitalism to modern managerial and financial capitalism, analogous to other emerging economies (e.g., in Africa and South Asia).

Through several short cases and exercises, a concluding chapter (Chapter 9) contemplates the future.

References

Fukuda, K. J. (1988). *Japanese management style transferred: The experience of East Asia.* London: Routledge.

Smith, G. (2007). Management history and historical context: Potential benefits of its inclusion in the management curriculum. *Academy of Management Learning & Education, 6*(4), 22.

Acknowledgments

Deep appreciation to Professor Barry Richman at UCLA, whose path-breaking work in comparative management inspired my career-long interest in the subject. To my students, thank you for all your attention and feedback over the years.

Thank you, current and former colleagues, for your suggestions and encouragement at different stages in this endeavor, especially Les Jankovich, Nakiye Boyacigiller, Mary Yoko Brannen, Frans Tempelaar, Mark Fruin, Randy Stross, Joyce Osland, and Carol Reade.

Thanks to the editing and production team at Sage (Al Bruckner, Lisa Cuevas Shaw, Carla Freeman, Carol Anne Peschke, and MaryAnn Vail) for their patience and professionalism. Thanks also to the following (previously anonymous) academic reviewers for their constructive critique of content, structure, and chapter drafts:

Stephen Blank
Pace University

Brian Boyd
Arizona State University

Kate Cooper
London Metropolitan University

Angelica Cortes
The University of Texas–Pan American

Dharma DeSilva
Wichita State University

Juan Espana
National University

Mark Fenton
University of Wisconsin, Stout

Gerald Fox
High Point University

Nigel Holden
Nottingham Trent University

David Hopkins
Daniels College of Business

Phil Hunsaker
University of San Diego

Alain Joly
HEC Montréal

Jill Kleinberg
The University of Kansas

Gido Mapunda
University of South Australia

Heinz-Dieter Meyer
University at Albany, State University of New York

Management

A Conceptual and Contextual Overview

1

> *The real reason for the absence of management teaching in our . . . schools is absence of theory. . . . The general public is not in a position to pass judgment on managerial activity, hence the importance of establishing a theory of management as soon as possible. . . . Light would soon be thrown on the subject as a result of comparison and discussion.*
>
> —Henri Fayol (1949, p. 14)[1]

This book is about comparative management, that is, the similarities and differences in management practice in different national and regional settings. This chapter provides some history, concepts, and terminology pursuant to that task. For some readers, it will be a beneficial review of the management discipline, and for others, it will be an introduction to managerial terminology and theory.

Chapter Objectives

- To describe management in conceptual, historical, and contextual perspective, highlighting some broad currents of related thought and theory

- To call attention to contingency factors (i.e., context) influencing managerial patterns, practice, and performance

- To distinguish between the international, cross-cultural, and comparative dimensions of management

Management: The social process of identifying and accomplishing group objectives (Adizes, 1971, p. 5).

Getting things done through and with people in organized groups.

Creating and maintaining an environment wherein people operating in groups can efficiently attain group purpose and objectives (Koontz, O'Donnell, & Weihrich, 1990, p. 4).

Purpose of   To make work productive, the worker achieving, and to improve the
management: quality of life (Drucker, 1973b, pp. 40–43).

Management occurs wherever people collaborate purposefully in groups, beginning with early hunter–gatherers up until modern-day business, government, educational, and other organizations. However, the recognition of management is recent, following the emergence of ever larger business organizations in the late 19th century.[2] By the mid-20th century, management had become a recognized process, task, role, and discipline worthy of widespread professional and scholarly attention. Its theory and practice now engage countless practitioners, educators, writers, trainers, consultants, and students worldwide.

Management   A framework for integrating management knowledge, aiming to describe,
theory: explain, guide, and improve practice, performance, and research.

Management   The application of management techniques, tools, approaches, procedures,
practice: methods, and style.

Management   Organizational effectiveness and efficiency; if group purpose and
performance: objectives are achieved, management is *effective;* if done with economy of resources and effort, it is *efficient.* Effectiveness is more important than efficiency, but both are necessary for long-run success.

Conceptual and Historical Perspective

History reminds us that theory is eminently practical in almost any area of human endeavor. For example, sea travel was long delayed by fear that ships would sail off the edge when the prevailing theory of terrestrial geography viewed the earth as flat. Improved theories of tidal movements, wind, and ocean currents brought better navigation and ship design. Modern chemistry would have evolved far more slowly without a coherent conception of atomic structure, as in the periodic table of the elements and quantum theory (particle physics). In economics, Adam Smith's (1776/1937) ideas about the power of free markets continue to influence national and international economic policy. Similarly, perceptive management theories can contribute to more effective and efficient economic, social, educational, government, and other organizations and enhance overall quality of life.

By comparison with most academic fields, modern management theory is diffuse and eclectic, a tangle of terminology and conceptual frameworks

(Donaldson, 1995; see also Koontz, 1961) narrow and broad, with roots and branches in diverse disciplines, including the social sciences (e.g., psychology, sociology, anthropology, political science, economics), quantitative and technical fields (e.g., mathematics, statistics, industrial engineering), and business administration. Pfeffer (1993, pp. 615–616) observed that organization theory "has a very large 'tent,'" including "diversity in ideas and methodology," its domain resembling "more of a weed patch than a well-tended garden." Its conceptual origin and evolution have been mainly North American and Western European. Although the conceptualization of management is recent, relevant terminology emerged earlier, such as ideas about unity of command and chain of command coming from military organizations (George, 1972; Wren, 1972).

This chapter traces broadly the evolution of management thought and theory from the early 20th century to the present day. Its thematic coverage includes the management process foundation and the contributions from social and behavioral sciences, management science, and systems and contingency theory.

THE MANAGEMENT PROCESS (MANAGEMENT FUNCTIONS)

The management process perspective is also called the classical or functional view of management. Its conceptual origin comes from practicing managers (manager authors) rather than management professors. There were few management professors until management became an established academic discipline, mainly after 1950.

The most famous forerunner was Frederick Winslow Taylor (a production manager, industrial engineer, and consultant), who wrote what can be called the first book focused on management, *The Principles of Scientific Management,* in 1911. Taylor systematically studied work processes (time and motion studies) in pursuit of manufacturing efficiency. Industrial engineers of his time conceived techniques for the orderly planning and control of complex tasks and projects, including time-event tracking tools (e.g., the Gantt chart, named for creator Henry Gantt, and forerunner of network models such as the Program Evaluation and Review Technique). Taylorist thinking eventually gave rise to management science.

Taylor's book was unique in conceptualizing some distinct managerial functions, which he perceived to be planning, training, selecting, and controlling.

Another pioneer manager–author was Henri Fayol (general manager of a French mining and metallurgical firm), who wrote *General and Industrial Administration* (1916). He too suggested some management functions such as planning, organizing, commanding, coordinating, and controlling. These and similar lists were revised and refined over the years by others. Table 1.1 presents an updated example.

Table 1.1   The Management Functions (Management Process)

Management Function	Definition
Planning	The process of setting objectives and choosing from among alternative ways to achieve them
Organizing	The integration and coordination of resources and effort, attending to organization structure and flow of information and authority
Controlling	The process of measuring and correcting performance, that is, comparing results with objectives and adjusting actions or plans as needed
Directing	The influencing and guiding of human resources (includes leadership, communication, motivation)
Staffing	The identification, selection, recruitment, evaluation, and development of managers

NOTE: Other proposed managerial functions include *integrating* and *coordinating* (these are more usually included in organizing), *decision making* (usually part of planning but permeates all the management functions), and *representing* the organization to its external constituents (e.g., community, government, public interest groups, investors).

Peter Drucker

No person has influenced management thought and practice more than Peter Drucker (1909–2005). Born and raised in Europe, he immigrated to the United States at age 28 and developed a long professional life as a consultant, professor, and author. Drucker was neither a practicing manager nor a typical professor but was much sought out for his insight and wisdom about management practice. He had an acute awareness of the changing societal context in which management evolves. Drucker wrote little for academic journals and produced few textbooks but served a much broader audience. (However, his books and articles are read in many business and management courses.) His most comprehensive work was *Management: Tasks, Responsibilities, Practices* (1973b), which described many contributors to management thought, theory, and practice. Its coverage reflects the classic tradition (i.e., management process and functions). For example, in identifying "five operations in the work of a manager" (pp. 400–401) Drucker described the management process, including the setting of objectives and preparations to attain them (i.e., *planning*), organizing, motivation and communication (*directing*), measurement and performance appraisal (*control*), and choosing and developing people (*staffing*).

The management functions are viewed as generic and universal, that is, pertinent to all purposeful group endeavor regardless of economic system, ideology, polity, country, era, or culture. Over the years, they became the dominant framework for structuring introductory management textbooks. In effect, they guide many academic programs in business. In U.S. business schools, for instance, the subject of planning is covered in operation management courses and in the capstone business strategy course. Insights and tools for control are covered in accounting, finance, and quantitative method courses. Organizing shows up in all management courses and is perhaps the most discussed theme in the academic management literature. Directing is the focus of organization behavior and organization development courses. Staffing is covered in human resource management courses.

The management functions are not the same as organizational task functions; the latter are more institution specific. For example, the task functions in a business include finance, accounting, production, and marketing. University business degree programs commonly require a package of courses (called a specialization, concentration, or major) focused on a particular business function (e.g., marketing, finance). The task functions of a university include instruction, research, administration, and advising. In a hospital, they might include emergency services, pediatrics, obstetrics and gynecology, surgery, and internal medicine. However, in all organizations (e.g., businesses, universities, hospitals), the management functions are the same.[3]

If management is a true academic and professional discipline, it follows that its practice and performance should be grounded in fundamental laws or principles analogous to the natural laws that underpin the physical sciences. That idea surfaced in the books by Frederick W. Taylor (1911) and Henri Fayol (1916), including in Taylor's *The Principles of Scientific Management.*

Fayol's work presented 14 principles of management, including chain of command (a clear vertical line of authority with accountability to just one superior). He also mentioned esprit de corps, discipline, stability of tenure, equity, and initiative. Today, these are viewed more as buzzwords than carefully conceived and tested propositions. Because management is a soft discipline (i.e., not rigorous like the physical sciences), there will never be consensus about fundamental principles (as is true for all social science disciplines, e.g., political science, sociology, and history). Nonetheless, some proposed ones can yield insight into managerial practice and decision making (Table 1.2).

It has been argued (Heugens, 2005) that Max Weber's *Wirtschaft und Gesellschaft* (1920s) gave rise to organization studies as a self-contained discipline.[4] Weber (1864–1920) was a German social scientist interested in sociology, economics, and public administration. He famously articulated

Table 1.2   Principles of Management

Principle of parity of authority and responsibility	Responsibility for actions cannot be greater than that implied by the authority delegated, nor should it be less. (In essence, if someone is responsible for achieving results, he or she should be delegated sufficient authority to achieve them.)
Principle of unity of command	The more often a person reports to a single superior, the more likely it is that the person will feel a sense of loyalty and obligation and the less likely there is to be confusion about instruction.
The commitment principle (related to the time horizon for planning)	Logical planning encompasses a future period of time necessary to fulfill, through a series of actions, the commitments involved in a decision made today.
The span of management principle (in organizing)	In each managerial position, there is a limit to the number of people an individual can effectively manage, but the exact number varies according to the impact of underlying variables.
Harmony of objectives principle (in leadership)	The more managers can harmonize the personal goals of people with the goals of the enterprise, the more effective and efficient the enterprise will be.

SOURCE: Adapted from Koontz et al. (1990).

the value of more rational–legal organizational structures (i.e., bureaucracy) when organizations grow large. Formal bureaucracy can bring more efficiency and fairness (more logical and impartial division of labor based on technical competence) to structures previously grounded on traditional authority (that of kings, popes, and family patriarchs). For Weber, bureaucracy seemed foreordained, a natural progression when organizations grew large, akin to a principle of organization.

BEHAVIORAL CONTRIBUTIONS TO MANAGEMENT THEORY

Over the years, the management process perspective was much enhanced by social and behavioral theory. Its contributions have drawn heavily from the social sciences (e.g., psychology, sociology, social anthropology) especially as they relate to themes of leadership, motivation, conflict resolution, and communication. These gave rise to the fields of organization behavior (OB) and organization development (OD) (see French & Bell, 1984; Hersey & Blanchard, 1972).

Organization behavior (OB): A subset of management theory dealing with individual and group behavior in organizations, involving human relations skills, communication, motivation, cooperation, leadership, organization values (personal and group), social processes, and group culture

Organization development (OD): The application of behavioral science methods to improve organizational processes; can involve intervention by corporate trainers and consultants to facilitate change and improve internal communication (therapy for organizations)

Significant early behavioral impetus came from experiments done at the Hawthorne plant of the Western Electric Company in Illinois (the Hawthorne Studies, 1924–1932), where telephone component assemblers were exposed (by design) to changing physical conditions of work (e.g., to illumination, ventilation, rest) in order to assess implications for productivity. As physical changes were made (for better and worse), performance generally improved. Australian Elton Mayo (Harvard psychology professor) and others attributed this effect not mainly to the physical changes per se but rather to the degree of personal attention given the participants (the original Hawthorne effect). The results suggested that tight supervision and incentive pay alone wouldn't ensure superior performance and that the psychosocial dimensions of work and work groups were also important (Roethlisberger & Dickson, 1939).

In 1938, Chester Barnard, CEO of New Jersey Bell Telephone, authored *Functions of the Executive,* portraying the corporation as a social system that required balance between human social influences and organizational processes and goals. He viewed communication and leadership as keys to gaining employee commitment, cooperation, and loyalty.

In the 1940s, the Tavistock Institute of Human Relations (London) explored the relationship between social and technical dimensions of work (a sociotechnical systems perspective).[5] This inspired future experiments in worker participation, including semiautonomous work teams at Sweden's Volvo Corporation and other examples of workplace democracy in the United States, Europe, and beyond.

Behavioral thinking (from behavioral economics, cognitive psychology, and group social dynamics) permeated Herbert Simon's (1945/1997) *Administrative Behavior* and Simon and March's *Organizations* in 1958. Subsequently, Cyert and March's (1963) *Behavioral Theory of the Firm* addressed the human limitations of rational decision making in a complex and changing world.[6]

MANAGEMENT SCIENCE

In the 1940s, management science (also called operations research [OR]) emerged as a new subcurrent of management theory and practice, gaining impetus from British military applications during World War II (see Ackhoff & Rivett, 1963). This included mathematical and statistical techniques for decision making such as choosing optimal plant locations and designing production supply chains, distribution networks, and other quantifiable problems (see Lee, 1983). Business students today study management science tools in their quantitative method courses (some are listed in Table 1.3).

Table 1.3   Examples of Management Science (Operations Research) Tools and Techniques

Quantitative Methods, Applied Statistics	
Probability analysis	Break-even analysis
Queuing (waiting line) theory	Time series projection
Correlation analysis	Linear programming
Regression analysis	Gaming methods
Simulation	Inventory ordering and control models

Management science can be very useful but has limitations for many subjective nonquantifiable decisions that require seasoned wisdom, judgment, and intuition, such as those in the conception of organizational purpose, business strategies, and human resource selection.

A conceptual overview of the aforementioned broad currents of management theory is provided in Figure 1.1.

In the decades that followed, this foundation (management process, behavioral contributions, management science) was enhanced by attention to contextual dimensions of management, as in systems and contingency perspectives.

CONTEXTUAL DIMENSIONS OF MANAGEMENT

Most people will agree that management decisions and actions are influenced by context. In that regard, systems and contingency perspectives call attention to diverse factors, forces, relationships, and interdependencies within organizations and between these and the community and society (Figure 1.2).

Origins		
Pre-1920	**Late 1920s and Early 1930s**	**Early 1940s**
Classic Theory: The Management Functions	*Behavioral Contributions*	*Management Science*
Conception of the management process	Human relations Focus on the function of directing (leadership, communication, and motivation)	Quantitative methods, mathematical models, simulation Operations research Systems perspective Focus on decision making, planning, and control
Representative Terms, Concepts, Ideas		
Management functions (e.g., planning, organizing, controlling) Specialization and division of labor Pay-based productivity incentives Span of control Chain of command Unity of command Principles of management	Authority Power Influence Organization behavior Organization development Organization culture Leadership theory	Network modeling (e.g., Program Evaluation and Review Technique, Critical Path Method) Project management Management information systems Quantitative tools and techniques • Breakeven analysis • Inventory models • Linear programming • Queuing theory
Conceptual Roots		
Industrial engineering The experience of practicing managers	Behavioral sciences • Sociology • Psychology • Anthropology	Decision criteria Mathematics Statistics Computer science Industrial engineering Cybernetics Systems theory
Forerunners		
Frederick Taylor (scientific management, shop floor productivity) Henri Fayol (general management) Max Weber (rational bureaucracy)	Elton Mayo (Hawthorne experiments) Hugo Munsterberg (industrial psychology)	British military applications during World War II Frederick Taylor (scientific management)

Figure 1.1   Core Currents of Management Thought and Theory

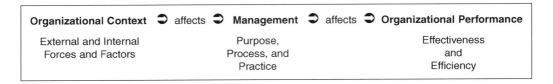

Figure 1.2   Context and Management

Systems Perspective

> A system is a whole which is defined by its function in a larger system. It consists of essential parts, each of which can affect the functioning of the whole, but none of which has an independent effect on the whole. (Ackhoff, 2002, p. 60)

Systems theory provides an integrated way to conceptualize a problem, project, process, or decision. Any organization (e.g., club, charity, company, university) can be seen as an integrated system, that is, a whole composed of interactive subsystems (e.g., divisions, departments, work units, projects, processes, people, subcultures). All human organizations are open systems, that is, influenced by their suprasystem (e.g., markets, industry, competition, community, country, culture). The organization, in turn, can influence its suprasystem.

The systems perspective can be useful for contemplating potential direct and indirect consequences of managerial action or inaction. For example, a company that is facing declining profits may see a quick solution in reducing labor costs and may begin layoffs. However, layoffs may affect employee morale, triggering preemptive departure of key personnel, creating a staffing problem. With loss of key people, external investors may get nervous, generating a financing problem, and so on. Systems thinking forces reflection about true sources of problems and the potential internal and external repercussions of any proposed managerial decision or action (or the lack thereof).[7]

Formal systems theory emerged in the 1940s and 1950s by way of the biological sciences (von Bertalanffy, 1950) and cybernetics (Boulding, 1956; Churchman, 1968; Weiner, 1950).

Contingency Perspective

The contingency view of management calls attention to situational factors, both internal and external to the organization, that can influence management process, practice, and performance. It suggests that the most effective management practice depends much on context and circumstance.

This view was apparent in Englishwoman Joan Woodward's 1958 study of the relationship between types of production technology (e.g., batch, assembly line, continuous flow) and organization structure in British manufacturing firms. She found fewer organization levels and wider spans of control (number of subordinates per manager) in batch technology enterprises (e.g., custom-made furniture) and assembly-line production (e.g., automobile engines) than in continuous-flow production (e.g., petrochemical plants). Her results suggested that the appropriate organizational structure depends on the production technology.

Contingency thinking is evident throughout the post-1950 management literature. For example, behavioralists Tannenbaum and Schmidt (1958) discussed leadership style in terms of a continuum ranging from authoritarian (managers announce their decisions without input from subordinates) to democratic (all bottom up). In their view, the most effective style depends on the characteristics of both the leaders and followers and on situational context. Fiedler (1967) viewed the appropriate leadership style as being situational depending on the nature of the task, the position power of the leader, and leader–member relations.

Alfred Chandler's (1962) study of structural change in major U.S. businesses tracked how circumstance (e.g., growth, strategic direction, competition) can lead to a shift away from structures centered around business functions (e.g., marketing, manufacturing, finance) to divisions based on product group or geographic market.

A contingency perspective permeated Lawrence and Lorsch's (1969) analysis of organizational differentiation (segmentation or division of labor) and integration (interunit coordination) in the plastics, container, and packaged foods sectors. They concluded that there was no one best way to structure and that "states of differentiation and integration in effective organizations can differ, depending on their environment" (p. 108). For instance, in a narrow–product line company in a stable industry (e.g., container manufacturing), organization structures remain undifferentiated, but in an industry experiencing rapid change (at the time, plastics), differentiation and integration contributed to more complex structures.

Table 1.4 lists several generic forces and factors external and internal to an organization that can directly or indirectly influence its managerial decisions and actions. These should be viewed as interdependent and in constant flux.

Global views of management invariably draw from contingency perspectives, as Peter Drucker (1973a) mentioned:

> Management concepts . . . and, above all, management tasks are the same the world over. . . . But there are very real differences when it comes to management structure and management career ladders, management values and management objectives, management policies, and management attitudes; these cannot be divorced from the economy, the society, the political tradition, and the general culture in which business and management live and of which they are a part. (p. 236)

Table 1.4   Generic Contingency Forces and Factors That Influence Management
                 Decisions and Actions

External Forces, Factors, and Constraints (National and International)	Factors, Forces, and Constraints Internal to the Organization
Economic	Organization purpose
Political and legal	Strategies
Ideological	Structure
Technological	Resources
Demographic	Strengths
Sociological	Weaknesses
Sociocultural	Experience
Educational	Scale and scope of operations
Other	Pace of growth
	Knowledge, skills, experience, and personal qualities of members
	Organization culture
	Synergies

According to Geert Hofstede (1993):

There is something in all countries called "management," but its meaning
differs to a larger or smaller extent from one country to the other, and it
takes considerable historical and cultural insight into local conditions to
understand its processes, philosophies, and problems. . . . Management is
not a phenomenon that can be isolated from other processes taking place in
a society. (pp. 88–89)

Global Context

The globalization of business has broadened interest in the international,
cross-cultural, and comparative dimensions of management.

International management is practiced wherever the management
process transcends national boundaries. For example, Intel Corporation
(U.S.) mobilizes, develops, transfers, and maintains resources worldwide

for the design, manufacture, and distribution of microprocessors and other digital computing products. In 2006, one third of its net property, plant, and equipment and almost half of its 94,000 employees were outside U.S. borders. Its operations included wafer fabrication plants in Ireland and Israel and assembly and test operations in Malaysia, the Philippines, China, and Costa Rica. It performed research and development in Israel, Malaysia, India, China, and Russia. It has depended on thousands of non-U.S. suppliers and subcontractors and is served by sales units and licensed distributors around the globe. Its 2007 global sales revenue was divided as follows: Asia-Pacific (51%), the Americas (20%), Europe (19%), and Japan (10%).

International management is invariably more complex than managing within a single country. For example, hiring decisions must consider linguistic and intercultural competence along with technical and professional ability. Planners must assess more information and respond to more diverse political, cultural, and economic pressures. Key information is commonly less available or less timely. National and local governments can intrude on company plans and planning. The extra complexity and uncertainty can lead to more frequent revisions of plans and more contingency planning. When designing organization structures, firms must balance country and region factors with product and function factors. It is more difficult to decide which tasks and decisions to decentralize to subordinate units and which to control centrally at headquarters.

Management is a social and political process influenced by societal culture. *Cross-cultural (or intercultural) management* refers to management and organizational processes involving culturally diverse groups. Leadership, motivation, and communication are influenced by the diverse mind-sets, values, attitudes, beliefs, norms, expectations, traditions, and behavior of culturally diverse participants. This occurs in Swiss-based Nestlé Corporation, for example, which has 95% of its operations outside Switzerland. In 2008, its senior management team (a 13-person executive board) included nine nationalities. Similarly, in Europe's Airbus Industrie an 11-member executive committee included French, German, English, Scottish, U.S., and Spanish nationals; these in turn interact with other managers, engineers, public officials, customers, creditors, and suppliers from various countries. In central Ohio, Japanese and U.S. nationals jointly manage Honda auto and motorcycle assembly plants, with intercultural dimensions coming into play. And in Saudi Arabia, the Bechtel Corporation (U.S.) has managed the construction of an industrial city (Jubail) involving more than 700 subcontractors and 40,000 workers from more than 40 countries. In Malaysia, indigenous Malays work with Chinese and Indic Malays.

The field of *comparative management* is concerned with similarities and differences in management methods, practice, style, and behavior in different settings. Such comparisons can be useful for assessing whether, how, when, or why patterns, practices, methods, and styles being tried in one setting could or should be adopted or adapted elsewhere. For instance, German law requires large companies to have employee representation on company boards of directors, raising the question of whether this practice might be suitable or desirable in other countries.

SOCIETAL CULTURE AND MANAGEMENT

Societal culture influences all human activity, including management. Through lifelong *enculturation* by family, school, workplace, community, and mass media, people continually acquire and modify personal values, attitudes, beliefs, and behaviors. When engaged in another culture, they *acculturate* to a greater or lesser degree; that is, they adopt or adapt to local patterns.

Intercultural encounters can also cause *culture shock,* a psychological response (e.g., surprise, discomfort, disorientation, amusement, puzzlement, fear, or frustration) experienced when perceptions deviate from expectations.

Table 1.5 briefly reviews some cultural terminology used in this book.

Table 1.5   Cultural Terminology

Definitions
Culture: "The collective programming of the mind that distinguishes one human group from another" (Hofstede, 2001, p. 9). Can refer to any group, such as a family, neighborhood, classroom, work unit, nation-state, or religion.
Ethnocentrism: The belief that one's own cultural patterns are fundamentally more normal, more universal, or better than others.
Components of Culture
Values: Ideas or viewpoints of fundamental importance (e.g., preference for monogamy over polygamy in marriage, degree of loyalty to be given one's leader, or degree of importance given to personal connections and family ties in hiring and promotion decisions).
Attitudes: Disposition toward or opinion about something (e.g., about work, wealth, age, gender roles, risk, change).
Beliefs: Perceptions of reality or truth.
Norms: Accepted patterns or standards of behavior.
Behavior: Human conduct, as reflected in personal manners, customs, and actions.

Hofstede's Dimensions of Culture

Dutch organizational anthropologist Geert Hofstede is renowned for developing a conceptual framework for comparing and interpreting cultures.

His terminology is used throughout this book. Hofstede's original work conceived four cultural dimensions (Table 1.6) based on data from 116,000 IBM employees (in about 40 countries) collected by that company in the 1970s (for other purposes).[8] With a numerical scoring system, he rank-ordered countries and classified them as high, medium, or low on each dimension (examples in Table 1.7). A fifth dimension (long-term time orientation) was added several years later (Hofstede & Bond, 1988).

In reference to his scoring system, Hofstede (1993) made the following observations:

> The table shows that each country has its own configuration on the four dimensions. Some of the values . . . have been estimated based on imperfect replications or personal impressions. The different dimension scores do not "explain" all the differences in management. . . . To understand management in a country, one should have both knowledge of and empathy with the entire local scene. However, the scores should make us aware that people in other countries may think, feel and act very differently from us when confronted with basic problems of society. (p. 90)

Table 1.6   Hofstede's Dimensions of Culture

Power distance (high vs. low)	The extent to which individuals in a society (culture, group) accept personal inequality in power
Individualism	The degree to which people identify and act more as individuals rather than as members of a group and to which private personal interests (i.e., self and immediate family) take precedence over collective ones (e.g., company, clan, or other group affiliation)
Masculinity	The degree to which tough values (e.g., assertiveness, aggressiveness, ambition, material success, competition) prevail over tender ones (e.g., concern for quality of life, warm and caring personal relationships, care for the weak)
Uncertainty avoidance (high vs. low)	The extent to which people accept and deal effectively with unstructured, unclear, or unpredictable situations
Long-term orientation (high vs. low)	The degree to which people are oriented toward the future (e.g., save their money or plan) rather than the past and present (e.g., respect for tradition and fulfillment of social obligations)

SOURCE: Hofstede (2001).

Table 1.7   Hofstede's Cultural Dimension Scores for 10 Countries

	Power Distance	Individualism	Masculinity	Uncertainty Avoidance	Long-Term Orientation
United States	40L	91H	62H	46L	29L
Germany	35L	67H	66H	65M	31M
Japan	54M	46M	95H	92H	80H
France	68H	71H	43M	86H	30*L
Netherlands	38L	80H	14L	53M	44M
Hong Kong	68H	25L	57H	29L	96H
Indonesia	78H	14L	46M	48L	25*L
West Africa	77H	20L	46M	54M	16L
Russia	95*H	50*M	40*L	90*H	10*L
China	80*H	20*L	50*M	60*M	118*H

SOURCE: Hofstede (1984b).
*Estimated.
H = top third; L = bottom third; M = middle third.

Hofstede has also suggested several business and management implications of these variables (Table 1.8).

High- Versus Low-Context Cultures

Another conceptual framework for classifying and analyzing culture is from Edward Hall (1959, 1976), who distinguished between high-context and low-context cultures on the basis of patterns in communication, personal relationships, and attitudes toward time (Tables 1.9 and 1.10). For example, in low-context cultures (e.g., northern Europe, United States), verbal communications are more often explicit and must be interpreted more literally. By contrast, messages in high-context settings (e.g., Mediterranean Europe, Middle East, Latin America) are more often implicit than in low-context ones. Their meanings must more often be interpreted from contextual clues (i.e., body language, nonverbal signals) rather than directly from the words. For example, an expressed "yes" from a Japanese executive may mean "no" when accompanied by other signals (Imai, 1975; Ueda, 1978).

Table 1.8   Some Suggested Implications of Hofstede's Variables in Work Organizations

Low Power Distance	High Power Distance
Decentralized decision structures; less concentration of authority.	Centralized decision structures; more concentration of authority.
Flat organization pyramids.	Tall organization pyramids.
Subordinates expect to be consulted.	Subordinates expect to be told.
The ideal boss is a resourceful democrat; sees self as practical, orderly, and relying on support.	The ideal boss is a well-meaning autocrat or good father; sees self as benevolent decision maker.

Low Individualism	High Individualism
Relatives of employer and employee preferred in hiring.	Family relationships seen as a disadvantage in hiring.
Poor performance reason for other tasks.	Poor performance reason for dismissal.
Less social mobility across occupations.	Greater social mobility across occupations.
In business, personal relationships prevail over task and company.	In business, task and company prevail over personal relationships.
Direct appraisal of performance is a threat to harmony.	Direct appraisal of performance improves productivity.

Low Uncertainty Avoidance	High Uncertainty Avoidance
Weak loyalty to employer; short average duration of employment.	Strong loyalty to employer; long average duration of employment.
Innovators feel independent of rules.	Innovators feel constrained by rules.
Belief in generalists and common sense.	Belief in specialists and expertise.
Power of superiors depends on position and relationships.	Power of superiors depends on control of uncertainties.

Low Masculinity	High Masculinity
Work in order to live.	Live in order to work.
Stress on equality and quality of work life.	Stress on equity, mutual competition, and performance.
More women in management.	Fewer women in management.
Resolution of conflicts through problem solving, compromise, and negotiation.	Resolution of conflicts through denying them or fighting until the best man wins.

SOURCE: Excerpted from Hofstede (2001, pp. 107, 108, 169, 244, 245).

Table 1.9   High- and Low-Context Cultures

Low Context	High Context
Northern European (Nordic, Germanic) and Anglo Cultures (United States, United Kingdom, Canada, Australia, New Zealand)	**Arab, Greek, Latin European, Latin American, Sinitic (Chinese, Korean, Japanese), and Indic cultures**
• Personal communications are more explicit more often than in high-context cultures.	• Personal communications are more often implicit and indirect than in low-context cultures; the full meaning of a message must more often be deduced from indirect contextual signals (body language, voice intonation, "reading between the lines") that accompany the words.
• Social relationships tend to be more impersonal; for example, business relations rely more on formal agreements (e.g., detailed written contracts).	• Relationships and commitments tend to be less formal and more personalized; more importance is put on interpersonal rapport, trust, and commitment; there is less reliance on formal written agreements.
• Time is more structured, more measured (monochronic view of time); punctuality is valued.	• Time is viewed as flexible (polychronic).

SOURCE: Conceptualized from Hall (1976).

Japanese Phrase That Says "No"	Interpretation by a Typical American
"That would be very hard to do."	Some adjustments are necessary, but the idea is still possible.
"I shall give it careful consideration."	Even more attention will be given.
"I'll do my best, but I'm in a delicate position."	It will be extremely tricky, but she or he will give it a shot.

Table 1.10 identifies several cultural clusters (multicountry groupings that share similar characteristics) and positions them on a spectrum from low to high. The Germanic, Nordic, and Anglo cultural clusters are at the low end of the spectrum (Germanic is lowest). On the high end are the Latin, Confucian, and Arab cultures (Arab is highest).

Hall's distinction has considerable business and management implications. For example, businesses in lower-context cultures tend to

Table 1.10   Cultural Clusters on a Continuum From Low to High Context

Low-Context Cultures		High-Context Cultures
◄——— Lower		Higher ———►
Germanic		Arab
Scandinavian (Nordic)		Confucian
	Anglo	Latin

SOURCE: Conceptualized from Hall (1959, 1976).

rely more, and more often, on formal contractual agreements and do more formal planning; in hiring and promotion they are likely to focus more on candidates' ability and performance rather than on their social connections (less nepotism and favoritism). There is a greater tendency to delegate authority (i.e., to extend decision-making rights to subordinates) rather than to control everything from the top.

The cultural frameworks of Geert Hofstede and Edward Hall used in this chapter (and throughout the book) won't preclude occasional reference to other cultural perspectives (see Kluckhohn & Strodtbeck, 1961; Trompenaars, 1993). Both Hofstede and Hall were much influenced by the ideas and scholarship of others. Both are highlighted here as two of the most recognized frameworks (especially Hofstede; cf. Kirkman, Lowe, & Gibson, 2006). Hofstede's influence contributed to a more recent comprehensive cultural research project, the Global Leadership and Organization Behavior Effectiveness (GLOBE) study (see House, Hanges, Javidan, Dorfman, & Gupta, 2004), which expands and reformulates his cultural dimensions. One of the GLOBE features was to compare respondents' values both as they are and where they want them to be.

The nine cultural dimensions of the GLOBE study are described in Table 1.11.

Cultural Clusters

Cultural categories certainly don't conform neatly to national boundaries. For example, some countries (e.g., India, Malaysia) are multicultural, and some cultural typologies transcend individual countries. For example, Persian culture is associated with Iran but includes fringes of neighboring nations. Iran, via Islam, shares socioreligious customs and beliefs with Arab, Pakistani, Indonesian, and other Muslims. Japanese and Korean cultures show some similarities with Chinese culture (and have a common Confucian heritage).

Table 1.11   Descriptions of the Nine GLOBE Cultural Dimensions

	GLOBE Cultural Dimensions
Power distance	Degree to which a culture's people are (should be) separated by power, authority, and prestige
In-group collectivism	Degree to which a culture's people (should) take pride in and (should) feel loyalty toward their families, organizations, and employers
Institutional collectivism	Degree to which people are (should be) encouraged by institutions to be integrated into broader entities with harmony and cooperation as paramount principles at the expense of autonomy and individual freedom
Uncertainty avoidance	Degree to which a culture's people (should) seek orderliness, consistency, and structure (Note: Because of different definitions of this dimension, a high score on Hofstede's uncertainty avoidance corresponds to a low one on the GLOBE scale and vice versa.)
Future orientation	Degree to which a culture's people are (should be) willing to defer immediate gratification for future benefits
Gender egalitarianism	Degree to which a culture's people (should) support gender equality
Assertiveness	Degree to which a culture's people are (or should be) assertive, confrontational, and aggressive
Humane orientation	Degree to which a culture's people are (should be) fair, altruistic, generous, caring, and kind toward others
Performance orientation	Degree to which a culture's people (should) encourage and reward people for performance

SOURCE: House et al. (2004).

The commonality permits broader classification or cultural clustering. Examples are listed in Table 1.12 (see also Ronen & Shankar, 1985).

Of course, culture is not the only influence on management practice unless one concludes that all things are culturebound. Ajiferuke and Bodewyn (1970) make that point (see also Farmer & Richman, 1965):

> One must keep in mind that in explaining social phenomena (e.g., management), there is no such thing as "the" explanation. Instead, one can only argue that a particular explanation—cultural, economic, psychological, or social—explains more or better than any other . . . since management is a complex phenomenon reflecting the influence of many environmental factors and affecting them in turn. (p. 162)

Table 1.12 Examples of Cultural Clusters

Anglo	Peoples and countries much influenced by British history and culture (e.g., United Kingdom, United States, Canada, Australia, New Zealand).
Germanic	Of Germany, Austria, and ethnic German minorities in neighboring countries (e.g., Switzerland, Poland).
Nordic	Of Scandinavia (Sweden, Norway, Finland, Denmark, Iceland).
Latin European	Of European countries linguistically linked to the Latin language of ancient Rome (e.g., Italy, Spain, Portugal, France, southern Belgium).
Latin American	Western Hemisphere countries (e.g., Mexico, Argentina, Peru, Brazil) that have long-standing historical and cultural ties with Latin Europe.
Sinitic or Sinic	Chinese (predominantly Confucian) cultural roots (e.g., Taiwan, Hong Kong, the Korean peninsula, Singapore, Japan) plus emigrant ethnic Sinitic peoples around the globe (e.g., the Overseas Chinese and Overseas Koreans).
Indic	Of India and Sri Lanka plus emigrant Indic peoples (including descendants) residing in Malaysia, Indonesia, Polynesia, East Africa, and North America.
Islamic	Of Muslim socioreligious heritage (includes much of the Middle East and North Africa and parts of South and Southeast Asia).
Arab	Of the Arabian peninsula (e.g., Saudi Arabia, Yemen, Oman, Kuwait, Qatar, United Arab Emirates) and Arabic-speaking peoples in the Near East (e.g., Syria, Jordan, Iraq) and North Africa (e.g., Egypt, Libya, Algeria, Morocco); most Arab countries are also Islamic.

Similarly, Negandhi (1983) cautions against overemphasis on culture to the exclusion of other factors:

> If one is interested in understanding and explaining interfirm and inter-country differences in management practices and effectiveness . . . there is increasing evidence that management practices, behavior and effectiveness are as much, if not more, functions of such contextual and environmental variables as size, technology, location, and economic, market, and political conditions as they are of sociocultural variables. (p. 18)

Apart from attending to culture, this book also attends to economic and political influences, including to economic, political, demographic, sociocultural, and technological trends.

ECONOMIC SYSTEMS

Economic systems are societal arrangements about the ownership, production, distribution, and disposition of investment, labor, goods, services, and property. In the conceptual world, polar opposite economic systems would be unbridled economic freedom (no government ownership or intervention) and totalitarian central planning (state socialism; neither free markets nor private ownership).

Although all economies are somewhere in between these extremes, the broad trend (not always linear) since the end of the cold war has been toward more economic freedom. The following are some brief descriptions of a few (mainly capitalist) systems.

- A *free enterprise system, market economy,* or *capitalism* is grounded in private ownership and control of resources; it emphasizes economic freedom, competition, and private initiative but with many variations, including the following:

Laissez-faire capitalism:

By definition the freest possible system; implies very limited government intrusion in the economy. No economy is completely laissez faire, but some are closer than others. The 2007 Heritage Foundation Index of Economic Freedom (annual) classified the following economies (in order) as the world's freest: Hong Kong, Singapore, Australia, United States, New Zealand, United Kingdom, Ireland, Luxembourg, Switzerland, Canada. Its rankings were based on a composite index of business freedom, trade freedom, fiscal freedom, freedom from government, monetary freedom, investment freedom, financial freedom, property rights, freedom from corruption, and labor freedom.[9]

Welfare capitalism (or welfare state capitalism):

Refers to a market-guided economy combined with high taxation and state social spending relative to gross domestic product, as in Scandinavia, Germany, and France. It aims to enhance social and material equality but at some cost of private liberty (some intra-European variations are described in Chapter 3).

Guided free enterprise system:

Predominantly free market but with notable government guidance and support (tax and financial incentives, direction setting, preferential purchasing) for particular firms and industries, as seen in East Asia (Japan, South Korea, Singapore, Taiwan, and China; more coverage in Chapters 6 and 7).

Capitalist systems also come with other labels, such as *frontier capitalism* (seen in countries in transition from socialism to capitalism, e.g., Russia, Ukraine, China, Vietnam). Here, business institutions, rules, and traditions are unsettled; there continues to be high uncertainty about rule setting, law enforcement, protection of property rights, dispute resolution, corruption, and crime.

Another variant is *family capitalism* (as in Latin America and other emerging economies), where family-controlled businesses and business groups prevail in the private sector (as compared with the *managerial capitalism* of the United States, Western Europe, and Japan, where ownership and management have become more separated, at least in most large firms).

The term *stakeholder capitalism* has been applied to Western Europe and Japan, where constituents other than shareholders (e.g., labor, community, government) get substantial managerial attention; this contrasts with U.S. *stockholder capitalism* (*investor capitalism, financial capitalism*), in which shareholder or investor interests and concerns get the most attention.

The term *employee capitalism* applies to places where law and culture discourage layoffs of full-time employees; for example, continental Western Europe requires long advance notice and large severance payments. In some European countries, there is employee representation on company boards of directors (more discussion in Chapter 3); the term can apply also to Japan, where ownership interests (shareholder return) have traditionally been kept subordinate to jobholder interests (employment security).

The terms *alliance capitalism* and *convoy capitalism* have also been applied to Japan and South Korea in reference to their prominent business group alliances (the Japanese *keiretsu* and South Korean *chaebol;* more coverage in Chapters 6 and 7).

Crony capitalism is the term for a market economy much influenced by long-standing personal preferential business ties; the cronies can also include public officials and government regulators, inhibiting economic freedom and open competition. (*Crony* is a term applied to a trusted person such as a relative or long-standing acquaintance, client, colleague, or friend; cronyism is common in higher-context cultures, e.g., Confucian, Latin, Arab.)

Network capitalism is the term applied to intranational and cross-national relational business networks (network enterprises) of Chinese family-controlled businesses and variously to the Japanese *keiretsu* and South Korean *chaebol* (more coverage in Chapters 6 and 7).

- *Mixed economies* include a combination of private and state ownership or control; although all economies are mixed to a degree, the term usually refers to a high degree of state ownership. It applies certainly to *transition economies,* that is, ones moving from socialism to capitalism (contemporary Russia, China, and Vietnam and much of former Eastern Europe). The transition seldom goes from capitalism to socialism (recent exceptions include Venezuela and Bolivia, but their future is uncertain).

- *Socialist economic systems* emphasize ownership in common, that is, government ownership or control of productive resources in tandem with central government economic planning (as in Cuba, North Korea, the former Soviet Union, and prereform China); one variation is *market socialism,* which allows limited economic freedom, as in Soviet-era Hungary (its "new economic mechanism") and in Yugoslavia before its breakup. At the microlevel, socialism also applies to communal enterprise and to some producer cooperatives where ownership is held in common (no individual property rights).

POLITICAL SYSTEMS

These are the societal frameworks for political direction, doctrine, policy, behavior, rules, and action.

- *Democracy:* Decisions are made by popular vote, including cases in which everyone votes on a matter (*direct democracy*) or elected representatives make decisions (*indirect democracy*); most democracies are *secular,* that is, with government independent from religion. Democracies can be *pluralistic* (or not) by order of degree, that is, accommodate diverse parties, perspectives, and interests across a broad political spectrum. In some cases, a single political party may dominate (be reelected) for a long period (*dominant party democracy*), as in Japan (its Liberal Democratic Party), Singapore (People's Action Party), and recently Russia (United Russia party), where the state controls much of the media and impedes political rivals.

- *Nondemocratic* (authoritarian) regimes can be *secular* (government and religion are separated) or *theocratic* (government and politics are controlled by religious leaders and doctrine). Degree of authoritarianism can vary by regime.

Secular

Communist: Single-party monopoly (the Communist Party, e.g., in Cuba, North Korea, China, former Soviet Union); Communist Party domination of the media and the political system.

Fascist: Single-party control but some pluralism tolerable; mobilization by the state, when needed, of private sector resources and institutions, including business and labor; strong appeal to nationalism (national chauvinism), as seen in World War II Nazi Germany and Mussolini's Italy and in Iraq (Baathist Party) under Saddam Hussein.

Military: Military officers in charge, as in Myanmar (Burma), Pakistan (Musharraf era), and Thailand; a military government can also be fascist.

Hereditary: Political succession through monarchies (Jordan, Saudi Arabia) or sultanates (Brunei, Oman).

Theocratic

Government and politics are the domain of religious leaders and doctrine, as in Iran, Afghanistan (under the Taliban), and pockets of Islamic fundamentalism (e.g., northwest Pakistan).

GLOBAL ENVIRONMENTAL PATTERNS AND TRENDS

Contemporary economic and political systems are not islands unto themselves but rather influence (and are influenced by) national and global patterns and trends. Table 1.13 lists some contemporary global economic, political, demographic, cultural, and technological trends.

Table 1.13   Global Environmental Patterns and Trends (partial list)

Political	Continuing erosion of national sovereignty; ascendance of problems that require regional or cross-national cooperation (e.g., protection of the natural environment, free and fair international trade, regulatory and legal harmony, protection of intellectual property rights, control of armed conflict, cybercrime, drug trafficking, and terrorism). Persistent but uneven spread of Western political values (e.g., attention to human rights, democracy, rule of law).
Economic	Continuing dialogue about the proper role of government in the economy (e.g., degree of state ownership and control of resources, regulation, taxation, social spending (education, health insurance, old-age pensions). Free market–oriented economic policies have been ascendant (e.g., privatization, less regulatory intervention, freer trade, more exchange rate flexibility); more cross-border business competition and cooperation (mergers, alliances). Since World War II, cross-border trade and investment have grown more rapidly than world output (gross world product), and international investment has grown even more rapidly than trade. Ascendance of labor-intensive manufacturing activity in lower-labor-cost locations (China, Southeast Asia, India).

(Continued)

Table 1.13 (Continued)

Economic (continued)	Ascendance of more information- and knowledge-intensive employment in advanced industrial countries.
	Rapid post–World War II economic emergence of East Asia; rapid recent ascendance of Brazil, Mexico, Russia, India, and China.
	Continuing inequality in productivity, wealth, and income of countries; much of the world's population remains materially poor, but with modest recent improvement.
Demographic	Birth rates declining and median age rising in most countries.
	Population growth near zero in the advanced industrial countries (increasing mainly from immigration).
	Urban share of the world population is rising.
	Population growth rates are highest in the least-developed countries but are declining.
	Significant flow of human resource talent (brain drain) from the less developed countries to the more developed ones.
Social and Cultural	Increasing educational and occupational opportunities for women.
	Cross-border dissemination of popular culture.
	Persistent ethnic, cultural, and religious tensions.
Technological	Rapid evolution of information, communication, and biological technologies.

Chapter Summary

This chapter has discussed management from a historical, conceptual, and contextual perspective (see Figure 1.3 for a thematic overview) and has introduced relevant managerial, cultural, economic, and political terminology to be used in this book.

- Management is about getting things done through and with people in organized groups.
- The purpose and process (functions) of management are universal; however, management practice (e.g., methods, style) is influenced by organizational context (external environmental factors and forces and internal organizational factors).
- Management practice affects performance, that is, organizational effectiveness (attainment of group purpose and objectives) and efficiency (economy in the use of resources).

- Management emerged as an academic discipline in the 20th century, with conceptual contributions from diverse sources, settings, and disciplines. Therefore, its thought and theory are eclectic and multidisciplinary.

- The conceptual components of management theory summarized in this chapter include its classic foundation (management process, management functions), behavioral contributions, management science, and systems and contingency perspectives.

- The management process (management functions) is the most widely used structure for organizing general management courses, study programs, and textbooks.

Context

(interdependent factors and forces in continual flux)

External Environmental Factors ↔ **Internal Organizational Factors**		
(national, regional and global)		

Cultural	Organizational culture (e.g., values, attitudes),	
Economic	competencies, and circumstance	
Political	Resources	Size
Legal	- Physical	Pace of growth
Ideological	- Financial	Previous performance
Social	- Technical	Strengths
Educational	- Information	Weaknesses
Technological	Knowledge	Organization culture
Demographic	Skills	Experience
Other		

Affects

Management Purpose, Process, and Practice

Organization Purpose	**Process** (functions)			**Practice**
	Planning			Style
Vision	Organizing			Approach
Mission ↔	Controlling	Judgment and ↔		Tools
Long-term	Directing	intuition (i.e., the		Behavior
objectives	(influencing)	ability to analyze		Techniques
Broad	- Leadership	and decide wisely)	↔	Methods
strategies	- Communication			Procedures
	- Motivation			
	Staffing			

Affects

Management Performance

Effectiveness (achievement of purpose and objectives) and **Efficiency** (economy in the use of resources)

Figure 1.3   Conceptual and Contextual Overview of Management

The remaining chapters focus on comparative management, that is, on similarities and differences in management practice and environment in different national, cultural, and regional settings.

Each chapter begins with an overview of the economic, political, and sociocultural setting, followed by an overview of managers and managerial tendencies. The management process (management functions) is the main framework for coverage of management practice.

Terms and Concepts

acculturation	intercultural management
comparative management	international management
contingency approach	management
cultural cluster	management functions
culture	management practice
effectiveness	management principles
efficiency	management science
enculturation	management theory
forms of capitalism	mixed economy
forms of socialism	organization behavior (OB)
Frederick W. Taylor	organization development (OD)
global environmental trends	Peter Drucker
Henri Fayol	systems approach
high-context versus low-context	types of economic systems
culture	types of political systems
Hofstede's dimensions of culture	

Study Questions

1. Define management and explain its social and economic significance.

2. Distinguish between management process, practice, performance, and environment.

3. Identify and discuss several broad currents of management theory (in terms of their origin, focus, concepts, pioneers).

4. "Managers are not taught in formal education programs what they most need to know to build successful careers in management." Discuss.

5. In your judgment, to what extent are management decisions and actions influenced by contextual factors or forces (organizational and societal environment) rather than individual free will?

6. Identify cultural patterns (e.g., values, attitudes, beliefs, behaviors) integral to a culture that is significantly different from your own. What might be some managerial implications of those differences?

7. Distinguish between at least three cultural clusters (groups of countries based on cultural commonalities).

8. Identify a global macroenvironmental trend or trends (economic, political, demographic, technological, social, other) other than the ones listed in Table 1.13.

Exercise 1.1

Review the table of contents, preface, and initial section or chapter of an introductory management textbook. How is management defined? Describe the topical framework the author uses to organize the material.

Exercise 1.2

One element of managerial control (in business, government, or elsewhere) is formal and informal evaluation of individual or group performance by administrative higher-ups. In many cases, feedback comes even coworkers and subordinates and from customers and suppliers. This approach is sometimes called *360-degree performance appraisal.* It is not uncommon in Anglo culture (e.g., at Dell Computer, AT&T, General Electric, Ford Europe, and several large British and Australian companies).

It occurs at U.S. universities where the professors and administrative staff periodically evaluate their department heads and school deans. Individual tenure-track professors are evaluated by their colleagues (individually or by committee) and by students. And in some classes, the students evaluate other students' performance in class.

In view of the differences in culture articulated by Hofstede and Hall, to what degree do you think 360-degree performance appraisal could be effectively used in business, education, or government institutions in non-Anglo settings (e.g., Indic, Chinese, Latin, Nordic)? Why or why not? Explain.

Exercise 1.3

From the list of global macroenvironmental trends (economic, political, demographic, technological, social, other) in Table 1.13, discuss some potential implications of one or more of them for an organization familiar to you (e.g., your current or former employer or university) or for your career.

Notes

1. Fayol (1949) was translated from Fayol (1916).

2. For an interpretive overview of the 20th-century management boom, see Chapter 2 in Drucker (1973b).

3. An alternative way to conceptualize management was offered in 1973 by Henry Mintzberg (McGill University, Canada), who observed that although managers plan, organize, and control, this doesn't tangibly describe what they do. Based on a systematic observation of managers over time, he conceptualized three key managerial roles (and corollary subroles): interpersonal (figurehead, leader, liaison), informational (monitor, disseminator, spokesman), and decisional (entrepreneur, disturbance handler, resource allocator, negotiator).

4. This and other Weber works were collected, revised, and published posthumously. His writings on bureaucracy first appeared in English in Henderson and Parsons (1947).

5. The research and practice of the Tavistock Institute revolve around the work of Eric Trist and Fred Emery (see Pasmore & Khalsa, 1993).

6. For a comprehensive overview and analysis of management research of the behavioral dimensions of management, see Miner (2006, Vol. 2).

7. Systems thinking is integral to Katz and Kahn (1966). See also Johnson, Kast, and Rosenzweig (1973).

8. Hofstede's conceptual schema and country scores have been widely published and cited. See Hofstede (1980, 1984b, 1993, 2001).

9. Information on the Heritage Foundation criteria, scoring, and latest annual rankings can be found at http://www.heritage.org/research/features/index/.

References

Ackhoff, R. (2002). Interview by Glenn Detrick. *Academy of Management Learning and Education, 1,* 56–63.

Ackhoff, R., & Rivett, P. (1963). *A manager's guide to operations research.* New York: Wiley.

Adizes, I. (1971). *Industrial democracy, Yugoslav style.* New York: Free Press.

Ajiferuke, M., & Bodewyn, J. (1970). "Culture" and other explanatory variables in comparative management studies. *Academy of Management Journal, 13*(2), 153–164.

Barnard, C. (1938). *The functions of the executive.* Cambridge, MA: Harvard University Press.

Boulding, K. (1956). General systems theory. *Yearbook of the Society for the Advancement of General System Theory, 1,* 11–17.

Chandler, A. (1962). *Strategy and structure.* Cambridge, MA: MIT Press.

Churchman, C. (1968). *The systems approach.* New York: Dell.

Cyert, R., & March, J. (1963). *Behavioral theory of the firm.* Upper Saddle River, NJ: Prentice Hall.

Donaldson, L. (1995). *American anti-management theories of organization: A critique of paradigm proliferation.* Cambridge, UK: Cambridge University Press.

Drucker, P. (1973a). Global management. In E. C. Bursk (Ed.), *Challenge to leadership* (pp. 228–274). New York: Free Press.

Drucker, P. (1973b). *Management: Tasks, responsibilities, practices.* New York: Harper & Row.

Farmer, R., & Richman, B. (1965). *Comparative management and economic progress.* Homewood, IL: Richard D. Irwin.

Fayol, H. (1916). Administration industrielle et générale [General and industrial administration]. *Paris, Bulletin de la Societe de l'Industrie Minerale, 10*(3), 5–162.

Fayol, H. (1949). *General and industrial administration* (C. Storrs, Trans.). London: Sir Isaac Pitman and Sons.

Fiedler, F. (1967). *A theory of leader effectiveness.* New York: McGraw-Hill.

French, W., & Bell, C. Jr. (1984). *Organization development.* Englewood Cliffs, NJ: Prentice Hall.

George, C. (1972). *The history of management thought.* Englewood Cliffs, NJ: Prentice Hall.

Hall, E. (1959). *How cultures collide.* Garden City, NY: Doubleday.

Hall, E. (1976, July). How cultures collide. *Psychology Today, 10*(2), 66–74.

Henderson, A., & Parsons, T. (Eds.). (1947). *The theory of social and economic organizations.* New York: Free Press.

Hersey, P., & Blanchard, H. (1972). *Management of organizational behavior* (2nd ed.). Englewood Cliffs, NJ: Prentice Hall.

Heugens, P. (2005). A neo-Weberian theory of the firm. *Organization Studies, 26*(4), 547–567.

Hofstede, G. (1980). *Culture's consequences: International differences in work-related values.* Beverly Hills, CA: Sage.

Hofstede, G. (1984a). The cultural relativity of the quality of life concept. *Academy of Management Review, 9*(3), 389–398.

Hofstede, G. (1984b). *Culture's consequences: International differences in work-related value* (Abridged ed.). Beverly Hills, CA: Sage.

Hofstede, G. (1993). Cultural constraints in management theories. *Academy of Management Executive, 7*(1), 81–94.

Hofstede, G. (2001). *Culture's consequences: Comparing values, behaviors, institutions and organizations across nations* (2nd ed.). Thousand Oaks, CA: Sage.

Hofstede, G., & Bond, M. (1988). The Confucius connection: From cultural roots to economic growth. *Organization Dynamics, 16,* 4–21.

House, R., Hanges, P., Javidan, M., Dorfman, P., & Gupta, V. (Eds.). (2004). *Culture, leadership, and organization: The GLOBE study of 63 societies.* Thousand Oaks, CA: Sage.

Imai, M. (1975). *Never take no for an answer.* Tokyo: Simul Press.

Johnson, R., Kast, F., & Rosenzweig, J. (1973). *The theory and management of systems.* New York: McGraw-Hill.

Katz, D., & Kahn, R. (1966). *The social psychology of organizations.* New York: Wiley.

Kirkman, B., Lowe, K., & Gibson, C. (2006). A quarter century of culture's consequences: A review of empirical research incorporating Hofstede's cultural value framework. *Journal of International Business Studies, 37*(3), 285–320.

Kluckhohn, F., & Strodtbeck, F. (1961). *Variations in value-orientations.* Westport, CT: Greenwood.

Koontz, H. (1961). The management theory jungle. *Academy of Management Journal, 4*(3), 174–188.

Koontz, H., O'Donnell, C., & Weihrich, H. (1990). *Essentials of management* (5th ed.). New York: McGraw-Hill.

Lawrence, P., & Lorsch, J. (1969). *Organization and environment: Managing differentiation and integration.* Homewood, IL: Richard D. Irwin.

Lee, S. (1983). *Introduction to management science.* Chicago, IL: Dryden.

Miner, J. (2006). *Organizational behavior.* Armonk, NY: M. E. Sharpe.

Mintzberg, H. (1973). *The nature of managerial work.* New York: Harper & Row.

Negandhi, A. (1983). Cross-cultural management research: Trend and future directions. *Journal of International Business Studies, 14*(2), 17–28.

Pasmore, W., & Khalsa, G. (1993). The contributions of Eric Trist to the social engagement of social science. *Academy of Management Review, 18*(3), 546–569.

Pfeffer, J. (1993). Barriers to the advance of organizational science: Paradigm development as a dependent variable. *Academy of Management Review, 18*(4), 599–620.

Roethlisberger, F., & Dickson, W. (1939). *Management and the worker.* Cambridge, MA: Harvard University Press.

Ronen, S., & Shankar, O. (1985). Clustering countries on attitudinal dimensions: A review and synthesis. *Academy of Management Review, 10*(3), 435–454.

Simon, H. (1997). *Administrative behavior: A study of decision making processes in administrative organizations* (4th ed.). New York: Free Press. (Original work published 1945)

Simon, H., & March, J. (1958). *Organizations.* New York: Wiley.

Smith, A. (1937). *An inquiry into the nature and causes of the wealth of nations.* New York: Random House. (Original work published 1776)

Tannenbaum, R., & Schmidt, W. (1958). How to choose a leadership pattern. *Harvard Business Review, 36*(2), 95–101.

Taylor, F. (1911). *The principles of scientific management.* New York: Harper & Row.

Trompenaars. F. (1993). *Riding the waves of culture.* London: The Economist Books.

Ueda, K. (1978). Sixteen ways to avoid saying "no" in Japan. In J. C. Condon & M. Saito (Eds.), *Intercultural encounters with Japan. Communication: Contact and conflict* (pp. 185–195). Tokyo: Simul Press.

von Bertalanffy, L. (1950). The theory of open systems in physics and biology. *Science, 3,* 22–29.

Weiner, N. (1950). *The human side of systems: Cybernetics and soyciety.* Boston: Houghton-Mifflin.

Woodward, J. (1958). *Management and technology.* London: Her Majesty's Stationery Office.

Wren, D. (1972). *The evolution of management thought.* New York: Ronald Press.

American (U.S.) Management 2

> *Every day an American banker working in Paris gets requests from French firms looking for Frenchmen "with experience in an American corporation." The manager of a German steel mill hires only staff personnel "having been trained with an American firm." The British Marketing Council sends 50 British executives to spend a year at the Harvard Business School—and the British government foots the bill. For European firms, so conservative and jealous of their independence, there is one common denominator: American methods.*
>
> —J.-J. Servan-Schreiber (1969, p. 35)

In the 20th century, the United States emerged as a mecca of management theory, practice, consulting, and research. Nowhere else was management so widely viewed as a unique and vital function and an academic and professional discipline. Early on, productivity engineer Frederick Winslow Taylor (1911) wrote *Principles of Scientific Management,* which can be called the world's first book focused on management. Other pathbreaking manager–authors included Chester Barnard, CEO of New Jersey Bell (*Functions of the Executive,* 1938), and Alfred Sloan, who led General Motors between 1923 and 1946 (*My Years at General Motors,* 1964). Management doyen Peter Drucker called the latter "the best book on management ever" (1990, p. 145). The United States produced the first large management consultancies (e.g., Arthur D. Little, McKinsey & Co.), executive recruiters (e.g., Korn/Ferry, Heidrick & Struggles), buyout equity firms (Kohlberg Kravis Roberts, Forstmann Little & Co.), and merger and acquisition specialists (investment banks such as Goldman Sachs and Morgan Stanley). It bred corporate business schools (e.g., General Electric's Crotonville Institute, IBM's Sandpoint School, and Motorola University). Today, management books and articles abound and U.S. business schools draw professors and students from around the globe.[1] Meanwhile, prominent American firms dominate global rankings of the most respected companies.[2]

This chapter examines some prevailing patterns in U.S. management and the setting (polity, economy, culture) that has shaped them.

Chapter Objectives

- To broadly describe the U.S. managerial macroenvironment
- To profile the personal backgrounds, pay, and career paths of American CEOs
- To note some distinctive U.S. management patterns and practices

The U.S. Macroenvironment

POLITICAL AND LEGAL SYSTEM

The U.S. government and political system are grounded in democracy, pluralism, and the rule of law, striving to balance the civil, economic, political, and other liberties of diverse constituents (e.g., business, consumers, employees, investors, workers, taxpayers, and public interest groups). An aggressive legal profession and inquisitive independent journalists keep managers alert to prevailing ethical standards, law, and the public interest. For business, government has been neither close partner nor adversary, offering less financial support than do other advanced industrial countries (except for the defense sector). There are few government-owned businesses.[3] Antitrust and investor and consumer rights rules are more forcefully protected than in most countries, as are individual civil rights in the workplace. There is more extensive disclosure of financial information by publicly held companies, required by the stock exchanges and securities market regulators.

The political voice of business is expressed through company public affairs offices, sponsored research groups, paid lobbyists, sectoral trade associations (e.g., Semiconductor Industry Association, Textile Manufacturers Institute), and broader spokesgroups (e.g., National Association of Manufacturers, Business Roundtable, Conference Board, and the U.S. and local chambers of commerce). These groups aim to inform and influence public officials, legislators, voters, the media, and others about pending legal and regulatory change. The political views of business are not uniform and can vary by sector, size, location, and other factors. For example, the textile industry has regularly sought protection from import competition, whereas most electronics firms haven't. Big steel wants restrictions, whereas small steel (mini-mills), specialty steel (niche steel makers), and steel buyers (machinery makers and car companies) are less likely to do so. Although trade protectionist pressures regularly surface in Congress (especially in the House of Representatives), proponents of freer international trade have generally prevailed over protectionists on most major trade policy initiatives (e.g., the creation of the North American Free Trade Agreement, General Agreement on Tariffs and Trade and World Trade Organization trade negotiations, and acceptance of China into the World Trade Organization).

These and other broad features of U.S. government and politics are listed in Table 2.1.

Table 2.1   U.S. Political and Legal Environment

Long-standing constitutional democracy that tries to balance the executive, legislative, and judicial powers of government.

Arm's-length relationship between business and government (neither preferential nor adversarial); less corporate welfare (subsidies, bailouts, preferential purchasing) than in other advanced industrial countries.

Orderly political succession; low political risk for business (legal and regulatory ground rules don't change without extensive debate and deliberation).

Political pluralism accommodates diverse viewpoints and interests (e.g., consumer, labor, environmentalist, business); leading business spokesgroups include the Business Roundtable, Business Council, National Association of Manufacturers, American Business Conference, Chamber of Commerce of the USA, National Federation of Independent Business, National Small Business Association, and many sectoral trade associations.

Common law legal tradition (roots in the English legal tradition).

Adversarial legal framework; proportionally more lawyers and lawsuits than in most countries; high incidence of class-action lawsuits; stiff negligence liability penalties (tort law).

Much business law is the domain of state and local government rather than national (federal, central) government; aggressive federal (central) government protection for individual civil rights in the workplace and for free and fair competition (antitrust rules).

An independent and active corps of press and television journalists keeps public officials, politicians, and business leaders alert to ethical and responsible behavior.

Less extensive and less intrusive federal labor law than in most countries; fewer legal restraints on laying off employees for economic reasons; more protection for equal opportunity in the workplace.

Political clout of unions has been weaker than in most advanced industrial countries.

Though mainly adversarial, union–management relations are much less confrontational than in the past.

Less unionized workforce than most countries; in 2008, about 12% of wage and salary employees were union members (vs. 36% in 1983) and less than 8% in the private sector;[4] fewer labor disputes than in most other advanced industrial countries (see Figure 2.1).

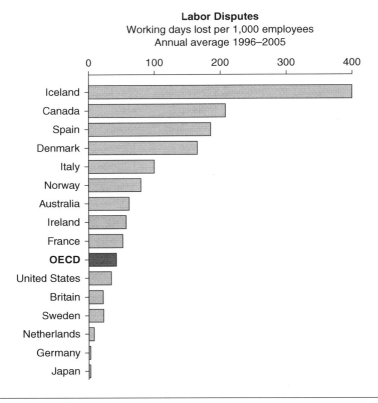

Figure 2.1   Labor Disputes

SOURCE: "Economic and Financial Indicators: Labor Disputes," *The Economist*, May 5, 2007, p. 121. Used by permission.

OECD: Organisation for Economic Co-operation and Development

Although most business law is the domain of state and local government, there is notable federal labor regulation (Table 2.2), although it is less burdensome than in most countries. U.S. managers have more liberty than peers abroad to determine labor relations policy and practices internally, whether unilaterally or in consultation with employees.

THE ECONOMY

The U.S. economy is based predominantly on private property and initiative; its internal markets for labor, goods, and capital are freer than those in most of the world.[5] It generates about one fourth of the annual gross world product with one twentieth of the world's workforce. Job creation and destruction have been high. Government taxation and

Table 2.2   U.S. Federal Government Involvement in Employer–Employee Relations

National Labor Relations Act of 1935 (Wagner Act)	Established rules for union organizing, collective bargaining, and the resolution of labor disputes
Social Security Act of 1935	Created a centrally administered retirement income security program funded by employee and employer payroll tax charges
Fair Labor Standards Act of 1938	Established a national minimum wage and required time-and-a-half pay for work beyond 40 hours per week
Civil Rights Act of 1964 (Title VII)	Banned discrimination in employment based on race, religion, gender, ethnicity, and national origin
Age Discrimination Act of 1967	Banned forced retirement until age 65 (was later raised to age 70)
Occupational Safety and Health Act of 1970	Workplace health and safety rules
Employee Retirement Income Security Act of 1974	Guidelines for investment of employee retirement funds and government insurance for private defined-benefit pension plans (Pension Benefit Guaranty Corporation)
Worker Adjustment and Retraining Notification Act of 1988	Guidelines for written advance notice in cases of large-scale layoffs and plant closings
Family and Medical Leave Act of 1993	Requires up to 12 weeks of unpaid personal annual leave for medical emergencies, newborn children, or child adoption

spending have been lower relative to national income than in most advanced industrial nations (Table 2.3).

Government employment (federal, state, local) has been low in relation to overall employment, accounting for about 16% of all jobs in 2008. These and other broad features of the U.S. economy are highlighted in Table 2.4.

CULTURE

Although U.S. society has become ever more diverse in ethnicity and culture, its dominant sociocultural tendencies draw much from Europe,

Table 2.3   Burden of Government as Percentage of Gross Domestic Product, 2006: United States, Western Europe, and Japan

	Total Government Expenditures	Total Government Revenues
United States	33.1%	36.6%
France	50.8	53.4
Germany	44.0	45.7
Italy	45.6	50.1
Spain	40.3	38.5
Sweden	57.6	55.5
United Kingdom	42.2	45.0
Japan	31.7	38.1

SOURCE: Data from *OECD in Figures 2007*, available at http://oberon.sourceoecd.org/vl=5391416/cl=12/nw=1/rpsv/figures_2007/en/page26.htm

Table 2.4   Profile of the U.S. Economy

High output and income per capita.
Mature economy (2%–3% average annual gross domestic product growth in recent decades); mild business cycles.
High incidence of business start-ups, buyouts, mergers, bankruptcies; high job creation and destruction.
Shrinking number and proportion of lower-skill manufacturing jobs; growth in knowledge-intensive service sector employment (e.g., education, health care, financial services, information technology).
High level of economic freedom and business competition; very flexible labor market.
Growth rates of U.S. trade have outpaced the overall economy. Exports have been high in monetary value but lower than in most other advanced industrial countries in proportion to output and population. No country hosts as much inward foreign investment or invests as much abroad. Since the late 1980s, the cumulative book value of foreign-owned assets in the United States (direct investment, portfolio investment, bank loans and deposits) has been greater than the value of U.S. assets abroad.[6]

Fluid financial markets; more shareholder-owned companies than in any other country.[7]

High value of securities (stocks and bonds) in proportion to gross national product; high ratio of equity (stock) relative to debt in corporate financial structures.

High turnover of share ownership; share purchases ever more the domain of institutional investors (mutual funds, pension funds); more than half of U.S. households directly or indirectly own corporate stock.

Predominantly stockholder-oriented capitalism; enterprise is more attuned to the interests of shareholders relative to other stakeholders (e.g., employees, lenders, bondholders, communities), although these others are by no means ignored.

Extensive public disclosure of corporate financial information.

Low price inflation (2%–4% per year on average, 1990–2008).

Public (government) spending and taxes have been lower in relation to national income than in most countries; minimal government ownership of business.

Government employment (federal, state, local) has been low in proportion to overall employment (16% of total jobs in 2008).

Home to the world's largest and most active venture capital investment community.

Much inequality in family wealth and income.

More privately run retirement and health insurance programs than in most countries.

from whence came most of the earliest U.S. immigrants, a trend that continued until after World War II. Since then, most immigration has come from Asia and Latin America. In 2008, about 13% (slowly rising) of the population was foreign-born.

Americans value personal independence (score high on Hofstede's individualism) and have high tolerance for risk and change (low uncertainty avoidance). That pattern draws partly from the early immigrants who fled social, political, and religious constraints in Europe. Driven by survival instincts and a strong work ethic, many persevered as workers, independent farmers, and small business owners. An ever-expanding westward frontier brought continual opportunity to start anew.

In general, Americans value equality of opportunity more than equal wealth and income. This brings less social and political pressure than in Europe to redistribute wealth and income through government taxation and social spending.

These and some other broad features of U.S. culture are listed in Table 2.5.

Table 2.5   Prevailing Sociocultural Tendencies in U.S. Society

Emphasis on individual rights, freedoms, and responsibilities.
Independence and self-reliance are valued.
Desire to be unique.
Belief in equality, but more in equality of opportunity rather than material equality.
At work, competence (how well you perform) matters more than social or family background; nepotism and favoritism have negative connotations.
High social and occupational mobility; weak loyalty of employee to employer (and vice versa); employer–employee relations have been more contractual than personal.
High acceptance of social, religious, and other diversity; less antagonism toward immigrants than in most countries.
Less stigma attached to failure (e.g., in school or business) and much opportunity to begin anew.
Extensive involvement of women in the workforce, including nontraditional roles such as management, although they are underrepresented in senior management in large companies.
High level of voluntarism on behalf of social, political, philanthropic, environmental, and other causes.
Optimism.
Ethnocentrism.
Openness, informality.
Friendships form quickly but without deep or long-term personal commitment.
Materialism.
Protestant ethic (strong achievement drive, thrift, diligence, orderliness, high tolerance for work).
Low-context culture; directness in personal communication.
Impatience (time is a resource; punctuality is valued).
Bias toward action (often just for action's sake).
In conversation, low threshold for silence (uncomfortable with silence).

> On Hofstede's cultural variables, a general profile of
> - Low power distance
> - Very high individualism
> - Moderate to high masculine-associated values (aggressiveness, assertiveness, competitiveness)
> - Low uncertainty avoidance (i.e., high tolerance of risk and change)
> - Short-term time orientation

The following section describes the personal backgrounds and pay of senior U.S. managers relative to their peers abroad. The description obviously won't fit all managers but rather highlights prevailing tendencies among senior executives in large firms. Additional comparison with peers abroad occurs in other chapters.

The U.S. Manager

Recent and historical evidence reveals several characteristics of contemporary U.S. CEOs. They include the following:

- Predominantly male and from middle- and upper-middle-class background
- A bit younger traditionally than peers in Europe and Japan
- Well educated but more likely than counterparts abroad to have been enrolled in business studies while in higher education
- More inclined to view management as a profession; high mobility between employers
- Very highly paid, and much of it tied to performance
- Less international life experience

PERSONAL BACKGROUND

Fortune magazine data from the mid-1980s portrayed the U.S. CEO in Fortune 500 firms as a well-educated male, median age 58, with an average of 8 years in office (McComas, 1986). Surveys from the 1990s showed all but three corporate chiefs in the BusinessWeek 1000 to have been male, mean age 56, with 8.5 years' tenure ("Corporate Elite," 1992, 1993). Their mean age at time of appointment to CEO was about 48–50 years, but some were notably younger, such as John Reed (Citicorp, age 44), Jack Welch (General Electric, 45), Michael Eisner (Disney, 42), and Richard Wagoner Jr. (General Motors, 45). The 1993 "Corporate Elite" included at least 10 CEOs in their 30s. According to executive recruiter Spencer Stuart (2004, 2006), the average CEO age in the largest 100 of Standard & Poor's (S&P) 500 companies fell from 59 to 56 years between 1980 and 2007. The median age (52 years) for new CEOs was lower than the S&P median for all 500 CEOs (Spencer Stuart, 2007). However, despite ever younger average age, only one S&P 500 CEO in 2007 was younger than 40 (Spencer Stuart, 2007). Median tenure (2007) was 6 years (Spencer Stuart, 2007). Whereas in 1980 a majority (51%) of the Fortune 100 CEOs were age 60–69, in 2006 a majority (68%) were age 50–59 (Spencer Stuart, 2006). Of those 100, about 2% were age 49 or younger in 1980, rising to 11% by 2005.

In regard to socioeconomic background, 46% of the Fortune CEOs (1986 Fortune 500) had come from upper-middle-class and wealthy households. Forty-four percent were from middle-class and 10% from less affluent families (McComas, 1986). About 45% were from rural or small-town settings, and 55% were from big cities or city suburbs. Fathers of 1 in 10 had been CEOs at the same company, either as founder or direct descendant of a founder. Half of the fathers had been businessmen (e.g., executive, manager, small business owner). Another one sixth had professional careers (e.g., law, medicine), and about one fourth had been in clerical, skilled or unskilled labor, or farm occupations.

Although most large-company CEOs are from wealthy and upper-middle-class backgrounds, their presence has lessened proportionally over time. As one indication, the percentage of S&P 500 CEOs who had bachelor's degrees from private Ivy League universities declined from 15% in 1998 to 9% in 2006 (Spencer Stuart, 2005, 2006). In 2005, there were equal numbers of CEOs (13 each) in the S&P 500 from the public University of Wisconsin and the private Harvard University (Spencer Stuart, 2005).

Few women have led large U.S. companies, but their numbers have been rising slowly. In 1996, only one woman led a Fortune 500 company. In 2007, several well-known large firms had female CEOs, including eBay, Avon Products, Xerox, Time Inc., Archer Daniels Midland, Sara Lee, and Pepsico (Benner, Levenson, & Rupali, 2007). Also, more women than men have been earning university bachelor's degrees, including those in business administration. At the MBA level, women earned 42% of degrees in 2004–2005 (U.S. Department of Education, 2007). Thus, there are now more female candidates than ever in the promotion pipeline.

FORMAL EDUCATION

Senior managers in large U.S. companies have substantially more formal higher education (measured in academic degrees) than does the general public. In 2007, about 10% of the U.S. population over age 25 held a master's degree or higher (U.S. Census data), compared with 67% of Fortune 500 CEOs (Spencer Stuart, 2007). Ninety-eight percent of the latter held bachelor's degrees (in diverse disciplines but above all in engineering [21%], economics [15%], and business administration [13%]) (Spencer Stuart, 2007). For postgraduate degrees, the MBA was the most prevalent (40%), followed by law degrees (10%). About 21% of non-MBA advanced degrees were PhDs. In 2003, the proportions of Fortune 100 and Fortune 700 CEOs holding MBA degrees were 37% and 35%, respectively. By contrast, in 1999, about 11% of European CEOs in comparably large firms held MBA degrees, a figure that has probably risen modestly since then.

Management is more widely accepted as an academic discipline in the United States than elsewhere. Nowhere else has there been so much higher education for business nor so much of it linked to universities. In 2004–2005, about one fifth (22%) of the 1,439,264 U.S. university undergraduate degrees and one fourth of the 574,618 master's degrees were in business or management (U.S. Department of Education, 2007). Formal higher education for business and management evolved more slowly in Europe, with enrollment there lower than in the United States, but growing (Antunes & Thomas, 2007).

Most of the premier U.S. graduate business schools offer doctoral studies in management, and many call themselves schools of management rather than schools of business administration, such as Yale (School of Organization and Management), UCLA (Anderson School of Management), MIT (Sloan School of Management), Northwestern (Kellogg School of Management), Case Western (Weatherhead School of Management), and Michigan State (Eli Broad School of Management). Undergraduate-level providers are more likely to be called schools of business administration.

In education, training, and development, a notable U.S. development was the "corporate university." Though not true universities, these learning centers offer in-house education and training (some delivered by internal staff and some outsourced) mainly for employees but often also for others. There were about 2,000 such institutions in 2007 according to the Corporate University Xchange (http://www.corpu.com). Some examples include Caterpillar University, Boeing Leadership Center, Motorola University, Hamburger University (McDonald's), Ingersoll Rand University, and Sears University.

MANAGEMENT AS A PROFESSION

The perception of management as a profession is more evident in the United States than elsewhere. A profession typically is a career field with a well-established body of knowledge, requires certification of mastery (e.g., medical exam for doctors, bar exam for lawyers, CPA exam for accountants, theological exam for clergy), and often has a profession-bound code of ethics (e.g., Hippocratic Oath for medical doctors). By these criteria, management isn't a true profession. As noted in Chapter 1, management knowledge is eclectic and multidisciplinary, and there is no consensus about what knowledge to master, much less about whether, when, or how to certify mastery.

Nonetheless, Peter Drucker (1973) once observed that management is "professional . . . a function, a discipline, a task to be done; and managers are the professionals who practice the discipline, carry out the functions, and discharge these tasks" (p. 6; see also Stone, 1998). He described managers as professionally accountable to their constituencies (e.g., owners, employees, customers, suppliers, society). In family businesses, a professional salaried manager is commonly brought in when enterprise size and complexity transcend the interest or ability of founder-owners to continue managing. Correspondingly, ownership becomes separated from management, a pattern that occurred earlier and more broadly in the United States than elsewhere (Berle & Means, 1932; Chandler, 1962). There are also professional associations that foster management education, training, and development, such as the American Management Association, the American Management Foundation, and the Society for the Advancement of Management. The Academy of Management (http://www.aomonline .org) encourages professionalism in management education and produces five professional publications.[8] Though oriented mainly toward professors, it also has some business representation (8% of members in 2008).[9]

Managerial professionalism is also reflected in the high mobility of U.S. managers between employers.

MANAGERIAL MOBILITY

> If you look at the resumes of 28- to 30-year-olds today, they've got three jobs listed already. Ten years ago someone with three jobs was a "job hopper." Today someone who is 30 and has had 10 years with one company, you ask if they're too conservative. (42-year-old U.S. executive Scott Adams, as quoted in Lublin & White, 1997)

In theory, a competent manager could lead any organization, and it is not unusual for seasoned U.S. CEOs to change employers. Many Fortune 500 CEOs have held similar posts at two or more companies, and some at three or more.

External hiring (as opposed to promotion from within) has become increasingly common, in tandem with shortening CEO tenure. In Fortune 500 companies, externally recruited CEOs reached a record high 43% of the total in 2005, up from 34% in 2004 ("Record-Breaking Churn in 2006"). In the S&P 500, 40% of new CEO hires in 2005 were external hires (Spencer Stuart, 2006).

Some past and present examples of this mobility include Thomas Graham, former chief at Jones & Laughlin (steel), who previously led U.S. Steel. Mark Hurd moved to Hewlett-Packard from NCR in 2005; Ed Zander at Sun Microsystems left for Motorola in 2004; Lou Gerstner of IBM (1993) previously led American Express and RJR Nabisco; Raymond Gilmartin moved from Becton Dickenson to Merck in 1994. AT&T's Michael Armstrong previously led Hughes Electronics. James McNerney (3 Com) went to Boeing (2005), and Michael Capellas (First Data Corp.) moved to Compaq Computer (2007).

There is occasional interim crossover from industry to government (e.g., Robert Rubin, cochairman of Goldman Sachs & Co., became treasury secretary in the Clinton administration). Former corporate CEOs who worked for President George W. Bush (2000–2008) included his vice president, Dick Cheney (Haliburton); treasury secretaries Paul O'Neil (Alcoa; International Paper), John Snow (CSX), and Henry Paulson (Goldman Sachs); and defense secretary Donald Rumsfeld (G. D. Searle; General Instruments). However, there is almost no crossover from a high-level government career to becoming CEO of a major company, as can happen in France and Japan.

Before 2001, U.S. CEO succession turnover was higher than in Western Europe, but they have been roughly equal since 2002 (Table 2.6). Their turnover rates have been lower than those in Japan because CEOs there are much older when they attain their positions and thus have less opportunity for long tenure.

Table 2.6   Worldwide Comparison of CEO Turnover (All Types of Succession, by Region), Including Regular (Normal, Planned), Performance-Related, and Merger-Driven Successions

	Percentage of CEOs Who Departed								
	1998	2000	2001	2002	2003	2004	2005	2006	2007
North America	10.6	17.9	13.4	11.0	10.1	12.9	16.2	15	15.2
Europe	6.2	9.8	8.2	11.4	10.0	16.8	15.3	15	17.6
Japan	12.5	14.5	17.1	9.7	13.5	15.5	19.8	15	10.6
Rest of Asia Pacific	2.3	3.7	1.9	9.1	5.6	17.2	10.5	10	—

SOURCE: Karlsson, Neilson, and Webster (2008); Lucier, Kocourek, and Habbel (2006); Lucier, Wheeler, and Habbel (2007); figures for 2006 are approximate (from reading a bar chart).

NOTE: Rates based on the world's 2,500 largest public companies ranked by market capitalization.

High U.S. managerial mobility is due partly to high personal acceptance of change (e.g., tolerance for restructurings, mergers, acquisitions) and high individualism. Managers are more driven by their personal goals than by loyalty to their employer. In addition, an active executive search and recruitment profession (headhunters) emerged earlier in the United States and is more well established than in other countries. In 2007, four of the world's five leading executive recruiters based on fee revenue were U.S. firms Korn/Ferry, Heidrick & Struggles, Spencer Stuart, and Russell Reynolds ("Hire and Hire," 2007, p. 16). In 2007, about 42% of global executive search market revenue was from the United States (Association of Executive Search Consultants, http://www.aesc.org/article/pressrelease2007111301/).

In 2006, *Fortune* magazine profiled a dozen U.S. companies that have been high-profile incubators of senior management talent that migrated to other firms. Table 2.7 lists the top five providers, some of their alumni, and destination employers.

CEO CAREER PATHS

The careers of future CEOs often follow specific business functional paths, some being more common than others. *Fortune* magazine data from the 1980s showed the career paths of Fortune 500 CEOs (industrial and service firms) to have been predominantly in marketing (32% of CEOs), production or operations (20%), and finance or accounting (27%) (McComas, 1986). In 2005, executive recruitment agency Spencer Stuart found in the S&P 500 that the finance function was most prevalent (27%), followed by operations management (25%) and marketing (24%) (Spencer Stuart, 2005). It also found that the proportion of CEOs who had stayed in one functional specialty throughout their careers fell from 25% in 2000 to 9% in 2006 (Spencer Stuart, 2006). In 2007, however, operations (33%) replaced finance (30%) as the most common path, followed by marketing (27%). Only 8% followed a purely "general management" path throughout their career (Stuart Spencer, 2007).

PAY

U.S. CEO pay in big companies has been much higher than in other countries. Consultancy Pearl Meyer & Partners reported average pay in the 200 largest U.S. companies (2005) to be $11.3 million, about 2.5 times that of the largest 100 companies on the FTSE index of the London Stock Exchange (Brush, 2006). For mid-sized businesses, Towers Perrin reported average U.S. CEO pay (year 2005) for firms with at least $500 million in sales to be $2.16 million, compared with $1.2 million, on average, in the United Kingdom, France, Italy, and Germany. (See Table 2.8; for additional CEO pay comparisons, see Tables 3.4, 6.9, 7.5, 8.11, and 8.12.)

Table 2.7   Notable Producers of CEO Talent

Source Company	Alumnus Name	Destination Company	Destination Title
Procter & Gamble	W. McNerney Jr.	Boeing	Chairman/president/CEO
	Gerald Johnston	Clorox	Chairman/president/CEO
	Douglas Baker Jr.	Ecolab	President/CEO
	Stephen Sanger	General Mills	Chairman/CEO
	Paul Charron	Liz Claiborne	Chairman/CEO
	Steven Ballmer	Microsoft	CEO
	W. Kiely III	Molson Coors Brewing	President/CEO
	Stephen MacMillan	Stryker	President/CEO
	Ronald DeFeo	Terex	Chairman/president/CEO/COO
	Mark Ketchum	Newell Rubbermaid	Interim president/CEO
General Electric	Kevin Sharer	Amgen	Chairman/president/CEO
	Barry Perry	Engelhard	Chairman/CEO
	Robert Nardelli	Home Depot	Chairman/president/CEO
	David Cote	Honeywell International	Chairman/CEO
	Mark Frissora	Tenneco	Chairman president/CEO
	Lawrence Johnston	Albertsons	Chairman/president/CEO
	W. McNerney Jr.	Boeing	Chairman/president/CEO
	Matthew Espe	Ikon Office Solutions	Chairman/president/CEO
	Christopher Kearney	SPX	President/CEO

(Continued)

Table 2.7 (Continued)

Source Company	Alumnus Name	Destination Company	Destination Title
General Motors	George Buckley	3M	Chairman/president/CEO
	John Finnegan	Chubb	Chairman/president/CEO
	José Alapont	Federal-Mogul	Chairman/president/CEO
	Michael Burns	Dana	Chairman/president/CEO
	Stanley O'Neal	Merrill Lynch	Chairman/president/CEO
	Lewis Campbell	Textron	Chairman/president/CEO
IBM Corp.	John Chambers	Cisco Systems	President/CEO
	Patricia Russo	Lucent Technologies	Chairman/CEO
	Jeffrey Joerres	Manpower	Chairman/president/CEO
	Steven Reinemund	Pepsico	Chairman/CEO
	Michael Cannon	Solectron	President/CEO
	Paul Curlander	Lexmark International	Chairman/CEO
McKinsey & Co.	Miles White	Abbott Laboratories	Chairman/CEO
	Kevin Sharer	Amgen	Chairman/president/CEO
	Gregory Case	AON	President/CEO
	W. McNerney Jr.	Boeing	Chairman/president/CEO
	Michael Jordan	Electronic Data Systems	Chairman/CEO
	John Malone	Liberty Media	Chairman/interim CEO
	William Foote	USG	Chairman/CEO

SOURCE: Partial list adapted from Colvin (2006); other firms mentioned in the *Fortune* magazine coverage (from a longer list) included Eastman Kodak, Chase, Exxon, General Mills, Pepsico, Ford, and AT&T.

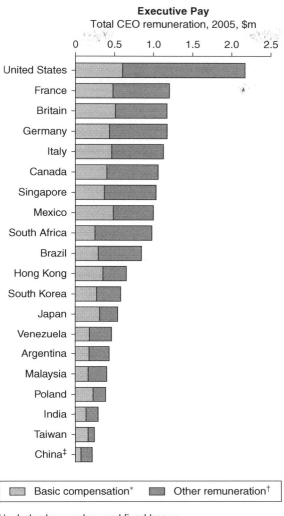

Figure 2.2   Executive Pay

SOURCE: "Real Pay," *The Economist,* January 21, 2006, p. 102. Used by permission.

The pay gap evident in Figure 2.2 is not mainly from base salary differences but rather from supplemental performance pay (e.g., cash bonuses and stock-based incentives) such as the following:

- *Stock options:* The right to purchase a specified number of employer shares at some future date at a price set today; until 2005, stock options in the United States didn't have to be expensed on enterprise financial reports, thus contributing to their use. They remain common but less so than previously.

- *Stock purchase:* Opportunity to buy employer stock either at cost or at a discount.

- *Grants of stock:* Direct gifts of company stock; shares typically vest (become salable) at some conditional future date.

- *Restricted stock:* Grant or purchase of employer stock that vests on some conditional future date.

- There can also be *phantom stock* and *stock appreciation rights* (SARs), bonuses that reward employees based on an increase in the value of the company's stock, the dividend performance of the stock, or both. Pension benefits offer opportunity for additional compensation.

One reason for the high nonsalary component of U.S. CEO pay is a $1 million annual cap (since 1993) on the tax deductibility (to the U.S. employer) of individual salary payouts. The cap doesn't apply to non-salary compensation. The form and amount of the variable pay can depend on the individual hiring contract, and the amount is typically higher for a person hired from outside the company than for someone promoted from within. For an external hire, the employer needs to at least match the person's prior pay and perquisites plus a suitable raise and incentives.

Though much publicized and frequently criticized, high CEO pay in the United States hasn't generated the same level of public criticism as it has in Western Europe.

INTERNATIONAL EXPERIENCE

U.S. CEOs generally have less international work, travel, and study experience than their European peers. For instance, in one study comparing U.S. CEOs (Fortune 100) with British CEOs (FTSE 100), one third of the Americans and two thirds of the British had lived or worked abroad (Guerrero & Pimlott, 2007b, p. 21). This experience is less often required in the United States, as noted by corporate recruiter Elisabeth Marx of Heidrick & Struggles:

> Many U.S. companies do not have a policy requiring executives to have had international experience in order to obtain a senior position. In the U.K., the better companies make it a requirement to have one or two. (Guerrero & Pimlott, 2007a, p. 21)

In a study of the perceived importance of previous travel and international relocation, 27% of European executives saw this to be extremely important (compared with only 15% of their North American peers). Also, 54% of North Americans (compared with 31% of the Europeans) said it wasn't at all important ("Executives Hold Traditional Values," 2007).

Another survey sought executive opinion about learning foreign languages, finding that "nearly 85% of [executive] recruiters in Europe, 88% of recruiters in Asia and 95% of recruiters in Latin America either 'strongly agreed' or 'somewhat agreed' that being at least bilingual is critical to succeed in today's business environment. Among recruiters in North America, the percentage was just 34%" (*Executive Recruiter News*, 2005).

Few Americans lead large firms in non-English-speaking countries.[10] Reasons include their more limited international backgrounds, legal restraints abroad on hiring of noncitizens, and lower pay. Also, large firms elsewhere are more likely to remain family owned longer, and are less inclined to hire outsiders, either local or foreign, for senior managerial posts. American-born CEOs of firms in non-English-speaking settings have included Frederick Reid (Germany's Lufthansa), Jeffrey Katz (Swissair), Peter Schutz (German-born, American-raised, former head of Germany's Porsche), John Mack (co-CEO, Credit Suisse), John Brock (Interbrew, Belgium), James Schiro (Zurich Financial, Switzerland), Thomas Middlehoff (Bertelsmann, Germany), Nancy McKinstry (publishing house Wolters Kluwer, the Netherlands), Simon Kukes (Yukos, Russia), Steven Theede (Yukos), Ben Lipps (Fresenius, German medical care firm), Gordon Riske (Deutz, German motor manufacturer), and William Amelio (Lenovo, Chinese firm based in Singapore).

By contrast, it is far more usual to find foreign-born leaders heading U.S. companies. Some examples in the present and recent past include the following CEOs: Antonio Perez (Spain) at Eastman Kodak, Sam Gibara (Egypt) at Goodyear Tire & Rubber, Indra Nooyi (India) at Pepsico, Rono Dutto (India) at UAL, Fernando Aguirre (Mexico) at Chiquita Brands, Roberto Goizueta (Cuba) and Douglas Daft (Australia) at Coca-Cola, Anthony O'Reilly (Ireland) at Heinz, David O'Reilly (Ireland) at Chevron, Alex Trotman (Scotland) and Jacques Nasser (Lebanese-born Australian) at Ford, Eric Benhamou (France and Algeria) at 3Com, Durk Jager (Netherlands) at Procter & Gamble, Andrew Grove (Hungary) at Intel, Rajat Gupta (India) at McKinsey & Co., Eckhard Pfeiffer (Germany) at Compaq Computer, Michael Spindler (Germany) at Apple Computer, Rakesh Gangwal (India) at U.S. Airways, Enrico Pesatori (Italy) at Tandem Computer, and Piers Marmion (United Kingdom) at Heidrick & Struggles. Others include Fred Hassan (Pakistani) at Schering-Plough, Michael Patsalos Fox (Greek-Australian) at McKinsey & Co., Robert Bishop (Australian) at Silicon Graphics, Charles Bell (Australian) at McDonald's, E. Neville Isdell (Irish) at Coca-Cola, Sidney Taurel (Spain) at Eli Lilly, and Alain Belda (France and Morocco) at Alcoa (for additional examples, see Story, 2007, p. A1).

It is noteworthy that U.S. CEOs' international experience has been rising. For instance, *Chief Executive* magazine reported that prior work experience abroad was at 37% and 30%, respectively, for Fortune 100 and Fortune 700 CEOs in 2003 (Martin, 2004). For the S&P 500, the number was 37%, up from 21% in 2002 (Spencer Stuart, 2006), but dropped to 34% in 2007 (Spencer Stuart, 2007). For 2007, among CEOs of the largest 100 S&P firms, 47 had experience abroad (Spencer Stuart, 2007).

U.S. Managerial Tendencies

Some notable managerial patterns, pressures, and practices (general tendencies) have characterized bigger U.S. business in recent decades. The descriptions here draw from diverse sources, including the business press, academic researchers, consultancies, data gatherers, and opinions of practicing managers. The management process (i.e., the functions of planning, controlling, organizing, and directing) frames the discussion. Additional comparisons with other countries and regions appear in other chapters.

PLANNING

The process and function of planning focuses on organization purposes and objectives and possible paths to achieve them. Plans themselves can be broad (long term, strategic) or narrow (short-term budgets and operating plans). The planning process can be formal or informal, decentralized or centralized, or continuous or discontinuous. It can be done individually or by groups. It may or may not involve outsiders (e.g., customers, consultants, suppliers). Plans can be put in writing or remain mental maps in the minds of managers (for a comprehensive conceptual overview of the planning process, see Steiner, 1969).

History shows the following tendencies in large U.S. companies compared with their counterparts in Western Europe and East Asia:

- More formalized long-range planning
- More recourse to external consultants
- More willingness to accept change

Formal Planning

The "professional" general manager dotes on long-range planning. He will probably set up a staff for it, then hire consultants to reinforce the staff. He will encourage the preparation of a planning manual and a proliferation of forms to be filled out by many different units in the organization. He will stress the preparation and analysis of the numbers that summarize his plans and then demonstrate his mastery of the numbers in presentations to corporate management and the board of directors. (Wrapp, 1979, p. F16)

Compared with peers abroad, U.S. managers historically have been more likely to formalize their long-term planning. That pattern dates back to the early 20th century, when American industrial engineers sought ways to increase production efficiency (e.g., Frederick Taylor's push for scientific management) and new ways to formally track projects, such as the Critical Path Method at the DuPont Co. (mid-1950s) and the Program Evaluation and Review Technique. The latter was developed in the late 1950s for the Polaris submarine program, involving Lockheed Corporation, the U.S. Navy, and consultancy Booz Allen & Hamilton (Wren, 1972). When companies grew larger and more complex, their internal budgeting systems became more formal.

In 1969, corporate planning expert George Steiner observed that many large U.S. companies pioneered comprehensive formal long-range planning systems after World War II. He attributed this to increased environmental uncertainty, rapid technological change, organizational complexity, and ever longer time horizons needed for resource commitments. Many large U.S. firms created planning departments, detailed planning manuals, and planning flow charts. By the early 1960s, about 60% of the 500 largest American industrial firms (SRI study) and 85% of 420 large firms (National Planning Association study) had created formal planning systems. Steiner (1969) concluded that these numbers were "unquestionably far higher than comparable figures for West European countries" (p. 15).

That legacy gave rise to many books and articles on corporate planning and, in academia, to a related professional association (the Strategic Management Society). When U.S. firms spread aggressively into Europe in the 1960s, their planning systems were seen as superior to local ones (Servan-Schreiber, 1967/1968). Although Japanese firms also introduced long-range planning systems after World War II, Kono (1984) saw these to be less formal than American ones.

Canadian Professor Henry Mintzberg (1994a) has described the U.S. managerial bias for formal planning:

That the relationship [of planning to culture] exists is hardly open to question. . . . America is where the planning school first took root and grew; it is where the General Electrics and the Texas Instruments led the way with action planning, where ITT led the way with performance control. . . . It is America that has generated the vast majority of the vast planning literature, . . . given rise to the huge planning societies, . . . [and] spawned most of the strategic consulting boutiques. (pp. 414–415)

Over the years, attention shifted to strategic planning to more systematically address organization mission, purpose, long-term objectives, and strategic direction (Ackhoff, 1970; Ansoff, 1965; Hofer & Schendel, 1978; Steiner, 1969). That attention focused on questions of location, timing, size, and scope of operations. This brought more systematic assessment of pertinent political, economic, technological, social, and other forces and analysis of internal corporate strengths and limitations (and those of competitors). By the 1980s and 1990s, strategic planning was seen as integral to managing. A planning consultancy profession sprung up. At U.S. universities, the capstone business policy course was repackaged as "strategic management." Strategy has become an academic discipline in its own right (Hambrick & Chen, 2008).

Evolution of Corporate Planning	
1950s and 1960s	Formal long-range planning
1960s and 1970s	Attention to strategic planning
After 1980	Strategic management

Despite much formality in planning, U.S. company performance was often disappointing. Critics saw a failure to involve plan implementers enough in the planning process. According to Bartlett and Ghoshal (1994),

> As companies grew larger and more complex . . . senior executives needed elaborate systems and specialized staff to ensure that headquarters could review, influence and approve the strategic plans of specific business units. Over time, the workings of increasingly formalized planning processes eclipsed the utility of the plans they produced: sterile generalities to which frontline managers felt little affinity or commitment. (p. 80)

Mintzberg (1994a) observed that corporate strategic planning came to resemble strategic programming, with too little strategic thinking, noting that strategy should coalesce incrementally, less formally, and more intuitively (see also Mintzberg, 1994b; Hamel & Prahalad, 1990).

The scale of formal corporate planning in the United States fostered (and is fostered by) the world's largest management consultancy profession.

Recourse to Consultants

Modern-day management consultancies date back to the time-and-motion studies of late 19th-century industrial engineers, which eventually extended into other areas of information and expertise. Larger consultancies emerged earlier in the United States than elsewhere, including Arthur D. Little (1886), Booz-Allen & Hamilton (1914), and McKinsey & Co. (1926). Later (after 1960) came strategy consultancies such as the Boston

Consulting Group (1963), Management Analysis Center (Harvard and MIT professors), and Bain & Co. (1973). By the early 1970s, the major accounting firms (e.g., Arthur Andersen, Ernst & Young) were offering management advice to supplement their tax, audit, and financial advice.

Over the years the growth of consultancy revenue (strategic and other consulting) has outpaced the U.S. economy (Wooldridge, 1997). The global consulting market was estimated to have exceeded $300 billion in 2007 (Kennedy Information, 2008, p. 2). According to one source, 10 of the top 12 most prestigious consultancies in 2008 were based in the United States (Vault Europe, 2008). Kennedy Information reported that 11 of the 15 largest consultancies (by revenue) were American ("Largest Consulting Practices," 2007, p. 1).

Big U.S. consultancies now engage actively abroad and have large international staffs. In 2007, for instance, McKinsey & Co. had 90 offices in 51 countries, and more than half of its partners were non-U.S. nationals.

In other countries, the consulting profession emerged more slowly. One reason was less intense business competition. Also, big companies there tended to stay family controlled longer. In general, family firms are more conservative, less inclined to pay for external advice, and more skeptical of that advice.

Attraction to Change and Fads

Could fadless management be the next fad? ("Instant Coffee," 1997, p. 57)

We love panaceas, the quick fix which can solve everything. . . . One always pays the price for quick fixes. (P. Drucker in Poe, 1983, p. 37)

U.S. managers show high acceptance of change and new ideas, as reflected in a high level of entrepreneurship, rapid emergence of new industries, and high managerial mobility across firms. The pressure of competition forces managers to consider change in order to survive. Table 2.8 presents a partial list of change-oriented practices and buzzwords introduced by educators, consultants, trainers, and others offering help, hope, and hype for business (see also Abrahamson, 1996; Carson, Lanier, Carson, & Guidry, 2000; Colvin, 2004; Hilmer & Donaldson, 1987; Micklethwait & Wooldridge, 1997).

CONTROL

Managerial control assesses whether organizational objectives are being met and calls for corrective action (or maybe a change in objectives) when needed. Control can be both broad and narrow. Very broadly, enterprise is controlled by its external product, capital, and labor markets. For example, if sales and profits fall (or are expected to fall), company share price and debt rating normally fall, making new funding more costly until performance improves.

Table 2.8   Help, Hope, and Hype in the Management Jargon Jungle

Activity-based cost accounting	Kanban	Relationship investing
Boston Consulting Group matrix	Knowledge management	Scenario planning
Boundary spanning	Lean organization	Self-managed teams
Boundaryless organization	Lean production	Six Sigma quality control
Business process outsourcing	Learning organizations	Strategic framing
Competitive benchmarking	Leveraged buildup	Strategic management
Continuous improvement	Leveraged buyout	Strategic partnering
Core competencies	M-form organization	Strategic planning
Corporate culture	Management buyout	Strategic visioning
Cross-functional teams	Management by objectives	Strength analysis
Cross-impact analysis	Management by walking around	Stretch targets
Customer relationship management	Managerial grid	Supply chain management
Cycle time reduction	Mission and vision statements	System 4 leadership
Delayering	Modular corporation	Team building
Downsizing	Networked companies	Theory Z organization
Employee empowerment	Niche strategy	Time-based competition
Employee involvement program	Open-book management	Total quality management
Employee stock ownership plans	Organization culture	Total time management
Gainsharing	Performance-based pay	Transformation management
Game theory	Portfolio planning	Value-added chain
Hierarchy value analysis	Process mapping	Value engineering
High-performance workplace	Process reengineering	Value migration
Integrated diversity	Process teams	Virtual corporation
Internal customers	Quality control circle	Zero-based budgeting
Intrapreneurship	Quality-of-worklife program	Zero defects
Job enlargement	Reengineering	
Job enrichment	Relationship contracting	

Boards of directors normally are empowered to control management (e.g., hire, advise, counsel, evaluate, reward, persuade, or remove managers) on behalf of owners, and they do so with varying effectiveness. Internal control systems (e.g., financial controls, budgeting systems, quality control, supervision) are also part of the control process.

Some control tendencies in large U.S. companies (relative to peers abroad) include the following:

- Broader and more transitory shareholder base that is more inclined to flee (sell their holdings) rather than fight (engage with managers) for change
- More attuned to shareholder interests relative to other stakeholders
- More vulnerable to buyout and takeover pressures
- More focused on quantifiable performance criteria
- Shorter-term time orientation
- More bottom-up appraisal of managers

Broad (and Transitory) Shareholder Base

U.S. rules that protect investors don't just sustain market liquidity, they also drive a wedge between shareholders and managers. Instead of yielding long-term shareholders who concentrate their holdings in a few companies, where they provide informed oversight and counsel, the laws promote diffused, arms-length stockholding. (Bhide, 1994, p. 131)

More than half of U.S. households own corporate stock (either directly or through their mutual fund and pension fund holdings). However, few investors are inclined to engage much with management when disappointed with performance. Instead, they sell their shares and look elsewhere. These fluid shareholdings contrast with the more closely held and more engaged equity of Europe and Japan (La Porta, Lopez-de-Silanes, & Schleifer, 1999).

One reason is a very large U.S. equity market, which offers more liquidity for investors than do most markets abroad. Firms abroad rely more on debt financing (bonds, loans), and proportionately fewer go public. Shareholding tends to be more concentrated (La Porta et al., 1999), and more large companies remain longer in the hands of founders. There is also more cross-shareholding between firms. With less dispersed and less liquid holdings, block shareholders (blockholders) are strongly inclined to engage directly with management when displeased with performance. In the United States, by contrast, this "relational investing" is seen mainly in venture capital, private equity buyouts, investment holding companies, and large institutional investors unable to sell their holdings without causing a drop in share price. Examples include large hedge funds, big mutual funds (e.g., Fidelity

Magellan), and giant pension funds. For example, CALPERS, the huge California public employee pension fund ($245 billion in assets in early 2008), maintains a list of laggard companies (low-performing stocks) and regularly pressures their CEOs and boards for change. So does TIAA-CREF, the world's largest retirement and financial service firm (more than $435 billion in assets under management as of January 2008).[11]

Priority of Shareholder Interests

[The CEO is] . . . an employee of the stockholders, and *profit* is a shorthand term for the interests of . . . stockholders. . . . A really competitive enterprise can't sacrifice profit [to pursue social goals] unless he has some monopolistic power. (Milton Friedman in "The 'Responsible' Corporation," 1973, p. 56)

American managers and directors tend to be less oriented toward non-shareholder constituents (e.g., employees, creditors, suppliers, government, communities) than their European and Asian peers. Although these other interests are by no means ignored, shareholder value (share price appreciation and dividend payout) gets first attention. One explanation is that managerial pay bonuses are often tied to share price appreciation.

By contrast, in Japan, job security for employees and long-standing relational ties with suppliers usually take priority over dividend payout to shareholders (see Chapter 7). European managers and boards are more directly obliged, both socially and legally, to respond to other interests. For example, employees and creditors sometimes sit on company boards of directors (more discussion in Chapter 3). Also, governments there occasionally have partial equity stakes even in predominantly private firms.

High Exposure to Buyout and Takeover Pressures

Wider share ownership and higher share turnover expose U.S. managers to more buyout pressure than occurs abroad. A potential acquirer, whether welcome or not, may pursue a buyout or merger for strategic reasons. In some cases, firms are acquired by their own managers (management buyouts).

Buyouts and takeovers are commonly financed by exchange of stock or other assets or by borrowing (e.g., loans, bonds). Pressures intensified with the emergence of private buyout equity partnerships and associations in the 1970s (e.g., Kohlberg Kravis Roberts & Co., Forstmann Little, Blackstone Group, Carlyle Partners).[12] These groups mobilize substantial capital from diverse individual and institutional sources (endowments, pension funds, hedge funds, investment banks, insurance companies, sovereign investment funds) to buy underperforming firms they hope later to sell or take public for significant gain.

In Western Europe, similar buyout pressures were slower to emerge. Takeover attempts there are less often hostile than in the United States and often blocked by dominant shareholders. In some cases outsiders can own only nonvoting shares, and governments occasionally block acquisitions when the suitor is foreign. The high-risk "junk bonds" popularized in the United States to finance buyouts have been less available abroad and in some settings are illegal.

Attention to Numerical Performance Indicators

The difference between well-managed companies and not-so-well-managed companies is the degree of attention they pay to numbers, the temperature chart of their business. How often are the numbers reported up the chain of command? How accurate are those numbers? How much variation is tolerated between budget forecasts and actual results? How deep does management dig for its answers? . . . Does one set of numbers match the other? Is the actuality above or below the company's expectations? If it is either, what are you going to do about it? (Geneen, 1984a, p. 78; see also Geneen, 1984b)

For purposes of planning and control, managers commonly monitor and analyze indicators of earnings, profitability, productivity, sales, market share, and costs for their overall business and subunits thereof. Numerical indicators gained particular attention in the 1920s when the DuPont Corporation popularized a return-on-investment (ROI) approach to measuring and comparing performance (Davis, 1950).

In the late 1990s, additional indicators became popularized, including economic value added (EVA), market value added (MVA), and total shareholder return (TSR). EVA is the amount by which a company's return on its overall capital (equity and debt) exceeds the cost of that capital. Put differently, it is the company's operating profit after income taxes, interest, and dividend payout to investors.[13] MVA is the difference between the total funding (at book value) that stock and bond investors have put into a company and its current equity market value, a reflection of wealth created.[14] TSR is the sum of holders' share price appreciation (capital gain) and dividends earned.[15] Some companies tie changes in these and similar indicators to CEO pay bonuses.

In the opinion of some observers, U.S. managers give numbers more credence and attention than warranted. As Hayes (1985) noted, "Quantitative goals . . . tend to drive out non-quantitative goals. It is easy to believe . . . that anything non-quantitative is not important" (p. 113). In the same vein, Michael Porter (1992a, 1992b) concluded that fixation with numbers had become a significant barrier to efficient allocation of capital and suggested that American managers needed to focus more on grasping the assumptions underpinning their numbers. For other critics, the problem hasn't been the numbers per se but rather the short-term time horizon for tracking them.

Short-Term Performance Orientation

Too many public company managers are still chasing the wrong bottom line. They run their companies, make their investment decisions, and pay their subordinates according to short-term accounting numbers. (Rappaport, 1990, p. 99)

> Management is a balancing act between the short term and the long term, between different objectives at different times. You have to have performance concepts and measures that enable you to do different things at different times. And the present stock market and the constant pressure to make next quarter's numbers are a severe impediment to achieving that balance. (P. Drucker, in Schlender, 1998, p. 170)

Compared with peers abroad, U.S. firms tend to rely more on equity financing in proportion to debt (loans, bonds) and face more pressure to report higher earnings every reporting cycle. Hayes and Abernathy (1980) remarked that the tendency "to fix on profit centers necessitates, in turn, greater dependence on short-term financial measurements like return on investment (ROI) for evaluating the performance of individual managers and management groups," declaring that "maximum short-term financial returns have become the overriding criteria for many companies, [resulting in] inordinately market-driven (and insufficiently innovation-driven) business strategy" (p. 68; for a similar view, see Jacobs, 1991). Some reasons for short-termism include overmeticulous tracking and reporting of expected earnings by management (the so-called guidance provided to financial analysts). There is also much daily and weekly attention in the business press to small, near-term stock price fluctuations. Individual stockholders (and investment fund managers) seem to do more short-term trading rather than long-term investing. For example, between 1960 and 2002, the average holding period for a share of common stock in the United States dropped from 8 years to less than 1 (Porter, 1992a; see also Bhide, 1994).

> Indeed, between 1945 and 1965 annual portfolio turnover averaged a steady 17 percent, suggesting that the average fund held its average stock for about six years. . . . Compared to that earlier . . . standard that prevailed for some two decades, the average stock is now held by the average fund for an average of just eleven months. . . .
>
> If a six-year holding period can be characterized as long-term investment and if an eleven-month holding period can be characterized as short-term speculation, mutual fund managers today are not investors. They are speculators. (Bogle, 2005, p. 4)

Mutual fund and pension fund managers face constant pressure to report ever better near-term financial results, and stockbrokers generate more fee income when share turnover increases. Also, the growth of online stock trading has fostered a shorter-term trading mentality by many individual investors.

A short-term time horizon is also reflected in surveys about expected recovery time for new capital investment. For example, in response to a *Wall Street Journal* survey about their investment abroad, North American CEOs expected a payback period of 4.3 years, on average, compared with

5 years for European and Pacific Rim managers (apart from Japan) and more than 6 years for Japanese managers. When asked whether they were willing to consider a longer time period, only 32% of North American CEOs were so inclined, compared with higher numbers for their Pacific Rim (42%), European (49%), and Japanese (63%) counterparts ("Surveying the CEOs," 1989, p. R21).

In a similar survey of 300 large U.S. and foreign companies, 21% of U.S. respondents declared their investment projects to be long term, compared with 47% and 61%, respectively, for their Japanese and European counterparts (Porter, 1992a).

Short-term time orientation is attributable partly to high managerial mobility. Attainment of near-term profit goals can draw the attention of executive search firms and bring a new job offer at higher pay and more challenge or prestige with a different employer. Managers can also be motivated to postpone longer-term investment in order to report higher near-term earnings. Also, grants of executive stock options become valuable only when company share price rises. If these stocks vest too soon, they can bring about a short-term mind-set.

More Peer and Bottom-Up Performance Appraisal

Along with the traditional top-down review (e.g., by supervisory higher-ups and boards of directors), managers can be evaluated by their colleagues and even by subordinates (see Grote, 2005). In one survey, 32% of U.S. firms used bottom-up reviews to complement their top-down reviews (Seglin, 2001). The internal evaluations sometimes include forced ranking of all employees (e.g., at General Electric, Cisco, Hewlett-Packard, Sun Microsystems, Intel) (Grote, 2002). At General Electric, for instance, people ranked in the bottom 10% have been strongly encouraged to pursue other employment.

> General Electric, a company whose management techniques are closely followed, has long evaluated its managerial and professional employees on a curve. . . . Each year, individuals complete a long form in which they lay out their contributions and list both strengths and weaknesses and areas needing improvement. . . . Their supervisors use similar forms to evaluate their employees and to comment on the employee's own assessments. . . . The supervisor will also solicit the opinions of peers and subordinates. (Abelson, 2001, p. A1)

ORGANIZING

Organizing is concerned with the integration and coordination of resources and effort and the flow of information and authority. It considers what activities to decentralize and whether company structure should focus around business functions (e.g., marketing, finance, manufacturing), or around product group, geographic region, processes, projects, or some hybrid approach (e.g., a matrix). The preferred choice can depend on circumstances (e.g., organization size, strategy, performance, technology, people, goals). For example, a smaller business, or one with a narrow product line, will normally structure itself around the business functions. But if it grows or diversifies, then changing to a product or geographic area orientation can enhance coordination and integration of operations (see Chandler, 1962; Stopford & Wells, 1972). External factors (e.g., intensity of competition) can also influence change. High acceptance of change in American culture makes organizational change more welcome than in most cultures.

Two organizational tendencies in large U.S. corporations (relative to counterparts abroad) are as follows:

- More likely to decentralize authority (i.e., to delegate key tasks and decision-making authority to subordinates)
- More frequent organizational change

Decentralization of Authority

Decentralization (i.e., the delegation of decision-making authority to lower organizational levels) was necessary in the early nationwide expansion of American business. In that regard, the DuPont and General Motors pioneered so-called federal (multidivisional) structures in the 1920s (decentralized product divisions, each often a separate profit center, with autonomous revenue and cost accountability) (Chandler, 1962).

In Japan, by contrast, societal culture long favored more centralized authority. Businesses there were less likely to diversify quickly, so there was less pressure to decentralize. When expanding abroad, they were more likely to keep tight control at headquarters, ceding less autonomy to their foreign units. By contrast, U.S. firms were quicker not only to diversify but also to make structural changes during their surge into Europe in the 1960s (Servan-Schreiber, 1967/1968). They were quicker than Europeans to use cross-national structures within Europe (Franko, 1976). Dyas and Thanheiser (1976) found a tendency for French and German firms to stay organized around business functions even when circumstances (e.g., product and market diversification) favored a divisional structure (see Dyas & Thanheiser, 1976, pp. 299–303). By contrast, European competitors were slower to decentralize their operations, preferring closer "mother–daughter" ties between headquarters and regional subsidiaries (Franko, 1976). In that era, Servan-Schreiber (1967/1968) noted the following:

An American firm can change its methods in almost no time, compared to a European firm. . . . These U.S. subsidiaries have shown a flexibility and adaptability that have enabled them to adjust to local conditions. . . . One by one, American firms are setting up headquarters to coordinate their activities throughout Western Europe. This is true federalism—the only kind that exists on an industrial level. (p. 36)

A willingness to decentralize organizations can also be influenced by cultural factors. For example, in low power distance cultures (e.g., the United States) managers are more likely to cede authority to subordinates, and there is more ready acceptance of delegated authority by the subordinates. Conversely, where social class structures are more rigid (e.g., high power distance settings as in Asia, Latin Europe, and Latin America), there is generally less delegation and more reluctant acceptance of delegated authority by subordinates.

Frequent Organizational Change

The open U.S. economy and intense business competition contribute to many change-driven actions, such as mergers, acquisitions, split-ups, organization development interventions, structural reorganization, spin-offs, buyouts, startups, and bankruptcies. As one broad indicator of change over time, of the 500 U.S. companies in the S&P 500 index in 1957, only 74 remained in 1997 (Foster, 2001).[16]

Most of the world's biggest merger and acquisition (M&A) advisors (e.g., investment banks), and equity buyout firms originated in the United States. For years, their U.S. activity was much greater than in Europe, but the M&A gap is now largely eroded.

One practice conducive to U.S. mergers and acquisitions has been high severance payouts (golden parachutes) to senior managers displaced by change in ownership. According to one source, 60% to 70% of large U.S. firms had such parachutes in 1999, compared with only 15% of British ones and even lower numbers on the European continent. Also, the prevalence of managerial stock options has been conducive to organizational change and risk taking. These options have high potential for personal financial gain if change is successful but little risk if it isn't. Another contributing factor is broad U.S. cultural acceptance of change (low score on Hofstede's uncertainty avoidance).

DIRECTING

The managerial function of directing involves guiding, commanding, nudging, exhorting, and inspiring subordinates, colleagues, superiors, and others to higher performance. This requires skills of leadership, communication, and motivation, in turn influenced by culture.

Among some general tendencies of U.S. managers and subordinates (relative to many counterparts abroad) are the following:

- Much directness in interpersonal communication
- Aversion for authoritarian leaders
- Motivation mainly from money, ego gratification, and personal challenge (and less from loyalty and personal relationships)

Broadly speaking, U.S. managerial (and other) communications tend to be direct and straightforward, a defining trait of a low-context culture. As Edward Hall (1976) noted,

Context and communication are intimately interrelated. In some cultures, messages are explicit; the words carry most of the information. In other cultures, such as China or Japan or Arab cultures, less information is contained in the verbal part of the message, since more is in the context. That's why American businessmen often complain that their Japanese counterparts never get to the point. The Japanese wouldn't dream of spelling the whole thing out. To do so is a put-down; its like doing your thinking for you. (p. 64)

In a similar vein, Peter Lawrence (1996, p. 64) pointed out the following:

In the American meeting, rank and hierarchy differences will intrude less than say in France or Britain (though they are present). Power play will be more direct. Nothing that needs to be said will be unsaid for reasons of delicacy or interpersonal restraint. . . .

American meetings move things on. At the end of the meeting you know:

- What is going to be done
- Who is going to be responsible for what actions
- When it is going to be done

This directness can be seen in the highly detailed business agreements (formal written contracts with carefully crafted contingency clauses), detailed employment contracts, and performance appraisals.

Effective leadership style can depend on the people involved, the tasks at hand, and other situational factors. The low power distance and low uncertainty avoidance of U.S. culture are not conducive to an authoritarian or paternalistic leadership style.

U.S. CEOs are attracted to high pay and personal challenge but are less driven (than most foreign peers) by loyalty to family, colleagues, owner, or boss. As noted previously, CEO pay in large companies is very high by world standards, and the pay packages are more personalized. For many managers, the issue isn't so much the level of pay but rather how it compares with that of peers both inside and outside the company, a reflection of personal self-worth.

Chapter Summary

For decades, the traits, triumphs, and troubles of U.S. management have attracted global attention. The United States has contributed much to the emergence of management thought and theory, consulting, recruitment, education, and research; nowhere has there been so much dialog and debate about managerial topics.

U.S. managerial tradition and practice draw from a distinctive political, economic, and sociocultural setting that shows the following features:

- Business–government relations are more neutral than in most countries, so there is less government ownership, less public assistance for business, and more economic freedom. However, antitrust rules and civil rights are generally more protected; labor unionism and union political power are weaker than in Europe.

- In general, the U.S. economy has been more free, productive, and competitive than most. There is more entrepreneurship and employee mobility; the overall tax burden is lower in relation to income; unemployment and inflation have been low; corporate shareholdership is broad-based.

- U.S. culture reflects high individualism and high tolerance for risk, change, and diversity; power distance is low; equality of opportunity is valued more than material equality; the culture is predominantly low context, oriented toward direct (explicit) communications and an orderly view of time (life, including work life, is scheduled; punctuality is valued) and formality in business agreements (carefully worded contracts).

In regard to managers and management in large companies,

- U.S. CEOs are more mobile and higher paid than peers in Europe and Japan, but have less international experience than Europeans; the pay gap comes not mainly from salary but from supplemental pay (bonus and performance pay) and commonly includes employer stock and stock options.

- U.S. managers have been more likely than foreign peers to formalize their long-term planning activity; they rely more on external consultants, are more accepting of change, and are drawn more quickly to new ideas and fads.

- Managers rely heavily on numerical performance indicators and face more intense pressure from investors to improve near-term financial results; there is more exposure to external takeover tries and more attention directed to stockholder interests (shareholder value) relative to other stakeholders (employees, creditors, suppliers, communities).

- There has been a stronger tendency in the United States than abroad to decentralize organizations and to effect organizational change (acquisitions, mergers, restructurings, managerial mobility).

- Leadership, communication, and motivation style conform with the low-context nature of U.S. culture; in general, people prefer nonauthoritarian leaders; directness and frankness are valued in personal communication, including in performance evaluations; pay, public esteem, and personal challenge are stronger motivators than is loyalty to an employer.

Terms and Concepts

equity buyout (private equity) firm
executive headhunter
golden parachute
hostile takeover
management buyout
management performance indicators
multidivisional organization structure

performance pay
professional management
Protestant ethic
shareholder capitalism
stock option
total shareholder return

Study Questions

1. Describe what is distinctive about the American managerial macroenvironment (economic, political, sociocultural, demographic, educational). What features differ the most from those of another country or culture with which you are familiar? In your judgment, is the U.S. macroenvironment changing? Explain how this could influence managerial practice and performance.

2. Investigate the personal background of the CEO of a large U.S. company. Find out as much as possible about the person's age, education, family background, career path, time in rank, international experience, and the like. To what extent does the profile conform with the prototype presented in this chapter?

3. Describe prevailing patterns, pressures, strengths, and criticisms of contemporary U.S. managers and management.

4. By global standards, U.S. managerial pay has been substantially higher than in other countries. How can this be explained? Discuss the following opinion: In the continuing, probably everlasting debate about managerial compensation, most CEOs seem to believe they are worth every dollar they get. By contrast, many investors think executive pay is unfair, has little relationship to performance, and is out of control.

5. From a managerial perspective, discuss trade-offs (advantages, disadvantages) between a company going public or remaining privately held.

Exercise 2.1

Investigate what is distinctive about the U.S. system of higher education for business management in comparison with that of another country or world region.

Exercise 2.2

Investigate and discuss the corporate governance guidelines enacted by the U.S. Congress in 2002 (Sarbanes–Oxley Act). In your judgment, have the guidelines contributed to improved corporate governance and performance? Discuss.

Case Study

Board of Directors

In U.S. stock exchange–listed companies, boards of directors typically are empowered (by law and company bylaws) to counsel and oversee management on behalf of stockholders.

Critics of boards sometimes note that directors tend to rubber-stamp the plans, actions, and decisions of the CEO. This has been attributed partly to having too many "inside directors" (executive directors). Even though outsiders usually outnumber insiders, it is not unusual for a U.S. CEO, or a recently retired one, to chair the board and to set and control meeting agendas, filter information, and influence the nomination of directors. Also, some directors are (or have been) CEOs of other firms and may be likely to protect management more than shareholder interests when these interests diverge. It is alleged that this bias contributes to the high pay of American CEOs compared with their peers abroad. Some firms pick directors whom they also tap for professional services (e.g., consultancy, legal advice, loans), triggering potential conflicts of interest.

Questions

1. In your view, what are the traits of an ideal company board of directors in terms of its size, director selection process, composition, experience, tenure, and director pay?

2. Investigate the board of directors of a specific company. If you were hired as an independent external advisor, what changes would you to suggest to its board, and why? Many company Web sites provide director biographies. For information on a particular corporate board, check the site for headings such as "investor relations" or "corporate governance."

Notes

1. About 624,000 non-U.S. students were enrolled in U.S. higher education in 2007–2008, with about 1 in 5 concentrating on business and management studies (Institute for International Education, http://opendoors.iienetwork.org/?p=131534).

2. See "World's Most Respected Companies" (2005); in 2007, 8 of the world's 10 most admired in a *Fortune* magazine global ranking were U.S. firms (Fisher, 2008, p. 67).

3. Examples of U.S. government corporations include the U.S. Postal Service, Eximbank (export loan guarantor), Overseas Private Investment Corporation (political risk insurer for some U.S. direct investors abroad), Amtrak (rail transport), and the Tennessee Valley Authority (electric power generation).

4. U.S. Bureau of Labor Statistics (n.d.). http://www.bls.gov/news.release/union2/nr0.htm.

5. The United States ranked fifth on the 2008 Heritage Foundation/Wall Street Journal Index of Economic Freedom (O'Grady, 2008), behind Hong Kong, Singapore, Ireland, and Australia.

6. U.S. foreign investment figures are reported annually in the August issue of *Survey of Current Business* (U.S. Department of Commerce).

7. In February 2008, about 7,000 companies (some of them non-U.S.) were listed on the New York, American, and Nasdaq stock exchanges (the 3 largest of 12 U.S. stock exchanges); U.S. securities market regulation (Sarbanes–Oxley Act of 2002) has contributed to a gradual reduction in listings.

8. The five publications of the Academy of Management are the *Academy of Management Review, Academy of Management Journal, Academy of Management Perspectives, Academy of Management Learning & Education Journal,* and *Academy of Management Annals.*

9. Other academic professional associations include the Academy of Business Education, Academy of Business and Administrative Sciences, American Society of Business and Behavioral Sciences, Academy of International Business, and Institute of Behavioral and Applied Sciences.

10. Examples (past and present) of U.S. CEOs leading foreign firms in other English-speaking countries include Solomon Trujillo (Telstra, Australia, 2005), Robert Diamond Jr. (Barclays, UK, 2005), Marjorie Scardino (hired by The Economist Newspapers, Ltd., in 1993 and in 1996 picked to lead its parent firm, Pearson PLC, UK), Ann Iverson (Laura Ashley, UK, 1996), Richard Brown at Britain's Cable & Wireless PLC (1996), Jonathan Ornstein (Virgin Express, UK, 1996), Richard Giardano (BOC, UK, industrial gases), Gene Lockhart (Midland Bank, UK), Paul Anderson (Broken Hill Proprietary, Australia), Robert Joss (Westpac Banking Corp., Australia), Don Voelte (Woodside Energy, Australia), Tom Glocer (Reuters, UK news agency), and Nancy McKinstry (Dutch publisher Kluwer).

11. TIAA-CREF serves mainly educational and research institutions; see http://www.tiaa-cref.org/newsroom/quickfacts.htm1;TIAA-CREF.

12. More information on buyout equity investors can be found at the Private Equity Council Web site (http://www.privateequitycouncil.org/); see also "Kings of Capitalism" (2004).

13. EVA was conceived and popularized by New York consultancy Stern Stewart & Co. See Lieber (1996) and Topkis (1996).

14. *Fortune* magazine published annual EVA and MVA rankings for large U.S. corporations for a few years beginning in 1993.

15. See the *Wall Street Journal* annual shareholder scoreboard (since 1996), an annual ranking of 1,000 major U.S. companies according to "total stockholder return" for 1-, 5-, and 10-year time periods (http://www.wsj.com).

16. If a firm is dropped from the S&P 500 large-cap stock index, it hasn't necessarily disappeared because the index is picked and readjusted by committee. Also, a few firms in the index are non-U.S.

References

Abelson, R. (2001, March 19). Companies turn to grades and employees go to court. *New York Times*, p. A1.

Abrahamson, E. (1996, January). Management fashion. *Academy of Management Review, 21*(1), 254–285.

Ackhoff, R. (1970). *A concept of corporate planning*. New York: Wiley.

Ansoff, I. (1965). *Corporate strategy: An analytical approach to business policy for growth and expansion*. New York: McGraw-Hill.

Antunes, D., & Thomas, H. (2007). The competitive (dis)advantages of European business schools. *Long Range Planning, 40*(3), 382–404.

Barnard, C. (1938). *Functions of the executive*. Cambridge, MA: Harvard University Press.

Bartlett, C., & Ghoshal, S. (1994, November–December). Changing the role of top management: Beyond strategy to purpose. *Harvard Business Review, 72*(6), 79–88.

Benner, K., Levenson, E., & Rupali, A. (2007, October 15). Special report: The 50 most powerful women. *Fortune*, p. 107.

Berle, A., & Means, G. (1932). *The modern corporation and private property*. New York: Macmillan.

Bhide, A. (1994, November–December). Efficient markets, deficient governance. *Harvard Business Review, 72*(6), 128–139.

Bogle, J. (2005). The mutual fund industry sixty years later: For better or worse? *Financial Analysts Journal*. Retrieved August 22, 2008, from http://johncbogle.com/speeches/JCB_FAJ2005.pdf

Brush, M. (2006, July 26). *European CEOs make half the pay*. Retrieved August 24, 2008, from http://articles.moneycentral.msn.com/Investing/CompanyFocus/EuropeanCEOsMakeHalfThePay.aspx

Carson, P., Lanier, P., Carson, K., & Guidry, B. (2000, December). Clearing a path through the management fashion jungle: Some preliminary trailblazing. *Academy of Management Journal, 43*(6), 1143–1158.

Chandler, A. (1962). *Strategy and structure*. Cambridge, MA: MIT Press.

Colvin, G. (2004, June 28). A concise history of management hooey. *Fortune*, p. 166.

Colvin, G. (2006, February 6). Catch a rising star. *Fortune*, pp. 46–50.

Corporate elite. (1992, October 12). *BusinessWeek*, pp. 119–146.

Corporate elite. (1993, October 11). *BusinessWeek*, pp. 64–109.

Davis, T. (1950). *How the DuPont organization appraises its performance*. New York: American Management Association Treasurer's Department.

Drucker, P. (1973). *Management tasks, responsibilities, practices*. New York: Harper & Row.

Drucker, P. (1990, April 23). The best book on management ever. *Fortune*, p. 145.

Dyas, G., & Thanheiser, H. (1976). *The emerging European enterprise: Strategy and structure in French and German industry.* London: Macmillan.

Economic and financial indicators: Labor disputes. (2006, April 29). *The Economist,* pp. 100–101.

Executive Recruiter News. (2005, February). http://www.kennedyinfo.com/home?C=4kzwvwT9h04Pvy3L

Executives hold traditional values regarding job mobility and tenure. (2007, October 24). Association of Executive Search Consultants press release. Retrieved August 22, 2008, from http://www.aesc.org/article/pressreleases/

Fisher, A. (2008, March 17). America's most admired companies. *Fortune,* p. 65–67.

Foster, R. (2001, September 10). Managers journal: The Welch legacy—Creative destruction. *Wall Street Journal,* p. A18.

Franko, L. G. (1976). *The European multinationals.* Stamford, CT: Greylock.

Geneen, H. (1984a, October 1). The case for managing by the numbers. *Fortune,* p. 78.

Geneen, H. (with Moscow, A.). (1984b). *Managing.* New York: Avon.

Grote, D. (2002, November–December). Forced ranking: Behind the scenes. *Across the Board, 39*(6), 40–45.

Grote, D. (2005). *Forced ranking: Making performance management work.* Cambridge, MA: Harvard Business School Press.

Guerrero, F., & Pimlott, D. (2007a, December 4). Cultural melting pot not seen as necessary. *Financial Times,* p. 21.

Guerrero, F., & Pimlott, D. (2007b, December 4). U.S. bosses "lacking global perspective." *Financial Times,* p. 21.

Hall, E. (1976, July). How cultures collide. *Psychology Today, 10*(2), 66–74.

Hambrick, D., & Chen, M. (2008). New academic fields as admittance-seeking social movements: The case of strategic management. *Academy of Management Review, 33*(1), 32–54.

Hamel, G., & Prahalad, C. (1990, May–June). The core competence of the corporation. *Harvard Business Review, 68*(3), 79–91.

Hayes, R., & Abernathy, W. (1980, July–August). Managing our way to economic decline. *Harvard Business Review, 58*(4), 67–77.

Hayes, T. (1985, November–December). Strategic planning: Forward in reverse? *Harvard Business Review, 63*(6), 111–119.

Hilmer, F., & Donaldson, L. (1987). *Management redeemed: Debunking the fads that undermine corporate performance.* New York: Free Press.

Hire and hire, the recruitment industry never had it so good. (2007, June 20). *Financial Times,* p. 16.

Hofer, C., & Schendel, D. (1978). *Strategy formulation: An analytical concept.* St. Paul, MN: West Publishing.

Instant coffee as management theory. (1997, January 25). *The Economist,* p. 57.

Jacobs, M. (1991). *Short term America: The causes and cures of our business myopia.* Cambridge, MA: Harvard Business School Press.

Karlsson, P., Neilson, G., & Webster, J. (2008, Summer). CEO succession 2007: The performance paradox. *strategy + business.* Retrieved August 26, 2008, from http://www.strategy-business.com/press/freearticle/08208?pg=all

Kennedy Information. (2008). *Global consulting marketplace 2007–2010: Key data, trends & forecasts.* Retrieved August 22, 2008, from http://www.consultingcentral.com/research/service-line/global-consulting-marketplace/BTCC28207GLOB2007-LC01

Kings of capitalism: A survey of private equity. (2004, November 27). *The Economist* (Supplement).

Kono, T. (1984). *Strategy and structure of Japanese enterprise.* Armonk, NY: M. E. Sharpe.

LaPorta, R., Lopez-de-Silanes, F., & Schleifer, A. (1999). Corporate ownership around the world. *Journal of Finance, 54*(2), 471–517.

Largest consulting practices by revenue. (2007, November 19). *Financial Times,* p. 1.

Lawrence, P. (1996). *Management in the U.S.A.* Thousand Oaks, CA: Sage.

Lieber, R. (1996, December 9). Who are the real wealth creators? *Fortune,* p. 107.

Lublin, J., & White, J. (1997, September 11). Dilbert's revenge: Throwing off angst, workers are feeling in control of careers. *Wall Street Journal,* p. A1.

Lucier, C., Kocourek, P., & Habbel, R. (2006, Summer). CEO succession 2005: The crest of the wave. *strategy + business, 43.* Retrieved August 22, 2008, from http://www.strategy-business.com/press/article/06210?pg0

Lucier, C., Wheeler, S., & Habbel, R. (2007, Summer). The era of the inclusive leader. *strategy + business, 47.* Retrieved August 22, 2008, from http://www.strategy-business.com/press/article/07205?pg=0

Martin, J. (2004, January–February). The global CEO. *Chief Executive,* p. 24.

McComas, M. (1986, April 28). Atop the Fortune 500: A survey of CEOs. *Fortune,* p. 26.

Micklethwait, J., & Wooldridge, A. (1997). *Making sense of the management gurus.* New York: Time Books/Random House.

Mintzberg, H. (1994a). *The fall and rise of strategic planning.* New York: Free Press and Prentice Hall International.

Mintzberg, H. (1994b, January–February). The fall and rise of strategic planning. *Harvard Business Review, 72*(1), 107–114.

O'Grady, M. (2008, January 15). The real key to development. *Wall Street Journal,* p. A10.

Poe, R. (1983, February). A walk and talk with Peter Drucker. *Across the Board, 20,* 32–45.

Porter, M. (1992a). *Capital choices: Changing the way America invests in industry.* Washington, DC: U.S. Council on Competitiveness.

Porter, M. (1992b, September–October). Capital disadvantage: America's failing capital investment system. *Harvard Business Review, 70*(5), 65–82.

Rappaport, A. (1990, January–February). The staying power of the public corporation. *Harvard Business Review, 68*(1), 96–104.

Real pay. (2006, January 21). *The Economist,* p. 102.

Record-breaking churn in 2005. (2006, January 31). Burson-Marsteller press release. Retrieved August 22, 2008, from http://www.burson-marsteller.com/newsroom/lists/PressReleases/DispForm.aspx?ID=542&nodename=Press%20Releases%20Archive&subTitle=Record-Breaking%20CEO%20Churn%20In%202005

The "responsible" corporation: Benefactor or monopolist. (1973, November). *Fortune,* p. 56.

Schlender, B. (1998, September 28). Peter Drucker takes the long view. *Fortune,* pp. 162–173.

Seglin, J. (2001, June). Reviewing your boss. *Fortune,* p. 248.

Servan-Schreiber, J.-J. (1968). *The American challenge* (R. Steel, Trans.). New York: Atheneum. (Original work published 1967 as *Le défi Américan*)

Servan-Schreiber, J.-J. (1969). *The American challenge.* New York: Avon.

Sloan, A. (1964). *My years at General Motors.* Garden City, NY: Doubleday.

Spencer Stuart. (2004). *Route to the top 2004: Fortune 700 CEOs.* Retrieved August 26, 2004, from http://www.spencerstuart.com/ArticleViewer.aspx?PageID= 10096&ArtID=4074799

Spencer Stuart. (2005). *Route to the top 2005. Leading CEOs: A statistical snapshot of S&P 500 leaders.* Retrieved June 6, 2006, from http://www.spencerstuart .com/research/articles/936/

Spencer Stuart. (2006). *Route to the top 2006. Leading CEOs: A statistical snapshot of S&P 500 leaders.* Retrieved October 23, 2007, from http://www.spencerstuart .com/research/articles/975

Spencer Stuart. (2007). *Route to the top 2007. Leading CEOs: A statistical snapshot of S&P 500 leaders.* Retrieved May 26, 2008, from http://content.spencer stuart.com/sswebsite/pdf/lib/Final_Summary_for_2008_publication.pdf

Steiner, G. (1969). *Top management planning.* New York: Macmillan.

Stone, N. (Ed.). (1998). *Peter Drucker on the profession of management.* Cambridge, MA: Harvard Business School.

Stopford, J., & Wells, L. (1972). *Managing the multinational enterprise.* New York: Basic Books.

Story, L. (2007, December 12). Seeking leaders, U.S. companies think globally. *New York Times,* p. A1.

Surveying the CEOs. (1989, September 22). World business; business abroad. *Wall Street Journal,* p. R21.

Taylor, F. W. (1911). *Principles of scientific management.* New York: Harper & Row.

Topkis, M. (1996, December 9). A new way to find bargains. *Fortune,* p. 265.

U.S. Department of Education. (2007). *Digest of education statistics.* Retrieved August 22, 2008, from http://nces.ed.gov/programs/digest/d07/tables/dt07_279 .asp?referrer=list

Vault Europe. (2008). *Top 25 consulting firm rankings, the top 25 most prestigious.* Retrieved October 18, 2007, from http://europe.vault.com/nr/consulting_ rankings/euro-consulting-rankings.jsp?euroconsult2008=2&ch_id=252

Wooldridge, A. (1997, March 22). A survey of management consultancy. *The Economist,* p. 1–22.

World's Most Respected Companies. (2005, November 18). 8th annual survey. *Financial Times.* Retrieved August 26, 2008, from http://media.ft.com/cms/ 8209896e-576c-11da-b7ea-00000e25118c.pdf

Wrapp, H. E. (1979, April 8). A plague of "professional" managers. *New York Times,* p. F16.

Wren, D. (1972). *The evolution of management thought.* New York: Ronald Press.

Western European Management 3

> *Whether it be only a question of fashion in management—which, like all fashions, can change—or whether it be a question of looking for the best single road to industrial achievement, it would seem no more than sensible to consider as contenders other management systems than our own. . . . In this competition, Western Europe deserves a serious look.*
>
> —David Granick (1964, p. 15)

In the late 1960s, a Frenchman's best seller, *The American Challenge* (Servan-Schreiber, 1967/1968), drew global attention to a growing U.S. corporate presence in Europe. While praising the prowess of American management, it saw Europeans slow to adopt modern management methods. By the 1970s, though, perceptions were changing (Heller & Willat, 1975), and by the 1980s, European direct investment in the United States (cumulative book value) surpassed U.S. investment in Europe. By the late 1990s, European firms in the *Fortune* magazine annual Global 500 outnumbered ones from the United States and Japan. Prominent European businesses now rank among the world's most respected companies. They include dozens of well-known giants such as Nestlé, Nokia, Royal Dutch Shell, BMW, Unilever, and British Petroleum (see the longer list in the Appendix at the end of this chapter) and many lesser-known medium-size firms such as those from among Germany's *Mittlestand,* the *media industria* of northern Italy, and other "hidden champions" throughout the region (Simon, 1996).

Europeans have also contributed much to management thought and theory, including the word *management* itself:

The linguistic origin of the word [*management*] is from the Latin *manus*, hand, via the Italian *maneggiare,* which is the training of horses in the manege; subsequently its meaning was extended to skillful handling in general. . . . However, the word also became associated with the French *menage*, household, as an equivalent of "husbandry" in its sense of the art of running a household. . . . The Scot Adam Smith, in his 1776 book *The Wealth of Nations*, used "manage," "management," . . . and "manager" when dealing with the process and persons involved in operating joint-stock companies. (Safire, 1989, p. 18)[1]

Europe gave rise to the Industrial Revolution and transformational technological evolution (e.g., hydraulic and electrical energy, internal combustion engine), contributing to bigger business and more challenging management problems. For dealing with larger size, German Max Weber (1864–1920) famously explained the merits of more rational organizational practices, policies, and structures (i.e., bureaucracy) to replace ad hoc methods and personalism of the past.[2] Frenchman Henri Fayol, the manager of a coal mine, conceptualized several core management functions that have become the most common framework for introductory management courses and textbooks.[3]

Renowned management doyen Peter Drucker (author, consultant, and professor) was born in Austria of Dutch ancestry and lived in Germany and England before emigrating to the United States. Drucker (1973) once called German banker Georg Siemens the world's first CEO to have thought through the role, operation, and structure of a top management team (at Deutsche Bank, in the late 19th century) and to have created "the first such organ in economic and business history" (p. 606).

Other European contributors to management theory were Von Bertalanffy (systems perspective), Lewin, Trist, and Emery (employee involvement in decision making), the British military during World War II (management science), and Geert Hofstede (influence of societal culture) (see Hofstede, 1993; Hofstede & Kassem, 1976). Although formal management education had a slow start in Europe, it has expanded in recent decades, especially in France and the United Kingdom. So too have academic and professional associations and journals focused on management topics.[4]

Chapter Objectives

- To broadly describe the Western European managerial macroenvironment (polity, economy, culture) in current and historical context

- To note unique patterns in European labor relations (e.g., unionism, collective bargaining, and employee involvement in decision making)

- To profile the personal backgrounds of Western European CEOs (with some intra-European, U.S., and Asian comparisons)

- To highlight some distinctive managerial practices, pressures, problems, and styles in Western Europe

The Western European Macroenvironment

Western Europe extends from the Arctic to the Mediterranean and the North Atlantic to former Eastern Europe (now called Central Europe), on a land area about one third the size of the United States. It includes 15 European Union (EU) nations plus Norway and Switzerland (Table 3.1) and a population one third larger than that of the United States. Jointly, the 17 would be the world's largest market, largest exporter, and leading source and host of foreign direct investment. Figure 3.1 shows the area discussed in this chapter.

Figure 3.1   Map of Western Europe

Table 3.1   Western Europe Includes 15 (of 27) EU Nations Plus Norway and
                   Switzerland

	Population (2007)	Gross Domestic Product (adjusted for purchasing power)
Germany	82.4 million	$2.6 trillion
France	63.7	1.9
Britain	60.8	1.9
Italy	58.1	1.9
Spain	40.4	1.1
Netherlands	16.2	0.53
Belgium	10.4	0.34
Sweden	9.0	0.29
Austria	8.2	0.28
Portugal	10.6	0.21
Greece	10.8	0.26
Denmark	5.5	0.20
Finland	5.2	0.18
Ireland	4.1	0.18
Luxembourg	0.5	0.03
Norway	4.6	0.21
Switzerland	7.6	0.26
Western Europe	**398.1**	**12.2**
United States	**301.1**	**13.1**
World	**c. 6,600.0**	**c. 66.0**

SOURCE: Data from Central Intelligence Agency (2008).

POLITY AND ECONOMY

The conceptual recognition of Europe began to coalesce around the 9th century, with roots going back to imperial Greece and Rome, followed by several centuries of social, intellectual, political, economic, and technological change. That legacy continued through the Medieval era (c. 800–1200), Renaissance (14th and 15th century), Protestant Reformation (16th century), Industrial Revolution (late 1700s and early 1800s), and French Revolution (late 18th century), forging institutions and ideas integral to modern Western civilization. These include the rule of law, civil and economic freedom, and ingredients of modern capitalism (e.g., double-entry bookkeeping, capital markets, business law, insurance, and limited-liability companies). It also gave rise to the scientific method and emergence of modern science.

Adam Smith's *The Wealth of Nations* (1776) famously explained how individuals serve the common social and material good even when pursuing self-interest and why a freer economic system yields a higher material standard of living than can a collectivized (e.g., state socialist or communal) one.

Europe also gave rise to Marxist social and political theory (late 19th and early 20th centuries). German social philosopher Karl Marx (1818–1883) concluded that ordinary workers produced society's wealth but had long been denied due material reward. He believed that the economic inequality inherent in capitalism would eventually force its demise, and he predicted prolonged struggle between the proletariat (peasants and industrial workers) and their exploiters (private owners and administrators of farms and factories).[5] Until the proletariat invariably triumphed, many Marxists saw a need for socialized (collective) ownership and control of economic resources, spurring a turbulent transition to state socialism in 20th-century Soviet Union, Eastern Europe, China, and beyond. (The managerial traits, triumphs, troubles, and transition of state socialism are discussed in Chapter 4.)

Capitalism prevailed in Western Europe but was accompanied by more government economic intervention than in the United States. Labor troubles of the early Industrial Revolution (long work hours, low pay, substandard working conditions, child labor) gave rise to more government involvement in labor relations. In general, Europeans have aspired to more material equality and job and income security, in contrast to the U.S. interest in equal opportunity and labor mobility. For example, in a broad opinion survey U.S. and European respondents were asked "Which is more important for government?" and then asked to choose between "(A) to guarantee that no one is in need" and "(B) to provide freedom to pursue goals." Responses for Germany, France, Britain, and Italy all hovered around 60% for choice A, whereas about 60% of U.S. respondents favored B ("A Survey of America," 2003, p. 4). Western Europe's egalitarian leanings draw from its religious, political, and social heritage, including a Judeo-Christian value system that long frowned on unequal wealth and income.

There was some early experimentation with employee ownership and control, including Robert Owen's transfer of his cotton textile mill to its employees (New Lanark, Scotland, c. 1800). His experiment failed, but Owen and other so-called utopian socialists of his era inspired future producer, consumer, and other cooperative enterprises in Western Europe and beyond. (The merits and limitations of employee ownership and control are discussed in Chapter 5.)

Systemic welfare state capitalism coalesced in Western Europe after World War II to include extensive "free" (taxpayer-paid) public education, health insurance, old-age pensions, unemployment income, and other social services. Its social democratic agenda became more strongly entrenched in Scandinavia, France, Germany, Austria, and the Netherlands, and to a lesser degree in the United Kingdom, Switzerland, and Ireland. Sweden has had some of the world's highest levels of government social spending and taxation relative to national income (50%–60%) (see Table 2.3 in the previous chapter). However, the Swedish economy has relied mainly on private enterprise to produce goods, services, jobs, income, and tax revenue.[6]

Most Western European economies can be called mixed; that is, they show both private and government ownership in business. However, state ownership is now much diminished, and these nations rank high in global indices of economic freedom (see the Heritage Foundation *2008 Index of Economic Freedom* at http://www.heritage.org/index/). Business–government relations have been more collaborative than in the United States, with more central government industrial policy support (loans, grants, rescues) for certain companies and sectors (e.g., agriculture, steel, electronics, aircraft manufacturing, airlines).

Western European welfare state capitalism has slowed its economic growth and raised questions about long-term affordability (including pending shortfall in promised pension and health insurance benefits). Worries include a rising median age, ever more retirees, and a shrinking labor force. Strict regulatory barriers against layoffs induce firms to hire more cautiously and rely more on part-time and temporary employees. Long-term unemployment has been higher than in the United States and Japan, especially among the youngest and oldest working-age people.

Labor costs are high. Because of high income tax and social security taxes, take-home pay is less than one half of gross labor costs in continental Europe ("Taxing Wages," 2007). Generous unemployment pay and disability pay cause some people to work less, become voluntarily unemployed, or show up less regularly for work (see Alvarez, 2004; "Sweden's Welfare State," 2002). The egalitarian pay levels reduce individual incentive to change employers, thus slowing human resource movement from declining industries and sectors to the ascendant ones.

Table 3.2 identifies some broad demographic, political, and economic features of the Western European macroenvironment of the early 21st century.

Table 3.2   The Western European Macroenvironment at Turn of the 21st Century

Demographic	Seventeen nations (two non-EU); overall population about 400 million (2007), low birth rates; natural population growth declining but offset by immigration.
	High and rising median age.
Political and Legal	Parliamentary democracies.
	Gradual political integration, including regional political institutions (e.g., European Commission, Parliament, Court of Justice).
	High (but declining) level of unionization (though low in France and Spain).
	High percentage of the labor force works under collective bargaining contracts.
	Considerable sector-wide collective bargaining.
	Close ties between labor unions and political parties.
	Labor relations policies and practices have been more government regulated than in the United States; fewer issues are resolved through collective bargaining because so much is already covered by law.
	Mandatory employee involvement in workplace decision making (e.g., through elected workers' councils) and, in some countries, employee representation on employer boards of directors.
Economic	Produces about one fifth of annual global economic output with just one twentieth of the world's workforce; living standards among the highest in the world.
	Mature economies; slow economic growth.
	Regional economic integration (the EU) contributing to gradual harmonization of the economic environment, including a spreading common currency (the euro) and coalescing rules for antitrust enforcement, intellectual property protections, capital market regulations, environmental protection, consumer rights, labor law, and the like. Full integration is years away.
	High value of exports in proportion to gross domestic product (GDP) compared with the United States and Japan.
	Falling number and proportion of low-skill manufacturing jobs; growth in service sector jobs.
	Predominantly social market economic systems, that is, market guided but with more government intrusion than in the United States.
	Significant off-the-books employment and income, especially in southern Europe.

(Continued)

Table 3.2 (Continued)

Economic (continued)	Government spending and taxation are high in proportion to income.
	More inward and outward foreign direct investment (cumulative book value) than any world region.
	High personal income per capita and high marginal tax rates; high payroll-based taxation on employers; extensive value-added consumption taxes; high minimum wage.
	Rigid labor markets; lower labor force participation rates (and shorter work weeks) than in the United States and Japan; high job security for the already employed; high labor costs; low job mobility; low job generation; high unemployment, especially among the youngest and oldest working-age people; high long-term unemployment.
	Significantly underfunded long-term social security (retirement income) and health insurance commitments.
	Smaller proportion of companies (than in the United States) that sell common stock to the general public; less widespread share ownership.
Social Market Economies (Welfare Capitalism)	*Goals*
	Political democracy, social equality, job protection, income security.
	Government Role
	Generous social assistance benefits (welfare, health insurance, disability pay, education, unemployment compensation, parental leave, retirement income) funded by high taxation and borrowing; legal and regulatory barriers to layoffs.
	Significant financial support and protection for certain companies and industries (e.g., steel, airlines).

The region shows some variation between its social market systems, as follows (Sapir, 2005):

- The *Rhennish (or continental) model*, that is, of the Rhineland (Rhine River basin and surrounds) including Germany, Austria, France, the Netherlands, Luxembourg, and Belgium. Strong labor unions, generous unemployment benefits, below-average employment rate.

- The *Mediterranean model*, that is, Italy, Greece, Spain, and Portugal. Has the region's strongest job protections, least generous unemployment pay, smallest proportion of working-age population in jobs, youngest retirement age, and most generous retirement pensions in proportion to preretirement income; highest government debt/GDP ratio.

- The *Anglo-Saxon model,* that is, the United Kingdom, Scotland, and Ireland. Lowest unemployment rates, weakest labor unions, weakest job protections, lowest government debt burden, lowest welfare outlays, modest unemployment benefits, most flexible employment rules.

- The *Nordic (Scandinavian) model,* that is, Sweden, Norway, Finland, Denmark, Iceland. Highest taxes and most generous welfare benefits, highest equality of wealth and income, lowest long-term unemployment rates; has the most retraining and relocation support for unemployed people and tightest criteria for unemployment compensation; along with the Anglo-Saxon group, the highest proportion of working-age population holding jobs; oldest retirement age.

CULTURE

Western Europe's cultural legacy has evolved over centuries and has influenced other world regions since colonial times. Table 3.3 lists some broad cultural tendencies for the region and some intraregional differences. Some managerial implications of patterns and differences are suggested later in the chapter.

Table 3.3   Prevalent Sociocultural Patterns in Western Europe

Predominantly Judeo-Christian sociospiritual heritage (Protestant, Catholic, and Jewish)
Ethnic and cultural diversity; major cultural subcategories (cultural clusters) include the Nordic or Scandinavian, Germanic, Anglo, and Latin; growing Islamic immigrant minority; problematic assimilation of non-EU immigrants
Predominantly high-context cultures in the south (Latin, Greek) and low-context cultures in the north (Nordic, Germanic, Anglo)
An egalitarian social value system inclined to favor equality of end result (material equality), by contrast with the U.S. emphasis on equality of opportunity
Limited but growing participation of women in nontraditional work roles, especially in northern Europe, and more so in government positions than in business
More social stigma than in the United States for failure (e.g., in school or business) and less opportunity to begin anew

Despite extensive cultural mixing from centuries of intraregional travel, trade, and migration, significant cultural differences persist, notably between the Nordic (or Scandinavian), Germanic, Anglo, and Latin clusters (Figure 3.2).

Continental Europe (Southern and Northern)					Anglo (English-Speaking) United Kingdom and Ireland
Southern Europe		**Northern Europe**			
Greek	*Latin*	*Scandinavian*	*Germanic*	*The Low Countries*	
Greece	Portugal	Denmark	Germany	Belgium	
	Spain	Sweden	Austria	Netherlands	
	France	Norway	Switzerland (Germanic and Latin cantons)	Luxembourg	
	Italy	Finland			

Figure 3.2   A Geocultural Profile of Western Europe

SOURCE: Adapted from R. Calori, "The Diversity of Management Systems," in Calori and de Woot (1994).

Germanic Europe includes Germany and Austria plus ethnic German minorities in neighboring nations (e.g., Switzerland, Poland). Anglo Europe (predominantly English speaking) includes the United Kingdom and Ireland. Latin Europe (Italy, Spain, Portugal, and France) has languages based heavily on Latin, the language of early Rome. Four small nations (Belgium, the Netherlands, Luxembourg, and Switzerland) have mixed linguistic and cultural roots; for example, most southern Belgians (Walloons) speak French, whereas northerners (Flemish) speak Dutch. Switzerland is home to German-, French-, and Italian-speaking Swiss.

Western Europe's north is mainly low context, and the south (Mediterranean Europe) is mainly high context.

EMPLOYER–EMPLOYEE RELATIONS

In every work setting, decisions are regularly made about pay, fringe benefits, work schedules, layoffs, retirement, promotion, training, and the like. These can be decided unilaterally by management or in consultation with employees or by government regulation. In Europe, government has intervened more in labor relations than in the United States. Unionism, too, has some notable differences from North America.

European Unionism

West European labor unions have had more political power and influence than their U.S. counterparts. This comes from a long history of labor involvement in sociopolitical change in the late 19th and early 20th centuries (Kassalow, 1969). Unions have had closer ties to political parties and ideologies. For example, leftist unions (e.g., socialist, communist) are particularly strong in southern Europe (e.g., Italy, France, Spain), moderate left ones (e.g., Social Democratic) in Britain, Scandinavia, and Germany, and centrist to moderately conservative ones (e.g., Christian-Democrat, Catholic) in Belgium and the Netherlands.

In some cases (e.g., Sweden, Denmark, France), labor unions either administer or co-administer national pension benefit programs. Governments regularly consult with unions about labor policy, and several nations (e.g., France, Belgium, Germany, Italy, Sweden) have special labor courts to handle labor relations cases.

Unionization rates, though gradually dropping, are higher than in the United States (except in France), ranging from more than 80% in Scandinavia (which has extensive white-collar unionism) to 20% in Spain and less than 10% in France. (About 12% of the U.S. workforce was unionized in 2008 and below 8% in the private sector.)

Proportionately more European employees than Americans work under collective bargaining agreements. However, because labor relations have been more guided by government, the range of issues covered in those agreements tends to be narrower than in the United States. All told, European managers have less liberty than Americans to shape their labor relations policies and practices internally. There has also been more sector-wide collective bargaining (e.g., in France, Spain, and Germany) compared with the mainly company-based agreements in the United States. In Germany, for instance, Gesamtmetall, an employer group for the metalworking industry, negotiates with labor group IG Metall (more than 3 million members); another group covers the rubber, chemical, glass, paper, energy, mining, and recycling industries. There is another for the German construction industry and another for government employees.

There has been slow progress in harmonizing labor law throughout the EU. Cross-border collective bargaining may one day emerge, an idea endorsed by the European Trade Union Confederation (pan-European labor consultation group) but resisted by most employer groups.[7]

Democracy in the Workplace

Compared with much of the world, Europe has more government-mandated consultation and decision sharing between management and workers. That includes plant-level committees (works councils), self-managed work teams, and employee participation on company boards of directors in some countries.

Works Councils. These are required by law in most European countries (e.g., France, Sweden, Austria, West Germany, the Netherlands) and voluntary in others (e.g., Finland, Britain). The councils typically are elected by employees and can include union and nonunion members. They can be as large as 40 people in large plants and as few as 3 in small ones. The law obligates management to engage with them on many labor relations matters and sometimes on enterprise policy and strategy. In Germany and the Netherlands, for example, councils have had some voice on capital investment, director appointments, and proposed mergers and acquisitions.

Self-Directed Work Teams. Another approach has been self-directed work groups, an approach that gained intellectual impetus from the Tavistock Institute of Human Relations (London) in the late 1940s and later the Norwegian Institute for Industrial Social Research (Emory & Thorsrud, 1976).

One much-publicized example in that regard was a so-called sociotechnical systems approach to organizing automobile assembly at Volvo plants at Kalmar (1974–1994) and Uddevalla (1988–1993), Sweden. The system was based on ideas of job design, job enlargement, and job enrichment, and workers were involved in making plant layout decisions and setting work assignments and schedules (Peterson, 1976). They favored a team approach in which members could perform diverse tasks rather than the single repetitive ones common in traditional plants. This approach required fewer supervisors, improved morale, and lowered turnover and absenteeism. However, productivity wasn't high, and it was discontinued in 1993–1994 (Prokesch, 1991).

The experience nonetheless suggests that team-managed production can be feasible where labor costs aren't an overriding competitive factor and where societal and corporate culture are favorable, that is, settings that are low in power distance and have high tolerance for change and ambiguity (low uncertainty avoidance). Although Sweden has the right cultural profile, Volvo was handicapped by high labor costs and strong global competition.

Worker Directors. Employee representation on company boards of directors was pioneered in West German government-controlled coal and steel firms beginning in 1951. Known as *Mitbestimmung,* or codetermination, it was extended in 1976 to all large German companies in all industries. Big German companies have two boards: a management board (*Vorstand*) composed of senior-level managers and a supervisory board (*Aufsichtsrat*) representing broader stakeholders (shareholders, employees, creditors, the community). One half of supervisory board positions and votes are reserved for elected worker directors, including at least three union members. One labor director is elected by the white-collar employees. The chair of the supervisory board, a shareholder representative, can cast a tie-breaking vote, if needed. A two-thirds majority vote is required to select a new CEO. In smaller German firms (500–2,000 employees) employees elect just one third of the supervisory board.

There is also board-level employee participation in Sweden, Denmark, France, Luxembourg, and the Netherlands, but to a lesser degree. In Greece, Ireland, and Portugal, it is seen in state-owned companies (Knudsen, 1995). This approach has contributed to less confrontational labor–management relations in northern Europe than in the south and fewer labor disputes than in many countries. (See Figure 2.1 in Chapter 2.)

Flextime

Employee involvement, labor union pressures, labor law, and the collective bargaining system have also contributed to more flexible scheduling of work hours. Several European countries (notably Germany, Sweden, Switzerland, and the Netherlands) have widespread flextime arrangements. In the United States, flextime has more often been temporary and more for professionals rather than for ordinary workers (Berg, Appelbaum, Bailey, & Kalleberg, 2004). The U.S. Bureau of Labor Statistics indicated that about 28% of the U.S. labor force had flextime work schedules in 2007.

Some German employers implement flextime (*Gleitzeit,* "gliding time") on a monthly or yearly basis, as described in the following passage:

> At Beck-Feldmeier, a department store in Munich which started flexiyears as an experiment in 1978, . . . 900 employees choose how many hours they want to work during the next 12 months. Full-time staff work at least 173 hours a month; part-timers anything from 60–160 hours. . . . When they work . . . during the month is a matter of negotiation with their supervisor. . . . It is even possible to work six months and take the next six off. Flexiyears has helped Feldmeier cope with a problem common to all retail stores—idle shop assistants at quiet hours of the week or periods of the year and queues of customers . . . at busier times. . . . The scheme has already radically altered the makeup of the store's workforce. The ratio of 65% full-timers to 35% part-timers in 1978 has been reversed. ("Management: Flexiyears," 1983, p. 76)

The Western European Manager

This section turns to Western European CEOs' personal backgrounds, career paths, pay, tenure, and prevailing values, management practices, and style. It notes some intra-European variation and contrasts with the

United States. The generalizations here do not describe all managers but rather reflect general tendencies among ones for which the most information is available: CEOs of large companies.

Terms for CEO or Equivalent in Several Western European Languages

English	*Chief executive officer (CEO), managing director*
German	*Vorsitzender, Generaldirektor*
French	*Président-directeur géneral, président du comité exécutif, administrateur délégué du conseil d'administration*
Italian	*Direttore generale, amministratore delegato di consiglio di amminstrazzione, presidente*
Spanish	*Presidente*
Portuguese	*Presidente*
Swedish	*Konzernchef, verkstallande direktor*
Danish	*Koncernchef*
Finnish	*Konzernchef*
Norwegian	*Konsernsjef*
Dutch	*Voorsitzer van het Uitvoerend comité*

SOCIAL STATUS OF BUSINESSPEOPLE

Until the 20th century, Europe's businesspeople were not often viewed as social peers by societal elites. Before then, businesses were small and commercial livelihood a less genteel way to earn a living. Some exceptions included founder–owners of long-standing family businesses. Serge Grosset describes the pattern:

> During the nineteenth century in Europe and America, the new business-men, the nouveaux riches, had to "break into" the well-established group composed of the heirs to family businesses. As a rule, the longer a family had been in business, the greater was its social prestige. In turn, the prestige of the established business families varied from country to country. The United States was the only country where businessmen and nonbusiness-men alike considered "business" something to be proud of. In Europe . . . the greatest honor was to serve the state and not to work for individual profits. Careers in the army, civil service, or the professions consequently ranked above business, even if these careers did not bring as many material rewards. (Grosset, 1970, p. 65)

By late 19th and early 20th century, though, businesses grew bigger and managerial talent became more valued and rewarded, but this occurred more slowly in Europe than in the United States.

AGE, GENDER

Like their North American peers, Western European CEOs are predominantly well-educated men appointed at around age 48–50.[8] Proportionally fewer women (than in the United States) are CEOs or board directors in large companies. In 2008, for example, companies on the FTSEurofirst 300 had seven female CEOs, three of them European and four American (the U.S. S&P 500 had 15 in 2007). For the same years, 9.7% of the FTSEurofirst 300 board directors were female (compared with 16% of the S&P 500). Female directorships are more common in Scandinavia, accounting for 18% to 26% of large firms in Sweden, Finland, and Denmark; in Norway (44%), the law mandates at least 40%. In other nations, numbers were lower: the Netherlands, 12.3%; United Kingdom, 11.5%; Germany, 7.8%; France, 7.6%; Spain, 6.6%; and Italy, 2.1%.[9]

MANAGERIAL MOBILITY

In times past, CEO turnover and mobility in Europe were lower than for American peers. One reason was more egalitarian pay, and hence less financial incentive to change employers. There was also a stigma associated with mobility. Barsoux and Lawrence (1990) made that point in regard to France:

> In France mobility is not a universal sign of professional success and ambition. Indeed it is just as likely to be construed as the result of successive failures, or even instability. . . . Indeed, bright young graduates are warned not to be too anxious to the offers of headhunters since they may get a reputation for instability. (p. 5)

Percy Barnevik, former chairman and CEO of Asea Brown Boveri (a Swedish–Swiss engineering firm) once expressed skepticism about the notion of a professional manager who can manage different companies in different industries, remarking (as quoted in Jackson, 1998), "You have to respect people who know the business deep down. The idea that a professional chief executive can run anything is plain wrong. The person who runs Nestlé will not be the right person to run ABB" (p. 16).

Robert Frank (1998) expressed a similar view:

> European managers still follow the "escalator" model of career advancement, where employees start at the bottom of a company at an early age and

slowly move up the ranks over 20 or 30 years, regardless of results. In Europe, workers who jump from job to job are blackballed as "unstable." In the U.S. they are "ambitious." (p. B1)

Today, however, U.S. and European CEO turnover rates (voluntary and involuntary) are about the same according to the Booz Allen Hamilton annual survey of the world's 2,500 largest companies (Karlsson, Neilson, & Webster, 2008).[10] (See Table 2.6.) Booz Allen surveys indicate that between 1995 and 2006, the average tenure of European CEOs who had been forced from office (i.e., involuntary turnover) was 2 years less than in the United States (5.2 years vs. 7.1 years). Their survey analysis attributed this shorter tenure to hedge fund and equity buyout activity bringing record numbers of mergers and acquisitions. Also, European boards of directors have become less tolerant than before of subpar financial results. In essence, stockholder capitalism has gained ground there. The increased mobility is also seen in more firms (especially in Britain, Germany, and the Netherlands) pursuing CEO talent beyond their own borders. Tagliabue (2008) reported growing numbers of nonnationals leading firms on the major national stock exchange indices, including 7 firms on the French CAC 40, 5 on the German DAX 30, and 34 on the British FTSE 100. Some recent and current examples are as follows:

CEO Name	Nationality	Employer
Anders Moberg	Swedish	Ahold (Dutch food and beverage retailer)
Hakan Samuelsson	Swedish	MAN (German mechanical engineering firm)
Jurgen Dorman	German	ABB (Swedish–Swiss engineering firm)
Jean-Pierre Garnier	French	GlaxoSmithKline (British pharmaceutical company)
Philippe Varin	French	Corus (British–Dutch steel maker)
Josef Ackermann	Swiss	Deutsche Bank
Wolfgang Mayrhuber	Austrian	Lufthansa (German airline)
Lindsey Owen-Jones	Welsh	L'Oreal (French cosmetics firm)
Harry Roels	Dutch	RWE (German utility company)
Louis Schweitzer	Swiss	Renault (French auto manufacturer)

Helmut Maucher	German	Nestlé (Swiss food company)
Paul Bulcke	Belgian	Nestlé
Peter Brabeck	Austrian	Nestlé
Peter Loscher	Austrian	Siemens (German telecom conglomerate)
Oswald Gruber (co-CEO)	German	Credit Suisse (Swiss bank)
Jose Luis Duran	Spanish	Carrefour (French retailer)
Robert Polet	Dutch	Gucci (Italian luxury goods)
Patrick Cescau	French	Unilever (British–Dutch consumer goods)

A few ways in which European CEOs in big companies differ from their North American peers include the following:

- Less likely to have studied business and management during their higher education

- More international experience (work, travel, study, living)

- Lower pay

- More balance between work life and private life

FORMAL MANAGEMENT EDUCATION

Cox and Cooper (1985) note that Europeans have traditionally sought educational and experiential breadth in their business leaders:

> A tendency to believe in the stereotype of the local manager or administrator as a classically educated and widely cultured gentleman, who because of his breadth of knowledge and general understanding of how the world works will be able to cope with every situation—the "gifted amateur" tradition. Even where this is not seen as the ideal manager, it still has an appeal as an ideal sort of person to be. This valuing of a broad classical education runs parallel with a suspicion of anyone trained in what is seen as a narrow specialization. . . . Thus . . . there is very little chance that a relatively young and imprecise specialization such as the behavioral sciences is going to be taken very seriously. (p. 32)

European managers are well educated but less likely than U.S. counterparts to have studied business and management during their formal higher education. For example, a 1999 survey of leading companies worldwide noted that just 11% of European CEOs held an MBA degree, compared with 39% of their American peers (*Which MBA?* 1999). In 2001, about 13,000 MBA degrees were awarded in the United Kingdom, highest in all of Europe. Germany had about 5,500 MBA students in 2004 (Foundation for International Business Accreditation, http://www.fibaa.com/engl/ mba.htm). By comparison, the United States graduated 142,617 MBAs in 2004–2005 (about one fifth were non-U.S. citizens, including some Europeans) (U.S. Department of Education, 2007).

Nonetheless, European higher education in business studies has been growing. Several schools such as the Institut Européen d'Administration des Affaires (INSEAD) (France), the International Institute for Management Development (IMD) (Switzerland), Nijenrode (the Netherlands), and Theseus (France) were initially started by private companies and eventually spun off. A 2008 *Financial Times* ranking of full-time global MBA programs (FT Business Education, January 28, 2008) listed 29 European entries among the top 100 (there were 63 from North America, including 57 from the United States and 6 from Canada). Average program enrollment numbers are much lower in Europe than in the United States.

The extent of European higher business education varies by country, being widespread in the United Kingdom and France but much less so in Germany and Italy. However, Germany has been changing course, with 70% of its current MBA programs founded between 1999 and 2004, notably after the German parliament officially approved business bachelor's and master's programs as part of university education (Foundation for International Business Accreditation, http://www.fibaa.com/engl/mba .htm). Except for the United Kingdom, management education is offered less often in universities and more often in specialized schools or institutes. European programs are commonly shorter than American ones. For bachelor's-level business studies, 3 years has been the norm there (compared with 4 in the United States). Many European MBA programs run 12–18 months (compared with 18–24 months in the United States) (Bradshaw, 2001). Also, European providers rely more on part-time practitioner–instructors than on full-time academic PhDs. That too is changing. For example, in 1970, only one instructor at INSEAD (the leading private international school in France) held a doctoral degree ("Management Theory," 1995). By 2008 nearly all did. Also, the leading European MBA programs have been more international in terms of student mix, curriculum, and instructional staff than most U.S. rivals. However, English is often the main language of instruction in the more well-known programs, including those in Europe. Schools have less independent funding than their major U.S. rivals (Antunes & Thomas, 2007).

Proportionally, Europe emphasizes executive education (evening and weekend study, open enrollment, and customized programs) rather than full-time in-residence study. Recently, about two thirds of 65 top-ranked custom MBA programs were European (FT Business Education, May 14, 2007).

There are now European national and regional academic accreditation review boards for business studies[11] and professional educator associations. The European Academy of Management accommodates scholars in the field of management (membership around 1,000 in 2008). The European Group of Organisational Studies had about 1,650 members in 2007 (mainly European but from 46 countries around the world). There is also the British Academy of Management and the European Foundation for Management Development (Brussels). There are also more management academic journals and more full-time faculty with doctoral degrees.

INTERNATIONAL EXPERIENCE

There is no European specificity in management techniques, whether they be in finance, marketing, IT, management control or corporate governance. There is, however, specificity in the art of managing people, based on a more internationally diverse body of managers who are multilingual, who have had multiple international experiences, and who are therefore skilled at applying their international experience at corporate headquarters level. (Vic Luck,[12] as quoted by T. Dickson, 2000, p. 15)

In general, European CEOs have more international experience than their U.S. peers. In one *Wall Street Journal* survey (Anders, 1989), 47% had worked abroad (compared with 32% for a comparable U.S. sample), 37% had managed a business abroad for their current employer (compared with 16% for the U.S. sample), and 28% had studied abroad (compared with 15% for the U.S. sample). More recently, based on biographical information from comparable populations of firms, 40% of European CEOs (FT 2005 Europe 500) have international experience, compared with just 24% of U.S. peers (S&P 500) (Hamori & Koyunku, 2007, p. 11).

One clear reason is the close proximity in Europe of different cultures and languages. Most European young adults speak English and one or two other languages. Also, international trade and investment are more prominent in their economies. For example, Germany has led the world in merchandise exports, which represent about 40% of its GDP (compared with 12% in the United States). The merchandise produced abroad by German companies surpasses even their home exports ("Germany's Best Kept Secret," 2006). Recently, firms listed on France's main stock index (CAC 40) generated two thirds of their revenue outside France (Schwartz & Bennhold, 2008). Across the EU, merchandise trade in proportion to GDP has been regularly above the Organisation for Economic Co-operation and Development country average, whereas the United States and Japan have been below that average.

In view of their international experience, Europeans seem better prepared than Americans and Asians to manage a cross-national or cross-cultural workforce and to accommodate cultural differences (Calori & de Woot, 1994; Calori & Dufour, 1995). They are more likely than either Americans or Japanese to place host country nationals in charge of their foreign subsidiaries. They also have more nonnationals on their boards of directors. In 2005, 90% of Europe's largest firms (ranked by market value) had one or more foreign directors, versus 45% for a comparable U.S. sample (S&P 200).[13]

PAY

CEO pay has been lower in Europe than in the United States. However, different sources, samples, and degree of disclosure make precise comparisons difficult, even within Europe. The 2005–2006 Towers Perrin Worldwide Total Remuneration report ("Real Pay," 2006, p. 102) showed average total pay of U.S. CEOs ($2.3 million) to be about twice that of German, British, French, and Italian peers in companies with at least $500 million in sales. (See Table 2.8 in Chapter 2.) Scandinavian and Dutch CEOs earned even less.

A 2008 Hay Group report on the 50 largest companies showed a similar pay gap, about €13 million versus €5 million, respectively, for U.S. and European CEOs (Burgess, 2008). That source showed European base salaries to be 20% higher than for U.S. peers, but their bonuses and long-term incentives were much lower. The Towers Perrin report indicates that variable bonuses and incentives amounted to about 30% to 40% of compensation in Europe and 62% in the United States.

Table 3.4 presents some additional comparative pay information.

Table 3.4   CEO Compensation

Country	Median Compensation	Sample	Year
United States	$6.8 million	Mercer U.S. 350[a]	2005
United Kingdom	$4.3 million	FTSE 100[b]	2005
France	$3.0 million	CAC 40[c]	2004
Netherlands	$1.47 million	75 publicly traded companies[d]	2004

a. From Mercer Human Resource Consulting (largest 350 companies in the United States).

b. From Independent Remuneration Solutions, London (largest 100 companies listed on the Financial Times Stock Exchange).

c. From Proxinvest (40 firms on the French benchmark stock index).

d. From Hewitt Associates (75 publicly traded companies, including small, medium, and large stock values) as cited in Fabrikant (2006, p. 1).

Equity-based incentive pay has been gaining ground in Europe, and the pay gap with the United States has been shrinking. Stock options are now widespread in Europe, especially where share ownership is most dispersed (United Kingdom, Ireland, Sweden, the Netherlands). Large French firms also use them extensively (Ferrarini & Moloney, 2005).

Europeans are more inclined than Americans to criticize high CEO salary, severance pay, and retirement payouts (see Olson, 2002). British board directors are obliged by law to vote on management pay packages, an advisory vote that influences but doesn't set pay). In Germany, employee directors on company boards have been a moderating force. Until 2007, German companies weren't required to disclose individual pay of the senior management board (*Vorstand*) members.

BALANCE BETWEEN WORK LIFE AND PERSONAL LIFE

Some evidence suggests that Western European executives achieve (or at least aspire to) more balance between their work and other life interests than do U.S. peers. In one broad inquiry in the 1980s, senior executives (930 executives in 10 countries) were asked whether their personal career, home life, or other outside interests brought them the most personal satisfaction (Posner & Schmidt, 1983). Only one third of the European sample indicated career (compared with one half of Americans), one half said home life (compared with 40% of Americans), and 14% said other interests (compared with 10% of Americans). Another survey (Arbose, 1980) showed executive personal satisfaction from career to be higher in Europe's north (Scandinavia, Germany, the Netherlands) than in the south (Spain, France, Italy, Greece). In addition, proportionately fewer Europeans than Americans expressed willingness to attend an important corporate function at the expense of an important family function, and more declared they had already achieved their life's ambition, suggesting that their career wasn't likely to bring much new personal or professional challenge.

In general, Europeans seem less inclined "to live to work" than Americans. Vacations are more protected and enjoyed. A common German expression for *vacation* is "July," and for the French, "August," when holiday pull is strong. In 2007, the average number of U.S. vacation days (13) was well below that of Italy (42), France (37), Germany (35), and the United Kingdom (28) (World Tourism Organization information retrieved from Infoplease, http://www.infoplease.com/ipa/A0922052 .html). However, it is doubtful that big-company CEOs take much extended holiday time.

NATIONAL DIFFERENCES IN MANAGERIAL BACKGROUNDS

The educational background and career paths of Western European CEOs have differed somewhat by country and era. In the past, for example, *The Economist* magazine ("European Management," 1988) highlighted some differences between French, British, German, and Italian managers in large private and state-owned firms. It acknowledged that its observations were a "caricature to be sure . . . but not so grotesque . . . as to be unrecognizable" (p. 89). And in retrospect, many of the perceptions have stood the test of time (Klarsfeld & Mabey, 2004; Mayer & Whittington, 1999).

For France, the magazine noted the highly elite academic preparation for business leadership in renowned *grandes écoles,* including the Ecole Nationale d'Administration (ENA), elite engineering schools (e.g., Ecole Polytecnique, known more simply as "X"; Ecole de Mines), and economics, business, and management schools, all operating outside the French university system.

In the late 1980s, graduates of prominent *grandes écoles* accounted for about three fourths of CEOs of large private and public French companies (Handy, Gow, Gordon, Randlesome, & Maloney, 1987). Schwartz and Bennhold (2008) reported that at least half of the French CAC 40 (largest 40 French firms) were led by graduates of either ENA or X. It is noteworthy that many French CEOs began their careers in the civil service. Thornhill (2007) reported that former civil servants were managing 63% of the CAC 40 index.

France is also home to INSEAD, a premier international business school. Also, French local chambers of commerce, industry, and the professions support a national network of business schools that offer 3-year study programs analogous to U.S. university undergraduate business programs. One distinct feature is student work internships inside and outside France.

For the United Kingdom, *The Economist* observed that just like the French, big British industrial companies and civil service have favored well-rounded administrators ("European Management," 1988, p. 89). However, the British have seldom had much crossover between government and industry. It concluded, "The British stress social and political skills, with a little bit of accounting thrown in, [and] in-house training." For the typical large company, promising young British candidates are put on fast-track promotion, and a "privileged few . . . [are] whisked quickly up to the penthouse offices at the top, working briefly in each of the company's divisions as they go," in 2- to 3-year cycles.

The Handy Report (Handy et al., 1987) on European management education noted that in comparison with German and French peers, proportionately fewer top British managers had university degrees, but this is no longer so. The proportion of CEOs in the FTSE 100 companies (Britain's largest firms) not holding a university degree fell from 37% in 1996 to 12% in 2005 (Marx, 2006).

Whereas continental European CEOs often have backgrounds in technical fields and their career paths are in production and engineering, senior British managers are more likely to have accounting and finance backgrounds. Currently, about 38% of Britain's CEOs (FTSE 100) have such backgrounds, followed by sales and marketing (23%) and general management (18%) (Marx, 2006). That profile partly explains long-standing British weakness and relative disinterest in durable goods manufacturing and their prowess in finance, the media, retail, and advertising.

Britain is noteworthy for its many very large firms. For example, in a recent annual ranking of firms based on their market value (the FT Global 500, 2008), 35 were British, compared with only 31 and 22, respectively, for France and Germany. The FT Europe 500 (2008) listed 87 British firms, compared with 49 for Germany and 73 for France. However, when the comparison is based on sales revenues (Fortune Global 500, 2008), numbers look more balanced: Britain (35 firms), France (39), and Germany (37).

CEOs of 18 of the 20 most admired firms in the British FTSE 100 had previous international experience. One half of the 18 were non-British (Marx, 2006).

Whereas in the 1980s, British CEO pay was among the lowest in Western Europe, it is now higher than most, and in 2007 was close runner-up to France in the Hay Group numbers (Burgess, 2008). Towers Perrin data (2005, reported in "Hot Topic," 2006) showed a wider gap in Britain than on the continent between average CEO pay and that of an average manufacturing worker. In the United Kingdom, the spread was a multiple of 22, compared with 15 in France and 222 in the United States.

Formal postsecondary schooling for business is more widely available in Britain than on the continent, but its elite universities (Oxford and Cambridge) didn't provide any until the 1990s. Until the 1970s, British higher education for business, as in engineering, was domain of polytechnic institutes. Thereafter, the universities of London, Manchester, Cranfield, and others started MBA programs, and eventually so did Oxford (1991) and Cambridge (1997). Recently, 15 of the 28 top-ranked full-time European MBA programs were in the United Kingdom (FT Business Education, 2008). So were 14 of the world's top 100 global MBA programs, more than in any nation except the United States.

In Germany, *The Economist* noted a strong educational emphasis on technical subjects and much on-the-job training ("European Management," 1988, p. 89). Managerial promotion was slower than for British and French peers, and career paths were more narrow (Stewart, Barsoux, Kieser, Ganter, & Walgenbach, 1996).

Lawrence (1980) noted high German regard for the enterprise builder (*Unternehmer,* or chief entrepreneurial executive), such as the founder–CEOs of thousands of *Mittelstand* (middle-size manufacturing firms).[14] Although most *Mittelstand* are still owner or founder managed, they have become less so over time (Simon, 1992, 1996).

German managerial aspirants usually begin their careers at a later age (mid- to late 20s) than peers throughout Europe. University degree programs there have been longer (although now being shortened through an EU effort to standardize higher education systems).[15] One reason is a long-standing German tradition of apprenticeship training. Although this is mainly for craftspersons rather than managers, the apprenticeship mind-set can slow fast-track promotion of younger people by their higher-ups.

German university students are attracted to business careers but have been less likely than American, British, or French peers to choose business studies. In recent years, just 10% of German university students received degrees in business (the BWL diploma), compared with 22% of students in the United States (undergraduate bachelor's degree). About twice as many German students as Americans earn science degrees, which has contributed to German prowess in manufacturing (equipment, machinery, high-end consumer goods, chemicals). Many German CEOs have science and engineering degrees, including several with PhDs.

Recently, German higher education for business has been expanding (*The MBA Guide 2009,* 2008). Much of it was previously done in higher technical schools (*Fachhochschulen,* or universities of applied sciences) and at some universities (usually in their departments of economics rather than in separate business schools).

In 2008, not one German MBA program (other than one jointly administered with Dutch and British partners) was listed on the *Financial Times* European ranking (28 ranked schools) or the global MBA ranking (100 schools).

A new German provider (the European School of Management and Technology, in Berlin) was started in 2002 with backing from German companies, initiating a 1-year MBA program in 2006. Also, a handful of private universities now offer business studies, spurred by the 2003 formation of the Foundation for International Business Administration Accreditation (FIBAA), a business studies accreditation agency. As of 2006 FIBAA quality certification had been granted to 53 master's programs in 41 institutions in Germany, Austria, and Switzerland (see http://www.fibaa .com). Also, many large German companies provide internal management education and training programs. For example, the global insurance giant Allianz has a management institute that serves internal needs and became the first German in-house "corporate university" to gain FIBAA quality certification (Williamson, 2005).

For Italy, *The Economist* ("European Management," 1988) noted,

> Like West Germany, Italian industry favours technicians and distrusts administrative elites. Though businessmen and government officials rub elbows on the 7 AM Milan–Rome shuttle, they tend not to swap each other's jobs, as in France. . . . Italy's few big private business groups tend to be run by small teams loyal to the boss: an Agnelli, a Gardini, or a De Benedetti. But in the management level just below, there is now a lot of movement from firm to firm

according to Mr. Corrado Masturo of ORGA, Italy's oldest and biggest head-hunting firm. The strengths of the Italian manager, he thinks, are hard work, a good sense of strategy and an ability to take quick decisions. The weakness, except at the very top, is that managers still think in provincial terms. (p. 89)

Although it was the world's twelfth largest national economy in 2008, Italy has a very high proportion of small and medium-size businesses and few giant private ones. In 2003, 43 of its largest 100 companies were still family owned and controlled (Becht, Betts, & Morck, 2002). The 2008 *Financial Times* Global 500 listed only 7 Italian companies, and the *Fortune* Global 500 showed just 10. There were only 28 Italian firms (many of them state owned) on the 2008 FT Europe 500.

Despite few large private manufacturers, Italy has many very competitive small and medium-size ones (*media industria*) in various industries (vehicle parts, ceramic tile, high-fashion apparel, furniture, footwear, machine tools) situated mainly in the Italian north and northeast (Piedmont, Lombardy, Veneto, and Emilia Romagna provinces).

Italy hasn't produced much formal higher education for business and management but has a prominent graduate school, the SDA Bocconi at the University of Bocconi in Milan. Another is the University of Modena and Reggio Emilia school of economics. In 2003, only 10% of Italy's working-age population held a university degree, compared with 38% for the United States and 24% for Germany.

European Management
Perspective, Process, and Practice

When for two thousand years you have seen yourself as part of the most dominant continent, from which all important thinking has been initiated and which has had far reaching effects on the rest of the world, it requires a large readjustment to accept influence from elsewhere. This is not, of course, to say that there would not be value in accepting such ideas. The reverse is, undoubtedly, true, but the ideas have to be tested for appropriateness and absorbed slowly into the culture. (Cox & Cooper, 1985, p. 34)

Although it can be easy to overgeneralize about Western European managerial pressures, patterns, traits, trends, and traditions, there is sufficient informed opinion from diverse sources to offer a general profile and note some contrasts with the United States. Nonetheless, pressures of globalization and regional integration are contributing to some gradual convergence in the region.

At the mid-20th century, Harbison and Burgess (1954) described Western European managers as more risk averse than their American rivals and more inclined to understaff their businesses.[16] (Long-standing

European legal protections for job security still discourage aggressive hiring.) They saw European decision making as more centralized and organizational practices more improvised. In their view, Europeans were less intensely competitive, disinclined to favor rapid growth, more cautious. They were adept at cost control and likely to emphasize lower volume and higher per-unit profit margins (compared with the American penchant for rapid growth regardless of margin). These traits, with high and inflexible labor costs, have helped to explain European attention to product quality (rather than product volume and diversity) as the key to gaining and sustaining competitive commercial advantage.

In 1962, David Granick surveyed several dozen British, German, French, and Belgian senior managers and sensed stronger tendency for secrecy among Europeans than among Americans. He noted less interfirm mobility and less inclination to see management as a profession. In that same era, an American business professor noted some similarities between U.S. and British managers but some differences from peers on the mainland (Kast, 1964). The latter were less mobile between firms, their decision making more centralized, and their leadership more paternalistic. They also relied less on staff specialists and committees. About the same time, Otto Nowotny (1964), CEO of Swiss pharmaceutical firm Hoffman Laroche, wrote in the *Harvard Business Review* that European and American managers differed in terms of their management philosophy. Europeans, he suggested, were more reverent of the past and more inclined toward incremental growth (rather than rapid growth). When appointing managers, they valued more the qualities of wisdom and experience and were less likely to promote younger people very quickly. Americans emphasized personal energy and vitality and were more likely to place promising candidates on fast-track promotion paths. He also saw Europeans as more formal in their business demeanor, especially the northerners (Scandinavians, Dutch, Germans). Others also note more formality:

> Given any three executives attending any international convention—one American, one British, one continental—it is a safe bet that before it ends the two Anglo-Saxons (at the American's instigation) will be addressing each other by their Christian names, while both will continue to address the European, Herr Doktor Schmidt, say, as Herr Doktor Schmidt. (Heller & Willat, 1975, p. 82)

> One sales manager at a German manufacturer . . . who was born and raised in France and speaks five languages fluently was . . . taken aback when employees of his Indiana (U.S.) client called him by his first name. "In Germany you don't do that until you know someone for ten years—and never if you are at a lower rank," says the manager, who asked his name not be used for fear of offending customers. (Hymowitz, 2000, p. B1)

Rudy Knoepfel (1974), CEO of Solvay (a Belgian chemical firm), observed that whereas American managers pursued sales growth "to the point of worship," Europeans were more cost conscious and less comfortable with change. In his view, Europeans were less wasteful of resources and better able to handle resource scarcity. In the 1980s, *The Economist* described European CEOs as being less driven by fads, less prone to buy and sell their companies, and less entrepreneurial than Americans (Sandeman, 1984; see also Kirkland, 1986). One reason given was that European firms, even many large ones, were likely to remain family owned longer, favoring stability and continuity rather than the opportunity and risk of faster-paced growth.

In the 1980s, perceptions began to change. By the mid-1980s, the U.S. business press described European management and managers as less parochial, more competitive, and more in tune with modern management practices. They were less reluctant to promote younger managers quickly and more willing to look for managerial talent beyond their own borders ("Europe's New Managers," 1982).

The next sections present additional comparisons from the viewpoint of the management process (management functions).

PLANNING

As mentioned in Chapter 2, European companies have been less inclined than U.S. counterparts to formalize their long-term planning activity. A 1970s study of strategy and structure in 79 large diversified French and 78 German firms found that proportionately fewer of them had a separate planning staff than American ones. It concluded that "preparation of strategic decisions could be significantly improved by . . . more systematic collection of information and more sophisticated processing" (Dyas & Thanheiser, 1976, pp. 299–303). A study of German business in the 1980s noted less detailed long-range planning and less comprehensive environmental scanning than in their American rivals. It also noted less communication between headquarters and foreign subsidiaries concerning planning (Negandhi, 1986).

One contributing factor to less formal planning has been the historical tendency of European manufacturers, even large ones, to diversify less often and later than their American rivals. In the United States, more than 85% of the largest 500 companies had diversified into two or more products by the late 1960s (Franko, 1974). Diversification is generally conducive to a shift from functional organization structures to divisional ones, that is, organization around product group or geographic area divisions, each led by a general manager.[17] At headquarters, the main focus then becomes corporate strategy rather than operations. That includes deciding what businesses to be in, when and where, and pace of growth and change (divestments, expansions, mergers, acquisitions, alliances). It involves investment allocations between and within the various divisions. That requires more formal, structured analysis of internal competencies, competitors, market trends, and technological and other change. In the United States, strategic planning consultancies sprang up to assist with that task. In Europe, by contrast, business diversification was slower, and strategy consultancies emerged later (although they are now widespread, and many of them are American).

Also, German and French CEOs are more likely than U.S. peers to have engineering and technical backgrounds and therefore are less inclined to diversify away from products and technologies they know best. Moreover, the marketing function has historically received less attention in Europe than in the United States. As Dyas and Thanheiser put it, "'To make what the market wants' rather than 'to sell what we can make' was not an easy change of mentality for the European industrialist" (1976, p. 297). And when they diversified, they often favored holding company structures rather than divisional ones.[18] Another obstacle to diversification or divisionalization has been more diverse viewpoints on company boards (more diverse stakeholders, e.g., creditors, government, and employees), which make consensus building more difficult.

A study sponsored by the European Roundtable (Calori & de Woot, 1994) concluded that although European CEOs were less inclined to formalize their planning, they didn't ignore it, and they often had a longer-term planning horizon than the Americans (though shorter than the Japanese). Other evidence supports that view, such as a study of the expected payback period (recovery of capital) for new investment abroad. European CEO respondents expected payback in 5.1 years, on average, compared with 4.3 years for American counterparts and 6.6 years for Japanese. Similarly, a study of financial return on investment projects in 300 companies reported that 61% of European respondents (compared with just 21% of Americans) didn't expect to make money for at least 5 years (Porter, 1992a).

Another contributor to a long-term planning horizon in Europe has been more concentrated shareholdership. Large blockholders are less able and less predisposed to sell their shares quickly. In Sweden, for instance, two very prominent investment firms, Industrivarden and the Wallenberg family holding company Investor AB, hold stakes in diverse small and large businesses. In 2007, Investor AB holdings accounted for about one third of Swedish stock market capitalization ("The Monday Interview," 2007). Also, continental financial institutions (banks and insurance companies) have been more prominent corporate funders than private external shareholders. European equity markets (except London) remain small, so their shareholdings are less liquid. Also, accounting and auditing rules have allowed annual or semiannual financial reporting rather than the short-term (quarterly) reporting required in the United States, exerting less pressure on CEOs to focus on the near term. In northern Europe, the predominantly consensual (and slower) decision-making style is conducive to longer-term planning.

The higher incidence of family control (except for the United Kingdom) also favors longer-term planning. So does government intrusion in business decisions and operations (e.g., in locating and closing of plants, and review of buyouts, mergers, and acquisitions). Governments sometimes hold partial equity stakes in private firms (e.g., in France, Sweden, and Germany) and sometimes bend to labor union and other pressure to delay or block strategic, structural, or other change.[19]

Formality in planning is also influenced by societal culture. In higher-context cultures (e.g., Mediterranean Europe), time deadlines are more flexible and less driven by the tight schedules inherent in formal planning and control. Moreover, there are proportionately fewer big private businesses in that region than in the north. Smaller firms are less likely than larger ones to formalize their planning processes.

Despite past differences in formal planning, consultancy Bain and Co.'s 2007 global management tools and trends survey suggests U.S. and European convergence with respect to using some planning tools. Its list of tools includes 'comprehensive strategic planning" (90% of respondents from among 334 European and 287 North American firms), "scenario/contingency planning" (Europe 74%, North America 72%), and "mission/vision statements" (Europe 76%, North America 83%) (Rigby & Bilodeau, 2007).[20]

An oft-cited contingency-driven planning system has been used for several decades at oil giant Royal Dutch Shell. With its worldwide petroleum operations (drilling, refining, distribution) continually being shaped by shifting technological, political, and economic forces, its managers discuss alternative scenarios that could affect plans and action.[21]

CONTROL

The managerial function of control checks whether performance meets expectations (objectives). Deficiencies call for corrective action (or changes in objectives) or may require new managers or owners, alliances, mergers, or liquidation. Success requires responsiveness to markets and to owner and other stakeholder interests. European-style stakeholder capitalism (as opposed to U.S. stockholder capitalism) generally requires more explicit accommodation of nonshareholder voices (employees, government, loanholders, bondholders, suppliers, public interest groups, communities). Notes F. Piech, CEO of Volkswagen (as quoted by Guyon, 1999),

> I don't say shareholders don't count for Volkswagen, but they count on the same level as our customers and our employees. This is very European. If I would need a lot of capital, we would have to adapt. (p. 102)

Thierry Breton (2006), former CEO of France Telecom and French economics minister, stated,

> The French minister of the economy is an obvious stakeholder and therefore entitled to ensure that further developments take into account the interests in his care. Other stakeholders such as employees, management, customers, suppliers and local authorities, also have the right to state their opinion. . . . The success of the future company and its shareholders is also a function of stakeholders' consensus. (p. 17)

Although European company boards of directors aren't as international as their firms, in 2007, 18% of board directors in the top 300 European companies were nonnationals, compared with just 7% for U.S. peers (S&P 200) (Heidrick & Struggles, 2007; Spencer Stuart US Board Index, 2007).

Broader stakeholder pressures have also contributed to lower company return on investment and lower dividend payout compared with North American rivals (Gugler, Mueller, & Yurtoglu, 2003). One reason is greater European reliance on debt funding (loans, bonds) in proportion to equity (stock) ("Survey: International Banking," 2004). The legal environment there has long favored creditor interests over shareholder ones (La Porta, Lopez-de-Silanes, Shleifer, & Vishney, 1998). Creditors (e.g., German and Swedish insurance companies and banks) commonly sit on debtor boards of directors, positioned to monitor and influence management. In Germany, for instance, both Deutsche Bank and Allianz (insurance company) have stakes in dozens of debtors (Dresdner Bank, Frankfurt, 2001) and often sit on their supervisory boards (Andrews, 2000). German banks get additional influence by controlling proxy votes of many nonbank portfolio investors. In the United States, by contrast, banks cannot own debtor stock, sit on their boards, or vote on behalf of other owners.

Given their lower reliance on equity, European companies have been more likely to downplay (or even understate) their reported earnings. In some cases, the accounting rules have allowed a shift of pretax earnings into untaxed reserve accounts. In any case, when profits look high, unwelcome pressures can emerge, such as those from unions for pay hikes and from government for more taxes.

Continental Europe's less diffuse stock ownership makes for fewer freely held shares and therefore less opportunity for outsiders to buy a controlling stake in an underperforming firm. In some nations (e.g., Germany, France, Italy) cross-shareholdings between companies inhibit takeovers. As Ferrarini and Moloney (2005) noted,

> Concentrations of direct voting power by shareholders are intensified into block-holdings and control groups by cross shareholdings between dominant block-holders, [and] the exercise of control through complex pyramidal ownership structures which allow control to be exercised through cascades of companies, proxy voting by financial institutions connected to the company, and voting pacts. (p. 3)

Often, owners' shares (frequently family owned) are golden, that is, carry superproportional voting rights, and therefore are able to block outsiders from gaining control even if they acquire a majority of the common stock. The blockholding by banks and others is conducive to more "relational investing" (active engagement with senior management), in contrast with the more arm's-length (passive) investing prevalent in the United States and the United Kingdom. If displeased with performance, blockholders are compelled to communicate directly with management instead of selling their shares.

Moreover, governments commonly block takeover attempts for political reasons, for example, to protect local firms from foreign ownership. In 2005, for instance, the French government blocked a PepsiCo (U.S.) buyout of Danone (food products) and an Enal (Italian utility company) offer for utility firm Suez. Similarly, trade union and worker involvement in decision making can restrict takeovers. Consequently, there have been many fewer hostile takeover attempts in Europe than in the United States.[22] Schneper and Guillen (2004, p. 264) noted that between 1988 and 2003, "478 hostile takeover attempts were announced in the United States and 273 in Britain. By contrast, there were just 19 announced in France, 18 in Norway, 7 in Germany."

Recently, pressures of globalization and regional economic integration have made the Western European business and financial climate ever more similar to those of the United States.

ORGANIZING

The managerial function of organizing is concerned with coordination and integration of tasks, resources, and effort. It considers division of labor, flow of authority, span of supervision, and whether to decentralize particular decisions or actions. As firms evolve, they adjust structurally to accommodate changes in goals, personnel, product mix, and markets.

American business professor and historian Alfred Chandler (1962) famously tracked the evolution of strategy and structure in early U.S. business giants. From his perspective, a small or slow-growing company with a narrow product line, or in a limited geographic market, will normally structure itself around business functions (e.g., marketing, finance, production) to benefit from specialized division of labor (see also Scott, 1971; Stopford & Wells, 1972). But if its product mix or geographic market broadens, then integration and coordination can be improved by a change to a divisional structure (e.g., product group or geographic area divisions). As Dyas and Thanheiser (1976) observed,

> Divisional organization permits faster and more effective co-ordination of production and sales, and economic decisions can be taken closer to where the marketing and technological competences lie. (p. 20)

The capability to envisage the exploitation of opportunities outside a firm's current scope of activities represents one of the fundamental strengths of the divisional structure. (p. 301)

In a study of structural transition in Europe, Franko (1976) noted that local firms were slower than American rivals to diversify. And when diversifying, they were less likely to try divisional structures,[23] often preferring holding companies (see Whittington & Mayer, 2000). (A holding company doesn't produce anything but rather holds equity stakes in a portfolio of companies.)

Moreover, European takeover and merger activity didn't attain U.S. levels until recently. Most of the world's major merger advisors (mainly investment banks) and equity buyout firms were first active in the United States. However, with continuing regional economic integration and global competition, the level of European acquisitions, mergers, and buyout activity is now near U.S. levels. Multidivision structures have become common, in line with the Chandlerian analysis (Whittington & Mayer, 2000).

DIRECTING

If there is an identifiable European management style, it would tend towards extensive consultation. (Vic Luck, quoted in T. Dickson, 2000, p. 15)

In all organizations, societal and corporate cultures influence directing (leadership, communication, motivation). Cultural diversity within Western Europe makes it impossible to generalize about the whole region. However, some scholars conclude that European CEOs have a stronger orientation toward people than do Americans and are more skilled at discussing and negotiating their decisions with others (Calori & de Woot, 1994; Calori & Dufour, 1995). As for cultural differences and their impact on management, Table 3.5 profiles some Western European countries along Hofstede's cultural dimensions and suggests some organization and management implications.

Where uncertainty avoidance is high (Mediterranean Europe), one should find fewer mergers and acquisitions, more resistance to internal organizational change, tighter supervision of subordinates, stronger personal bonds between managers and subordinates, and less managerial turnover. By contrast, where uncertainty avoidance is low, as in the United Kingdom, the Netherlands, and the Scandinavian countries, personal bonds between an employee and manager tend to be weaker, and there is easier acceptance of change. With other factors being equal, this contributes to more managerial mobility and more flexible supervision of subordinates.

Where individualism is low and collectivism high, wage and salary rewards tend to be weaker motivators. There is more psychic reward from performing well-recognized work. Personal lives and work life intersect more. Only two Western European countries (Greece and Portugal) have low individualism (just mildly low), whereas Spain, Austria, Germany, and Finland are mildly high; the rest are high.

Table 3.5   A Profile of Western European Countries Along Hofstede's Cultural
Dimensions and Some Organization and Management Implications

Individualism: The degree to which people act as individuals (vs. a primary orientation toward the group)			
High	**Medium–High**	**Medium–Low**	**Low**
Sweden	Finland	Portugal	None
Norway	Germany	Greece	
Denmark	Austria		
Netherlands	German Swiss		
Belgium	Spain		
United Kingdom			
Ireland			
Italy			
France			

Higher Individualism ←——————→ *Lower Individualism*

• More emphasis on individual motivation, achievement, and rewards	• Emphasis on group motivation and accomplishment
• More separation between work life and personal life	• Less sharp separation between work and nonwork life
• Importance (e.g., in hiring and promotion) of personal achievements	• Strong loyalty of employee to employer
	• More importance (e.g., in hiring and promotion) of candidates' loyalty, commitment, and personal connections
	• Seniority-based pay

Power Distance: Acceptance of inequality in power			
High	**Medium–High**	**Medium–Low**	**Low**
None	Portugal	Spain	Scandinavia
	France	Italy	Germany
	Belgium	Greece	Austria
			United Kingdom
			Ireland
			Netherlands

Higher Masculine-Associated Values ←——————→ *Lower Masculine-Associated Values*

• More acceptance of autocratic leadership styles (benevolent authoritarian)	• More collegial, consultative leadership styles
• Less participation in decision making by subordinates	• Less emphasis on hierarchy; less boss-centered direction and guidance
• More awareness of social and occupational hierarchies	• Tendency for flatter organizations (fewer levels)
• Tendency for taller organizations (i.e., more organizational levels)	• More delegation of authority
• Less occupational mobility	• More decentralized decision making
• Less delegation of authority	• More occupational mobility
• More centralized decision making, action taking, and guidance	

(Continued)

Table 3.5 (Continued)

Masculinity: The predominance of masculine-associated values rather than feminine ones			
High	**Medium–High**	**Medium–Low**	**Low**
Germany Austria Italy Ireland United Kingdom	Greece Belgium	France Spain	Nordic countries Portugal

Higher Masculine-Associated Values ⟵⟶ *Lower Masculine-Associated Values*	
• More traditional gender roles • Emphasis on performance and competition • Success- and career-driven leaders	• Less gender stereotyping • Less managerial stress and burnout • Relative pay equality • Age and seniority more respected

Uncertainty Avoidance: Tolerance for risk, change, and ambiguity			
High	**Medium–High**	**Medium–Low**	**Low**
Belgium France Spain Portugal Greece	Austria Italy Germany	Norway Finland Netherlands	United Kingdom Ireland Denmark Sweden

Higher Uncertainty Avoidance ⟵⟶ *Lower Uncertainty Avoidance*	
• Conducive to stronger personal bonds with one's employer and manager • More emphasis on job security; less managerial mobility • Closer supervision of subordinates	• Weaker personal bonds with one's employer and manager • More managerial mobility between firms • Looser, more flexible supervision and control of subordinates

SOURCE: Adapted from Hofstede (1984); see also Hoecklin (1995) and Jackofsky, Slocum, and McQuaid (1988).

High (this category includes countries ranked in the top quartile in Hofstede's original study, i.e., those ranked from 1 to 13 on the dimension from among 50 countries and 3 world regions).

Medium–high (second quartile, that is, countries ranked 14–26).

Medium–low (third quartile; countries ranked 27–39).

Low (bottom quartile; countries ranked 40–53).

Differences in power distance can influence leadership style. For example, managers and employees in low–power distance cultures (Scandinavian, Germanic, Anglo) tend to be less attracted to autocratic and paternalistic leaders than are their higher–power distance Latin peers and more receptive to a consultative, participative decision making. In the German *Vorstand* (senior management board), for instance, decision making is largely collegial, with much consultation and negotiation between colleagues; the same tendency prevails in Scandinavia.

> When American CEOs decide to do something, they do not need to ask anybody, they just do it. When Americans say, "It's a great idea, okay let's go, let's do it now!" they are expressing a temperamental inclination toward positiveness and non-fatalism. . . . The German, Danish or Dutch manager who has that same purposeful temperament would not be able to act like this. The European reaction is more likely to be: "This is a great idea. We will now discuss it with the supervisory board, then we'll discuss it with our trade unions. And we should perhaps let the worker representative comment on it. And since we're a fairly big company we'd better consult government." (Barsoux & Lawrence, 1991, p. 216)

Conversely, where power distance is high (e.g., Mediterranean Europe) managers and subordinates are less likely to share decision making, and there is more acceptance of an authoritarian leader. Here job security and personal relationships are stronger motivators than in low–power distance cultures.

Edward Hall's (1976a, 1976b) distinction between high- and low-context cultures (see Chapter 1) also can have implications for directing. In the lower-context cultures (e.g., Nordic, Germanic, and Anglo), communication is more direct (frank, to the point, to be interpreted more literally). By contrast, in higher-context settings (e.g., Mediterranean Europe), messages often must be deciphered from the context in which they are expressed, that is, from body language and from reading between the lines.

In lower-context settings (Nordic, Germanic, Anglo), managers are more likely than in higher-context ones to cede decision-making authority to subordinates. Power distance is lower and therefore more conducive to decentralized authority. With other factors being equal, low-context cultures are more conducive to flatter organization structures (fewer levels, less hierarchy) and more bottom-up communication. They depend more on explicit messages (e.g., detailed memos, reports, written contracts). Professional and managerial relationships are less personal. On a spectrum from high to low, Hall views Germanic and Scandinavian culture as low context (lower than the United States and United Kingdom). Greece is the highest-context Western European country (higher than Italy, Spain, or Portugal). Here, the preferred leadership style is often personal and paternalistic, with less inclination toward employee involvement in decision making. Motivation and commitment are based more on relationships and rapport between managers and subordinates. Attitudes toward time are more flexible, and there is less rigid conformance to tight time schedules and deadlines (Table 3.6 and Figure 3.3).

Table 3.6   High-Context and Low-Context Cultures in Western Europe

Lower-Context Cultures	Higher-Context Cultures
Germanic, Nordic, Anglo, Northern France	**Greece, Italy, Spain, Portugal, Southern France**
• Propensity for direct (explicit) communications; frankness is expected. • Meanings of messages come more often directly from the words alone (that is, are more explicit rather than implicit). • More emphasis on written agreements (e.g., formal detailed contracts). • Monochronic view of time (more measured and scheduled).	• Communication is more often implicit (than in low-context settings). • In general, more information must be deciphered from the context of a message (than in low-context cultures), that is, "from listening between the lines" and from body language. • Verbal agreements are more important than in low-context cultures; more emphasis on trust, rapport, personal relationships; less importance on a piece of paper (written contract). • Polychronic view of time (more flexible and open-ended).
Managerial Implications	
• More reliance, in hiring and promotion, on impartial merit-driven selection criteria • More extensive delegation and decentralization of authority • More bottom-up communications • More at ease with participative leadership styles	• More emphasis on personal power, relationships and interpersonal influence • Tendency to centralize and hoard authority • Less bottom-up communication • More acceptance of personalistic, paternalistic, authoritarian (benevolent authoritarian) leaders

SOURCE: Based on ideas expressed in Hall (1976b).

Figure 3.3   West European Low- and High-Context Cultural Spectrum

SOURCES: Adapted from Hall (1976b).

Context variations can also occur within countries. For example, the north of France (e.g., Paris and Alsace, Normandy and Calais provinces) is predominantly low context, whereas Mediterranean France (e.g., Provence) leans toward high context. Lombard Italians (far north, in Lombardy) are much less high-context than southerners (Neapolitans and Sicilians). Flemish Belgians (northern Belgium, Dutch speaking) are generally lower context than Walloons (southern Belgium, French speaking); Bavarian Germans (south) are not as low context as northern Germans (from Hamburg or Kiel). In general, urban settings are lower context than rural ones.

Chapter Summary

- Western Europe attracts global attention for its advanced economies and high standard of living. Despite slow economic growth in recent years, its managers and workers produce about one fifth of the gross world product with just one twentieth of the world's workforce.

- European social and political history gave rise to predominantly social market economic systems that aim for political and economic freedom in tandem with employment security and social and material equality. By late 20th century, this welfare state capitalism included extensive government economic and social spending, funded by high taxation and borrowing. Government intervenes more (than in the United States) in labor relations; job security is more protected, at least for people already fully employed. Long-term unemployment has been higher than in the United States and Japan; rigid labor markets and low labor force participation rates have contributed to slower economic growth. There is more formalized employee involvement in decision making (e.g., plant-level "works councils" and sometimes employees on company boards of directors), though more so in Europe's north than in the south.

- European managers in large companies historically have been less mobile than their North American peers, but today tenure and turnover are about equal. Upward managerial promotion in Europe has been slower and CEO pay lower; there has been less performance-based pay, but this too is in flux. Although CEOs there were once slightly older than their North American peers, they are now about the same age. Europeans tend to have more international experience and are less likely to have had as much formal higher education in business (MBA degrees). They are more likely to pursue better balance between work life and private life.

- In general, European managers have a long-term planning horizon. High manufacturing labor costs force more attention on product quality. In general, when compared with their U.S. counterparts, they are less singularly stockholder oriented. Firms were slower to diversify their product mix or to adopt multidivisional organization structures, but this too has been changing. In general, Europeans have been more conservative, less attracted to fads, and better prepared to manage a culturally diverse workforce. Cultural differences between the north and south of Europe influence leadership, communication, and motivation. In the south, people are more at ease with a benevolent authoritarian leader. In the north (Scandinavia, Germany), there is more decision consultation.

Terms and Concepts

Adam Smith
codetermination (*Mitbestimmung*)
European cultural typologies
European Union (EU)
flextime
golden shares (preference shares)
Industrial Revolution
Karl Marx

relational investing versus
 arm's-length investing
social democracy
social market economy (welfare
 capitalism)
sociotechnical system
stakeholder capitalism
works council

Study Questions

1. Identify distinctive features of the Western European managerial macroenvironment (economic, political, sociocultural, demographic, educational).

2. What distinguishes U.S. and Western European patterns of employer–employee relations?

3. What is distinctive about the Western European management perspective, practice, and style?

4. Identify some differences between a few European countries in regard to questions 1, 2, and 3.

Exercise 3.1

Investigate the CEO of a large European company and a similar U.S. company. Compare their personal backgrounds. How do they compare in terms of age, education, social background, employment history, career path, time in rank, and international experience. Identify your sources of information. For specific company names, you might check the *Fortune* magazine Global 500 list (an annual ranking based on sales revenue) or the FT Global 500 (ranking based on the market value of the firm). Company Web sites often include CEO background information. (Look for a link on their site titled "investor relations," "corporate governance," or similar. You could also Google the executive's name and see what turns up.)

Exercise 3.2

In large stockholder-owned companies in most countries, a key instrument of control is the board of directors (group of 5–20 people that meets several times annually) and the general meeting of the shareholders (usually meets annually).[24]

Board purpose, size, member selection, structure, rules, and procedures vary by country and also by individual company bylaws. Board members can include insiders (company executives such as the CEO or other senior officers) or outsiders (independent nonexecutive directors; nonemployees).

Directors are empowered to monitor the interests of shareholders and other stakeholders (e.g., employees, creditors, government, local communities). Their advice, voice, and vote influence company management to a greater or lesser degree. Boards are empowered to replace an underperforming CEO and to recruit successors. Internal committees of the board can decide or approve CEO pay packages and severance and retirement payouts. They can verify company compliance with law, auditing standards, and financial disclosure.

In most countries, board structure is unitary, that is, only one board. However, some settings (e.g., Germany, Italy, France, the Netherlands) have dual boards.

• By law, Germany requires a dual-board structure in its largest firms. This includes a supervisory board (*Aufsichtsrat*) made up mainly of shareholder and worker members and a management board (*Vorstand*) composed of senior general and functional managers.

The supervisory board guides and advises management on behalf of shareholders and appoints and dismisses members of the *Vorstand;* it has no legal authority to approve specific management action not identified in internal company statutes or by mutual agreement. In firms with 500 to 2,000 employees, one third of its members are elected by employees. In companies with more than 2,000 employees, employee representation increases to one half of the board. Decisions are made by majority vote, with the chair having the tie-breaking vote if needed. The chair is elected by the members, but if a majority is not obtained, he or she is elected by representatives of shareholders.

The German *Vorstand* (management board) is composed entirely of senior company executives. In firms with more than 2,000 employees, one *Vorstand* member (*Arbeitsdirektor*) gives full attention to employee concerns.

• In Italy, a main board (*consiglio di amministrazione*) is supplemented by a board of auditors (*collegio sindacale*) elected by the shareholders.

• In France, the single-tier board (*conseil d'administration*) is most prevalent; this can have a combined chairperson and chief executive, or those roles can be separated. Some firms, though, have a dual-tier structure: a supervisory board (*conseil de surveillance*) and management board (*directoire*).

• In the Netherlands, a dual-board system prevails, with separate supervisory and management boards, but some boards are unitary.

• In the United States, boards are unitary, and the chair normally is elected from among the members; the company CEO (or recently retired CEO) commonly chairs the board. (This is less common and sometimes not allowed in Europe, where the CEO may even be excluded from voting.) U.S. company director nominations (new board members) can come from company management or from the board itself and are usually approved at annual shareholder meetings. There are few restrictions as to residency or citizenship of board directors and no requirement for a labor director. Board decisions are generally approved by majority vote unless company bylaws state otherwise; a supermajority vote (up to and including unanimity) may be required for some decisions (e.g., mergers and acquisitions). The law generally allows only directors to declare and pay dividends, over which they have broad discretion.

QUESTIONS

1. In the country where you reside, should the law require a labor director in every private corporation? Why or why not? Explain.

2. Is it a good idea for the CEO of the company (or its former CEO) to also chair the board of directors? Why or why not? Explain.

Notes

1. Safire (1989) also notes that English political economist John Stuart Mill used the term *managing director* in 1861.

2. Weber's original work, *Wirtschaft und Gesellschaft*, was published posthumously in 1922. See Weber (1968) for first complete edition in English.

3. Early conceptualization of management functions (e.g., planning, organizing, control) can be found in American Frederick W. Taylor's *Principles of Scientific Management*, published in 1911, and Henri Fayol's *General and Industrial Administration*, first published in French in 1916; both books predate modern management textbooks and represent the beginnings of management as an academic discipline.

4. The European Group for Organizational Studies has about 1,500 members (2008) and publishes the journal *Organization Studies* (social science orientation). The UK-based Strategic Planning Society has two publications, *Long Range Planning* and *Strategy Magazine*. Other international publications from Europe include *The British Journal of Management, Journal of Management Studies, European Management Journal, European Management Review, Journal of Management and Governance, Management Learning, International Journal of Crosscultural Management, Journal of International Management, Journal of Management History, European Journal of Innovation Management, Management Decision, International Journal of Management Reviews, Management International Review,* and *Corporate Governance Journal.*

5. Karl Marx's *The Communist Manifesto* was first published in German in 1848, and *Das Kapital* (*Capital*) was published in 1867.

6. Today, less than 10% of Swedish industrial equity is government owned; another 5% is in cooperatives and the rest in private hands. In 2006, the state had partial stakes in about 60 companies.

7. Some national and cross-national employer groups include the Confederation of Italian Industry, the Confederation of British Industry, the Federation of German Employers' Associations, and the French employers' association (Patronat); there are also a few pan-European groups, such as the European Roundtable, a forum for industrialists; and the Union of Industrial and Employers' Confederations of Europe (UNICE). As of January 23, 2007, this organization is called BusinessEurope (http://www.businesseurope.eu).

8. The Booz Allen annual surveys documented CEO age at time of appointment for the years 1995–2001 (world's 2,500 largest companies ranked by market value) in Lucier, Spiegel, and Schuyt (2002). Its 2002–2007 surveys make no reference to age when appointed, which changes slowly; annual turnover figures appear each year in the summer quarterly issue of *strategy + business* (a Booz Allen Hamilton publication).

9. European numbers are from the Third Bi-annual European PWN BoardWomen Monitor 2008, a survey of the FTS Eurofirst 300 by the European Professional Women's Network in partnership with Egon Zehnder; a survey report and press release are posted at http://www.EuropeanPWN.net. The S&P 500 numbers are from the Spencer Stuart Board Index 2007, at http://www.SpencerStuart.com; the FTS Eurofirst 300 consist of the 300 largest European companies based on market capitalization; the S&P 500 consist of the 500 U.S. large-cap companies trading on the New York and Nasdaq stock exchanges.

10. Firms are ranked by the current market value of their common stock.

11. Accreditation bodies include the Association of MBAs (United Kingdom), European Quality Improvement System (Equis), and European Programme Accreditation System of the European Foundation for Management Development. As of February 2006, there were 57 Equis-accredited schools in Europe. Equis also accredits some non-European institutions. See http://www.efmd.org/html/home.asp. Germany's Foundation for International Business Administration Accreditation accredits German, Austrian, and Swiss programs.

12. Vic Luck is managing partner of the PricewaterhouseCoopers management consulting practice in Europe, the Middle East, and Africa.

13. Based on survey data from executive search firms Spencer Stuart and Heidrick & Struggles International, cited in "Globalizing the Boardroom" (2005).

14. Germany's *Mittelstand* are firms with 50 to 2,000 employees and annual sales revenues between US$50 million and $2 billion.

15. Europe's Bologna Accord (1999) established regional commitment to create a common Higher Education Area by year 2010. Its goal is compatibility of educational structure, curriculum and degree qualifications across the region. For Germany, this means shortening its traditional university first degree from 6 years to 3.

16. Survey based on interviews with 50 British and 55 continental middle- and top-level managers (French, Belgian, German).

17. The pioneers of multidivisional structures were General Motors and DuPont (Chandler, 1962).

18. From European enterprise studies based at the Harvard Business School (cf. Dyas and Thanheiser, 1976; Whittington & Mayer, 2000).

19. In 2003, the French government held equity stakes in more than 1,400 companies, including large ones such as Air France (45% ownership), Renault (16%), and France Telecom (42%); in some of them, it was the sole shareholder, e.g., at Sncf (railways), Areva (nuclear fuel), Giat (military vehicles), and Sanef (motorways).

20. For more information on the annual Bain global management tools and trends survey, go to http://www.bain.com/management_tools/home.asp.

21. For discussion of the Shell scenario planning system, see Schwartz (1996) and Wack (1985).

22. The first significant large-scale cross-border hostile takeover in Europe was the acquisition of Germany's Mannesman by Britain's Vodaphone in 2000.

23. See Chandler (1962). For a succinct analysis of this perspective as applied to multi-national enterprise, see Chapter 2 in Stopford and Wells (1972).

24. Some of this information is available on the Spencer Stuart Web site (http://www.spencerstuart.com/research/) and in PricewaterhouseCoopers Guides for Doing Business.

References

Alvarez, L. (2004, July 25). Norway looks for ways to keep workers on the job. *New York Times,* Sec. 1, p. 4.

Anders, G. (1989, September 22). Going global: Vision versus reality. *Wall Street Journal,* p. 1.

Andrews, E. (2000, March 12). The metamorphosis of Germany Inc. *New York Times,* Sec. 3, p. 1.

Antunes, D., & Thomas, H. (2007). The competitive (disadvantages) of European business schools. *Long Range Planning, 40*(3), 382–404.

Arbose, J. (1980, July). The changing life values of today's executives. *International Management, 35*(7), 12–19.

Barsoux, J., & Lawrence, P. (1990). *Management in France.* London: Cassell.

Barsoux, J., & Lawrence, P. (1991). Countries, cultures and constraints. In R. Calori & P. Lawrence (Eds.), *The business of Europe* (pp. 198–217). London: Sage.

Becht, M., Betts, P., & Morck, R. (2002, February 3). The complex evolution of family affairs: Corporate dynasties. Part I. *Financial Times,* p. 12.

Berg, P., Appelbaum, E., Bailey, T., & Kalleberg, A. (2004). Contesting time: International comparisons of employee control of working time. *Industrial and Labor Relations Review, 57*(3), 331–349.

Bradshaw, D. (2001, January 22). MBA trends. *Financial Times,* p. iv.

Breton, T. (2006, February 6). It is the stakeholders' duty to assess mergers. *Financial Times,* p. 17.

Burgess, K. (2008, January 28). French bosses are best paid in Europe. *Financial Times,* p. 17.

Calori, R., & de Woot, P. (Eds.). (1994). *A European management model. Beyond diversity.* New York: Prentice Hall.

Calori, R., & Dufour, B. (1995). Management European style. *Academy of Management Executive, 9*(3), 59.

Central Intelligence Agency. (2008). *The world factbook 2008.* Retrieved August 30, 2008, from http://www.odci.gov/cia/publications/factbook/index.html

Chandler, A. (1962). *Strategy and structure.* Cambridge, MA: MIT Press.

Cox, C. J., & Cooper, C. L. (1985, Winter). The irrelevance of American organizational sciences to the UK and Europe. *Journal of General Management, 11*(2), 27–34.

Dickson, M. (2000, July 14). Corporate governance; complexities will pose challenges. *Financial Times,* p. 6.

Dickson, T. (2000, April 13). A model of cooperation: Management European business: As the European way comes under pressure from shareholder value economics, Tim Dickson weighs opinions on its prospects. *Financial Times,* p. 15.

Dresdner Bank, Frankfurt. (2001, June 12). Survey: Germany. *Financial Times,* pp. 7–8.

Drucker, P. (1973). *Management tasks, responsibilities, practices.* New York: Harper & Row.

Dyas, G., & Thanheiser, H. (1976). *The emerging European enterprise: Strategy and structure in French and German industry.* London: Macmillan.

Emory, F., & Thorsrud, E. (1976). *Democracy at work.* Leiden, the Netherlands: Martinus Nijhoff.

European management: Discordant national anthems. (1988, October 15). *The Economist,* p. 89.

Europe's new managers: Going global with a U.S. style. (1982, May 24). *Business Week,* p. 116.

Fabrikant, G. (2006, June 16). U.S.-style pay deals for chiefs become all the rage in Europe. *New York Times,* p. 1.

Fayol, H. (1949). *General and industrial administration* (C. Storrs, Trans.). London: Sir Isaac Pitman and Sons.

Ferrarini, G., & Moloney, N. (2005, April). *Executive remuneration in the EU: The context for reform.* European Corporate Governance Institute Law Working Paper No. 032/2005. Retrieved May 5, 2006, from http://ssrn.com/abstract= 715862

Fortune Global 500. (2008, July 21). *Fortune,* pp. 165–182.

Frank, R. (1998, June 15). Chasing the American dream around the world. *Wall Street Journal,* p. B1.

Franko, L. (1974). The move toward a multidivisional structure in European organizations. *Administrative Science Quarterly, 19*(4), 493–506.

Franko, L. (1976). *The European multinationals.* Stamford, CT: Greylock.

FT Business Education. (2005, January 24, September 12; 2006, January 30, March 20, May 15, September 11, October 23; 2007, January 29, May 14, September 17, October 22; 2008, January 28). *Financial Times* special reports.

FT Europe 500 2007. (2007). *Financial Times.* Retrieved January 10, 2008, from http://www.ft.com/cms/s/0/ad53b3b2–2586–11dc-b338–000b5df10621, dwp_uuid=95d63dfa-257b-11dc-b338–000b5df10621.html

FT Europe 500 2008. (2008). *Financial Times.* Retrieved August 31, 2008, from http://www.ft.com/cms/s/0/05b22652–413c-11dd-9661–0000779fd2ac, dwp_uuid=4ca4e366–413b-11dd-9661–0000779fd2ac.html

FT Global 500. (2008). Retrieved August 28, 2008, from http://media.ft.com/ cms/889d77f0–4142–11dd-9661–0000779fd2ac.pdf

Germany's best kept secret: How its exporters are besting the world's manufacturing. (2006, May 19). *Financial Times,* p. 11.

Globalizing the boardroom. (2005, October 31). *The Wall Street Journal,* p. B1.

Granick, D. (1964). *The European executive.* New York: Anchor.

Grosset, S. (1970). *Management: American and European styles.* Belmont, CA: Wadsworth.

Gugler, K., Mueller, D., & Yurtoglu, B. (2003, January). *Corporate governance and the returns on investment* (Finance Working Paper No. 06/2003). European Corporate Governance Institute. Retrieved May 26, 2006 from http://papers .ssrn.com/s013/papers.cfm?abstract_id=299520

Guyon, J. (1999, March 29). Getting the bugs out at VW. *Fortune,* pp. 96–102.

Hall, E. T. (1976a). *Beyond culture.* New York: Anchor Books/Doubleday.

Hall, E. T. (1976b, July). How cultures collide. *Psychology Today,* pp. 66–74.

Hamori, M., & Koyunku, B. (2007). *International experience and career advancement: A multilevel analysis.* IE Working Paper WP07–03, March 21, 2007. Retrieved August 31, 2007, from http://latienda.ie.edu/working_papers_ economia/WP07–03.pdf

Handy, C., Gow, I., Gordon, C., Randlesome, C., & Maloney, M. (1987). *The making of managers: A report on management education, training and development in the U.S.A., West Germany, France, Japan and the U.K.* London: National Economic Development Office.

Harbison, F., & Burgess, E. W. (1954). Modern management in Western Europe. *American Journal of Sociology, 60*(1), 15–23.

Heidrick & Struggles. (2007). *Raising the bar: Corporate governance in Europe* (5th ed.). Retrieved December 7, 2007, from http://www.heidrick.com/NR/ rdonlyres/666FC928–1933–4F4B-B184-FBBE141313A9/0/HS_CorpGov Europe2007.pdf

Heller, R., & Willat, N. (1975). *The European revenge.* London: Barries & Jenkins.

Hoecklin, L. (1995). *Managing cultural differences.* Reading, MA: Addison-Wesley.

Hofstede, G. (1984). *Culture's consequences, international differences in work-related values.* Thousand Oaks, CA: Sage.

Hofstede, G. (1993). Cultural constraints in management theories. *Academy of Management Executive, 7*(1), 81–94.

Hofstede, G. (2001). *Culture's consequences: Comparing values, behaviors, institutions and organizations across nations* (2nd ed.). Thousand Oaks, CA: Sage.

Hofstede, G., & Kassem, M. (Eds.). (1976). *European contributions to organization theory.* Assen, the Netherlands: Van Gorcum.

Hot topic: Are CEOs worth their weight in gold? (2006, January 21). *Wall Street Journal,* p. A7.

House, R., Hanges, P., Javidan, M., Dorfman, P., & Gupta, V. (Eds.). (2004). *Culture, leadership, and organization: The GLOBE study of 63 societies.* Thousand Oaks, CA: Sage.

Hymowitz, C. (2000, August 15). Companies go global, but many managers just don't travel well. *Wall Street Journal,* p. B1.

Jackofsky, E., Slocum, J., & McQuaid, S. (1988). Cultural values and the CEO: Alluring companions? *The Academy of Management Executive, 2*(1), 39–49.

Jackson, T. (1998, February 6). When the big chair is vacant. *Financial Times,* p. 16.

Karlsson, P., Neilson, G., & Webster, J. (2008, Summer). CEO succession 2007: The performance paradox. *strategy + business.* Retrieved August 26, 2008, from http://www.strategy-business.com/press/freearticle/08208?pg=all

Kassalow, E. (1969). *Trade unions and industrial relations: An international comparison.* New York: Random House.

Kast, F. (1964, Winter). Management concepts and style. *Business Horizons, 7*(4), 25–26.

Kirkland, R. (1986, September 29). Europe's new managers. *Fortune,* p. 58.

Klarsfeld, A., & Mabey, C. (2004, December). Management development in Europe: Do national models persist? *European Management Journal, 22*(6), 648–649.

Knoepfel, R. (1974, November–December). American and European entrepreneurs and managers. *Managerial Planning,* pp. 1–14.

Knudsen, H. (1995). *Employee participation in Europe.* London: Sage.

La Porta, R., Lopez-de-Silanes, F., Shleifer, A., & Vishney, R. (1998, December). Law and finance. *Journal of Political Economy, 106*(6), 1113–1153.

Lawrence, P. (1980). *Managers and management in West Germany.* New York: St. Martin's Press.

Lucier, C., Spiegel, E., & Schuyt, R. (2002). Why CEOs fall: The causes and consequences of turnover at the top. *strategy+business.* Retrieved August 22, 2008, from http://www.strategy-business.com/press/article/20306?pg=0

Lucier, C., Wheeler, S., & Habbel, R. (2007, Summer). The era of the inclusive leader. *strategy+business, 47.* Retrieved August 22, 2008, from http://www.strategy-business.com/press/article/07205?pg=0

Management: Flexiyears. (1983, March, 5). *The Economist,* p. 76.

Management theory: The advent of the Euroguru. (1995, March 11). *The Economist,* p. 66.

Marx, E. (2006). *UK route to the top 2006. Executive summary.* Retrieved January 3, 2008, from http://www.heidrick.com/NR/rdonlyres/C4053B9E-4270–4F8B-9DBA-B3156163CC22/0/HS_RouteToTop2006.pdf

Mayer, M., & Whittington, R. (1999). Euro-elites: Top British, French and German managers in the 1980s and 1990s. *European Management Journal, 17*(4), 403–408.

The MBA guide 2009. (2008). Köln: Wolters Kluwer Deutschland.

The Monday interview (Jacob Wallenberg): Scion of Sweden's financial dynasty. (2007, November 12). *Financial Times,* p. 16.

Negandhi, A. R. (1986). Role and structure of German multinationals: A comparative profile. In K. Macharzina & W. Staehle (Eds.), *European approaches to international management* (pp. 51–66). Berlin: Walter de Gruyter.

Nowotny, O. (1964, March–April). American vs. European management philosophy. *Harvard Business Review, 42*(2), 101–108.

Olson, E. (2002, April 25). Swiss blush, but reveal some salaries. *New York Times,* p. W1.

Peterson, R. (1976, June). Swedish experiments in job reform. *Business Horizons, 19*(3), 219–226.

Porter, M. (1992a). *Capital choices: Changing the way America invests in industry.* Washington, DC: U.S. Council on Competitiveness.

Porter, M. (1992b, September–October). Capital disadvantage: America's failing capital investment system. *Harvard Business Review, 70*(5), 65–82.

Posner, B., & Schmidt, W. (1983, March). U.S. and European executives begin to think alike. *International Management, 38*(3), 58–60.

Prokesch, S. (1991, July 7). Edges fray on Volvo's brave new humanistic world. *New York Times,* Sec. 3, p. 5.

Real pay. (2006, January 21). *The Economist,* p. 102.

Rigby, D., & Bilodeau, B. (2007). Bain's Global 2007 management tools and trends survey. *Strategy & Leadership, 35*(5), 9–16.

Safire, W. (1989, February 19). On language: How "managing" is managing. *New York Times Magazine,* p. 18.

Sandeman, H. (1984, December 22). Managing America's business. *The Economist,* pp. 91–112.

Sapir, A. (2005, September 9). *Globalisation and the reform of European social models.* Bruegel Policy Brief, Issue 2005/01. Retrieved April 21, 2006, from http://www.bruegel.org/Public/Publication_detail.php?ID=1169&publicationID=1255

Schneper, W., & Guillen, M. (2004, June). Stakeholder rights and corporate governance: A cross-national study of hostile takeovers. *Administrative Science Quarterly, 49*(2), 263–295.

Schwartz, N., & Bennhold, K. (2008, February 17). Where the heads no longer roll. *New York Times,* p. B1.

Schwartz, P. (1996). *The art of the long view.* New York: Doubleday/Currency.

Scott, B. (1971). *Stages of corporate development.* Boston: Harvard Business School Press.

Servan-Schreiber, J.-J. (1968). *The American challenge* (R. Steel, Trans.). New York: Atheneum. (Original work published 1967 as *Le défi Américan*)

Simon, H. (1992, March–April). Lessons from Germany's mid-size giants. *Harvard Business Review, 70*(2), 115.

Simon, H. (1996). *Hidden champions: Lessons from 500 of the world's best unknown companies.* Boston: Harvard Business School Press.

Spencer Stuart US Board Index. (2007). Retrieved January 23, 2008, from http://www.spencerstuart.jp/research/boards/1212/

Stewart, R., Barsoux, J., Kieser, A., Ganter, H., & Walgenbach, P. (1996). A comparison of British and German managerial roles, perceptions and behavior. In P. Joynt & M. Warner (Eds.), *Managing across cultures: Issues and perspectives* (Chap. 12). London: International Thompson Business Press.

Stopford, J., & Wells, L. (1972). *Managing the multinational enterprise.* New York: Basic Books.

A survey of America. (2003, November 8). *The Economist,* p. 4.

Survey: International banking. Just deserts? (2004, April 17). *The Economist,* pp. 8–10.

Sweden's welfare state. (2002, October 26). *The Economist,* p. 49.

Tagliabue, P. (2008, June 8). In hiring, Europeans go global. *New York Times,* p. C1.

Taxing wages. (2007, March 24). *The Economist,* p. 109.

Taylor, F. W. (1911). *The principles of scientific management.* New York: Harper & Row.

Thornhill, J. (2007, April 16). Why France may find its social model extracts too high a price. *Financial Times,* p. 9.

U.S. Department of Education. (2007). *Digest of education statistics.* Retrieved August 22, 2008, from http://nces.ed.gov/programs/digest/d07/tables/dt07_279.asp?referrer=list

Wack, P. (1985, November–December). Scenarios: Shooting the rapids. *Harvard Business Review, 63*(6), 139–150.

Weber, M. (1968). *Economy and society: An outline of interpretive sociology* (C. Wittich & G. Roth, Eds.). New York: Bedmister Press.

Which MBA? (1999). London: The Economist Intelligence Unit.

Whittington, R., & Mayer, M. (2000). *The European corporation: Strategy, structure, and social science.* Oxford, UK: Oxford University Press.

Williamson, H. (2005, March 21). Insuring a well-trained workforce: Allianz Management Institute. *Financial Times,* p. 5.

APPENDIX

50 Largest Western European Firms, Ranked by Market Value, 2008

NOTE: The 2008 FT Europe rankings (500 companies) from which this list came included Russian and other non–Western European firms. Four Russian entries (Gazprom, Rosneft, Lukoil, and Sherbank) were ranked at 1, 23, 41, and 42, respectively. These were deleted from this list and replaced with the next four largest Western European firms to complete the 50.

Rank	Company	Country	Market Value ($ billion)	Sector
2	Royal Dutch Shell	United Kingdom	220.1	Oil and gas
3	Nestlé	Switzerland	197.2	Food
4	HSBC	United Kingdom	195.8	Banking
5	BP	United Kingdom	191.8	Oil and gas
6	Total	France	178.6	Oil and gas
7	Roche	Switzerland	165.2	Pharmaceutical and biotech
8	Vodafone Group	United Kingdom	159.3	Mobile telecommunication
9	EDF	France	159.1	Electricity
10	Telefonica	Spain	137.7	Telecommunication
11	ENI	Italy	137.1	Oil and gas
12	Novartis	Switzerland	134.9	Pharmaceutical and biotech
13	Banco Santander	Spain	125.1	Banking
14	E.On	Germany	124.0	Utilities
15	Nokia	Finland	120.6	Tech hardware and equipment
16	Arcelor Mittal	France	119.1	Industrial metals
17	GlaxoSmithKline	United Kingdom	114.8	Pharmaceutical and biotech
18	Rio Tinto	United Kingdom	103.8	Mining

(Continued)

(Continued)

Rank	Company	Country	Market Value ($ billion)	Sector
19	Sanofi-Aventis	France	102.8	Pharmaceutical and biotech
20	Unilever	Netherlands, United Kingdom	101.6	Food
21	Volkswagen	Germany	101.0	Automobiles and parts
22	Siemens	Germany	99.4	Electronic and electrical equipment
24	StatoilHydrdo	Norway	95.8	Oil and gas
25	BNP Paribas	France	91.7	Banking
26	Intesa Sanpaolo	Italy	90.0	Banking
27	Unicredito Italiano	Italy	89.7	Banking
28	Allianz	Germany	89.5	Insurance
29	France Telecom	France	88.0	Telecommunication
30	Daimler	Germany	87.0	Automobil
31	Suez	France	86.1	Utilities
32	ING	Netherlands	84.4	Insurance
33	BBVA	Spain	82.8	Banking
34	Anglo American	United Kingdom	79.6	Mining
35	L'Oreal	France	77.9	Personal goods
36	Iberdrola	Spain	77.7	Electricity
37	BG Group	United Kingdom	77.6	Oil and gas producers
38	British American Tobacco	United Kingdom	75.8	Tobacco
39	AXA	France	75.1	Insurance
40	Deutsche Telekom	Germany	72.9	Telecommunication
43	Xstrata	United Kingdom	68.5	Mining
44	RWE	Germany	68.3	Gas, water, and multiutilities
45	Royal Bank of Scotland	United Kingdom	67.2	Banking
46	BASF	Germany	66.3	Chemicals

Rank	Company	Country	Market Value ($ billion)	Sector
47	Enel	Italy	65.9	Electricity
48	BHP Billiton	United Kingdom	65.6	Mining
49	Generali	Italy	63.6	Nonlife insurance
50	ABB	Switzerland	62.4	Electronic and electrical equipment
51	SAP	Germany	62.2	Software and computer services
52	Bayer	Germany	61.5	Chemicals
53	UBS	Switzerland	60.5	Banking
54	Deutsche Bank	Germany	60.3	Banking

SOURCE: Adapted from FT Europe 500 2008. Retrieved September 16, 2008, from http://media .ft.com/cms/fcdd2be4–41db-11dd-a5e8–0000779fd2ac.pdf.

Soviet Socialist Management 4

> *Management, one might say, was discovered before there was any management to speak of. The great English economists . . . Adam Smith (1723–1790) to David Ricardo (1772–1823) to John Stewart Mill (1806–1873) and their successor and antagonist Karl Marx (1818–83) knew no management. To them the economy was impersonal and objective.*
>
> —Peter Drucker (1974, p. 21)

Adam Smith and Karl Marx knew no management, but if still around they would surely view it as a vital resource, role, task, function, and practice worthy of widespread attention. History informs us that whether in a state socialist, free enterprise, or mixed economy, organizations must produce results (achieve objectives). History also carries lessons and clues about what might work well, and what won't, and where, why, and when.

The Soviet experience vividly demonstrated how societal macroenvironment can shape management practice and performance. Although the Soviet economy collapsed, its lessons are relevant today and for the future. After all, socialist ideals, aspirations, and practice haven't vanished from the human psyche; witness their endurance in Cuba and North Korea and the recent push by leaders in Venezuela and Bolivia toward "21st-century socialism" (see Wilpert, 2006). And many economies today are mixed, that is, include significant state-owned enterprises in tandem with private ones. The Soviet legacy still influences public economic and business policy today in Russia and other states in transition toward greater commercial, financial, and political freedom. Difficulties there stir doubt about quick and easy adoption or adaptation of capitalist ideas, institutions, solutions, and practices. Previous culture, practice, memories, and mind-set get in the way (May, McCarthy, & Puffer, 2005). Even in long-standing capitalist firms in the West, Soviet-type scenarios can emerge (e.g., in a department, task force, project, or internal cost center) when goals or decisions lack the discipline of markets (valid price signals).

This chapter is positioned here (after the Europe chapter) because of Marxism's European roots. Also, there is brief coverage of the Chinese transition from state socialism in Chapter 6.

Chapter Objectives

- To describe the former Soviet Union (polity, economy, culture)
- To profile the Soviet industrial manager (factory director)
- To highlight patterns, strengths, limitations, and lessons of socialist management practice and behavior
- To identify management scenarios and situations today (anywhere, including in free enterprise systems) similar to those facing former socialist managers

Soviet Polity, Economy, and Culture

Socialism: "A theory or policy of social organization which aims at or advocates the ownership and control of the means of production, capital, land, property, etc., by the community as a whole, and their administration or distribution in the interests of all" (Oxford English Dictionary, 2007); invariably comes with limits on personal civil liberties in order "to protect the common good"; can refer to a small communal enterprise or a nation state.

State socialism: Central government ownership and control of the means of production (e.g., property, tools, funds) in tandem with monopoly political control (e.g., by the Communist Party). In 2008, there were two state socialist economies (North Korea and Cuba); many former ones are now mixed economies (e.g., Russia, China, Vietnam, Belarus, Ukraine, Moldova), some with more economic freedom than others.

Socialist thought and theory drew significant early impetus from German social philosopher Karl Marx, whose *Communist Manifesto* (1848/1964) and *Capital* (*Das Kapital,* 1867/1906) were published long before any nation went socialist. Marxist ideology brought revolution in Russia (1917) and the post–World War II transformation of Eastern Europe (now called Central or Middle Europe), China, Mongolia, North Korea, Vietnam, Cuba, Chile, Cambodia, Algeria, Angola, Myanmar (Burma), Ethiopia, Guyana, Libya, Madagascar, Mozambique, Nicaragua, Tanzania, and others. True believers saw hope for transcending problems they perceived in capitalism, such as redundant and wasteful competition, unequal wealth and income, boom-and-bust business cycles, job dislocation, bankruptcies, homelessness, and resource diversion to frivolous ends (e.g., clothing for pets) rather than basic human needs. State socialist systems have varied in their degree of central state control. For example, the Soviet Union was highly centralized, whereas Yugoslavia and Hungary were less so (market socialism). Table 4.1 briefly describes some differences between some states of that era.

Table 4.1   State Socialist Economic Systems

Union of Soviet Socialist Republics (USSR, or Soviet Union)	Coalesced after the Russian Revolution of 1917, becoming the world's first large industrial economy to be run by a central government bureaucracy. Table 4.2 highlights some overall features of its industrial system; Table 4.3 profiles main features of Soviet society in the late 1980s, just before its collapse (c. 1990).
Former East Germany (or German Democratic Republic)	Fell within the Soviet sphere of influence after World War II, at first with a centralized system but in the late 1970s emphasized semiautonomous production associations (*combinate*), some of them subordinate to central government and others under regional control; was reunited with West Germany in 1992.
The former Yugoslavia (included today's Slovenia, Macedonia, Croatia, Serbia, Montenegro, Kosovo, and Bosnia and Herzegovina)	Went socialist after World War II but with a more decentralized model; decisions about what to produce and how were made by each enterprise within price and wage parameters set by the state; provided for election of managers by employees and review of enterprise policy, plans, and action by elected workers' councils.
Hungary	Went socialist in 1948, initially trying central economic planning but in 1968 began its New Economic Mechanism, which made prices more flexible and reduced directives from central government. It allowed private ownership of small businesses (up to 30 employees) and encouraged agricultural and industrial cooperatives.
The People's Republic of China	Turned socialist after its 1949 Red Revolution; was initially patterned after the Soviet Union but in 1978 began forging a mixed economy while retaining state control of natural resources and heavy industry (e.g., steel, petroleum, cement).
Cuba	Turned socialist after a 1959 revolution; since then reluctant to allow much private enterprise beyond small in-home restaurants and room rentals.

Table 4.2   The Soviet Industrial Enterprise System (pre-1990)

Overall direction and control	By a Communist Party political infrastructure, including its leadership organs (Politburo, Secretariat, Central Committee) and pervasive party hierarchy permeating every ministry, agency, region, community, and factory. Coordination by a council of ministers and several dozen sectoral branch ministries. Specialized state policy committees established guidelines for planning, pricing, quality control, and pay; the State Planning Committee (Gosplan) was charged with coordinating and integrating enterprise planning and plans; a central statistical agency tracked and analyzed performance.
Industrial production	Role of thousands of production units (factories), each accountable to a sectoral branch ministry or department (*glavki*) thereof; some factories were part of multienterprise production associations under regional or local control.
Pricing	The role of the State Price Committee and price departments of each sectoral branch ministry and those of republics and municipalities; a cost-plus system that allowed modest price variation based on production efficiency, product enhancement, quality, season of purchase, whether new or old version of the product, whether for export, and special packaging requirements, plus an increment of profit (about 15%); consumer prices for most basic goods and services (e.g., food, housing, public transportation, energy) were kept artificially low.
Quality control	Responsibility of the State Standards Committee and State Quality Inspectorate.
Pay	Pay guidelines were set by the State Committee on Labor and Wages; there was modest variation based on occupation, skill, education, industry, geographic location, economic sector, and enterprise size.

Enterprise (factory) resources	Working capital was administered through the State Bank (Gosbank); the bank also effected payments and receipts between enterprises[1] by debiting or crediting their respective accounts.
	The Construction Bank (Stroibank) funded new capital investment, product development, and plant renovation.
	A portion of enterprise "retained earnings" was distributed through each factory's Enterprise Fund as bonus pay or social outlay (e.g., for housing, recreation, child care for employees and families).
	Supplementary funding possible (e.g., for research and development) from specialized state agencies.
Material	Supply deliveries were supervised and coordinated by the territorial wholesale network of the State Committee on Supply (Gossnab) and the supply offices of individual branch ministries and other distribution centers authorized by Gossnab; delivery typically depended on a production order and formal supply contract between producer and customer in alignment with the official plan.
Technology	Domain of the State Committee on Science & Technology and specialized research institutes of individual branch ministries or multienterprise production associations.
Labor	Individuals could be assigned to an employer or be hired directly.

SOURCE: Synthesized from many sources, especially Berliner (1988), Bornstein and Fusfeld (1974), Polyakov and Rakhmilovich (1977), and Richman (1965).

Labor unionism was controlled by the state, with employees being de facto members. Union leaders were paid by the state and enforced compliance with labor laws and regulations and proper political education. Infrequent efforts to form independent unions were suppressed on the grounds that workers' needs and interests were already protected by the state.

Employees were docile and compliant, conditioned by their ideology, their culture, and the law to obey higher-ups. They had a nominal voice in setting work norms, hiring, firing, training, working conditions, and promotions through their elected committees and production conferences (analogous to the Western European works councils described in Chapter 3). They also had a voice, in principle, regarding bonus pay (Grancelli, 1988). Large factories sometimes supplied significant social support services (e.g., housing, education, health care services) for employees and families.

Table 4.3   Profile of the Soviet Union (late 1980s) Just Before Its Collapse (1990–1991)

Demographic context	Population 285 million (1990); Russia (148 million) was the largest of 15 Soviet republics, followed in size by the Ukraine (50 million); others were Belorussia, Georgia, Azerbaijan, Armenia, Moldavia, Estonia, Latvia, Lithuania, and the Uzbek, Turkmen, Tadzhik, Kazakh, and Kirgiz republics.
	Ethnic and cultural diversity; predominantly Slavic heritage in the north and Muslim in the south.
Political context	Centralized Communist Party control of economic, social, political, educational, labor, media, and other institutions.
	Significant limits on personal civil liberties "in order to safeguard the common good."
Economic context	State socialist system based on central government economic planning coordinated by Gosplan (State Planning Agency).
	Government-administered cost-plus pricing system; prices for many basic goods and services (housing, food, energy, public transportation) were kept artificially low.
	No business cycles, price inflation, or unemployment.
	Significant shortages, waiting lines, delays.
	Largely egalitarian pay but modest variation based on occupation, skill level, industry, geographic location, economic sector, and enterprise size; bonuses were possible if production goals were met on time.
	Preference for large (often vertically integrated) enterprises in order to gain economies of scale.
	Underdeveloped transportation and communication infrastructure.

Economic context (continued)	About one fourth of the workforce was engaged in agriculture, mainly in large state-run farms and cooperatives.
	High priority for national security, heavy industry, space program, Olympic sports.
	Considerable off-the-books economic activity (unofficial underground economy).
	Low-quality consumer goods.
	Low unemployment; much redundant employment (labor hoarding, overstaffing).
Labor relations	No autonomous labor organizations; unions were controlled by the Communist Party.
	Provision for employee production conferences (analogous to Western European works councils) with nominal employee voice in workplace decisions.
	Individuals could change employers, but there was not much financial incentive to do so.
Social context	Social and economic privileges for the *nomenklatura*, that is, party-controlled rosters of the more competent, well-educated, well-connected, and politically correct individuals (leaders and candidates for political and economic leadership).
	Extensive participation of women in the workforce but seldom at top levels of enterprise or government.
Work ethic	Long tradition of passive subservience to authority; citizenry conditioned by culture and ideology to follow directions and rules from higher-ups.
	Much patience, fortitude, and endurance in face of adversity.
Cultural context	High-context culture; importance of personal relationships and trust.
	On Hofstede's cultural dimensions:[2] <ul><li>Medium individualism</li><li>High uncertainty avoidance</li><li>High power distance</li><li>Medium masculinity</li><li>Short-term time horizon</li></ul>
Educational context	Universal primary and secondary education; nationally standardized curricula.
	Dual-track system (general and technical/vocational).

SOURCE: This material is drawn from diverse newspaper and magazine sources *(e.g., New York Times, Wall Street Journal, The Economist)* and academic sources.

People could change employers, but there was seldom much financial incentive to do so unless one was choosing more dangerous work, joining a mobile work brigade, or transferring to a remote geographic region. Without personal connections, it was difficult to obtain residence permits in the most coveted locations (big cities such as Moscow and Leningrad). Overall, the labor supply was constrained by slow population growth and almost no immigration. A young retirement age (60 for men and 55 for women) and a tendency for factories to hoard labor contributed to labor shortages in many endeavors.

The Soviet Manager

PERSONAL BACKGROUND

Soviet-era managers had high social status. Heads of the 50–60 or so sectoral branch ministries topped the industrial hierarchy, controlling many thousand factories (and some multifactory production associations). The branch ministries appointed the factory directors, although some were picked by regional and local political authorities. Candidates came from the Communist Party–controlled rosters of proven or precertified people (the *nomenklatura*) and were also reviewed by labor and community officials.

Russians factory directors were favored over other Soviet nationalities, and they commonly had backgrounds in engineering or technical fields (Andrle, 1976; Freris, 1984). More than half of directors eventually became Communist Party members, a proportion much higher than among the general population.

Promotion to factory director was usually slow, starting on the factory floor and eventually progressing to chief engineer and then director (Granick, 1961). Berliner (1966) described the pattern:

> The young Soviet engineer who goes into industry starts at the bottom of the managerial ladder, as chief of a production shop, or the design or maintenance departments of an enterprise. As new job opportunities develop, he faces the choice of continuing in direct production or taking one of the staff jobs in the enterprise, such as the planning department. If he stays in production proper, his career path may lead to chief engineer of an enterprise or to one of the higher economic agencies. If he moves into staff work, his career may lead to the directorship of an enterprise or of one of the higher organs. Either career leads to the pinnacle of Soviet management. (p. 114)

And Conyngham (1982) stated,

> In the normal pattern of promotion, a plant manager has been successfully advanced to foreman, shop head, and chief engineer, a process that might consume twenty years. Traditionally, the move to a directorship is most easily achieved by the chief engineer. A study in one ministry noted that chief engineers won 72% of the directorship appointments. (pp. 19–20)

In the late 1950s, Granick (1961) noted some similarities between U.S. CEOs and Russian factory directors. Both were almost exclusively male and from white-collar family backgrounds. However, the Russians were more production oriented, had more hands-on work experience, and had more postsecondary formal schooling (Table 4.4).

A perennial dilemma in choosing managers was the degree of importance to put on candidates' ideological credentials or professional competency, that is, whether to choose party loyalty or expertise when these didn't coincide. Post–Soviet era interviews with emigrant former factory directors found that their education, training, and experience were more important than their Communist Party ties (Linz, 1988). By the 1980s,

Table 4.4   Similarities and Differences in Personal Backgrounds of Soviet and U.S. Managers (c. 1960)

- Both groups came from reasonably similar social classes, mostly white-collar family backgrounds.
- The proportion of college graduates was higher among Soviet managers than among U.S. managers, and more of them had engineering degrees.
- The Soviet manager was far less likely than the American to have formal training in human relations. On the other hand, because of Young Communist League activities, he probably had more people experience while in school.
- The Russian's first major practical experience in business occurred in his final college year, a bridge between education and the world of work.
- Russian managers had an earlier and larger dose of work experience directly in the manufacturing function.
- Russian managers were more likely to have begun their career as low-level executives. American managers were more likely to have started in staff or technical positions.

SOURCE: Adapted from Granick (1961, pp. 80–81).

previous experience in line positions (e.g., production) was generally preferred over staff (advice and support) experience.

MANAGEMENT EDUCATION

Promotion to factory director was often accompanied by short-term
management courses (3 to 6 months) in special engineering and economics. These emphasized socialist economic theory along with engineering
and technical studies surrounding the production (manufacturing) function (Puffer, 1981).

Formal higher education for management expanded after 1980 with
founding of specialized business schools. Managerial studies were also
supplied by high-level economic institutes such as the Plekhanov Institute
of the National Economy (elite Russian undergraduate management
school) and the Academy of the National Economy (elite graduate-level
management program begun in 1978). Another was the Institute of the
Management of the Economy, created in 1978, tied to the State Committee
on Science and Technology. The Council of Ministers coordinated management education for the business institutes of the respective industrial
branch ministries. In addition to their coverage of socialist politics and
economics, there was also attention to business subjects, sometimes using
Western textbooks (Puffer, 1981).

Most of this education was descriptive and prescriptive rather than
analytical, with much coverage of management science (quantitative
methods) applied to planning and decision making and much less on
behavioral dimensions of management (Puffer, 1981).

MANAGERIAL ROLE AND TASKS

In essence, the role of the Soviet factory director was analogous to that
of a production (manufacturing) manager in a Western capitalist firm,
but broader, and involved interaction with ministry technocrats and
Communist Party and local officials. In contrast to their counterparts in
capitalist countries, they didn't need to worry about independently raising
capital because that came from the state rather than from (nonexistent) capital markets. Also, no marketing was required because state planners identified the customers. There was no need or desire to be entrepreneurial in the
sense of developing new products, technologies, or markets. However, there
was a need to be creative in negotiating attainable production targets and
sufficient resource allotments. Also, managers often had to round up scarce
material resources outside official channels when suppliers couldn't deliver
on time. Overall managerial autonomy was very constrained (Table 4.5).

Table 4.5   Soviet Managerial Decision Autonomy at the Enterprise Level (Factory Director)

Nearly No Autonomy	Moderate Autonomy	High Autonomy
Appointment of factory director and key deputies (chief engineer, controller)	Negotiation (with supervisory branch ministry) of annual production targets and material, financial, and human resource allocation	Day-to-day scheduling, integration, and coordination of tasks, resources, and effort
Disposition of fixed assets (plant, machinery)	Disposition of unused buildings and material resources	Recruiting and hiring
Division of earnings between the enterprise and the state	Minor realignments in product mix	Employee training and development
Capital investment	Procurement of supplemental resources to offset unforeseen or unplanned contingencies such as late delivery from suppliers	
	Production and sale of limited goods and services beyond the commitments of the official plan	
	Disposition of the Enterprise Fund (earnings retained by the enterprise for bonuses and social expenditures, such as housing and recreation)	
	Layoffs, dismissals	

NOTE: For an overview of the Soviet industrial enterprise system, see Polyakov and Rakhmilovich (1977) and Richman (1965).

The Management Process

The Soviet enterprise system gave rise to some distinctive managerial patterns, pressures, and problems. Several of them are identified in the following sections from the viewpoint of the management process (management functions).

PLANNING

The Soviet Union had a centrally planned economy. In most respects, its managers (factory directors) had much less autonomy than their counterparts in free enterprise systems. There were no worries about takeover attempts by outsiders, no criticism from stockholders (there weren't any), no consumer rights activists (not an organized constituency), few environmentalists, few human rights champions (they were jailed or exiled), and minimal philanthropic requests because "the state already looked after everyone's needs."

At the enterprise (factory) level, strategic planning wasn't a worry because there were no competitors, no business cycles, and no commercial risk or credit risk. Capital was free to its users, and there was a seller's market for goods and services. However, there was strong pressure from the state bureaucracy (branch ministries) and the Communist Party for timely completion of production goals according to plan.

Each factory negotiated a provisional (typically annual) plan with a ministerial department (*glavki*) in the supervisory branch ministry (in some cases with a multienterprise production association or regional or municipal authority). After give-and-take negotiation, production goals were decided (and announced) and seen as legally enforceable contracts. This led to a ratchet system of planning in which targets were increased incrementally each year if goals were met. If not actually met, numbers could be fudged to make it seem so, to qualify for bonuses and to ensure equivalent resource allotments for the next cycle.

The negotiation of targets and resources was often based on incomplete, inaccurate, and hidden information. Factory directors wanted attainable goals and were inclined to understate their true production capability and to exaggerate their resource needs. They were especially concerned about material shortages and delivery delays. Their resource allotments, whether or not actually used up, became officially used up (at least so reported) to protect future allotments. Unused inventory could be hoarded to be used, sold, or traded on the side, as necessary.

Delivery delay from suppliers could be overcome by dispatching *tolkachi* (pushers, expediters) to ply their personal and political connections to barter or bribe for supplies hoarded by other factories or sitting in state supply offices.

The system was conducive to *autarky* (self-sufficiency) in the repair and service of equipment and the making of supplies, spare parts, and subassemblies when suppliers couldn't deliver on time (Kontorovich & Shlapentokh, 1985). There was resistance to innovation and plant modernization lest these jeopardize future production timelines. And things were sometimes produced for which there was no urgent need, as in the following example:

> The Soviet Union has 3m tractors; 250,000 of them are broken down at any one time. . . . Farms do not repair their own tractors; specialist repair shops do that. Each has its own plan for the number of tractors it is supposed to repair in a year. . . . So the repair shops forced the farms to send tractors to be repaired even when they didn't need it . . . [thus] repair becomes an end in itself; repair doesn't exist for the tractor. The tractor exists to fulfill the repairmen's plans. (*The Economist*, 1989, p. 101)

Tight time schedules and supply irregularities were conducive to storming (*schturmovschina*), that is, a flurry of activity near the end of each production cycle. For example, in a factory functioning on a monthly schedule, the pace of work early in the month would generally be slow, a time to recover from the rush that ended the previous cycle. Also, many resources weren't yet in hand. As the month progressed, the work rhythm would pick up as more supplies arrived and deadlines drew near. Near the end of the cycle, the pace of work could be frenetic, with people working overtime and being assigned, as needed, to tasks outside their specialties (putting engineers on the assembly line). The phenomenon is described by *New York Times* journalist Hedrick Smith (1976, p. 286):

> It is a practice so endemic and essential to the Soviet system that Russians have coined the fancy term *shturmovshchina* to denote the entire national phenomenon of crash programs and the wildly erratic work-rhythm of Soviet factories, large and small, civilian and military. Storming to fulfill the monthly, quarterly or annual Plan turns every month into a sort of crazy industrial pregnancy, sluggish in gestation and frenzied at the finish.

A common consequence was poor production quality. As an Uzbek factory foreman declared, "The whole population knows all about this because everyone works. . . . So normally when someone buys a household appliance, he tries to buy one with a certificate saying that it was produced before the 15th of the month and not after the 15th" (Smith, 1976, pp. 287–288).

Table 4.6 highlights some contrasts between enterprise planning in the USSR and a free enterprise setting.

CONTROL

In any organization, effective management involves monitoring of performance and making adjustments, as needed, to operations (or to objectives). In the Soviet industrial system, a central government economic bureaucracy (Gosplan and the sectoral branch ministries) and the Communist Party had broad supervisory oversight. Success involved completion of output targets within the timelines of the official plan.

The notion of profitability had no substantive meaning because true profit is not knowable in an arbitrary pricing system. The Soviet *khozraschet* (business responsibility; self sufficiency) accounting system recognized about 15% profit, defined as the difference between enterprise revenue and costs computed at artificial government-set prices. In the words of Soviet economist Nikolay Shmelyov (as quoted in "Toward a Soviet Market Economy," 1987, p. 1),

> Our suspicious attitude toward profit is a historical misunderstanding, the result of the economic illiteracy of people who thought that socialism would eliminate profit and loss. In point of fact, the criterion of profit under socialism is in no way tainted. It simply tells whether you are working well or not.

Table 4.6   Enterprise-Level Plans and Planning

Free Enterprise System (United States, Western Europe)	Former Soviet Union
High managerial autonomy in regard to what to make or sell and how much, how, where, when, with what, and by whom.	Limited autonomy. Provisional production plan was negotiated or reconciled annually with a supervisory branch ministry. Subsequent adjustments were possible for unforeseen contingencies, including amended state priorities and delays in receiving supplies.
Plans and planning influenced directly or indirectly by diverse stakeholders (employees, shareholders, creditors, government, environmentalists, local communities).	Overall planning and plans coordinated by ministry technocrats and Communist Party officials, with nominal consultation with employees and community officials. The Communist Party monitored its social, political and ideological interests in each enterprise.
Attention to strategic planning (continual adjustment of the firm to evolving market opportunities, competition, and macroenvironmental change).	No need for enterprise-level strategic planning. Emphasis on year-to-year production plans and day-to-day operations. Overall planning was the domain of each supervisory branch ministry and the central government planning office (Gosplan).

From a Western perspective, the system breached a core tenet of management: parity of responsibility and authority. In effect, directors lacked sufficient authority to achieve what they were being held accountable for. (One example was no autonomous contact with state-designated suppliers.)

Table 4.7 identifies some differences in the control system in a free enterprise setting and a state socialist one.

ORGANIZING

The Soviet industrial system was structured around sectoral branch ministries (and their subordinate departments, *glavki*) for each product sector (e.g., one for pulp and paper and another for household appliances).

From 1957 to 1965, a geographic area orientation (with regional economic councils) was tried.

Enterprise units (factories) were typically large and with narrow product lines, and they focused around the production function. Factory directors dealt with a dual line of supervisory authority, one from their industrial branch ministry and another from the Communist Party, often with different priorities.

Table 4.7 Control

Free Enterprise System	Former Soviet Union
Main performance criterion is profitability; other indicators include position and trends in sales, market share, and market rank.	Enterprises (production units and associations) were conceptually cost centers rather than profit centers;[3] although profit was mentioned, it was impossible to know because of non–free market pricing.
Success entails satisfying the autonomous purchasing decisions of customers.	The main performance criterion was the on-time production of planned output; efforts were made to include additional criteria (e.g., reduction in production costs and improvements in productivity, quality, and delivery).
Senior management is overseen by an enterprise board of directors charged with stewarding the interests of shareholders and other acknowledged stakeholders.	Performance was monitored by branch ministry bureaucrats and party officials.
Regular detailed public financial reporting is required of companies that raise capital from the general public. Auditors (external and internal) monitor compliance with prescribed accounting and reporting standards.	There was no public disclosure of internal financial information; a factory auditor reported directly to the supervisory branch ministry; a government bank (Gosbank) controlled payments between enterprises (no direct control over cash flow by factory directors).
Unsatisfactory performance can lead to transfer, resignation, or discharge of a manager or maybe restructuring, merger, sale, or bankruptcy. Over time, this tends to weed out ineffective managers, who then have difficulty gaining similar employment or who can learn from their experience and become successful in the future.	Unsatisfactory performance could lead to dismissal and loss of valued perks and privileges; similar future appointment was unlikely.

The branch ministry system was conducive to weak integration and coordination between the various ministries, state committees, and factories, and there was much fragmentation and overlap of policy oversight (and bureaucratic intrusion) by administrative higher-ups. In the following quotation, a factory director expressed frustration with the bureaucracy.

> Today there is much talk about whether it is necessary to eliminate ministries, and how many of them there should be. . . . In no other place in the world are there so many ministries and things are going so terribly. . . . To tell you the truth, we don't need ministries. . . . But this doesn't mean we don't need a central agency to coordinate things. But they should work and earn their keep from us and not from the central budget. Let the ministries catch the mice. If they don't, they don't eat. . . . Enough. I can't stand this proliferation of paperwork. . . . I understand one thing. It's useless to fight the forms, you've got to kill the people producing them. (Vladimir P. Kabaidze, general director, Ivanovo Machine Building Works, quoted in Taubman, 1988, p. 1)

Table 4.8 describes some differences in regard to the organizing function between a free enterprise setting and the former Soviet system.

Table 4.8   Organizing

Free Enterprise System (e.g., United States)	Former Soviet Union
Companies usually are structured around function, product, geography, or a combination thereof.	Industrial branch ministries were organized along product lines; enterprises (factories) were structured around the production function.
Periodic restructuring (e.g., reorganization or consolidation, merger, acquisition, spin-off) to accommodate internal and external change.	No enterprise-level autonomy to restructure or merge; bias toward large-scale factories in order to gain economies of scale; some multiplant production associations.
Interfirm integration and coordination (e.g., between suppliers, customers) guided mainly by market forces (supply and demand) and managerial initiative.	Integration and coordination between enterprises were desired, but the branch ministry system was not conducive to much interfactory or interindustry synergy or interaction.

DIRECTING

Motivation

They pretend to pay us, and we pretend to work. (Soviet-era refrain)

From a Marxist perspective, employee motivation would cease to be an issue once society was rid of capitalists and capitalist incentives. Socialism would bring comparable worth and wealth for all. An enlightened citizenry would contribute ceaselessly and selflessly for the common good, and as Marx expressed in his *Communist Manifesto* (1848/1964), all would contribute according to their abilities and be rewarded according to their needs. The Soviets did it differently, though—"From each according to their ability, and to each according to their work"—allowing pay differences for more critical tasks and higher productivity. However, these differences were seldom large enough to be meaningful motivators.

A factory director's pay was about three times that of an ordinary worker but could vary by enterprise size, sector, and performance. Heads of large enterprises received more than those of small ones. Pay could be increased with bonuses when production goals were met on time. There were also valued perquisites such as a personal driver, shopping privileges in special stores, access to a countryside cottage (*dacha*), priority medical attention, and access to preferred schools for one's children.

Another motivator was potential criminal liability for not fulfilling the plan, demotion, loss of party membership, and foregone future bonuses and perks. Employees could be sent to corrective labor camps if unemployed for more than four consecutive months. In essence, there was no right to be voluntarily unemployed, as expressed by a Russian engineer:

> Moscow News, January 3, 1988. . . . I would like to discuss and to express my own opinion in relation to the "right to work" which we proclaim. Soviet people enjoy the first part of this right—to work. But the second part of this right—the right not to work—is utterly lacking. In our country a person cannot choose not to work—it is a crime (so-called parasitism). Therefore, the right to work in its full meaning is nonexistent in our society, and what we have is not a right but an obligation. A person enjoys the right not to work in practically all countries except ours. . . . I think that articles on parasitism should be deleted from the new criminal code, and the labor code should allow for the possibility of not working, without any especially unpleasant consequences. A. Ivanov, engineer. (Shipler, 1988, p. 1)

There was also socialist competition. This didn't mean competition against other producers but rather the opportunity to surpass one's own production goals. For example, a labor management committee could propose a counterplan more ambitious than the official one, and workers would receive bonuses for achieving it. In theory, this would generate peer pressure from coworkers wanting bonuses. However, it could also lead to unrealistically high production targets in the next planning and production cycle and jeopardize future bonuses.

Other rewards included praise, ribbons, and medals for high-performing employees and factories. Shock workers (*udarniki, peredoviki*) were recognized for high productivity. A much-heralded model worker movement emerged in the 1930s, named after miner Aleksei Stakhanov, who was reported to have produced 227 tons of coal in a single work shift (the norm was 7 tons). From this came a Stakhanovite Movement that waxed and waned over the years.

There was some evidence of personal motivation based on self-interest in (illegal) moonlighting away from regular jobs, even during regular working hours, using employers' tools, equipment, and supplies. Rewards came both in cash and in kind (goods, favors) from appreciative customers.

It is noteworthy that some visible successes of the Soviet era drew from capitalist values (self-interest and survival of the fittest). This was apparent in sports and the performing arts, where high achievers got extra pay and travel privileges. In world competitions, Soviet athletes could earn substantial cash bonuses for medal-level performances. At the 1988 Olympic Games (in Seoul, South Korea), rewards included 12,000 rubles for a gold medal, 6,000 rubles for a silver, and 4,000 rubles for bronze; by comparison, the median annual income for an ordinary industrial worker was about 3,500 rubles. (Occasionally, cash prizes were reduced for silver or bronze medal winners from whom gold had been expected.) Outstanding athletes and artists often got preferential housing and access to special stores and medical services. Training was time-intensive rather than material-intensive, less dependent on logistical ties to suppliers. Achievements were the result of intense competition favoring the fittest coaches, athletes, dancers, and musicians.

Leadership

Marxist political doctrine emphasized democratic centralism, that is, the nominal opportunity for everyone to have a voice in decisions but one person having the final say. Once the decision was made, it was to be accepted and implemented by everyone. If there was doubt about action, it was wise to protect oneself from criticism by deferring to higher-ups, as Berliner (1988) described:

> In the centrally-planned economy, each organizational unit is held to account for the administration of some line of state policy, and it demands some control over all decisions taken elsewhere that may affect its own plans and instructions. Moreover, the mistrust is not always directed downward but extends upward as well. There is a widespread tradition of the voluntary seeking of written approval of important decisions by one's senior official and other, as a sort of protection against incrimination in case the decision later proves to have been a bad one. Even in the absence of formal procedures, the practice of "collecting signatures" tends to widen the network of organizations brought into decision making. (p. 368)

The ideal was one-man management with an unambiguous unified chain of authority. However, many decisions required negotiation and discussion between different offices, agencies, and committees. The rules, policies, and pressures of the state ministries and policy committees constrained factory directors' abilities to get things done. So did rigid separation of ministries, which prevented cross-fertilization of ideas, resources, technology, and skills between industrial sectors and factories.

The system did little to encourage the initiative, insight, judgment, or creative instincts of its implementers. Moreover, administrators were overwhelmed by the complexity of it all, as economist Friedrich Hayek (1988) once insightfully explained:

> What cannot be known cannot be planned. . . . The totality of resources that one could employ in such a plan is simply not knowable to anybody, and therefore can hardly be centrally controlled. (p. 85)

Managerial Performance

A Briton, a Frenchman, and a Russian are viewing a painting of Adam and Eve in the Garden of Eden:

"Look at their reserve, their calm," muses the Brit. "They must be British."

"Nonsense," the Frenchman disagrees. "They're naked, and so beautiful. Clearly they are French."

"No clothes, no shelter," the Russian points out, "they have only an apple to eat, and they're being told this is paradise. They are Russian."
(Source unknown)

A central concern of all managers is the attainment of goals. Soviet society did achieve some goals of state socialism. For example, average living standards for most people improved gradually over time. There was full employment, near universal literacy, improving life expectancy, and not much dire poverty. There was largely egalitarian distribution of income and wealth despite some privileges for party and professional elites. However, many people, especially in the countryside and among the elderly, lived at the margin of poverty compared with peers in North America, Western Europe, and Japan.

There were also technological advancements in metallurgy, hydroelectric power generation, and medicine and a path-breaking space program that placed the first human in Earth orbit. There was consistent excellence in Olympic sports, classical music, ballet, and chess. These successes raised the question of why the system couldn't also produce first-rate cars, houses, or computers. One reason was the allocation of resources to results that would demonstrate the superiority of socialism to the outside world. The most competent engineers and scientists were routinely assigned to the defense and space programs. Also, some Soviet successes came in areas where a command economy can have a competitive edge, that is, in mobilizing, concentrating, and coordinating resources quickly for a high-priority purpose (analogous to the 1969 U.S. moon expedition) but at the expense of other goals.

Overall economic performance was disappointing for the true believers, who expected so much more. So noted Berliner (1988):

> Imagine a managerial official who fell into a deep sleep in 1941 and awoke to find himself in a typical enterprise in 1986. He would surely be overwhelmed by the visible changes. . . . On the one hand he could scarcely believe that his country's technology had advanced so far in the 45 years of his sleep. On the other, he finds about him an air of gloom at the prospect that unless something is done, the USSR will enter the next century as a second-rate industrial and technological country. (pp. 271–272)

Despite inexpensive housing, free education, universal health care, and a guaranteed job, the average citizen had a living standard well below that of peers in the capitalist West. Per capita consumption of many consumer goods and services was low, and quality was low. More money was paid in wages and salaries than there were goods and services to buy at the artificially set prices. Underpriced essential goods sold quickly, bringing rationing (and corollary waiting lines), and overpriced shoddy items accumulated unsold. The quality of housing was low in terms of living space, amenities, and maintenance. These and other problems are reflected in the following excerpt from a Communist Party Conference ("Key Parts of Soviet Plan for Change," 1988, p. 13):

> The economic structure remained, on the whole, cost intensive. Scientific and technological progress is yet slow, and the plans for increasing the national income and resource saving are not fulfilled. There is no notice-able improvement in product quality. The country's finances are still in a bad state. Tensions remain in the supply of foodstuffs and consumer goods, and the population's demand for services is not fully met. The housing problem remains acute.

A more pronounced sign of failure was the lack of immigration from other countries.

ECONOMIC REFORMS

Many wondered whether the system's lackluster performance was inherent in the system or whether it just needed better managers. It is noteworthy that in the 1920s Soviet leader Vladimir Lenin sensed need for more enterprise autonomy and sought to encourage some private entre-preneurship, especially in agriculture. After Lenin, however, Stalin refo-cused on central planning. Thereafter, reforms were tried over the years, some of which are chronicled in Table 4.9.

Most reforms were neither fully nor effectively implemented and didn't salvage the system, leading eventually to the more substantial Mikhail Gorbachev reform initiatives of the late 1980s. With emphasis on *glasnost* (candor, openness, transparency) and *perestroika* (restructuring), he pro-posed the changes listed in Table 4.10.[4]

> The principles of self-financing, self-support, self-management must be introduced everywhere. Glasnost must be affirmed, and initiative by local bodies and local public opinion must be stimulated. ("Key Excerpts," 1988, p. 14).

The Gorbachev period brought the end of Soviet state socialism in 1990–1991. Today, Russia and most other former Soviet republics are transitioning to market-guided economies, but progress has been much slower than anticipated (Table 4.11).

Table 4.9   A Selection of Soviet Economic and Managerial Reforms

Date	Nature of the Reform	Fate of the Reform
1921–1927	Lenin's New Economic Policy linked pay to individual qualification and performance, allowed private ownership for small farmers and entrepreneurs, and reinstated individual inheritance rights.	Superseded by Stalinist central planning in 1928; no comparable reforms until the Gorbachev era.
1931	Pay was re-linked to individual productivity.	Wage and salary differences were never large enough to be effective motivators.
1956	Workers were allowed to change employers; pay could vary by geographic region and type of work.	Pay differences were not large enough to promote labor mobility; political barriers to mobility (residence permits) continued.
1957	Shift from an industrial branch ministry system to one based on geography (regional economic councils).	The territorial system was unsuccessful; the industrial branch ministry system was reinstated in 1965.
1962	Revenue of the government industrial research institutes was to come from contracts with individual enterprises.	Never fully implemented.
1964	Price surcharges were allowed for product enhancements if they led to higher production costs.	Tried for a time; however, there were many other barriers to product-enhancing innovation.
1965	Liberman reforms and 1965 Statute of the Socialist State Enterprise brought reversion to the pre-1957 industrial branch ministry system. Managerial pay was to be based on "profits," and some enterprises were allowed to sell directly to end users.	Much was never fully implemented; at the time, they were considered revolutionary but couldn't overcome the lack of enterprise autonomy, invalid price signals, and inadequate incentives.

Date	Nature of the Reform	Fate of the Reform
1965 (continued)	"Profit and loss" (*khozraschet*) accounting and modest profit sharing between the enterprise and the state were introduced; some of each factory's earnings could be distributed as employee bonuses, enterprise social expenditures, or capital investment; supplementary performance criteria were added to gross output, including output sold and attention to quality. Interest was to be charged on working capital and investment capital from the state. Voluntary people's control committees were formed at plants for purposes of quality control; factory directors were given more authority to hire and fire employees, within the constraints of their overall wage fund.	
1967	The Shchekino experiment allowed some enterprises to keep the same overall wage fund even when reducing their workforce; laid-off workers were retrained for other enterprises.	Some improvement in efficiency at the enterprise level; it was extended to many enterprises, but factory directors remained reluctant to trim their workforce.
1973–1974	Branch ministry bureaucracy was reduced in an effort to improve interbranch cooperation; factories were grouped into multienterprise production associations and industrial associations to gain synergy and economies of scale.	Modest improvement.
1983	Andropov reforms, Law on Labor Collectives: crackdown on labor indiscipline and absenteeism; proposal for more worker involvement in decision making; renewed effort to link bonuses to improvements in output quality. A brigade teamwork system was tried in some firms.	Modest short-term improvement in productivity; the Andropov reforms were superseded by the Gorbachev reform initiatives (Table 4.10).

SOURCE: Synthesized from diverse press reports leading up to the Gorbachev reforms of the late 1980s.

Table 4.10   Gorbachev Reform Initiatives, Post-1985

More enterprise-based planning, pricing, and marketing initiatives; less reliance on production orders from central planners.

Greater voice for employees in decision making, including in the selection of managers.

Plan to reduce ministerial and party control of economic planning and eliminate 700,000 jobs in the industrial branch ministries.

Greater regional control of light industry, construction, and other services; provision for local taxation of enterprise to fund local public services.

Acceptance of self-financed enterprise, more exposure to external commercial and financial risk, and provision for bankruptcy (Law on the State Enterprise, effective January 1988).

Encouragement of direct contacts and contracts between producers (including foreign ones).

General price reforms (more market-guided pricing), including gradual phaseout of state subsidies, and transition to a socialist market economy; intent to create viable financial markets and a foreign exchange–convertible ruble.

Permission (after mid-1988) for small private cooperatives and sole proprietorships (Law on the State Enterprise of January 1, 1988); in January 1989 there were more than 75,000 functioning cooperatives, employing 1.4 million people (Keller, 1989, p. 1).

Collectivized leases; opportunity for individuals and groups to rent land, buildings, and production equipment and to work on a contract basis for other firms or for the state.

Proposed draft law giving workers the real right to strike.

Banking reform in 1988: formation of special banks for consumer and agricultural needs; scale-back of Gosbank and its conversion to a central bank.

Encouragement of inward direct foreign investment (beginning in 1987, allowing up to 49% foreign private ownership in joint equity ventures); proposed creation of pilot enterprise zones allowing up to 100% private foreign ownership.

Table 4.11   Russia in Transition, 2008

Demography	Population 143 million (and shrinking), most of it located west of the Ural mountains.
Politics and Government	A government-guided democracy dominated by the United Russia Party; strong presidency and weak legislature; suppression of political opposition; government domination of key media.
	Problematic legal and regulatory system; uncertain enforcement of business and commercial law (property rights, shareholder rights, contract enforcement).
	Cumbersome state bureaucracy and much red tape.
	Considerable public and private economic crime and corruption.
	Weak labor unions.
Economy	State-guided capitalist system (mixed economy); problematic progress toward a mature free enterprise system.
	State ownership of most major natural resource firms and government stakes in many partially privatized enterprises.
	Growing presence of private enterprise in the economy (produced more than two thirds of gross domestic product in 2008).
	Underdeveloped small business sector; slow new enterprise formation.
	High economic growth spurred by natural resource export boom. Inflationary pressures.
	Ambiance of frontier capitalism; unfamiliar with business law and ethics of a well-functioning free market economy.
	Problematic corporate governance; predominantly insider control; weak protection for minority shareholders.
	Slow emergence of viable banking and capital markets; gas and oil sectors dominate the stock market.
	Widespread accounting irregularities and opaque financial reporting and disclosure.
	Arbitrary taxation and extensive tax evasion.
	Substantial unreported and underreported personal and corporate income.
	Emerging middle-class affluence in major cities; decline in poverty rates.
	Well-educated, low-cost labor force.
	Handful of large financial–industrial conglomerates headed by business tycoons (oligarchs).
	Senior government officials and cronies or associates dominate boards of directors of large state-owned enterprises.

(Continued)

Table 4.11 (Continued)

Eonomy (continued)	Aging and inadequate transportation and communication infrastructure.
	Economic nationalism bringing discriminatory treatment of imports and foreign investment.
	Expansion of higher education for business.
Culture	Uneasiness with capitalist values; economic inequality evokes envy and sense of injustice.
	Nostalgia for the equality, security, and predictability of the Soviet era (especially in the older generation).
	Suspicion and distrust of outsiders; importance of trust and relationships in getting things done.
	Preference for order rather than freedom.
	Attraction for authoritarian leadership.
	See also the cultural traits listed in Table 4.3.

SOURCE: Drawn from diverse academic and journalistic sources, including the *New York Times, The Economist, Financial Times, Wall Street Journal,* and Russian English-language news Web sites (e.g., *Moscow News, Moscow Times*). See also Broadman (2001); Desai and Goldberg (2000); "FT Russia" (2006); "FT Series Russia Resurgent" (2006); Puffer, Shekshnia, and McCarthy (2005); and "Special Report Russia" (2006).

Chapter Summary

- Management transcends ideology, but ideology, via politics and economics, can profoundly influence management practice and performance. This was apparent in the former Soviet Union and other state socialist systems.

- Even though most socialist economies collapsed, their management lessons continue today in any group where decisions occur without guidance of markets, including inside work groups, departments, and divisions of private companies and in government-administered health, education, and other services.

- The Soviet industrial system was based on government ownership and control of the means of production, allowing neither private property nor autonomous price signals. Central coordination came from a national planning office (Gosplan) and branch industrial ministries organized around product group. Factories were accountable to their supervisory branch ministry, with which they negotiated annual production targets and resource allotments.

- The personal backgrounds of the Soviet-era managers (factory directors) were similar to those of their free-world peers in regard to gender (male), age, level of education (high), and social status (high). However, their managerial concerns, problems, and practices were very different. The Soviet manager had much less autonomy and was more focused on the production function and largely oblivious (by design) to matters of strategy, finance, and marketing. Engineering and technical expertise were key criteria in selecting factory directors; ideological fidelity was also important but not (usually) the main factor. Nomination and selection often came from Communist Party–approved rosters (*nomenklatura*) of positions and candidates.

- Central government was successful in mobilizing resources quickly for certain high-priority goals (e.g., space program, national security) but at high opportunity cost to consumers and the overall economy. A ratchet pattern of planning evolved, with factory production goals increased each year if production targets were achieved. When negotiating the annual production plan with higher-ups, the factory director was inclined to hide and distort information about capabilities in order to have viable goals and sufficient resources to accomplish them. Tight time deadlines and irregular delivery from suppliers contributed to storming, that is, a flurry of activity near the end of the production cycle, hampering product quality.

- When resources didn't arrive on time, they were manufactured or improvised internally or otherwise hustled up through bribe or barter through nonofficial channels.

- Overall control involved dual lines of supervision: one from the Communist Party hierarchy and another from the branch ministry technocracy. Factory directors were responsible for fulfilling their plans but lacked adequate authority and autonomy to get things done. Each factory was essentially a cost center rather than a profit center, expected to achieve its goals within its resource allotments. There was no true measure of profit or of cost efficiency because prices were set arbitrarily by the state rather than guided by (nonexistent) free markets.

- Factories were commonly large and vertically integrated in order to gain economies of scale. Overall, the system saw poor coordination and integration of resources and effort between the various ministries, sectors, and enterprises.

- Managerial motivation came partly from salary, but the pay gap with ordinary workers wasn't large. Bonuses were possible if goals were achieved on time. There were also some valued managerial perquisites (e.g., preferential access to shopping, schooling, and medical services). People were expected to work diligently for the common good and glory of socialism.

- In the end, the system couldn't produce living standards comparable to those of its capitalist rivals, and there were persistent shortages, waiting lines, low-quality goods and services, and resistance to change.

- Despite many tries at reform over the years, the system ended in 1990–1991, followed by a problematic transition to a market-guided system. Political, economic, and cultural change has progressed more slowly than expected.

Terms and Concepts

democratic centralism
economy in transition
enterprise as a cost center
  (vs. profit center)
frontier capitalism
Karl Marx

nomenklatura
shturmovshchina (storming)
socialism
state socialism
tolkachi
underground economy

Study Questions

1. Describe broadly the economic, political, and sociocultural characteristics of the pre-1990 Soviet Union.

2. From the perspective of the management process (planning, organizing, controlling, directing, staffing) discuss distinctive patterns, strengths, limitations, and problems of the former Soviet industrial management system.

Exercise 4.1

Explain how each of the following situations raises issues analogous to the ones faced by the former Soviet enterprise system. What could be done in each instance to reduce or prevent negative consequences?

1. The delivery of health benefit services in a nationalized (government-run, e.g., Canada, United Kingdom) health care delivery system.

2. Scenario in which executives qualify for significant pay bonuses if they achieve specified goals (e.g., sales revenues, production volume, profits, or meeting a budget) within stipulated time deadlines.

3. Negotiations between a public school principal and a superinten-dent concerning budget and allocation of resources or between pub-lic university administrators and a system chancellor or other public officials (education offices, legislators, governors), and the formulas used for those decisions.

4. Individual or team salary caps placed on professional athletes.

5. Crowd flow management in a large amusement park (e.g., Disneyland) under conditions of single-price entry that allows patrons to select their activities in the park.

6. Add and explain a scenario of your own. Consider a cost center within a private corporation (any budget-driven administrative unit, department, division, or project team) or maybe a multilateral agency such as the European Union, World Bank, or United Nations or a military organization, government tax agency, post office, or government-owned airline. You could comment on the significance for staffing practices; pay structure; purchasing practices; planning, scheduling, and budgeting practices; plans; organization structure; and attitude toward change.

Notes

1. In socialist states, *enterprise* is a more appropriate term than *corporation*. Private corporations were illegal in the USSR. Each enterprise was in essence a cost center (analo-gous to a nonautonomous department or division in a nonsocialist firm) and expected to attain production goals within its resource allotments.

2. Russia was not measured culturally in Hofstede's initial work. Using Hofstede's parameters, Elenkov (1997) culturally compared samples of managers from Russia, Sweden, and the United States.

3. A cost center is an organizational unit (department, division) that must achieve results within the resources it is allocated; unlike a profit center, it has no autonomous profit and loss responsibility.

4. For coverage of the Soviet industrial performance, see Berliner (1976), Granick (1961), and Richman (1965).

References

Andrle, V. (1976). *Managerial power in the Soviet Union*. Westmead, Farnsborough, Hants, UK: Saxon House/Lexington Books.

Berliner, J. (1966). Managerial incentives and decision making: A comparison of the United States and the Soviet Union. In M. Bornstein & D. R. Fusfeld (Eds.), *The Soviet economy: A book of readings* (Rev. ed., pp. 109–140). Homewood, IL: Richard D. Irwin.

Berliner, J. (1976). *The innovation decision in Soviet industry.* Cambridge: MIT Press.

Berliner, J. (1988). *Soviet industry: From Stalin to Gorbachev.* Ithaca, NY: Cornell University Press.

Bornstein, M., & Fusfeld, D. (Eds.). (1974). *The Soviet economy* (4th ed.). Homewood IL: Richard D. Irwin.

Broadman, H. (2001). Competition and business entry in Russia. *Finance & Development, 38*(2), 22–25.

Conyngham, W. (1982). *The modernization of Soviet industrial management.* London: Cambridge University Press.

Desai, R., & Goldberg. I. (2000). Stakeholders, governance, and the Russian enterprise dilemma. *Finance & Development, 37*(2), 14–18.

Drucker, P. (1974). *Management.* New York: Harper & Row.

The Economist. (1989, November 25). [Review of book by N. Shmelev and V. Popov, *The turning point: Revitalizing the Soviet economy*], p. 101.

Elenkov, D. (1997). Differences and similarities in managerial values between U.S. and Russian managers. *International Studies of Management and Organization, 27*(1), 85–106.

Freris, A. (1984). *The Soviet industrial enterprise.* New York: St. Martin's Press.

FT Russia. (2006, April 21). *Financial Times* Special Report.

FT series Russia resurgent. (2006, June 19, June 27, July 5). *Financial Times.*

Grancelli, B. (1988). *Soviet management and labor relations.* Boston: Allen & Unwin.

Granick, D. (1961). *The red executive: A study of the organization man in Russian industry.* Garden City, NY: Anchor Books.

Hayek, F. (1988). The fatal conceit: The errors of socialism. In W. W. Bartley III (Ed.), *The collected works of F. A. Hayek* (Vol. 1). Chicago: University of Chicago Press.

Keller, B. (1989, March 19). The world; waiting for a new Soviet economy. *The New York Times,* p. 1.

Key excerpts from speech by president (Mikhail Gorbachev). (1988, October 2). *New York Times,* p. 14.

Key parts of Soviet plan for change. (1988, July 5). *New York Times,* p. 13.

Kontorovich, V., & Shlapentokh, V. (1985, January 11). Soviet industry grows its own potatoes. *Wall Street Journal,* p. 1

Linz, S. (1988, Spring). Management's response to tautness in Soviet planning: Evidence from the Soviet interview project. *Comparative Economic Studies, 30*(1), 65–103.

Marx, K. (1906). *Capital: A critique of political economy, Vol. I. The process of capitalist production.* Chicago: Charles H. Kerr. (Original work published 1867)

Marx, K. (1964). *The communist manifesto.* New York: Washington Square Press. (Original work published 1848)

May, R., McCarthy, D., & Puffer, S. (2005). Transferring management knowledge to Russia: A culturally based approach. *Academy of Management Executive, 19*(2), 24–35.

Oxford English Dictionary. (2007). Retrieved September 1, 2008, from http://www.writing.upenn.edu/~afilreis/50s/socialism-def.html

Polyakov, V., & Rakhmilovich, V. (1977, May–June). The state undertaking in the USSR: Its legal status and management. *International Labour Review, 115*(3), 367–377.

Puffer, S. (1981). Inside a Soviet management institute. *California Management Review, 24*(1), 90–96.

Puffer, S., Shekshnia, S., & McCarthy, D. (Eds.). (2005). *Corporate governance in Russia.* Cheltenham, UK: Edward Elgar.

Richman, B. (1965). *Soviet management with significant American comparisons.* Upper Saddle River, NJ: Prentice Hall.

Shipler, D. (1988, April 24). Now, dear Moscow editor, about the socialist plague. *New York Times,* p. 1.

Smith, H. (1976). *The Russians.* New York: Ballantine.

Special report Russia. (2006, July 15). *The Economist,* pp. 23–25.

Taubman, P. (1988, June 30). Soviet party conference delegates turn anger on press and economy. *New York Times,* p. 1.

Toward a Soviet market economy. (1987, August 26). *Wall Street Journal,* p. 1.

Wilpert, G. (2006). *The meaning of 21st century socialism for Venezuela.* Retrieved September 1, 2008, from http://www.venezuelanalysis.com/analysis/1834

Management 5
by Democracy

The Employee-Controlled Organization

Democracy and democratic control permeate public political life but are seldom seen in the workplace. However, some sources predict more of it in the future:

A study carried out by the Economist Intelligence Unit for a Korn/Ferry International report . . . surveyed 160 senior executives in a broad sweep of businesses across the world and interviewed a further 75 top executives. . . . They [described] future leaders as entrepreneurial, visionary and prepared to share information and power. . . . Does this mean that companies will more closely mirror the governments of settled democracies? It seems a logical development. (Donkin, 1998, p. 24)

Contrarians say otherwise:

The extreme contrast between . . . widely accepted organizational norms and those that naturally arise when democratic principles are introduced generates significant resistance within the organization and greatly limits the effectiveness of workers' participation. (Witte, 1980, p. 7)

Whatever your perspective, the theme of employee control stirs perennial interest, debate, and practice worldwide, hence its inclusion in this book. One noteworthy trait is compatibility with all variants of socialism, capitalism, and mixed economic systems. In the United States, for example cooperatives are widespread and take different forms (credit co-ops, purchasing co-ops, marketing co-ops, housing and electric co-ops, and even some manufacturing co-ops).[1] The United States also has some mutually owned financial institutions, including some savings and loan associations, insurance companies, and stock exchanges. Professional partnerships (e.g., in consulting, architecture, medicine, law, accounting) are often managed democratically (or can be) to a degree.

Cooperative or communal agricultural enterprise was pervasive in the former Soviet Union and Eastern Europe and continues in the post-Soviet era. Western Europe has many cooperatives. In the Middle East, both Jewish and Arab cultural traditions support communal and cooperative ventures, mostly in rural areas. In South America, Venezuelan president Hugo Chavez has actively supported cooperatives (there called "social production enterprises") in pursuing 21st-century socialism.

The subject of management by democracy also surfaces regularly in academic circles. For example, the Academy of Management (professional association for management educators) chose the theme for its 2003 annual meeting. Many courses and textbooks bring up the subject. Also, at many universities, most academic departments are run democratically by the professors, who decide matters of curriculum, academic standards, hiring, professional development, and the like.

Outside the workplace are many voluntary organizations that rely on democratic member-based governance, such as homeowners' associations, philanthropies, industry trade associations, public interest groups (e.g., environmental groups), labor unions, enterprise boards, consumer advocates, political campaigns, amateur sports leagues, and affinity groups of all kinds (e.g., gardeners, pet owners, musicians).

In the workplace, management by democracy has been effective at times, but often not, for reasons mentioned later.

Chapter Objectives

- To present the subject of employee control
- To note some examples from diverse contextual settings
- To discuss its strengths and limitations
- To suggest circumstances in which it is most likely to succeed

The Concept

Documented rationales for democracy in civil and political life go back to Plato (c. 400 BC), preceding broader attention among European intellectuals of the 17th and 18th century, such as Rousseau (views on equality, freedom, political legitimacy), Voltaire (attention to civil freedom, as in speech and religion), and Locke (government by consent of the governed). These and others contributed to ever more economic, social, and political freedoms that eroded long-running dominion by monarchs, feudal lords, and the church.

In business, the onset of the Industrial Revolution (late 18th century) famously saw Robert Owen transfer his cotton mill to its workers at New Lanark, Scotland (c. 1800). Owen later organized a communal venture at New Harmony, Indiana, in 1824. His ventures and those of other utopian socialists of his era, such as Frenchmen Fourier (1772–1837) and St. Simon (1760–1825), were unsuccessful but inspired later efforts in Europe and beyond. One milestone was a successful consumer cooperative at Rochdale, England, in 1844, where founders (the Rochdale Society of Equitable Pioneers) articulated several cooperative principles:

- Voluntary and open membership
- Democratic control by the members
- Member economic participation
- Autonomy and independence
- Education and training in cooperative practices and ideals
- Cooperation between cooperatives
- Concern for community

The idea of workplace democracy also draws from socioreligious values. For example, Christian and Judaic doctrine invoke themes of social justice, brotherhood, fairness, and equality. Judaic social and communal traditions inspired the Israeli kibbutzim. In Catholicism, a 1991 Vatican Encyclical encouraged more employee participation in the workplace:

> The [Catholic] church offers . . . social teaching as an indispensable and ideal orientation, a teaching which . . . recognizes the positive value of the market and of enterprise, but which at the same time points out that these need to be oriented toward the common good. This teaching also recognizes the legitimacy of workers' efforts to obtain full respect for their dignity and to gain broader areas of participation in the life of industrial enterprises so that . . . they can in a certain sense "work for themselves" . . . through the exercise of their intelligence and freedom.

In the late 19th century, English Fabian Socialists saw in cooperativism a path for capitalism without capitalists, some even favoring worker control of the state. Most mainstream European political parties today (e.g., Socialist, Social Democrat, Christian-Socialist) support employee involvement in the workplace. A 2002 European Union directive obligates all large employers to inform and consult with employees in some way on a regular basis.

DEGREES OF WORKPLACE DEMOCRACY

The level of workplace democracy to be discussed in this chapter is more extensive than the Western European works councils and worker directors described in Chapter 3. Table 5.1 distinguishes between degrees of participation in management ranging from complete employee control to none at all. This chapter focuses on complete employee or member control.

Table 5.1   Workplace Democracy, by Order of Degree

Complete employee (or member) control	*Highest Member Involvement* Managers are directly or indirectly elected by the members and accountable to the collective or to an elected representative council that oversees organization policy and performance (e.g., in some cooperative, communal, and partnership enterprises).
Co-control, joint management	*High Involvement* Employees (or their representatives) and managers share decision-making authority on fundamental questions; may include members' right to veto some decisions (e.g., worker directors on enterprise boards).
Co-influence	*Moderate Involvement* Employees offer suggestions, but management has final decision authority; managers seek out, welcome, and follow up employee or member recommendations and explain their decisions and actions (threshold of democratic participation) (e.g., workers' councils, labor–management committees, quality control circles).
Token consultation	*Low Involvement* Employees offer suggestions, but they get low attention and priority; management may or may not explain decisions and actions (e.g., the suggestion box approach).
No influence or control	*No involvement* All decisions are made from the top, without explanation or employee input.

SOURCE: Adapted from Bernstein (1982, p. 58).

Democracy can be direct (i.e., one vote per person) or indirect (through elected representatives). In the workplace it can be combined with economic democracy, that is, employee ownership rights and profit sharing.

In its purest form (communitarian organizations), the management process can differ notably from conventional hierarchical organizations (Table 5.2). In the former, planning includes both economic and noneconomic objectives. There is equal voice and vote for each member. There is collective review of group purpose and performance, and there is equitable, envy-free sharing of decisions, tasks, risks, and rewards. Communitarianism abhors hierarchy and aims for self-direction and control. The position of manager is rotated among the members; individual monetary and material rewards (e.g., pay and perquisites) emphasize equality.

Table 5.2   Management Process in Traditional and Democratic Organizations

Conventional Hierarchical Enterprise		Communitarian, Democratic, Horizontal Enterprise
Emphasis on economic objectives and pursuit of economic efficiency. Planning is the responsibility of top management.	*Planning*	Emphasis on economic and noneconomic objectives. Attention to social processes and democratic values. Goal of sustainable economic efficiency. Plans and actions are reviewed and approved by the overall membership (or by their elected representatives).
Intentional formal structure to coordinate roles, tasks, resources, and effort. Division of labor by task specialization. Hierarchical line of organizational authority (pyramid form).	*Organizing*	A nonhierarchical structure is the ideal, analogous to a spoked wheel rather than a pyramid, that is, a flat "horizontal organization" with just one level. Authority is diffused and resides in the collective as a whole. Can include delegation of authority (e.g., to an elected manager) by the collective membership.

(Continued)

Table 5.2 (Continued)

Conventional Hierarchical Enterprise		Communitarian, Democratic, Horizontal Enterprise
Top-down review and control of performance. Overall control exercised by providers of risk capital (stockholders, typically one share, one vote). Overall performance reviewed by a board of directors accountable mostly to owners.	*Control*	Self-control and social control by the members (one vote per member), who are individually and collectively accountable to themselves, their work units, and the general membership.
Centralized vision or direction. Leadership from the top. Emphasis on vertical communication channels. Monetary and material rewards are the main motivators.	*Directing*	Self-direction. Leadership can emerge from anyone. Extensive horizontal communication. Motivation mainly from moral, social, and political values and less from ego, money, and material rewards.
The chief executive is appointed or approved by a board of directors. Senior managerial pay (salary, bonuses, perquisites) is usually much higher than for most employees.	*Staffing*	Managerial selection or election by the general membership (one person, one vote). Rotation of members in managerial positions. Managerial pay not much different from that of other employees.

Management by democracy also differs in terms of core norms and values, including some suggested by Rothschild and Whitt (1986). (See Table 5.3.)

ORGANIZATION THEORY AND EMPLOYEE CONTROL

Some management theorists see merit in and a promising future for bottom-up control. For instance, it is argued that traditional hierarchies are ill suited to an emerging postindustrial era in which well-educated people want more voice in the workplace. These are self-driven Theory Y (to use McGregor's [1960] terminology) and self-actualized (Maslow, 1943) people.

Table 5.3   Contrast Between Norms and Ideals in Conventional Bureaucratic
Organizations Versus Communitarian (Collective/Cooperative/Communal)
Organizations

Dimensions	Conventional-Bureaucratic	Collective-Democratic
Authority	Authority resides in individuals by virtue of incumbency in office and/or expertise; hierarchical organization of offices. Compliance is to universal fixed rules as these are implemented by office incumbents.	Authority resides in the collectivity as a whole; delegated, if at all, only temporarily and subject to recall. Compliance is to the consensus of the collective, which is always fluid and open to negotiation.
Rules	Formalization of fixed and universalistic rules; calculability and appeal of decisions on the basis of correspondence to the formal, written law.	Minimal stipulated rules; primacy of ad hoc individuated decisions; some calculability possible on the basis of knowing the substantive ethics involved in the situation.
Social control	Organizational behavior is subject to social control, primarily through direct supervision or standardized rules and sanctions, tertiarily through the selection of homogeneous personnel, especially at top levels.	Social controls are primarily based on personalistic or moralistic appeals and the selection of homogeneous personnel.
Social relations	Ideal of impersonality; relations are to be role based, segmental, instrumental.	Ideal of community; relations are to be wholistic, personal, of value in themselves.
Recruitment and advancement	Employment based on specialized training and formal certification. Employment constitutes a career; advancement based on seniority or achievement.	Employment based on friends, sociopolitical values, personality attributes, and informally assessed knowledge and skills. Concept of career advancement not meaningful; no hierarchy of positions.
Incentive structure	Remunerative incentives are primary.	Normative and solidarity incentives are primary; material incentives are secondary.

(Continued)

Table 5.3 (Continued)

Dimensions	Conventional-Bureaucratic	Collective-Democratic
Social stratification	Isomorphic distribution of prestige, privilege, and power (i.e., differential rewards by office); hierarchy justifies inequality.	Egalitarian reward differentials, if any, are strictly limited by the collectivity.
Differentiation	Maximal division of labor: dichotomy between intellectual work and manual work and between administrative tasks and performance tasks. Maximal specialization of jobs and functions; segmental roles. Technical expertise is exclusively held: ideal of the specialist expert.	Minimal division of labor: administration is combined with performance tasks; division between intellectual and manual work is reduced. Generalization of jobs and functions; wholistic roles. Demystification of expertise: ideal of the amateur factotum.

SOURCE: From J. Rothschild and J. A. Whitt, *The Cooperative Workplace,* 1986, Cambridge University Press, pp. 62–63. Reprinted by permission of Cambridge University Press.

NOTE: The authors define collectives and cooperatives as "any enterprise in which control rests ultimately and overwhelmingly with the member–employee–owners, regardless of the specific legal or national political framework through which it is achieved."

Organizational theorist Rensis Likert (1961, 1967) conceptualized a range of participation possibilities in his System 4 leadership spectrum (Table 5.4), including System 1 (exploitative–authoritarian, no participation), System 2 (benevolent–authoritarian), System 3 (consultative), and System 4 (decentralized, bottom-up, participative). According to Likert, System 4 is the preferred choice.

There are also some pragmatic reasons (Walker, 1974) for more bottom-up involvement and control. For example, it can bring more good ideas. Decisions will be more readily accepted and implemented. People are more motivated to work diligently and intelligently for the common good. It can reduce disputes, thus improving efficiency. De Jong and van Witteloostuijn (2004, p. 54) noted, "Democratization, apart from being a good thing in itself and for the organization involved, also plays an educational role and may thus produce important spillover effects. . . . [It] is educative because participation develops and fosters specific qualities— e.g., skills to argue, to understand, to empathize, and to develop compromises." Moreover, it can enhance managerial legitimacy, promote loyalty, reduce turnover, and encourage change (See Chapters 2 and 3 in Heller, Pusic, Strauss, & Wilpert, 1988).

Table 5.4   Likert's Management Systems

System 1: Exploitative–Authoritarian	System 2: Benevolent–Authoritarian	System 3: Consultative	System 4: Democratic
Leaders have no confidence or trust in subordinates. Motivation by fear, threats, punishment, and occasional rewards. Most decisions made at the top. Little communication or interaction with followers. Highly centralized control.	Leaders have very limited confidence and trust in subordinates. Little communication and interaction with followers. Motivation by rewards and actual or potential punishment. Predominantly centralized control (partial delegation).	Leaders have confidence and trust in subordinates. Motivation by rewards (occasional punishment) and partial involvement in decisions. Broad policy decisions still made at the top. Much two-way communication and interaction. Some sharing of review and control responsibility.	Complete confidence and trust in subordinates. Motivation through participation in goal setting and implementation and by consensus-driven material rewards. Full individual and group involvement in decisions. Open communication and interaction (up, down, lateral). Universal responsibility for review and control.

SOURCE: Adapted from Likert (1967).

Examples of Employee or Member Control

Bottom-up control can occur in various enterprises (e.g., collectives, cooperatives, communes, professional partnerships, research laboratories, and think tanks). It is seen in start-up ventures, family businesses, and employee buyouts. It can emerge from restructuring out of bankruptcy, as in the following example from Argentina:

> *Buenos Aires, Argentina.* . . . When sacked workers at Ghelko, a bankrupt maker of ingredients for ice cream, discovered earlier this year that the firm's owners were selling its assets, they . . . started camping outside their former workplace to protest. Two months later their campaign bore fruit, when the court handling the bankruptcy hearings leased the factory to them for a peppercorn rent. Now, minus the managers who accounted for over a third of Ghelko's 90 employees, the factory is working again.

Ghelko is just one of 130 Argentine companies that over the past four years have risen from the ashes of bankruptcy under employee management, . . . not to be sniffed at where one [person] in five is unemployed. ("Under Workers' Control," 2002, p. 40)

Beyond work, examples include nonprofit organizations, condominium associations, school boards, student living groups, clubs, and student team projects.

The examples of management by democracy to be highlighted in this section include the following:

- A national system of "self-management socialism" that evolved over nearly four decades in the former Yugoslavia (Until its breakup after 1990, Yugoslavia encompassed the states of Slovenia, Croatia, Serbia, Montenegro, Bosnia-Herzegovina, Vojvodina, Macedonia, and Kosovo)

- Communes and other intentional communities

- Cooperatives

- Professional partnerships

THE SELF-MANAGED ECONOMY, YUGOSLAVIA, 1950–1990

After World War II, Yugoslavia (then a federation of several republics) fell within the Soviet socialist sphere of influence. In 1951, though, it moved away from centralized economic planning to try an employee-managed socialist economy (participatory socialism, or market socialism), seen as a third way, an alternative to both laissez-faire capitalism and centralized state socialism (see Vanik, 1970, 1971; Ward, 1953). The Yugoslav approach had the following features (Vanik, 1971):

- Ownership of the means of production by all of society, that is, by the state (but allowed for small private enterprises)

- Enterprise autonomy

- Employee control

- Labor mobility

Yugoslav enterprises were empowered to make their own production, marketing, and hiring decisions. However, state bureaucrats set limits on prices and wages (including a national minimum wage and regulated pay differences between the highest- and lowest-paid employees). Initially, the central government guided overall capital investment flows, had a monopoly on international trade, and captured some enterprise earnings for broader social purposes such as public housing and education.

In the workplace, employee control was at first indirect, through elected workers' councils (1-year term limits) with elections supervised by Communist Party–controlled labor unions. The councils were as small as 3 people in small firms and as large as 20 or more people in big firms. Each council elected a general manager (administrative director) to a 4-year term and reviewed senior administrative appointments (which were also reviewed by trade union, municipal, and Communist Party officials).

In the 1960s, decision authority for enterprise planning and policy shifted from the workers' councils to a general assembly of all the workers in each enterprise, with important decisions decided by referendum and consensus. In the 1970s, decision autonomy was decentralized even further through so-called units of associated labor. The core unit was the basic organization of associated labor (BOAL), which could be any work group or department whose performance could be measured independently from other units (Prasnikar & Prasnikar, 1986). Each BOAL was a profit center (had autonomous revenue and expense responsibility) but an imperfect one because of interdependencies between the BOALs and between BOALs and higher units of associated labor, such as worker organizations of associated labor (WOALs) and composite organizations of associated labor (COALs). BOALs included 80 or so people but occasionally as many as 400. The WOAL (an integrated cluster of autonomous BOALs) was the unit most comparable to an autonomous company in a free market economy. WOALs could associate freely with other WOALs and with COALs, the latter analogous to a multiplant or multidivision enterprise in a free enterprise economy.

Each BOAL had nominal authority to make investment and hiring decisions and set production targets, prices, conditions of work, wages, and salaries and pursue alliances with other units of labor.

At each level (BOAL, WOAL, COAL), general assemblies of members were empowered to elect a council, which in turn elected the management board and general manager. Councils of BOALs elected the councils of associated WOALs, which in turn elected those of yet higher composite organizations (regional and national producer associations). At each level, enterprise plans were developed by technical specialists and administrators and were reviewed by pertinent councils or assemblies. Operating plans were discussed, negotiated, and integrated between affiliated WOALs through self-management agreements to handle interunit hiring and transfer pricing. Any unit of associated labor (BOAL, WOAL, COAL) could freely pursue international trade, arrange external financing, and establish links (e.g., joint ventures and licensing agreements) with foreign firms. Their autonomy was not total, however, because key decisions (e.g., production and investment decisions and managerial appointments) were also reviewed by municipal and communist party officials.

The Yugoslav system was a model for similar experiments elsewhere, such as an industrial community system of producer co-ops tried in Peru in the 1970s (Adizes, 1971b; Stephens, 1980).

COMMUNES AND OTHER INTENTIONAL COMMUNITIES

Whereas Yugoslavia's self-management socialism was cooperativism writ large, the purest form of democracy is direct, as in small communal enterprises. Ideally, communes strive for strict egalitarian values with the following features:

- Social ownership, that is, property and resources owned in common by the members (no individual property rights)

- Shared division of labor and material rewards

- Direct election (one person, one vote) of supervisors and managers

- Job rotation, including supervisory and managerial positions

- Important decisions made by consensus of all the members

- Mostly nonmonetary compensation (e.g., food, lodging, clothing) rather than cash

One classic example is the Jewish *kibbutz* (pl., *kibbutzim*) rural commune pioneered in Palestine around 1909, which gained prominence after the creation of Israel in 1948. In 2006, about 268 or so kibbutzim employed about 2% of the Israeli workforce (Central Bureau of Statistics, 2006). Another form is the Mexican *ejido,* a small collective farm created from land transfers to peasants after the 1917 revolution. In 2000, about 3 million people were working 30,000 or so *ejidos* reported to involve about one half of all land under cultivation ("Mexico, Farmed Out," 2000). Another was the self-sustaining Walden II communities in the United States, Canada, and Mexico, inspired by behavioral psychologist B. F. Skinner's (1948) book, *Walden Two,* emphasizing community sharing, cooperation, and equality.

Former Soviet agriculture relied on communal farms known as *kolkhoz* (*kollektivnoye khozyaystvo*). In 1967, about 36,800 *kolkhoz* supported some 18 million members (about 14% of the civilian labor force; about 400 households per collective) (Keefe et al., 1971). These used internal funding, loan capital, and subsidies from the state. Workers were paid in both cash and kind. Many *kolkhoz* continue today in post-Soviet Russia, where perhaps half of all farmland is still in collectives (including communes and cooperatives).

Another example is intentional communities, which include many collective arrangements such as cohousing, residential land trusts, student cooperatives, and ecovillages. In 2008, the Fellowship for Intentional Community (FIC) Web site (http://directory.ic.org/iclist/geo.php) listed 1,391 U.S. member groups and dozens more abroad.

In distinguishing between communes and intentional communities, the FIC describes the latter as more diverse:

Many people use these terms interchangeably, however, it is probably more useful to use the term "commune" to describe a particular kind of intentional community whose members live "communally" in an economic sense—operating with a common treasury and sharing ownership of their property. Most intentional communities are not communes, though some of the communities most active in the communities movement are. . . . Some communities are wholly secular; others are committed to a common spiritual practice; many are spiritually eclectic. Some are focused on egalitarian values and voluntary simplicity, or mutual interpersonal growth work, or rural homesteading and self-reliance.

Internal governance practices of intentional communities are commonly, though not necessarily, democratic:

Of the hundreds of communities [we] have information about, 64% are democratic, 9% have a hierarchical or authoritarian structure, 11% are a combination of democratic and hierarchical, and 16% don't specify. Many communities which formerly followed one leader or a small group of leaders have changed in recent years to a more democratic form of governance.

COOPERATIVES

A cooperative (or co-op) is a voluntary mutual association pursuing a shared economic goal of its members. By contrast with communes, co-ops can include individual ownership rights and differing financial or material rewards. Work needn't be shared equally, and there may be employees who are not members. A co-op can be profit or non–profit oriented, and its funding can come from members, or from earnings or loans.

The International Labor Organization (2008) estimates that cooperatives employ more than 100 million people around the world. Many national and international support organizations promote and assist cooperativism. One is the Swiss-based International Cooperative Alliance (ICA), a private group (since 1895) with regional offices worldwide.[2] It serves more than 200 cooperative organizations from 92 countries representing more than 750 million individual members. Another is the International Committee for the Promotion and Advancement of Cooperatives, formed in 1971; its members include the ICA, the World Council of Credit Unions, the United Nations Food and Agricultural Organization, and the cooperative branch of the International Labor Organization.

One enterprise of this type is a manufacturing co-op (workers' co-op or producer co-op, that is, a factory or farm owned and controlled by its employees). There are a few manufacturing cooperatives in the United States. One source (Benello, 1984) reported that about 1,000 were being formed annually in the late 1970s and called this "the largest and most vital burgeoning of cooperatives in [U.S.] history," but this is probably an overstatement. There is a documented history of worker-owned plywood and forest worker co-ops in the Puget Sound region of the Pacific Northwest (for case study examples of U.S. co-ops, see Rothschild & Whitt, 1986; for plywood co-ops, see Berman, 1967; Greenberg, 1986). Some were founded in the 1930s and 1940s by Scandinavian immigrants. By the 1980s, most had been sold by their owners (i.e., their workers) to large private forest product companies.

More common are consumer co-ops, credit co-ops, procurement (purchasing) co-ops, and housing co-ops. Consumer cooperatives are found throughout the United States but on a much smaller scale than in Europe (and numbers are shrinking). In 2008, there were about 10,000 U.S. credit unions, with more than 79 million members (National Credit Union Administration, http://www.ncua.gov/). Because of tax advantages, these can pay slightly higher interest rates on member deposits than can commercial banks, and they also charge members lower interest rates on loans than do banks.

Cooperatively owned apartment buildings can make housing more affordable for member–owners (and preserve opportunities for financial gain if property values rise). Cooperative purchasing groups can obtain quantity discount pricing by buying in bulk (e.g., supplies, materials, electricity, transport services) for their members and also return patronage refunds (or voting rights) based on proportional volume of purchase or use. Such cooperatives (e.g., food and hardware distributors) help small independent store owners compete with big stores or store chains.

Thousands of U.S. agricultural cooperatives assist member growers in buying farm supplies and marketing crops.[3] In 2008, the National Rural Electric Cooperative Association (http://www.nreca.org/AboutUs/Overview.htm) had more than 900 member cooperatives serving 40 million people in 47 U.S. states. Most of its 865 electric distribution systems were consumer cooperatives; some were public power districts.

Many former Soviet collective farms continue today as agricultural cooperatives. When the Soviet state socialist system collapsed in 1991, thousands of small state-owned businesses were privatized as cooperatives through transfer or sale to the employees.[4]

The British famously pioneered food distribution co-ops in the 19th century (at Rochdale in 1843). Today a network of private British retail societies (consumer co-ops) has several million members. These in turn are part of the Co-Operative Group (formerly the Cooperative Wholesale Society) that includes bank, insurance, and other businesses. Switzerland's two largest retailers, named Migros and Coop, are cooperatives. The Migros umbrella group (Migros-Genossenschafts-Bund) is involved in retailing, banking, insurance, travel, mortuary, and other services.

Many Italian cooperatives have ties to national political parties, including about 28,000 associated with the Christian Democrat party. The Italian Communist and Socialist parties have ties to several thousand producer, construction, and agricultural cooperatives that make up the *Lega*

(*Lega Nazionale della Cooperative e Mutue*). France also has extensive cooperativism.

In the former Eastern Europe (now Central Europe), cooperativism predates the state socialist era (e.g., in the Czech and Slovak republics, Poland, and Hungary). In the 1990s, Cuba converted some of its state farms into cooperatives (however, the state has continued as the landowner).

The World Bank is a kind of global cooperative owned by its member countries. The size of each country's shareholding is determined by the size of the country's economy relative to the world economy. The bank offers technical support and lends money at low interest rates to less developed countries for infrastructure projects (e.g., schools, electrification, road building, sanitation) (World Bank, http://web.worldbank.org/WBSITE/EXTERNAL/EXTABOUTUS/0,,pagePK:50004410~piPK:36602~theSitePK:29708,00.html).

THE MONDRAGON COOPERATIVE SYSTEM, SPAIN

One of the most publicized producer co-op systems functions in the Basque region of northern Spain. It began with a single metalworking factory in the city of Mondragon in 1956, followed by others to make machinery, household appliances, and other consumer goods, including for export. By the end of 2006, the group had 264 companies (most of them co-ops, with overall sales equivalent to Spain's seventh largest industrial group and with 81,800 employees). Some Mondragon co-op firms now have foreign operations, including joint ventures and licensees in France, Egypt, Russia, China, and the Americas (Mondragon Cooperative Corporation, http://www.mondragon.mcc.es/ing/quienessomos/presidente.html).

By design, most Mondragon producer co-ops limit their membership to 500 employees. Each new employee typically buys a capital holding, either from personal resources or with a loan from the co-op.[5] Co-op earnings are distributed annually in the amount of 20% to an internal investment fund, 70% to a capital fund, and 10% for the broader co-op community to support schools and other social services. The cash value of each member's holding in the capital fund increases over time if the enterprise is profitable (it shrinks if it doesn't) and must be taken out when the member leaves (up to 80% withdrawal) or retires (100% withdrawal).

The Mondragon system includes some secondary support co-ops, including a bank, a technology development center, education and training institutions, and housing, health, and cultural service providers ("Cooperate and Prosper," 1989). The system supports retirement pension plans, day care centers, health care services, and unemployment compensation. The entrepreneurial department of the cooperative bank does feasibility studies and offers management advisory services for new co-ops (BBC, 1980).

Mondragon wage and salary levels are influenced partly by members' skill level and experience, but differentials are low. In the beginning (the 1950s), the ratio between the highest- and lowest-paid members was set at 3:1 but more recently has risen to 4.5:1 and in some cases 6:1.

In principle, major decisions are made democratically, with each member having equal voice and vote in a Workers' Assembly. The assembly meets at least once yearly to review policy decisions and elect representatives to a management board (4-year terms, one half elected every 2 years) that in turn chooses the general manager.

PROFESSIONAL PARTNERSHIPS

Democratic management can also be found in professional service partnerships (e.g., law, architecture, consulting, accounting, and medicine). Here, the partner–owners elect officers from among their ranks and bring collective judgment to key decisions. Conceptually, their organization structures are flat and flexible.

However, not all the employees are owners, nor do they have equal voice or vote in management. Some partners carry more influence than others by virtue of their productivity or seniority (e.g., general partner, associate partner, limited partner). A junior professional who performs well may eventually become general partner with full voice and vote in management and qualify for extraproportional pay. The support staff (nonprofessionals) usually has no ownership or voting rights.

Compared with communes and cooperatives, professional partnerships are driven more by monetary rewards than by social and democratic ideals. That would apply, for example, to McKinsey & Company, the renowned management consultancy, and reflected in the following interview (by Singh, 2001) with its then managing director, Rajat Gupta:

J. V. Singh: In some ways McKinsey must be like an academic organization, with its tenured faculty, and less like a Fortune 500 firm. . . .

Rajat Gupta: You're absolutely right. It is very much, in many dimensions like an academic organization. We have senior partners who are very much like tenured faculty; they are leaders in their own right. . . . So when you have a firm, which consists essentially of leaders, then you must give them an enormous amount of room to exercise their leadership capabilities. It's a firm which is a very flat, horizontal structure, with a great deal of independence. . . . We have about 80 to 100 performance cells—a geographic office or industry practice or functional practice. They are very much autonomous and they are not organized in any hierarchy beyond that.

J. V. Singh: The very fact that you're in your third term, which, I understand, is the most terms permitted at McKinsey, is a testament to your success as a leader of the firm. How would you characterize your leadership style?

Rajat Gupta: One of the important principles that I always have is rotation of leadership. Because if you're a firm of leaders, and we have hundreds of leaders, they're all capable of doing the task. In order to keep them motivated, in order to bring in fresh energy and perspective, you need to change people in positions. . . . So we have a typical spirit of rotation every three to five years. . . . You're not anybody's boss. . . . I've been elected at the pleasure of my fellow partners (pp. 36–37).

Performance

The diversity of democratically run enterprises raises the questions of how well they perform compared with conventionally managed (hierarchical) ones and why they aren't more common. Experience worldwide shows them to be occasionally successful, especially procurement (purchasing) co-ops, marketing co-ops, credit co-ops, and cooperative housing. In former socialist countries such as Poland, Hungary, and Czechoslovakia, cooperatives were demonstrably more productive (and more flexible users of capital) than were state enterprises (Jones, 1985). Yugoslav self-management socialism was more efficient than was Soviet state socialism in regard to quality and variety of consumer goods.

The most egalitarian enterprise of all, the commune, has seldom been successful when judged solely on economic grounds. For example, most Israeli kibbutzim struggled when the Israeli economy became more open, having difficulty competing with imports and local private business. Their survival has relied heavily on financial and other support from the Histadrut (General Confederation of Labor), a labor-controlled organization with stakes in many Israeli companies, which has long supported workers' cooperatives and communes.

When kibbutzim spread into manufacturing (mainly after 1960), their difficulties grew. Most of the remaining ones survive only with state subsidies, have often strayed from communal principles, and are heavily in debt. In 1995, total kibbutz sector debt obligations to banks and other institutions were more than $10 billion, or about $56,000 per member (Israeli Ministry of Finance study cited in Melman, 1995, p. 45).

Kibbutz communal values and ideals were also eroded by changing political and cultural values, including increased individualism and personal freedom. So notes Eliezer Ben-Rafael (1997):

> All efforts had failed to create communities based on sharing and equality and able to flourish economically.... Members, re-questioning every arrangement, spared no aspect of kibbutz life. Some kibbutzim now charged members for meals in the collective dining room, or alternatively, closed down the dining room and transferred the meals to the private apartment. Others instituted financial rewards to gratify extra work or public functions, and in some cases, introduced differential rewarding as a general practice.... The number of hired workers was increasing.... Many kibbutzim abolished the General Assembly, the heart of kibbutz life for decades, and replaced it by a restricted elected Council. (p. 1)

Kibbutzim were also weakened by departure of grown children to pursue livelihoods beyond the communes (Leviatan, Oliver, & Quarter, 1998). There are reports of many kibbutz members owning their own homes and private investment portfolios. Many kibbutzim have started private commercial ventures. Also, the Israeli government has ceased gifting of land and water subsidies for kibbutzim (Leggett, 2005). In addition, member pay has become more tied to work contribution rather than to the principle of equality (Steinberg, 2004).

In Mexico, *ejido* communal farms were highly inefficient and not able to boost the productivity or incomes of member small farmers. Plots were too small. Public reforms begun in 1992 now allow *ejido* lands to be privately owned, or rented, and become collateral for bank loans. Plots can be combined to gain economies of scale.

Despite the economic and managerial shortcomings of democratic collectivism, proponents often point to their noneconomic achievements, such as social solidarity and equality, as is expressed in the following passages:

> The actual effect on productivity ... is not clear.... In any case ... any improvement in productivity can be viewed as an added bonus. (Spinrad, 1984, p. 211)

> Alternative gauges of success—for example, the level of democratic control in the organization, the social utility and quality of the goods or services provided, the fulfillment of human needs of the workers, and the contribution of the enterprise to progressive societal social change—may be far more important to the participants in democratically organized firms. (Lindenfeld & Rothschild-Whitt, 1982, p. 10)

Kamusic (1970) makes a similar point in reference to the former Yugoslavia:

> If we compare impartially our system of self-managing relationships both in enterprises and in the society at large to the model of capitalist enterprises and the system of the capitalist economy of the mixed type as to their

economic efficiency we should admit that the latter fulfills its economic function, at least in the economically most advanced countries and for a long period, better than the first. But in saying this we must take into account the psychological and moral–political advantages of self management. (p. 112)

However, it is apparent that noneconomic goals and member control can't be sustained if a group can't efficiently deliver a product or service valued by its members or by outsiders. Also, the evidence is mixed about whether many purported noneconomic benefits of cooperativism truly occur and whether members value them highly. It is generally assumed that an employee-controlled company is more egalitarian, more participative, and more supportive of its workers or members than are conventional firms. However, research findings raise doubts about whether employees are truly more satisfied or less alienated from their bosses or from their work and whether labor relations are really more harmonious.

One cross-national study (Tannenbaum, 1975) examined the social and psychological effects of workplace democracy in five countries, each reflecting varying degrees of member involvement in management. At one extreme was the Israeli kibbutz (the most democratic of the five), followed in declining degree of democracy by Yugoslav, U.S., Austrian, and Italian enterprises, the latter the least democratic and most hierarchical in structure and style. That study examined employee psychological adjustment and their attitudes toward the work group and the work itself. Although the U.S. sample reflected a wider hierarchy gap between employees and managers than did the kibbutz and Yugoslav groups, there was no apparent difference in psychological adjustment in the workplace (measured by respondents' perceptions of esteem, depression, and resentment). Surprisingly, the U.S. employees scored significantly higher than the other four groups on job satisfaction.

In any case, the elimination of authority is often an illusory and irrelevant goal, as Peter Drucker (1974) once observed:

Authority is an essential dimension of work. It has little or nothing to do with ownership of the means of production, democracy at the workplace, worker representation at the board of directors, or any other way of structuring the "system." (p. 192)

In another case (a 2-year field study of member participation in a Canadian employee buyout firm), the employees were pleased to participate in management but showed no measurable change in their attitude toward work. Once the novelty of their purchase (and their involvement) wore off, member participation in meetings gradually declined (Long, 1982).

LIMITATIONS OF WORKERS' COOPERATIVES

The historical evidence shows that many manufacturing cooperatives have had disappointing performance when measured solely on economic grounds and are less enduring than are user or member co-ops (e.g., credit, consumer, procurement, and housing co-ops). In the latter, member livelihood (e.g., job, income) is not a main concern; in a producer co-op, it is paramount. Producer co-ops generally do well when the economy around them is doing well. However, in difficult times, weaknesses in efficiency and competitiveness become apparent, especially in free enterprise economies.

One weakness is that labor is a fixed cost, so workforce downsizing, when needed, is nearly impossible because members won't support layoffs. The same applies to automation of production (i.e., it won't reduce labor costs if the workforce can't shrink). And if the enterprise does well, there is reluctance to add new members lest these become a burden when sales decline. Moreover, profits and wages become more diluted when membership grows. In the real world, when competitive pressures arise, cooperative principles are commonly ignored. So it was with the Puget Sound plywood cooperatives, which in good times took on extra workers from the surrounding community (at lower pay than that of member–owners). They had neither voting rights nor job security and were the first to be laid off when sales and earnings slumped.

Furthermore, members must choose between higher near-term pay and long-term capital investment (e.g., expansion, modernization). High pay can undercapitalize a firm in the long run and force more borrowing. Additional debt becomes burdensome during business downturns, when cash flow declines but loan repayment must continue.

In the former Yugoslavia, the state sought to resolve this dilemma by mandating a capital maintenance (investment) requirement (Bonin, 1985). However, this reduced enterprise flexibility by forcing additional investment even when it was untimely or unnecessary. The state was also reluctant to let troubled firms fail, offering emergency loans. In Israel, faltering kibbutzim have received tax relief and other financial support from the state, causing moral hazard, that is, the solution (government bailout from debt obligations) makes the problem (excessive borrowing) more likely to recur. Employees won't be much inclined to reduce their personal pay if they know the state will eventually jump in with rescue money.

Additional limitations to management in workers' cooperatives include the following:

• Decision making by assemblies, councils, and committees is very time-consuming, with excessive compromise and difficulty in changing directions quickly.

• There is a heavy burden on the participants (members or employees) to be sufficiently prepared for meetings, that is, to have enough of the right information and the time, ability, experience, and good judgment to make sense of it all.

• There is higher risk (than in conventional firms) that sensitive information will be leaked to competitors because more people have access to it.

- There can be difficulty in getting the most able candidates to serve as leaders because the egalitarian pay scale doesn't compensate for the extra pressures and responsibilities of the job. In the early years at Mondragon, Spain, managerial pay was constrained to three times that of the lowest-paid employee. After Spain's economic reforms (privatization and deregulation in the late 1980s and 1990s) and entry into the European Union, the competitive pressures grew. In the 1990s, the pay multiple for some Mondragon managers had risen to more than 6:1 (see http://www.mondragon.mcc.es/ing/contacto/faqs17.html).

- There will also be suboptimal use of human resources when certain tasks and responsibilities are shared or rotated among all employees; in other words, specialists won't always be doing what they do best.

- Managers often lack authority to achieve what they are held accountable for because they must get approval from the membership (or a representative council) for many decisions.

- There can be problems with member shirking and free riding when they are accountable to the group rather than to an individual manager or supervisor, especially when everyone is paid the same regardless of their contribution.

- There is a tendency to underestimate the complexity of the managerial role and to see management as a routine administrative task (Benello, 1984, p. 390).

- There is risk to the employees of having the fruits of their lifelong labor bound to the success of their employer, that is, having all their retirement eggs in one basket. Whereas suppliers of capital to a firm can spread their risk by diversifying across many firms, the suppliers of labor (employees) cannot easily diversify their income (an argument articulated by Meade, 1972).

In general, user or member service sector co-ops (e.g., consumer co-ops, credit co-ops) have had more staying power than have producer co-ops. Nonetheless, overreliance on cooperative principles and ideals can hinder efficiency and competitive strength, and the noneconomic goals often conflict with economic ones. For example, consumer co-ops sometimes serve hard-to-reach customers not served by other providers. And some purposefully refrain from selling high-margin upscale brand name products in favor of low-margin generic ones. Social goals have precedence over profits. For instance, the Migros consumer cooperative chain in Switzerland chooses not to distribute tobacco or alcohol products.

ARE DEMOCRATIC ORGANIZATIONS REALLY DEMOCRATIC?

In many cases, it is questionable how much democracy truly occurs in a nominally democratic organization. Employees or members often are little interested in managerial decision making and insufficiently prepared to participate. In the former Yugoslavia, Obradovic (1975) noted that there was a strong tendency to reelect the same people to the various councils, committees, and managerial posts and that "deliberations in these councils are largely dominated by high-level managers and technical experts . . . with the result that rank-and-file members participate less actively than theory might suggest" (p. 32) (see also Adizes, 1971a; Prasnikar & Prasnikar, 1986).

In the Israeli kibbutz, especially after 1980, bottom-up participation proved problematic. According to Ben-Rafael (1997),

> A close look at the kibbutz industries actually shows that, long before the mid-1980s crisis, directors and managers were already in charge of policy making and implementation in the factory. Most kibbutz factories never saw any genuine rank-and-file participation in executive processes. (p. 108)

> In practice . . . as partners in an enterprise, the kibbutzniks soon understood that their manpower was one of their most crucial economic resources and that their interest was to exploit it rationally. Hence they soon developed evaluative criteria which in effect differentiated between various kinds of work . . . [which] . . . became the axis of a whole stratification system which transformed the social structure of the community. (p. 115)

Walker (1974)[6] synthesized and analyzed the findings of several studies of employee participation in several countries, concluding that participation was seldom very extensive:

> It is unwise to assume a universal desire among workers to participate personally in all decisions, and that older, more educated and more skilled workers tend to participate more, as do men rather than women. Workers at lower levels of the enterprise tend to have only a "calculative" involvement, based on the "cash nexus." For many workers, work is not a central life interest. (p. 16)

> Experience in Socialist and non-Socialist countries alike reveals considerable difficulty in getting all workers to participate, no matter what the structures and processes of participation available to them. (p. 23)

Similarly, in the former Yugoslavia, Ramondt (1979) noted, "The management and staff play a predominant role in decision-making and have more influence than one would expect. The workers have far less say in decision-making and that too is unexpected" (p. 83), a view shared by Ben-Rafael (1997) in regard to Israel:

> Egalitarianism is, of all collective values, the least appreciated, and in fact, also the one perceived as the least implemented. (p. 176)

> We have learned that decentralized democratic enterprises . . . [are] not an exception to the universality of power processes. . . . The kibbutz teaches us that even here technocrats are able to achieve privileges and a liberty of action, which the rank-and-file are hardly able to control. (p. 227)

For workplace democracy to succeed, participants need the appropriate knowledge and proper mind-set, judgment, and motivation to be fully involved. In practice, members are likely to cede decision-making authority to incumbent administrators and specialists. Individual personal involvement usually amounts to little more than attending occasional meetings to routinely approve proposals and decisions developed, discussed, and decided by others. A de facto hierarchy controls the decision making, and therefore the experience of the typical member differs little from that in a conventional firm.

For Yugoslavia, Veljko Rus (1984) noted a tendency for cooperative ideals to degenerate. Initially equality, democracy, and ideological commitment were high, but as time passed, a de facto organizational hierarchy emerged (pp. 376–377). That conforms with Robert Michels's (1966) iron law of oligarchy (from political science), which notes the tendency for a minority of people to dominate decision making, even in democracies. It also conforms with Pareto's law, which holds that much of the performance of an organization can be attributed to a small proportion of its input (resources, people). For example, 80% of a company's sales are made by 20% of its sales force, and 75% of its profit comes from 17% of the product line. The implication for management is that they cannot expect much participation by very many people even when they have the right and the opportunity to participate.

On the other hand, isn't this the way most civil political democracies work? Unless people are required to vote, the voter turnout is often low, and voters tend to favor the incumbent over the challenger. Or does it really matter whether participation is complete as long as voters have the opportunity to express their views at the ballot box?

Critical Success Factors

Under what circumstances would management by democracy have the highest probability of success? Historical evidence suggests the following.

Management by democracy has the highest probability of success when members are carefully chosen, as at Mondragon, Spain, where candidates are carefully screened and have a year of probation before final acceptance. In U.S. professional partnerships (e.g., consultancies, law firms), there is high selectivity, including an up-or-out evaluation system that retains the best revenue producers.

The probability of success is highest when government legal and regulatory rules interfere with labor mobility. In Europe, for example, labor law commonly requires long advance notice and large severance payments for layoffs. Also, egalitarian pay levels and high marginal personal income taxes tend to impede mobility, which makes for a less competitive business environment.

A stable political and regulatory environment and weak competition, as in pre–European Union Spain when Mondragon and other enterprises were protected by tariff and nontariff trade barriers, also increase the probability of success. Today, Spain faces more competitive pressures as a member of the European Union, threatening the long-term viability of its producer cooperatives. Recent reports show that Mondragon's cooperative principles have eroded. In 1990, an umbrella organization, the Mondragon Cooperative Corporation (MCC), was formed to coordinate international expansion opportunities and respond to increased global competition. The MCC has initiated investment abroad (startups and buyouts). Managerial pay has risen, and many non–co-op members have been accepted as employees (Huet, 1997).

The probability of success is highest when members or employees have high participation potential, that is, when they are willing and able to participate (Walker, 1974, p. 12), a pattern more common where knowledge capital is at a premium, as in legal and consulting partnerships.

The probability of success is also highest where egalitarian values are strong, that is, when members reflect low power distance and are neither too independent nor too conformist (medium individualism), are tolerant of risk and change (low uncertainty avoidance), and are likely to favor and accept compromise (low masculine value orientation).

A small, slow-growing organization has the highest probability of success. When an organization is small, peer pressure to perform is stronger, reducing the tendency to shirk; also, the decision making process is less cumbersome. By contrast, large size and rapid growth tend to bring more specialized division of labor, and management must be more professional. For example, when professional partnerships grow, their management structures tend to become more hierarchical despite the nominal democracy.

The probability of success is highest when member participation is direct rather than indirect and when individuals are willing to actively participate. (Rubenowitz, Norrgren, & Tannenbaum, 1983, p. 243)

The probability of success is highest when personal and cultural bonds between the members are strong, as at Mondragon, Spain, with a shared Basque language, history, and work ethic. The Basque region was long isolated geographically and politically, and after World War II, it received autonomy to administer its own tax system, health services, schools, retirement benefits, job training, and other programs. More recently, the Spanish economy has grown rapidly, and job mobility has eroded Basque cultural cohesion.

Intermember cultural bonds were similarly strong in the U.S. Pacific Northwest plywood manufacturing cooperatives dominated by Scandinavian, mainly Swedish, immigrants. In Israel, the kibbutz movement was driven mainly by Jews of European origin (the Ashkenazi Jews) who had strong socialist political views and were the backbone of the dominant Israeli political party of the time (Labor Party). By contrast, Israel's Sephardic Jews (non-European, mainly of Middle Eastern and North African origin) were less attracted to communitarian ideals.

The probability of success is highest when the members have an expressive rather than an instrumental view of work, that is, when the work is valued for itself rather than as means to support life outside work. An expressive view of work is found most often in creative and professional pursuits and in upper levels of management, as Tannenbaum (1975) noted: "Whether organizations are participative or not, top management finds life more fulfilling than do workers at the bottom. In all plants, the bosses report more chances to do their thing, and those below find work less interesting" (p. 43).

The probability of success is highest when members have a significant personal financial stake in their firm and when it can grow and eventually be withdrawn. In reviewing the research on employee-owned companies, Tannenbaum (1983) concluded that the beneficial social and psychological "effects are likely to be realized to the extent that ownership is substantial rather than merely nominal" (p. 263). At Mondragon, members' capital holdings typically have grown with each passing year because its ventures have been profitable in most years. The same is true in the Breman Group (a successful democratically run engineering and construction firm) in the Netherlands (De Jong & van Witteloostuijn, 2004).

Employee stock ownership and profit sharing are conducive to a longer-term perceptual horizon that helps to resolve the trade-off between high near-term pay and long-term capital investment.

Chapter Summary

- Management by democracy has been tried in many places throughout modern history; its intellectual roots draw from Christian socialist ideals and modern organization theory, especially its humanist and human relations subcurrents.

- Democratic management practice and style differ from conventional management in regard to the management process and traditional organizations; its ideals are purest in communitarian settings (communes and producer cooperatives) and to a lesser degree in private professional partnerships and knowledge-driven service organizations (e.g., accountancies, consultancies, universities, public policy research institutes).

- The examples of management by democracy described in this chapter include the system of self-management socialism tried nationwide in the former Yugoslavia (1950–1990) and various communes, cooperatives, and professional partnerships in diverse settings.

- Communitarian enterprise strives to balance economic and noneconomic objectives; it aims for less hierarchy and more self-direction and control than are found in traditional organizations. The position of manager is usually, but not necessarily, rotated, and the pay differences between members are small.

- History shows employee control to be problematic, but it has had some success in some settings. In the former socialist countries (e.g., Eastern Europe and the Soviet Union), cooperatives outperformed state enterprise. However, the most democratic enterprise of all (a commune) has been the least successful when judged solely on economic grounds.

- Circumstances that offer the best probability of success include small size; careful selection of members; a stable legal and regulatory environment; close intermember personal and cultural bonds; and an expressive view of work, a significant ownership stake, and direct rather than indirect participation by members.

- In general, service sector co-ops (e.g., consumer co-ops, purchasing co-ops, credit co-ops) have had more staying power than producer (manufacturing) cooperatives.

- There is doubt about whether many purported noneconomic benefits of member democracy truly occur and whether members value them highly. It is generally presumed that a worker-controlled enterprise is more egalitarian, participative, and supportive than a conventional one; however, much research suggests otherwise.

- Participants need the proper knowledge, mind-set, and judgment to engage effectively in decision making. Despite egalitarian ideals and goals, a minority of members commonly dominate the decision making.

- Management by democracy has limits in terms of efficiency and competitive survival, especially in a free market economy. In effect, labor becomes a fixed cost, and members can experience a conflict of interest in balancing the desire for higher pay with the need for long-term investment. Also, decision making can be more time-consuming than in traditional organizations, there is more risk of leaking information to competitors, free riding is more likely, and there is higher risk (to employees) of having the rewards of their lifetime of labor tied up in the well-being of just one organization (their employer).

Terms and Concepts

democratic organizational forms
direct democracy
economic democracy
ejido
horizontal organization
iron law of oligarchy
kolkhoz
kibbutz
market socialism

Mondragon experiment
producer cooperative
representative democracy
Robert Owen
Rochdale principles
social ownership
utopian socialist
workers' cooperative

Study Questions

1. Describe differences in the management process (i.e., planning, organizing, directing, controlling, staffing) in conventional and democratic, communitarian organizations.

2. Discuss several strengths and limitations of employee control.

3. Under what conditions and circumstances do co-ops and communal organizations have the highest probability of success?

4. Consider the idea of democracy in university academic programs (i.e., having the students design their own study programs and set academic standards and graduation requirements). Discuss the advantages and disadvantages of such a system.

5. Investigate and report on what remains today of management by democracy in the former Yugoslavia (or its main remnant, Serbia).

6. What if the law required that all industrial organizations be managed democratically? Discuss.

Exercise 5.1

Investigate and discuss the pattern and performance of democratic management in a real-life example such as one or more of the following. To what extent does it adhere to the democratic structure, process, principles, and values described in this chapter?

Research laboratory

University faculty senate

University academic department

School board

Co-housing

Campus student organization

Homeowner (or condominium owner) association

Social or recreational organization (e.g., a private swim or tennis club, sports league)

Student team project

Public policy think tank

Credit union

City council

Business partnership

Semco Group, Brazil (Ricardo Semler)

Scott Bader Company (United Kingdom)

An example of your own choosing

Exercise 5.2

Venezuelan President Hugo Chavez has been pressing for "socialism of the 21st century." By contrast with the centralized state socialism of the 20th century (Russia, China, former Eastern Europe), his approach emphasizes the Empresa de Producción Social (EPS, or Social Production Enterprise). EPSs are "economic entities dedicated to the production of goods or services in which there is substantive equality between members, where planning is participatory and with collective ownership" (Wilpert, 2006). Core principles include social responsibility and commitment to community.

Chavez states that the number of these cooperative enterprises has grown from a few hundred several years ago to maybe 150,000 or more today (numbers are hazy) employing maybe 10% of the nation's adult population. From oil export revenue, the state helps EPSs with cash, tax exemptions, training, subsidized loans, and preferential purchasing of their output. In addition, some faltering private businesses have been expropriated and turned over to their employees to be run as collectives.

Assignment: Investigate and evaluate the progress (plans, successes, uncertainties) of "21st century socialism" in Venezuela. In your judgment, what are its prospects for the future? Explain.

Notes

1. The Swedish immigrant father of this book's author was an early shareholder and employee for nearly three decades in a plywood manufacturing cooperative (Peninsula Plywood, or PenPly) in Port Angeles, Washington.

2. The ICA Web site (http://www.ica.coop/al-ica/) has information on cooperative ventures in different sectors: agriculture, banking, credit, consumer, energy, fisheries, housing, insurance, workers, tourism, and health care, from all continents.

3. It is estimated that about 30% of U.S. farm output is distributed through cooperatives (http://www.ica.coop/coop/statistics.html#members).

4. In 1989, there were 133,000 private Soviet cooperatives employing about 5 million people ("The Search for Decentralized Socialism," 1990, p. 12).

5. The initial capital holding cost 9,000 euros in 2001.

6. This report of the International Comparative Research Project study, organized by the International Institute for Labor Studies, included research studies from France, Germany, India, Israel, Japan, Poland, Spain, the United Kingdom, the United States, and Yugoslavia.

References

Adizes, I. (1971a). *Industrial democracy: Yugoslav style.* New York: Free Press.

Adizes, I. (1971b, October–December). The role of management in democratic (communal) organizational structures: A study of the Yugoslav self-management, the Israeli kibbutz and the Peruvian comunidad industrial. *Annals of Public & Cooperative Economics, 42*(4), 399–420.

BBC (Producer). (1980). *The Mondragon experiment* [Videotape]. London: Nova–Horizon Series.

Benello, C. (1984). Workplace democracy in the United States: Present trends and counter-trends. *Economic Analysis and Workers' Management, 18*(4), 385–397.

Ben-Rafael, E. (1997). *Crisis and transformation: The kibbutz at century's end.* Albany: State University at New York Press.

Berman, K. (1967). *Worker-owned plywood companies: An economic analysis.* Pullman: Washington State University Press.

Bernstein, P. (1982). Necessary elements for effective worker participation in decision making. In F. Lindenfeld & J. Rothschild-Whitt (Eds.), *Workplace democracy and social change* (pp. 51–81). Boston: Porter Sargent.

Bonin, J. (1985). Labor management and capital maintenance. In D. Jones & J. Svejnar (Eds.), *Advances in the economic analysis of participatory and labor managed firms* (Vol. 1, pp. 55–70). Greenwich, CT: JAI Press.

Central Bureau of Statistics. (2006). *Statistical abstract of Israel 2007.* Retrieved September 4, 2008, from http://www.cbs.gov.il/reader/?MIval=cw_usr_view_Folder&ID=141

Cooperate and prosper. (1989, April 1). *The Economist,* p. 61.

De Jong, G., & van Witteloostuijn, A. (2004). Successful corporate democracy: Sustainable cooperation of capital and labor in the Dutch Breman Group. *The Academy of Management Executive, 18*(3), 54–66.

Donkin, R. (1998, September 2). Democratic revolution. *Financial Times*, p. 24.

Drucker, P. (1974). *Management: Tasks, responsibilities, practices.* New York: Harper & Row.

Greenberg, E. (1986). *Worker democracy: The political effects of participation.* Ithaca, NY: Cornell University Press.

Heller, F., Pusic, E., Strauss, G., & Wilpert, B. (1988). *Organizational participation: Myth and reality.* Oxford, UK: Oxford University Press.

Huet, T. (1997, November–December). Can coops go global? Mondragon is trying. *Dollars & Sense*, p. 16.

International Labor Organization (cooperative branch). (2008). *Cooperatives worldwide.* Retrieved September 4, 2008, from http://www.ilo.org/dyn/empent/empent.portal?p_docid=WOLDWIDE&p_prog=C

Jones, D. (1985). The cooperative sector and dualism in command economies: Theory and evidence for the case of Poland. In D. Jones & J. Svejnar (Eds.), *Advances in the economic analysis of participatory and labor managed firms* (Vol. 1, pp. 195–218). Greenwich, CT: JAI Press.

Kamusic, M. (1970). Economic efficiency and workers' self management. In M. Broekmeyer (Ed.), *Yugoslav workers' self management* (pp. 76–116). Dordrecht, the Netherlands: D. Reidel.

Keefe, E., Boucher, A., Elpern, S., Giloane, W., Moore, J., Ogden, T., et al. (1971). *Area handbook for the Soviet Union.* Washington, DC: Government Printing Office.

Leggett, K. (2005, May 26). Pay-as-you-go kibbutzim. *New York Times*, p. B1.

Leviatan, U., Oliver, H., & Quarter, J. (Eds.). (1998). *Crisis in the Israeli kibbutz.* New York: Praeger.

Likert, R. (1961). *New patterns of management.* New York: McGraw-Hill.

Likert, R. (1967). *The human organization.* New York: McGraw-Hill.

Lindenfeld, F., & Rothschild-Whitt, J. (Eds.). (1982). *Workplace democracy and social change.* Boston: Porter Sargent.

Long, R. (1982). Worker ownership and job attitudes: A field study. *Industrial Relations, 21*(2), 196–215.

Maslow, A. (1943, July). A theory of human motivation. *Psychological Review, 50,* 370–396.

McGregor, D. (1960). *The human side of enterprise.* New York: McGraw-Hill.

Meade, J. (1972, March). The theory of labour-managed firms and profit sharing. *Economic Journal, 82,* 402–428.

Melman, Y. (1995, February). Kibbutz: Is the dream dead? *Moment, 20*(1), 44–60.

Mexico, farmed out. (2000, April 1). *The Economist*, p. 34.

Michels, R. (1966). *Political parties: A sociological study of the oligarchical tendencies of modern democracy.* New York: Free Press.

Obradovic, J. (1975). Workers' participation in management: Who participates? *Industrial Relations, 14*(1), 32–44.

Prasnikar, J., & Prasnikar, V. (1986, May). The Yugoslav self-managed firm in historical perspective. *Economic and Industrial Democracy, 7*(2), 167–191.

Ramondt, J. (1979, March). Worker's self management and its constraints: The Yugoslav experiences. *British Journal of Industrial Relations, 17*(1), 83–94.

Rothschild, J., & Whitt, J. (1986). *The cooperative workplace: Potentials and dilemmas of organizational democracy and participation.* Cambridge, UK: Cambridge University Press.

Rubenowitz, S., Norrgren, F., & Tannenbaum, A. (1983). Some social psychological effects of direct and indirect participation in ten Swedish companies. *Organization Studies, 4*(3), 243–259.

Rus, V. (1984). Yugoslav self-management: 30 years later. In B. Wilpert & A. Sorge (Eds.), *International perspectives on organizational democracy* (pp. 371–389). New York: Wiley.

The search for decentralized socialism: A survey of perestroika. (1990, April 28). *The Economist,* p. 12.

Singh, J. (2001, May). McKinsey's managing director Rajat Gupta on leading a knowledge-based global consulting organization. *Academy of Management Executive, 15*(2), 34–44.

Skinner, B. (1948). *Walden two.* New York: Macmillan.

Spinrad, W. (1984). Work democracy: An overview. *International Social Science Journal, 36*(2), 195–215.

Steinberg, J. (2004, April 20). In soy food, kibbutzim find manna for a modern age. *New York Times,* p. 1.

Stephens, E. (1980). *The politics of workers' participation: The Peruvian approach in comparative perspective.* New York. Academic Press.

Tannenbaum, A. (1975, September). Rank, clout and worker satisfaction: Pecking order, capitalist and communist style. *Psychology Today,* pp. 41–43.

Tannenbaum, A. (1983). Employee-owned companies. In L. L. Cummings & B. Staw (Eds.), *Research in organization behavior* (Vol. 5, pp. 235–268). Greenwich, CT: JAI Press.

Under workers' control. (2002, November 9). *The Economist,* p. 40.

Vanik, J. (1970). *The general theory of labor-managed market economies.* Ithaca, NY: Cornell University Press.

Vanik, J. (1971). *The participatory economy.* Ithaca, NY: Cornell University Press.

Vatican Encyclical Letter. (1991). *Centessimus annus, by Pope John Paul II, on the hundredth anniversary of "Rerum Novarum"* (Chapter 4, Section 43). Retrieved September 4, 2008, from http://www.cin.org/jp2doc.html

Walker, K. (1974). Workers' participation in management: Problems, practice and prospects. *Bulletin of the International Institute for Labor Studies, 12,* 3–35.

Ward, B. (1953, September). The firm in Illyria: Market syndicalism. *American Economic Review, 48*(4), 566–589.

Wilpert, G. (2006, July 22). *The meaning of 21st century socialism for Venezuela.* Retrieved September 4, 2008, from http://www.zmag.org/znet/viewArticle/3525

Witte, J. (1980). *Democracy, authority and alienation in work: Workers' participation in an American corporation.* Chicago: University of Chicago Press.

The Legacy of China **6**

> *In the Far East, for the Overseas Chinese and arguably the Japanese and Koreans also, there are no indigenous textbooks, no recognizable management theory, and the Western textbooks penetrate hardly at all. . . . The design of organizations is more instinctive, less openly discussed, somehow more natural. Organizations are cultural artifacts just as are their Western equivalents, but in the search for productive efficiency, they appear to have found a formula closer to the needs of their participants.*
>
> —S. Gordon Redding (1990, p. 238)

Rapid economic progress in East Asia has spurred much interest in Confucian zone business and management practices for many reasons, including the following.

Here are the only non-Western nations other than oil exporters to have attained a high material standard of living. Japan was first, followed by the Four Tigers (Hong Kong, Singapore, Taiwan, and South Korea), all now advanced industrial economies.

The Overseas Chinese (emigrant ethnic Chinese) have proven their entrepreneurial prowess in East and Southeast Asia and beyond. Unique, too, have been the private Korean *chaebol* business groups and China's emergent state-favored "national champions."

China holds one fifth of the world's population, but produced just one ninth of world output in 2007 (adjusted for purchasing power; cf. Central Intelligence Agency, 2008). If its economic reforms continue, and with well-managed organizations, it could astonish the world in the years ahead. It might also disappoint.

It can be debated whether traditional Chinese management practice and style are compatible with global competitiveness. For example, few private ethnic Chinese businesses grow very large. However, through extensive business networking some have overcome limits of scale and breadth. Some sources view their networks as a pathbreaking structural prototype worldwide. (Schlevogt, 2002).

Outsiders see a growing need to understand and engage more effectively with East Asian customers, suppliers, rivals, regulators, and allies both at home and abroad.

Chapter Objectives

- To profile the culture, economy, and polity of Confucian East Asia (China, Taiwan, Singapore, Hong Kong, and South Korea)
- To note prevailing management practices, pressures, and problems, including intraregional and Western comparisons

The Chinese Macroenvironment

CHINA LEGACY

Chinese civilization was one of seven major ones to emerge independent from others.[1] Its origins go back to agricultural villages in the Yellow River valley of northern China around 5,000 BC. It eventually spread to include today's China, Taiwan, Hong Kong, and Singapore (three fourths ethnic Chinese) and influenced Korean and Japanese society and culture. China coalesced politically in the Qin (Ch'in) Dynasty (221 to 206 BC), from which came its name in English. It often surprises Westerners to hear about early Chinese technological advancements (gunpowder, block printing, paper, magnetic sailing compass, complex pest control systems) that predate exposure to Western science (Needham, 1954). There were grandiose public works projects such as the Grand Canal (1,200-mile north–south waterway, part natural, part constructed), started in the 6th century AD, stretching from Tianjin in the north nearly to Shanghai; there was the Great Wall (about 1,500 miles long) in the north, begun in 220 BC. Early Chinese traders traveled the Silk Road to Central Asia, and fleets reached India, the Arabian peninsula, and east Africa before the Spanish and Portuguese crossed the Atlantic (*The Explorers Map,* 1998; *History of China,* 1991).

Figure 6.1 and Table 6.1 characterize the area covered in this chapter.

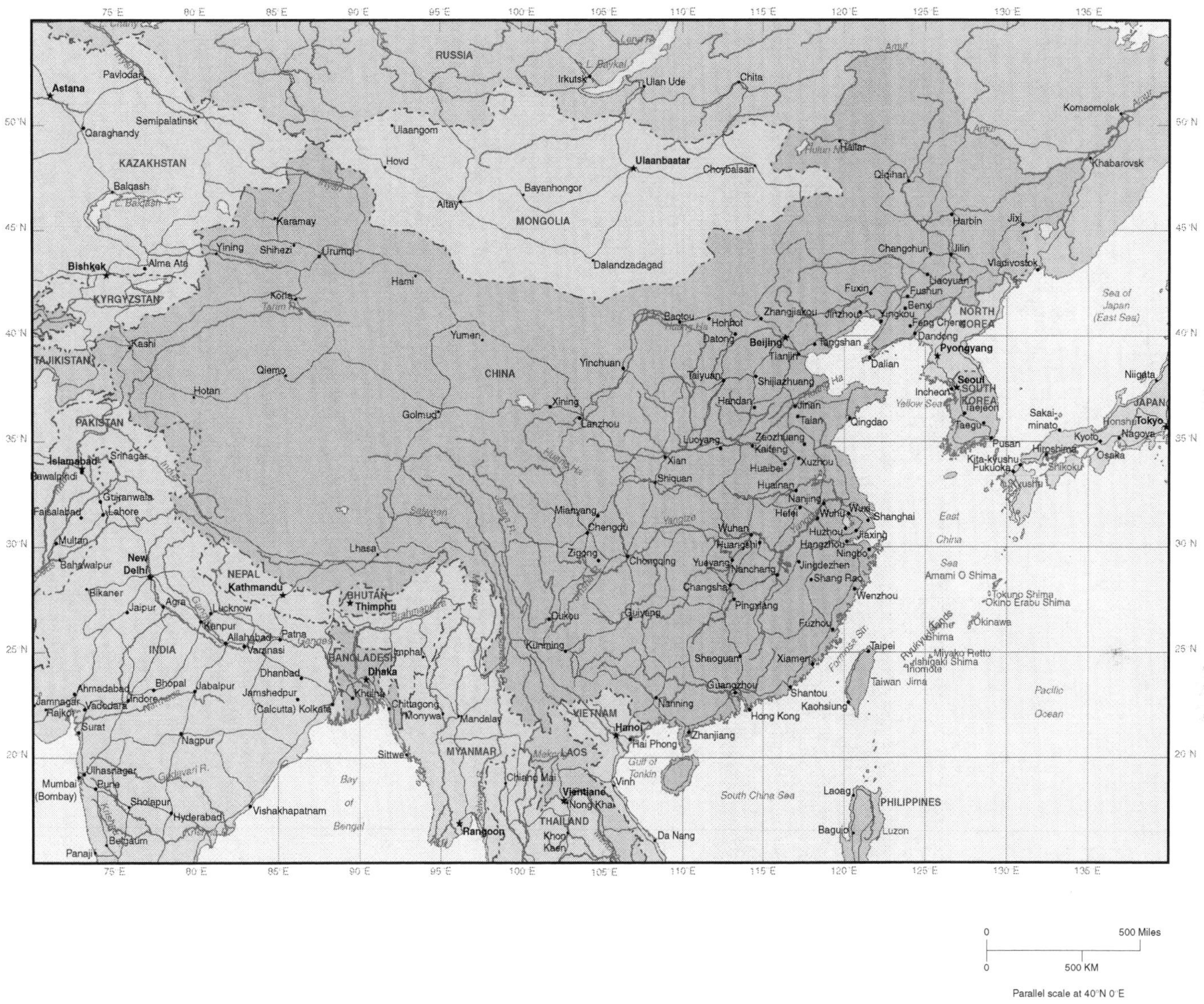

Figure 6.1 Map of East Asia

Table 6.1   The East Asian Economies

	Population (million)	Gross Domestic Product per Capita (U.S. dollars)
China	1,322	5,300
Taiwan	22	29,800
Hong Kong	7	42,000
Singapore	5	48,900
South Korea	49	24,600
North Korea	23	1,900
Japan	127	33,800

SOURCE: Estimates; gross domestic product numbers adjusted for purchasing power from Central Intelligence Agency (2008).

CULTURE

Chinese culture is called Confucian in reference to its early, long-revered, and oft-cited sage Confucius (Kung Fu-tzu, c. 500 BC), whose thinking and teaching influenced its social value system (Leys, 1997). Confucian tradition draws mainly from custom rather than from religion, ideology, or law, and with the following features.

The social structure values order, hierarchy, and deference to authority, as reflected in long-standing *wu-lun* rules of deference (e.g., of child to parent, student to teacher, young to old, wife to husband, citizen to ruler, and, by extension, employee to employer or boss). In this respect, Chinese culture is high on Hofstede's power distance, that is, it readily accepts interpersonal differences in power.

Group consciousness is strong (high collectivism, low individualism); daily life, including business, relies heavily on personal connections and trust, based variously on family and kinship ties, community, geographic region, language dialect, school, or other bonds. The following is an example based on family surname:

> Dateline, San Jose, California: About 1,000 people from 20 countries are here for the seventh Teo-Chew International Convention, which unites Chinese from all over the world whose ancestors hail from the same region in China, a cluster of provinces on the country's southeast coast near Hong Kong. . . . There are nine Teo-Chew associations in the United States, and scores of others scattered around the world, though they are concentrated in Southeast Asia. . . . Family Associations are common in Chinese communities, providing scholarships, financial help, community services and a

social network to Chinese with the same surname. The Teo-Chew group is similar, though its communality is based on linguistic and regional, rather than family ties. (Gomes, 1993)

In Southeast Asia, local Chinese chambers of commerce, benevolent associations, and surname groups nurture and sustain family business networks. For instance, Malaysia has thousands of Chinese associations and guilds. In Taiwan, mutual aid societies mobilize capital for small business (Pao-an, 1991). In lower Manhattan (New York), immigrant Fujianese and Cantonese help newcomers of similar origin to find lodging and sustenance (Sachs, 2001).

Personal relationships are nurtured and sustained through *guanxi* (mutual reciprocal trust, favors, influence, obligations) (Tsui, Farh, & Xin, 2000).

> The lifeblood of a Chinese company is guanxi connections. Penetrating layers of quanxi [is] like peeling an onion: first come connections between people with ancestors from the same province in China; then people from the same clan or village; finally the family. It does not matter much whether a Chinese businessman is in Hong Kong or New York, he will always operate through guanxi. (Cowley, 1991, p. S6)

> La (pulling) guanxi is the most commonly used strategy by the Chinese in network construction. Pulling guanxi means the efforts to establish and build up relationships with others where no previous relationships existed, or where an existing relationship is not close enough to be useful. There are many ways of pulling guanxi, involving a wide range of skills and strategies. Depending on these to manage their daily relations, the Chinese living in mainland China have rightly used a special term, guanxixue (relationology) to describe this complicated phenomenon. (Chen, 1995, pp. 53–54)

Confucian culture shows a predominantly masculine value orientation (i.e., competitive, aggressive, work oriented). A patriarch commonly heads the family business, a role that normally passes eventually to a son or other male relative. Women have subordinate social status, and upon marriage they join their husband's family.

Confucian culture is characterized by an aversion for shame, emphasis on saving face, and self-conscious awareness of the expectations of others (e.g., parents, siblings, friends, colleagues, teachers, the boss).

Confucian culture emphasizes social harmony.

Major spiritual influences include Taoism (a Chinese folk religion) and Buddhism (introduced from South Asia after the 2nd century AD). Both emphasize selflessness and harmony with nature. Although Confucianism is sometimes called a religion, it is more of a code for living and has no institutional infrastructure. However, one feature is reverence for ancestors.

Patience, perseverance, and maintenance of composure are emphasized; people tend to suppress expressive emotions in public.

The culture includes a flexible, transcendental view of time with a long-term perceptual horizon. These and some other cultural tendencies are listed in Table 6.2.

Table 6.2   Sinitic[2] Cultural Tendencies

Confucian sociocultural foundation; emphasis on order and hierarchical relationships, embodied in deference or submission of child to parent, student to teacher, young to old, wife to husband, citizen to ruler.

Predominantly high-context culture (Hall, 1959, 1976), that is, inclined toward indirect and implicit (rather than blunt) communications; relationships in business (and life) depend heavily on trust; polychronic view of time (flexible, unregimented); in organizations, the tendency to centralize (and to hoard) decision-making authority at the top.

Strong core group identity (family, clan, village, province, language dialect, school) and basis for developing and sustaining *guanxi* (mutual favors, connections, obligations); low trust of outsiders.

Propensity for personalism, favoritism, nepotism.

Taoism and Buddhism have been the dominant spiritual traditions.

Reverence for the past, including ancestor worship.

High regard for learning.

Tendency for introspection and humility.

Importance of preserving personal honor and saving face; aversion for embarrassment and shame.

Comfortable with benevolent, patriarchal leaders.

Subordinate social and occupational status for women.

Patience, diligence, perseverance, frugality, thrift.

Emphasis on harmony in social relations.

On Hofstede's cultural dimensions, the following tendencies (for some intercountry variations, see Table 6.3):

- High power distance
- Low individualism
- High masculinity
- High uncertainty avoidance
- Long-term time orientation

Despite a common Confucian heritage, Sinitic nations are neither homogeneous nor cultural clones. For example, northern Chinese (e.g., from Beijing, mainly Mandarin speaking) tend to be more reserved, less expressive, and less entrepreneurial than Cantonese-speaking southeasterners in Guangdong province and Hong Kong (Schlevogt, 2001). The Taiwanese

Table 6.3 Sinitic Countries and the United States Scored on Hofstede's Cultural Dimensions

Hofstede's Dimensions[a]	China	Hong Kong	Taiwan	Singapore	South Korea	Japan	United States
Power distance[b]	80	68	58	74	60	54	40
Individualism[c]	20	25	17	20	18	46	91
Masculinity[d]	50	57	45	48	39	95	62
Uncertainty avoidance[e]	60	29	69	8	85	92	46
Long-term time orientation[f]	118	96	—	—	—	80	29

SOURCE: Hofstede (1980).

a. Hofstede conceptualized the dimensions (except for long-term time orientation) and scoring system based on employee attitude surveys done within (and by) the IBM Corporation (116,000 employees in 53 countries collected from 1967 to 1973). The IBM surveys did not include the People's Republic of China (PRC); PRC scores here are Hofstede estimates.

b. Power distance (high versus low), the degree of social inequality considered to be normal.

c. Individualism (high versus low), the degree to which people act as individuals rather than as members of groups.

d. Masculinity (versus femininity), the degree to which tough values (e.g., assertiveness, performance, success, and competition) prevail over tender ones (e.g., quality of life and warm, caring personal relationships).

e. Uncertainty avoidance (high versus low), the degree to which structured situations are preferable to unstructured ones; degree of tolerance for risk and uncertainty.

f. Long-term time orientation (versus short-term), the degree to which emphasis on the future takes priority over the near-term time horizon; numbers in this row are Hofstede and Bond (1988) estimates and not derived from the original IBM data.

Chinese are described as more individualistic, self-centered, competitive, materialistic, and pragmatic than peers in Singapore and Mainland China (Hsu, 1987). Hong Kong and Singapore show much lower on Hofstede's uncertainty avoidance than mainlanders, as reflected in stronger entrepreneurial tendencies.

Confucian peoples generally accept high power distance, but mainland and Singapore Chinese are higher on this dimension than are South Koreans and Japanese. South Koreans are less collective than Chinese and Japanese, and their work ethic and education ethic have been called the strongest in East Asia. In this regard, South Koreans take fewer holidays and work more hours than the Japanese. They are also more likely to pursue a university education.

South Korea and Hong Kong have been the most open to certain Western influences. For example, about one fourth of South Korea's population is Christian, and there is much interfirm labor mobility and notable labor union militancy.

POLITICAL AND LEGAL SETTING

After World War II, the Sinitic region divided politically into socialist states (China, North Korea) and nonsocialist ones (Taiwan, Singapore, South Korea, Hong Kong, Japan). Even for the latter group, political democracy was slow to emerge, partly for cultural reasons. For example, the Confucian affinity for affiliation, conformity, order, and harmony seems inconsistent with the personal civil liberties and political pluralism of democracy. Kristof (1991, p. 8) observes that the "Chinese expressions for 'freedom,' or 'privacy' still have a negative connotation in Chinese, showing traditional lack of concern for individual rights." China's Communist Party has anti-Confucian traits (e.g., putting ideology above family); however, other communist values have been Confucian-friendly (e.g., material equality and hierarchical political structure).

Even where national elections are well established in East Asia, one political party has often dominated for long time periods. In Japan it has been the Liberal Democratic Party, and in Singapore it has been the People's Action Party.[3] In Taiwan, the Nationalist Chinese party (Kuomintang) was in charge from 1949 until 2000, at first under Chiang Kai-shek, who fled the mainland when the communists took control (1949). When Chiang died (c. 1975), his son replaced him. Only after the son's death (1988) did opposition political parties compete openly. Taiwan's first fully free national presidential election was in 1996, and the first transfer of leadership to an elected opposition party was in 2000. In post–World War II South Korea, the military was either in charge or main powerbroker for 40 years. The 1988 South Korean presidential election was its first openly democratic one. Not until 1993 was there presidential changeover, by election, to a nonincumbent political party. In state socialist North Korea, Kim Il Sung ruled for nearly five decades until his death in 1994, when he was succeeded by son Kim Jung Il.

For centuries, the Chinese central state remained weak because of China's widely dispersed (and predominantly rural) population and an underdeveloped transportation and communication infrastructure (*Area Handbook,* 1972). In that regard, Chinese philosopher Lin Yu-tang (1935/1966) cites an ancient proverb, "Heaven is high and the emperor is far away," and observes, "The Chinese people can always govern themselves, have always governed themselves. If the thing called 'government' can leave them alone, they are always willing to let government alone" (p. 205). The central state didn't acquire significant control until 1949.

Table 6.4 lists several core features of government and politics in East Asia.

Table 6.4   Government and Politics in Chinese and Korean East Asia

- Preference for strong benevolent authoritarian leaders; weak legislatures.
- Dominant party political systems; weak opposition parties.
- Slow, historically, to pursue and protect individual civil liberties and democratic values.
- For centuries, the family (rather than the state) was foundation for Chinese sociopolitical order.
- Chinese business has long been guided by custom rather than by formal commercial law; foundations of such law are only now emerging in the PRC.
- Limited social welfare role for the state (more the role of family).
- Minimal spontaneous or independent labor unionism (except in post–World War II South Korea).

ECONOMY

The Confucian zone economies include the predominantly capitalist Four Tigers (South Korea, Hong Kong, Singapore, Taiwan) and a newly marketizing China. Hong Kong and Singapore are the most affluent, and both regularly rank at or near the top of global indices of economic freedom.[4] Regional economic growth has been high in recent decades. The Shanghai region, Pearl River delta, and other areas of coastal China have seen rapid export-led growth analogous to what occurred previously in Hong Kong and Singapore.

Singapore, Taiwan, and South Korea have seen significant state guidance and support for certain companies and industries (a state-guided form of capitalism similar to Japan's). That has included indicative planning, aimed to influence (but not dictate) investment patterns. China can be called frontier capitalist, social market, or a mixed economy in transition toward more economic freedom.

In general, government spending in the Four Tigers has been lower in proportion to national income than in North America and Europe, but it is rising. These and some other general economic tendencies are described in Table 6.5.

Table 6.6 tracks the economic transition in the People's Republic of China (PRC) after the communist revolution of 1949.

By international standards, East Asia has few large private firms except for several within South Korean *chaebol* and Japanese *keiretsu* business groups. A *chaebol* (literally "financial house") is a group of independent firms with members engaged in diverse businesses. They remain largely controlled by their founder families. Table 6.7 identifies Confucian zone firms (other than Japanese) ranked in the 2008 Fortune Global 500 (based on sales revenue). It is noteworthy that only 13 (and just 5 of them private) were in the top 200, and there were only 51 among the 500. All 25 listed for the PRC have 50% or more state ownership. All but 1 of 14 from South

Table 6.5   Economic Patterns and Trends in Taiwan, Singapore, Hong Kong, and
                 South Korea

- Rapid export-led economic growth in recent decades
- State-guided capitalism (except in Hong Kong), that is, mainly market-guided economies but with government indicative planning and selective support or protection for certain sectors
- Bank-dominated financial systems; government-dominated banks
- Underdeveloped but functioning (and modernizing) capital markets
- Proven entrepreneurial prowess of emigrant ethnic Chinese (the Overseas Chinese)
- High personal savings rates
- Low tax collection and low government spending in proportion to output compared with the United States and Europe; fewer state social welfare commitments
- Significant trade and investment protectionism (except in Hong Kong and Singapore) but diminishing
- In the private sector, predominance of small and medium-size family businesses; few private companies grow very large (except for South Korean *chaebol* enterprises)

Table 6.6   The PRC: An Economy in Transition

1949

The Communist Party and Red Army (led by Mao Zedong) win a long-running civil war; the PRC is founded, bringing a state socialist economy modeled after the Soviet Union.

1953–1957

First 5-year central economic plan; conversion of private farms into agricultural collectives.

1958–1962

Second 5-year plan (the Great Leap Forward) consolidated agricultural cooperatives into rural agroindustrial communes; administrative decentralization of light industry to the provinces.

1966–1976

Period of the Great Proletarian Cultural Revolution; party purists try to reinvigorate communist values and ideals; revolutionary committees form in factories and communes; contrarian intellectuals and other "capitalist roaders" are assigned to manual labor in rural farms and factories.

1976

Mao Zedong dies; economic pragmatists gain control and begin market socialism.

1978

The contract responsibility system is tried in Sichuan province (the Sichuan experiments), by allowing farmers to keep or sell privately any production above their quota obligations to the state; agricultural productivity rises dramatically.

1980

The contract responsibility system is extended to almost all Chinese agriculture and to many small and medium-size manufacturing firms.

Creation of several Special Economic Zones (mainly in coastal areas) where free market economic conditions are allowed; Shenzhen Special Economic Zone (contiguous to Hong Kong, in Guangdong province) becomes the most active.

Citizens are allowed to "jump into the sea" (i.e., to establish private businesses).

Township/village enterprises (TVEs) coalesce from rural industrial communes and become managed as municipal, provincial, or private enterprises (including some cooperatives).

Reduced political intervention by the Communist Party in enterprise management; factory directors get more autonomy.

1990 to present

The economy is in transition.

Gradual privatization of state enterprise continues.

Some central government–owned enterprises are converted to provincial and municipal enterprises.

Legal and judicial system (e.g., protections for property rights, contract enforcement, dispute resolution) emerges slowly.

Ongoing improvements in communication and transportation infrastructure.

Slow development of private banking and capital markets; stock exchanges opened in Shanghai (1990) and Shenzhen (1991).

Problems with price inflation, corruption, trade protectionism, foreign exchange controls, nonperforming loans (private and public), unemployment and underemployment, opaque accounting and reporting practices, and ambiguities and inconsistencies in the tax and legal system

Subsidies and loans for state-owned enterprises (SOEs); high volume of nonperforming bank loans.

In 2006, there were an estimated 140,000 Chinese SOEs, including several thousand military-controlled ones ("A Survey of China," 2006). SOEs accounted for about one third of national economic output, one half of industrial assets, and 40 million jobs.

The private sector has grown dramatically (Tsui, Bian, & Cheng, 2006), with many small family businesses and individual proprietorships. The private sector, including foreign investors, accounted for at least two thirds of the economy in 2006 (and this proportion is rising).

SOURCE: Information from Child (1994), Henley and Nyaw (1986), Laaksonen (1988), Miljus and Moore (1990), and periodic survey issues in *The Economist*.

Korea are private. The Korean *chaebol* are well represented, including three Samsung entries, Hyundai with two, and one each for SK, LG, and Hanwha. Among six Taiwanese entries, only one is state owned (CPC, a petroleum company). The four Hong Kong firms are private.

Table 6.7   Chinese and Korean Firms listed on the 2008 Fortune Global 500
                 (and their rank in the 500 based on sales)

Taiwan (6 firms)	PRC (25 firms; all SOEs)
132 Hon Hai Precision Industry	16 Sinopec
300 Cathay Financial	24 State Grid
324 CPC (government owned)	25 China National Petroleum
344 Quanta	133 Industrial & Commercial Bank of China
363 Asustek	148 China Mobil
395 Formosa Petrochemical	159 China Life Insurance
South Korea (15 firms)	171 China Construction Bank
38 Samsung Electronics	187 Bank of China
67 LG	223 Agricultural Bank of China
82 Hyundai Motor	226 China Southern Power Grid
86 SK Holdings	257 Sinochem
224 POSCO	259 Baosteel
245 Korea Electric Power (government owned)	288 China Telecom
247 Samsung Life Insurance	303 China FAW Group
267 GS Holdings	341 China Railway Group
278 Shinhan Financial Group	356 China Railway Construction
279 Woori	385 China State Construction
329 Hanwha	373 Shanghai Automotive
387 KT	398 COFCO
378 Hyundai Heavy Industries	405 China Ocean Shipping
461 Kookmin Bank	409 China National Offshore Oil
475 Samsung C&T	412 China Minmetals
Singapore (1 firm)	426 China Communications Construction
378 Flextronics	476 Aluminum Corporation of China
Hong Kong (4 firms)	480 China Metallurgical Group
286 Hutchison Whampoa	
349 Noble Group	
437 Jardine Matheson	
499 Lenovo Group	

NOTE: The four firms indicated for Hong Kong were listed with China in the *Fortune* ranking (*Fortune*, 2008). Although Hong Kong is not a country, it has a separate economic system and is discussed separately in this chapter.

In recent times, the government of China has sought to foster "global champions." Eight of the 11 emergent champions listed in Table 6.8 are predominantly government enterprises.

The remainder of this chapter focuses on managerial themes. Before we proceed, an introductory observation is in order. (See box, p. 199.)

Table 6.8   A Sample of Prominent Chinese Companies (National or Global Champions)

	Sector	Sales Revenue (2007)
PetroChina	Oil and gas	$88.3 billion
Sinopec	Oil and gas	131.6
CNOOC	Oil and gas	19.0
Baosteel	Steel	22.7
Chalco	Aluminum	7.9
Lenovo (private)	PCs	14.6
SAIC	Cars	18.0
TCL (private)	TVs and electronics	39.4
Haier	Appliances	13.3 (2005)
Wanxiang (private)	Car parts	3.0
Huawei	Telecom equipment	11.0 (2006)

SOURCE: The names come from a list in "The Struggle of the Champions" (2005); the revenue numbers come from diverse (mainly corporate) Web sites; for a list of these and 30 other Chinese "champions," see the 2008 Boston Consulting Group 100 Global Challenger List (http://www.bcg.com/impact_expertise/publications/files/New_Global_Challengers_Feb_2008.pdf).

A Note on Western Management Thought and Theory and East Asian Business Organizations

For Western researchers and observers, the study of management in East Asia brings interesting complications. One is in selecting a suitable organizational unit (e.g., enterprise) for analysis. Whereas Western business generally has well-defined legal and institutional boundaries, in Asia "[the] boundaries of organization systems are unclear and undefined [and with] overlap between organizational systems and other systems such as family, community and clan" (Kyi, 1988, p. 216). This is observed in intranational and cross-national relational business networks (network enterprises, or network capitalism) of Chinese family-controlled business (Schlevogt, 2002).

(Continued)

(Continued)

Also, some people view the mind-sets and reasoning processes of East Asians and Westerners to be fundamentally different, with these differences compounded by written communication. For example, the pictorial script of Sinitic languages cannot replicate conceptual abstractions expressed in Western phonetic languages. Also, Western academic theory is grounded mainly on deductive reasoning, that is, the logic of Aristotle and Descartes, which gave rise to the scientific method and emergence of modern science. That logic underpins most Western academic research, including in management. By contrast, East Asian mind-sets and reasoning have been described as mainly inductive, and its scholars are less driven to conceive, confirm, or refute "scientific postulates" or principles. It is argued that East Asians have a more holistic and integrated understanding of the world around them and grasp better the complementarity, continuity, harmony, and synergy of human actions, actors, events, and circumstances (Maruyama, 1984; Nisbett, Choi, Peng, & Norenzayan, 2001).

For some Easterners, Westerners seem to be compartmentalized thinkers, prone to categorize, measure, and analyze, but lacking a coherent sense of the whole. In a similar vein, Kyi concludes that ethnographic case studies can offer superior insight into Eastern organizations than can the narrow empirical studies of Westerners (Kyi, 1988, p. 222).

For people analyzing life (including business and management) in another culture, there is inevitable tendency to frame things from personal mind-set and experience. One example involved Westerner scholars (Adler, Campbell, & Laurent, 1989, p. 62) investigating a "Chinese perspective relative to a number of key managerial concepts that have helped to explain European and North American approaches to management and organization." With a modified Western research instrument (the Laurent Management Questionnaire), they collected opinions from a sample of 100 Chinese participants in a management training seminar. The responses were inconsistent and difficult to interpret and seemed to reflect respondents' "politically correct" viewpoints rather than frank personal views. The results caused the researchers to question their own methods:

> We were learning more about the transferability of Western-based concepts and methodologies to the PRC than about the PRC itself . . . [and that] . . . oriental and occidental management conceptions may be so different on key dimensions as to render the results fairly meaningless. (pp. 67, 70)

S. Gordon Redding (1990) goes to the heart of the matter:

> To get outside one's own world-view sufficiently unencumbered to be able to empathize with, let alone understand, someone else's is a feat of mental agility beyond most of us. . . . All that one can realistically ask for is a suspension of disbelief and a willingness to accept the possibility that certain fundamental processes of the mind vary by culture. (p. 72)

With that caveat, the remainder of this chapter describes some prevailing managerial tendencies in East Asia from the viewpoint of a Western conceptual construct: the management process (planning, organizing, controlling, directing, and staffing). The coverage starts with managerial staffing.

The Confucian Zone Manager

By comparison with the West, information about CEOs in East Asia is lean. Few firms go public, and there is high secrecy in ones that do. Nonetheless, some information from academia, consultancies, and media sources is available.

SELECTION AND MOBILITY

The prototype Confucian zone private business (or business group) is family controlled and typically led by the patriarch. Favoritism and nepotism are common in hiring and promotion, and close relatives hold key positions without stigma of unfair preferential treatment. Although this pattern fits many family firms worldwide, it is stronger in the more collective (and higher-context) cultures than in individualistic ones. For Taiwan, Singapore, and South Korea, observers have described a nesting box pattern of staffing, with family members at the center and nonfamily on the periphery:

> In the small internal box are those core family members who own or will inherit the business; in the next box are more distant relatives and friends who owe their positions to their connection with the owners and who are in a position to influence and be influenced by them; in the next outer boxes are ranks of unrelated people who work in the firm for money. Depending on the size of the firm, the outer boxes may contain the ranks of professional managers, technicians, supervisors, and other craftspeople. The outermost box would include unskilled wage laborers. (Hamilton & Biggart, 1988, pp. S84–S85)

Hiring criteria heavily emphasize trust, as I-Ching Tu (1991) noted in reference to Taiwan:

> To most owners, when considering candidates for a management position, the most basic and important question is whether or not the candidate can be trusted. They will choose the most trustworthy persons to manage, and for added insurance, they will ask these people to invest in the firm and so have a stake in the ownership of the company themselves. From this, it is easy to understand why family members are often the favored candidates for higher-level jobs in an enterprise and why most general managers in Taiwan's enterprises are also shareholders. (pp. 122–123)

A similar tendency occurs in the South Korean *chaebol*. For example, six major industrial groups in the Hyundai *chaebol* have been led by sons of founder Chung Ju Yung. However, because of their large size, *chaebol* enterprises must also hire outsiders (non–family members). Some are recruited upon university graduation, including some who become assistants to senior family members to whom they develop strong loyalty (Choe, 2000; Steers, Shin, & Ungson, 1989). In an effort to ensure sufficient personal loyalty and trust, hiring managers often take the candidate's home region and university affiliation into account, as the following sources attest:

> In some . . . [Korean] companies, the top management group is dominated by executives who are all from the same geographical area, like Seoul, Yeongnam (a southeastern province), Honam (a southwestern province), or whatever the owner's home region may be. In some . . . companies, the executive group is dominated by graduates of certain universities (Seoul National, Yonsei, or Korea) or high schools (Kyunggi, Seoul or Kyungbook). (Chung & Lee, 1989, p. 156)

> When Korean managers are introduced, one of their first questions they ask each other [is] where they went to school. Discovering that both attended the same high school or university (even at different times) often brings an instant feeling of closeness. These ties help define who the employee is in the organization and provide a degree of status in a status-oriented society. They continue to affect the employee throughout his career. (Steers et al., 1989, p. 45)

An exception to this pattern is the occasional senior South Korean government official who takes a senior position in a major company after a long civil service career (analogous to a similar practice in Japan).

Given rapid recent industrial development, China is facing a shortage of managerial talent for its many enterprises, including foreign-owned ones ("Briefing: Asia's Skills Shortages," 2007). In Chinese SOEs, the Communist Party reviews key managerial appointments, often including political criteria in tandem with professional qualifications (Zhao & Zhou, 2004).

Throughout East Asia, there has been a tendency for strong personal loyalty of employees to employers (and vice versa) and hence less managerial turnover than in the West. For example, the Booz Allen Hamilton annual global survey of CEO turnover worldwide shows the lowest rates for the Asia Pacific region (compared with North America, Europe, and Japan).[5] Also, in 2007, that region accounted for just 16% of the global executive search market (executive recruitment firms), compared with 35% and 41%, respectively, for Europe and the United States (Association of Executive Search Consultants, http://www.aesc.org/article/pressrelease 2007111301/).

PAY

There is not much information on senior executive pay in East Asia, but a limited amount comes from human resource consultancies. For example, Towers Perrin produces CEO pay figures worldwide for a cross-section of firms with at least $500 million in sales. For 2005, average total CEO pay in Singapore was about the same as for Western Europe (about US$1 million). CEO pay in Hong Kong and South Korea was a bit lower (US$600–700,000), and in Taiwan and China (Shanghai) it was yet lower (around US$200–300,000) (Table 6.9).

Regarding senior-level pay in state-owned firms in China, a study (Chen, Guan, & Ke, 2008) noted that they generally draw from the same managerial candidate pool as non-SOEs. Researchers reported that the median annual cash income of the CEO or chairman in 83 red chip firms was approximately US$180,000 in 2005, plus an average US$140,000 in stock options. However, they noted that the executives rarely exercise vested stock options during their tenure with their firms. The 83 firms represented 52% of the total market capitalization of Mainland China's domestic stock market and 37% of the market capitalization of Hong Kong's Hang Seng stock index. The authors defined red chip firms as

Table 6.9   CEO Pay (Average, 2005)

Country	CEO Pay ($ million)
Singapore	$1.0
Hong Kong	0.7
South Korea	0.6
Taiwan	0.3
China (Shanghai)	0.2
Japan	0.5
United States	2.2
Canada	1.1
France, Britain, Germany, Italy	1.1–1.2

SOURCE: These Towers Perrin figures are for total pay (salary, variable pay if any, benefits, and perquisites) from a broad cross-section of companies with at least $500 million in sales. Numbers are approximate, based on a bar chart in "Total Worldwide Remuneration" (2006, p. 102).

mainland Chinese state-controlled companies incorporated outside China (e.g., in Hong Kong, Bermuda, and the Cayman Islands) that trade on the Hong Kong Stock Exchange. More than 90% of their shares are owned by the Chinese government.

BUSINESS AND MANAGEMENT EDUCATION

Except for a late start in China, higher education for business has been available in East Asia. South Korea got an early start in the 1950s when converting its former commercial colleges into schools of business that now strongly resemble U.S. university business schools.[6] Most universities in Hong Kong, Taiwan, and Singapore have schools or departments of management or business administration,[7] several with ties to Western institutions. For example, the Hong Kong University of Science and Technology has an MBA program run jointly with Northwestern University, in Illinois.

In Taiwan, academic programs in business disciplines are offered at National Sun Yat-Sen University (College of Management), National Taiwan University (its College of Management), and others.

Singapore providers were prominent in the 2007 *Financial Times* ratings of global MBA and executive education program. They included Nanyang (Technological University) Business School and the National University of Singapore, plus the Singapore-based programs of INSEAD (of France), ESSEC (France), the Helsinki School of Economics, and the University of Chicago. Singapore Management University was founded in 2000, a private school with several joint programs with Western schools.

Many East Asian university-age students study abroad, particularly in the United States, Japan, and Australia. In 2007–2008, for example, four of the largest six sources of enrollment in U.S. higher education were East Asian, including the PRC (81,127 students), South Korea (69,124), Japan (33,974), and Taiwan (29,001); another 8,286 came from Hong Kong (Open Doors, 2008). About one in five enrollees were in business study programs. It was once reported that about half the board chairmen in South Korea's 30 leading *chaebol* had studied for a time in the United States, and another one fourth studied in Japan (Mallaby, 1995).

China famously pioneered formal schooling for its civil servants in the 7th century AD,[8] an era when merchants had low status in the Confucian social hierarchy (below soldiers, civil servants, and peasants).[9] Today, business leaders have more prestige, and there is strong demand (and rising pay) for managerial talent. Over the years, foreign institutions have contributed educational support. In 1978, for example, the Chinese Enterprise Management Association began courses and seminars with support from Western corporations, universities, foundations, and other sources (e.g., European Union, World Bank, United Nations, and the foreign aid agencies of Japan, Germany, Canada, and the United States). The National Center for Industrial Science and Technology Management Development was started in 1980 at Dalian (northeast China). In 1984, several European business schools helped to establish the China–Europe Management Institute in Beijing, which has an executive MBA program administered by the European Fund for Management Development.[10] It later added a Shanghai campus. In 1994, the China–Europe International Business School started MBA and executive MBA programs administered by the European Fund for Management Development and Shanghai Jiaotong University. An MBA program at Beijing's Tsinghua University's School of Economics and Management has ties to U.S. Ivy League universities. More recently it was reported that 95 PRC universities were producing about 12,000 MBAs (Li, 2005). In addition, some foreign investors (e.g., Coca-Cola and Motorola) have internal management schools in China (Hagerty, 1997).

In academic circles, the Asia Academy of Management was founded in 1997 by local management scholars and publishes the *Asia Pacific Journal of Management*. Another group, the International Association for Chinese Management Research, emerged in 2004 with the involvement of Hong Kong University of Science and Technology and Peking University and publishes *Management and Organization Review*. Singapore's Nanyang Technological University publishes the *Chinese Business Enterprise Review*. Another regional interest group (since 1982) is the Asia-Pacific Researchers in Organization Studies, started originally in Australia (http://www.apros.org).

Management Practice

There are invariably differences in management practice and style in different organizations (big vs. small, state-owned vs. private, young vs. old, high-tech vs. low-tech, and whether allied or not with foreign firms). Other variations can result from CEO age, education, experience, and other factors. The discussion here focuses on general tendencies that apply broadly in private business. It draws from the opinions, perceptions, and research of scholars, managers, journalists, and others, both Eastern and Western but mainly Western. As China enterprise scholars Tsui, Bian, and Cheng (2006) noted, "Given the paradigm shaped by the common North American training of most scholarship on Chinese firms, we are not surprised that much of the current work . . . reflects the use of a Western lens" (p. 21).

PLANNING

Managerial planning is concerned with organization purposes and objectives and alternative ways to achieve them. As noted in previous chapters, the planning process can be formalized but can also be informal, especially in small firms. In general, the larger the company, the more formal its planning activity. Except for large SOEs in China and the South Korean *chaebol,* small and medium-size businesses are the norm in East Asia. In these, plans and planning are generally more intuitive and flexible than in the West. This is reflected in Bain & Company's 2007 global Management Tools and Trends survey, which reported that strategic planning was the most popular tool worldwide (from its list of 15 tools) but was less prevalent in the Asia-Pacific region than in North America, Europe, and Latin America (Rigby & Bilodeau, 2007a, 2007b; see also http://www.bain.com). Asia-Pacific also used less scenario and contingency planning, growth strategy tools, and mission and vision statements.

In describing Chinese enterprise in Hong Kong and Southeast Asia, Redding (1990) observed, "The Chinese businessman . . . denying the usefulness of formal planning, . . . prefers to absorb information and to use his intuition to process it" (p. 77). He noted, "The leader's intentions remain loosely formulated is a common observation in Chinese organizations. Equally common, and related, is the capacity for surprise leaps into unrelated ventures which speaks of a very open-ended view of an organization's mission" (p. 132).

Westwood (1997) noted the tendency among Overseas Chinese for business leaders to hoard information and be nonspecific about intentions, even to their own employees. (The Overseas Chinese, or *huaqiao,* are the 40 million or so China-born people and their descendants living abroad, mainly in Southeast Asia but also in the Americas and beyond.) Their personal plans "are . . . often loose . . . based on . . . intuitive judgment, grounded on . . . extensive experience and personal immersion in [the] business environment . . . rather than having been formulated systematically and objectively" (p. 469).

Informed opinion varies as to whether the flexible, intuitive, reactive planning style of the Overseas Chinese results from culture and other external factors or is normal in small family businesses anywhere. In general, small firms tend to be more flexible and reactive than large ones. Their objectives can also differ from those of large firms, often preferring stability, continuity, and preservation of family status and wealth rather than fast-paced growth or optimal earnings.

In China, the prevailing uncertainty about taxation, property rights, accounting and reporting practices, currency convertibility, trade policy, and government regulations forces more flexibility and more frequent revision of plans by local and foreign firms alike.

Nonetheless, formal planning is apparent in bigger enterprises in China (state-owned and large private firms). It is also apparent in medium and large high-tech contract manufacturers in Taiwan (e.g., Hon Hai, Acer,

HTC, Asustek, TSMC, Quanta) obliged to meet tight production, quality, and logistics commitments to Western and Japanese clients (e.g., Apple, Dell, Sony, Nokia) (Dean, 2007). Also, many of their founders, managers, and engineers were previously educated or employed in the West, where they were exposed to Western business practices, including more formal planning (Hempel & Chang, 2002).

Steers et al. (1989, p. 40) noted that most South Korean *chaebol* (e.g., Samsung, Hyundai) "have a planning group [and] . . . a central planning function that works closely with the group chairmen," which contributes to their extensive overseas business presence, including in the United States and Europe.

Throughout much of East Asia, the state has intruded more on corporate plans and planning than in the West. In Singapore, Taiwan, South Korea, and China, this has included subsidies, tax breaks, trade protectionism, preferential purchasing arrangements, and partial ownership stakes even in predominantly private businesses. Less-developed local capital markets make banks a major source of external funding. Most banks in the region are government owned. For South Korea, Moskowitz (1989) noted that the "power of the capital provider [mainly government banks] to determine policies and strategic direction of enterprises has been overwhelming, and the independent power of professional management in these decisions is extremely limited" (p. 72). That also applies to large PRC state-owned businesses, which are routinely favored and subsidized, including the "national champions" mentioned previously (see Table 6.8).

Private sector Chinese occasionally get inspiration for business strategy from ancient sages, as reflected in the following passage.

The Chinese Art of Management

Do the managers of China's factories need to read the works of Peter Drucker or Tom Peters or the other gurus of Western business? Of course not. They can bone up on China's own Classics. . . . It is Sun Tzu's "The Art of War" that offers most on market strategy: "launch an attack when it is least expected," "strong and weak can be reversed," "know yourself and your enemy."

Huo Xinyi and Yu Zaoyu are both deputy secretaries-general of the Society for the Study of China's Ancient Management Thinking. . . . Mr. Huo tells the tale of the king's horses and the computers of Liangxiang. There was once a commoner who raced three horses against three horses belonging to the king. The best was pitted against the best; the middling against the middling; and the slowest against the slowest. Each time, the king won because his horses were a little faster than the commoner's. Afterwards a clever person told the commoner that he should have raced his slowest horse against the king's fastest, his middling horse against the king's worst, and his best against the king's middling horse. In this way, he would have won two races out of the three. That is why the Liangxiang company sells its medium-range computer in the bottom-of-the-range international market.

SOURCE: "The Chinese Art of Management" (1991, p. 41). Used by permission.

CONTROL

The managerial function of control is about measuring and correcting performance. If results don't meet expectations, adjustments are made to actions or plans. In a free market economy, corporations and managers are broadly controlled by product and capital markets. Subpar performance can trigger a drop in share price or fall in credit rating that will spur change or bring a takeover try by outsiders. In East Asia, however, takeovers have been much less common than in the West (but are increasing). Stock markets are smaller, and fewer companies go public, making stock-financed buyouts less of an option.[11] In most stock exchange–listed firms, insiders (family members and sometimes the state) control a dominant block of stock (or votes). Boards of directors are dominated by insiders (owners, family members, and in SOEs, the state),[12] very reluctant to accept outsiders among their ranks, much less have them pass judgment on management. One source concludes that "many Asians find it hard to accept the idea of, say, an external auditor or an independent board director, since he might actually disagree with them" (Kluth, 2001, p. 3). Stockholder meetings are generally infrequent, short, and uneventful, and there is little tradition of shareholder activism. Family control (and sometimes government control) has priority over profits (to the dismay of independent minority shareholders).

China's stock markets (Shenzhen, Shanghai) have been more a venue for speculators than for prudent investors. This is due partly to unreliable financial information about companies and fuzzy and opaque accounting and reporting practices (see Ball, Robin, & Wu, 2001; "PRC Accounting Standards," 2006). One source notes, "It is said (with apparent sincerity) that some Chinese firms keep several sets of books—one for the government, one for company records, one for foreigners and one to report what is actually going on" ("Cultural Revolution," 2007, p. 63).[13]

When they need external capital, East Asian enterprises usually seek debt funding rather than equity. Whatever the source (private or government lenders), loans often are relationship driven rather than credit risk driven. In the 1990s, this contributed to a high volume of nonrecoverable loans, bringing a regional financial crisis (and economic slowdown) and eventual state bailout of lenders.

Private sector business in Hong Kong, Taiwan, and Singapore has a reputation for judicious cost control. For example, Redding (1990, p. 205) observed that small and medium-size Overseas Chinese businesses are "normally very sensitive to matters of cost and financial efficiency" and that money-mindedness and frugality are key competitive strengths. Attention to cash and cash management is also mentioned by longtime Hong Kong hotelier Robert Burns (Kan & KCTS/ Seattle, 1992):

Because [people] aren't speaking the King's . . . English [doesn't mean] they don't know what they're doing [about money]. They know better than you by about a factor of ten. They are five steps ahead, especially when it comes to banking, finance, money. I say that particularly the Cantonese are born counting. They know more about money and how to make it than anybody I've ever dealt with.

Long-standing Chinese aphorisms call attention to financial diligence. These include Fan Li's Sixteen Principles of Good Business (Table 6.10), written in the 5th century BC, especially Principles 7, 9, 11, and 13. These principles are reproduced today in Chinese wall hangings, calendars, and diaries, and they help to explain the reputation for tight cost control and cash management practices.

East Asian private family business has shown a tendency for hierarchical, centralized, informal control of human resources. In Overseas Chinese family-controlled business, Redding (1990) noted that personal supervision there is "more nebulous, less programmatic, more personalistic, and . . . likely to rely more on the sense of responsibility of key individuals" than in Western firms (p. 217). He noted that it is not common to allocate individual performance criteria or to assess performance on an individual basis objectively against any criteria (p. 220).

It is unusual in Confucian settings (and culturally inappropriate) to do formal face-to-face individual performance evaluations or to direct much personal criticism at subordinates. For South Korea, Chung and Lee (1989, p. 157) observed that "many . . . managers are . . . reluctant to evaluate their subordinates negatively" so as to preserve harmonious personal relationships. Among ethnic Chinese family firms in Singapore, Choy (1987, p. 139) noted reluctance to reprimand or to lay off underperforming employees. Jacob (2001) made a similar point:

There are cultural barriers that make standard [Western] procedures, such as career evaluations, difficult to pull off in the Asian context; . . . those employees doing well . . . hide their performance, preferring to share the credit even with lacklustre performers. . . . There is the pervasive issue of maintaining "face"—the overriding need not to embarrass people. Inevitably this tends to inhibit free-flowing evaluations and makes it hard to tell someone they are doing a poor job. (p. 14)

ORGANIZING

The managerial function of organizing is concerned with enterprise structure, distribution and flow of authority, and integration and coordination of roles, resources, tasks, and effort. Whether by choice or by chance, business structure can be simple or complex. In general, the larger the company, the more complex the structure (more hierarchy, departmentation,

Table 6.10   Sixteen Principles of Good Business, Expressed in Contrasting Active (yang) and Passive (yin) Forms

Yang	Yin
1. Be prudent and industrious in business.	*Laziness dooms all ventures.*
2. Keep expenditures to a minimum.	*Extravagance erodes capital.*
3. Be friendly in dealing with others.	*Impatience entails loss of business.*
4. Grasp the right moment to close a deal.	*Procrastination is the thief of golden opportunity.*
5. Be lucid in setting down the terms of the transactions.	*Ambiguity breeds contention.*
6. Be discreet in offering credit.	*Undue generosity erodes capital.*
7. Audit all accounts carefully.	*Laxity hampers flow of funds.*
8. Distinguish between the good and the bad.	*Indifference paralyzes the enterprise.*
9. Manage the inventory systematically.	*Perfunctory management creates a total mess.*
10. Be just and impartial to staff.	*Bias brings inefficiency.*
11. Exercise due caution in all payments and receipts.	*Negligence attracts costly errors.*
12. Examine the merchandise before acceptance.	*Indiscrimination causes unprofitability.*
13. Observe strictly the terms of payment.	*Late settlement damages trustworthiness.*
14. Be judicious and honest in money matters.	*Mismanagement promotes corruption.*
15. Be responsible in the face of adversity.	*Irresponsibility aggravates the problems.*
16. Be cool, calm, and confident.	*Recklessness hinders daily dealings.*

SOURCE: By Fan Li, under the pen name of T'ao Chu King, 5th century BC, from "The Management of Chinese Small-Business Enterprises in Malaysia," by Sin, 1987, *Asia Pacific Journal of Management,* *4*(3), 181–182. Reprinted by permission of Springer Science and Business Media.

task specialization, and cross-functional coordination). Small firms tend to be simply structured (flatter, less hierarchy, fewer levels; less differentiation and departmentation of roles and tasks) and commonly organized around business functions (e.g., production, marketing, finance). But when they grow and diversify, integration and coordination may improve by changing to a divisional structure (focused on product groups or geographic markets).

Firms can also be vertically integrated to a greater or lesser degree. If greater, they directly control a fuller range of resources, processes, and channels involved in the conception, design, production, and distribution of their product or service.

Prominent structural prototypes seen in East Asia include small private Chinese family business, vertically integrated conglomerates (Korean *chaebol,* Japanese *keiretsu*), and network structures (Taiwanese contract manufacturers).

Small Family Businesses

As noted previously, the traditional Overseas Chinese family business is small, patriarch led, and with simple structure. It can be flexibly and informally connected to suppliers and customers, bound personally by *guanxi* (reciprocal personal commitment, obligations, trust). Hamilton and Biggart (1988) described the pattern in regard to Taiwan:

> The family firm (jiazuqiye) and business group (jituanqiye) [are] the dominant organizational forms in industry, especially in the export sector. . . . [They show] conspicuous lack of vertical and horizontal integration, . . . absence of oligarchic concentrations . . . [and an] unwillingness or inability of . . . entrepreneurs to develop large organizations or concentrated industries [that] appears to have defied even the encouragement of government. [Therefore] . . . the small-to-medium size, single-unit firm is so much the rule in Taiwan that when a family business becomes successful, the pattern of investment is not to attempt vertical integration . . . but rather . . . to diversify by starting a series of unrelated firms that share neither books nor management. (p. S65)

Small size results partly from the limited range of interpersonal trust (seldom beyond kin) and reluctance of owner families to yield or dilute control. Another factor is underdeveloped equity markets, which constrain capital formation and inhibit mergers and acquisitions.

Conglomerates

By contrast, many Korean *chaebol* enterprises are huge and vertically integrated. As noted earlier, a *chaebol* (literally "financial house") is a group of independent firms; in a few cases just one large family ensures administrative control and guidance through direct stock holdings, cross-shareholdings, and holding pyramids between member firms. Where possible, operational synergies, complementarity, and coordination are sought between firms. The most visible *chaebol* groups are the Big Four (Samsung, LG, Hyundai, SK), but there are several dozen others (see http://wiki.galbijim.com/Chaebol#The_.22Big_Four.22).

The *chaebol* have many similarities with Japanese *keiretsu* business groups (discussed in the next chapter), including their large size, member cross-holding of stock, and much sharing of information and resources. There are also significant differences (Table 6.11).

Historically, the *chaebol* were nurtured by government protection and support after World War II. Previously, South Korean industry was very similar to peers in Taiwan and Hong Kong (small and medium-size businesses and business groups). The state support continued over the years but has been scaled back recently. By turn of the 21st century, high *chaebol*

Table 6.11   Differences Between South Korean *Chaebol* and Japanese *Keiretsu*[14]

Most *chaebol* are younger than most *keiretsu*, having emerged mainly after 1960, and are more closely tied to founders (founding families).
The *chaebol* have been more dominant in the South Korean economy than have the *keiretsu* in Japan.
The *chaebol* have had more government protection, loans, and other assistance (now diminishing) than have the *keiretsu*; they also have faced stronger recent government pressure to restructure and be more autonomously competitive.
The *chaebol* have fewer member firms but enter more diverse businesses than the *keiretsu*.
The *chaebol* show predominantly horizontal (unrelated product) diversification, whereas the *keiretsu* can be horizontal (e.g., *zaibatsu*-style *keiretsu*) or vertical (independent *keiretsu*).
In *chaebol*, fewer non–family member managers ascend to the top of the management hierarchy; the *chaebol* hire more from the outside (at every level), whereas *keiretsu* enterprise traditionally develops and promotes people from within.
Chaebol enterprises are more vertically integrated and less bound to particular networks of suppliers and subcontractors (Chen, 1995; Hattori, 1989).
The *chaebol*, unlike the major early *keiretsu*, have no commercial bank affiliates (South Korean banking laws restrict the nonbank ownership of banks).
The *chaebol* have higher debt/equity and debt/asset ratios than the *keiretsu*.

debt levels brought debt rescheduling, defaults, and government bailouts. In the process, government pressured the *chaebol* to reduce intragroup cross-shareholdings, spin off noncore businesses, reduce their debt ratios, and include more outside directors on their boards.

In private Chinese businesses, whether in Hong Kong, Taiwan, Singapore, Mainland China, or beyond, the large vertically integrated company is rare. Intuitively, that doesn't bode well for long-run competitiveness with Western, Japanese, and Korean rivals, who can gain and sustain advantages from the scale and breadth of their operations.

Network Organization

Many Chinese entrepreneurs, through extensive personal domestic, regional, and global business networks, are successfully partnering with other businesses, forming virtual extended enterprises that transcend size limitations.

One example is Hong Kong–based Yue Yen (the world's largest footwear firm), which has relational ties with thousands of suppliers and subcontractors throughout China, Southeast Asia, and beyond. It makes branded shoes for Nike, Adidas, New Balance, and others (Agtmael, 2007). Another example is Hon Hai, the largest of several Taiwan-based electronics contract manufacturers with extensive flexible production, supply chain, and distribution ties throughout East and Southeast Asia. Hon Hai makes a diverse mix products (e.g., cell phones, game players, monitors, cameras, personal organizers, and electronic parts and subassemblies) for Apple, Sony, Nintendo, Nokia, Dell, HP, and others (Dean, 2007).

Based on widespread personal contacts and constant exchange of information, these and similarly formed firms show ability to adapt to changing competitive conditions.

Some sources see this network structure as a new and unique structural form for which Chinese culture, with its personalism, cultural bonds, and reciprocal trust, is especially well suited. It is even suggested that such networks will replace traditional hierarchies and be the standard in global business. Schlevogt (2001, p. 556) concluded,

> We are entering the age of what can be termed "web capitalism," a concept that embraces the physical, social, and spiritual world. Asians in particular are renowned web masters. Their skill in weaving dense networks loaded with invisible capital accounts for much of their economic success. Undoubtedly, Westerners are well advised to learn from their techniques to master the challenges of the present and future in different fields of society.

Boisot and Child (1996) were similarly persuaded:

> The Chinese system of network capitalism works through the implicit and fluid dynamic of relationships. On the one hand, this is a process that

consumes much time and energy. On the other hand, it is suited to handling complexity and uncertainty. Networks offer greater capacities for generating and transmitting new information, and when they are sustained by trust-based relationships they offer a cushion against the possibility of failure that is a concomitant of uncertainty. (p. 625)

China is a system that in its transformation is giving rise to a distinctive institutional form—network capitalism. (p. 626)

By contrast, Chan (2000) sees no preordained permanence or superiority in the network systems of the Overseas Chinese and concludes that they "have developed their businesses within a very unique historical context, at a particular time and in a particular place where their skills are found to be appropriate. Many did not succeed, but the ones who did are much talked about in the world" (p. 326).

Continued interest in the subject (network theory) has generated discussion and debate about the conceptual parameters, strengths, and limitations of network structures (Kim, Oh, & Swaminathan, 2006; Uzzi, 1997; see also the July 2006 issue of the *Academy of Management Review*).

DIRECTING

If you do too many things you will make many errors; if you do few things you will make few errors; if you do nothing you will make no errors.

(Chinese proverb)

The managerial function of directing involves guiding and influencing colleagues, subordinates, and others. In cultural terms, given Confucian high power distance and high collectivism, managers expect subordinate compliance, cooperation, conformity, obedience, deference, and followership. There is much attraction to a benevolent patriarchal authoritarian leader; conversely, managers show paternalism toward subordinates (Westwood, 1997). Personalism and loyalty are key to ensuring individual performance, with the subordinates conditioned by culture to please the boss. Farh and Cheng (2000) note, "Personalistic leadership, which combines strong discipline and authority with fatherly benevolence and moral integrity couched in a personalistic atmosphere, has been found to be prevalent in overseas Chinese family businesses" (p. 84). For Taiwan, Javidan and Carl (2005) similarly noted the importance of the Confucian virtues of benevolence, propriety, trustworthiness, and human heartedness, with managers "expected to provide for and to protect the wellbeing of their employees" (p. 23). Accordingly, supervisory styles are more relationship oriented than task oriented.

The collectivism and egalitarianism in Confucian culture seem intuitively favorable to employee participation in decision making. However, other cultural traits work against it. These include high power distance, which inhibits voluntary and open communication; high uncertainty avoidance, which promotes resistance to change; and predominantly masculine value orientation, which is conducive to an authoritarian rather than a participative decision-making style. In prereform China, Communist Party lip service to worker participation brought false participation, with Walder (1984) noting that "patterns of worker participation in meetings on the shop floor appear to the worker not as an opportunity to influence decisions, but as part of the everyday reality of communication, command, and control, which they [the workers] view with a mixture of anxiety, indifference, and boredom" (p. 555).

In comparing the leadership styles of Hong Kong Chinese businesspeople with those of the Japanese, Fukuda (1988) noted a wider social hierarchy divide between managers and subordinates in Hong Kong than occurs in Japan. For Chinese business, Laaksonen (1988, p. 301) saw a wider influence gap between top and middle management levels than in similar-size Japanese and European firms and attributed it to the "traditional authoritarian and patriarchal Chinese culture" and to a Communist Party–controlled political system where important decisions come from higher-ups.

In regard to employee motivation, Herman Kahn (1979, p. 123) and former associates at the Hudson Institute called the East Asian Confucian ethic a key to explaining its rapid regional economic growth:

> We believe that . . . aspects of the Confucian ethic—the creation of dedicated, motivated, responsible, and educated individuals and the enhanced sense of commitment, organizational identity, and loyalty to various institutions—will result in all the neo-Confucian societies having at least potentially higher growth rates than other cultures.

In a similar vein, MacFarquhar (1980) concluded that "Confucian ideology [was] as important to the rise of the East Asian hypergrowth economies as [was] the conjunction of Protestantism and the rise of capitalism in the West" (p. 68). Hofstede and Bond (1988) viewed certain Confucian traits, but not all of them, as instrumental to regional economic development. They described a Confucian dynamic wherein the values of thrift, perseverance, and orderly structuring of human relationships contribute to economic success, for example, of many Overseas Chinese. Less relevant, in their view, is the valuing of tradition, personalism, and "protecting face."

Nevis (1983) discussed Chinese motivation from the viewpoint of Maslow's famous hierarchy-of-needs theory of motivation and saw reason to modify the hierarchy for Confucian settings. Maslow's (1954) original framework postulated five levels of human needs, two of them lower-order (physiological needs and safety and security) needs and the others, in ascending order, social needs (affiliation, belonging, and love), esteem needs (ego gratification), and self-actualization (personal psychological fulfillment) (Table 6.12). According to Maslow, lower-order needs must be largely met before higher-order ones have much motivational significance. The implication is that managerial styles and reward systems should be tailored to the need satisfaction profiles of the people involved.

Nevis's (1983) modified Chinese need hierarchy omits Maslow's esteem category altogether. In his view, belonging is the most basic Chinese need, followed in ascending order by physiological and safety and security needs, and then self-actualization, the latter derived from group accomplishment rather than individual accomplishment.

Table 6.12   Need Hierarchies: Western (Maslow) and Chinese (Nevis)

Maslow's Need Hierarchy (Maslow, 1954)	Nevis's Chinese Need Hierarchy (Nevis, 1983)
Self-actualization (defined in terms of individual development)	Self-actualization (in the service of society)
Self-esteem	Safety
Social (belonging)	Physiological
Safety	Belonging (social)
Physiological	

Chapter Summary

- Business and management trends in East Asia have captured global attention because of fast-paced economic development in its Four Tigers (Hong Kong, Singapore, Taiwan, and South Korea), transformational change in China, and corollary business opportunities and threats.

- The region's cultural heritage is predominantly Confucian, reflected in prevailing tendencies for groupism, acquiescence to hierarchy, deference to authority, and reverence for education; business depends on social bonds based on kinship, school, geographic, or other ties, nurtured and sustained through *guanxi* (reciprocal trust, favors, and obligations).

- The Four Tiger economies have been predominantly capitalist, with Hong Kong being the most free; South Korea, Taiwan, and Singapore have had a state-guided form of capitalism. China is a transitional mixed economy (incrementally becoming more free).

- Taiwan, Singapore, and South Korea have been dominant-party democracies; the Communist Party continues to control China.

- In the Chinese world, the family has long been the bedrock of social order, guided mainly by custom and tradition (Confucian social and ethical codes); Western-style civil liberties have gained belated interest and attention.

- The prototype private sector Confucian manager is a family patriarch leading a small or medium-size business. Nepotism and favoritism are common in staffing. CEO pay is lower than in the West (save for Singapore and Hong Kong, where it is high), but shortages of managerial talent are pushing pay higher.

- Chinese private sector business planning is generally informal, intuitive, adaptive, and opportunistic; except in Hong Kong, government intrudes considerably in private sector planning.

- Stock markets play a lesser role in corporate control than they do in the West; mergers and acquisitions are less common but increasing. Fewer companies go public, and corporate boards of directors have little independence. Problems with financial disclosure and accounting and reporting standards continue.

- In regard to organizing, the Chinese private sector seldom produces large integrated businesses. Some sources see Chinese network capitalism as an organizational prototype for the future worldwide. Where bigger private local companies appear in the region, the state usually is involved with support (e.g., in South Korean *chaebol* groups and some Chinese state-owned or state-supported "national champions").

- Leadership, communication, and motivation are much influenced by Confucian culture. High power distance and hierarchical social structure bring preference for older, benevolent, paternalistic authoritarian leaders. The need to belong is a strong motivational need. Personal bonds and trust are important for getting things done.

Terms and Concepts

chaebol
Confucius; Confucian culture
contract responsibility system
Four Tigers
guanxi
indicative planning
market socialism
network capitalism

network organization
Overseas Chinese
People's Republic of China (PRC)
Sichuan experiments
Sinitic culture
Special Economic Zones
state-guided capitalism
township/village enterprises

Study Questions

1. What is distinctive about the East Asian cultural, economic, and political environment?

2. Identify major tenets of Confucian culture and discuss ways in which they influence East Asian managers and management patterns and practices.

3. From the viewpoint of the management functions, discuss prevalent management patterns in the region.

Exercise 6.1

Guided by a theory of motivation such as Maslow's renowned hierarchy-of-needs (see Table 6.12), one could design a managerial compensation package (monetary and nonmonetary rewards) tailored to the personal wants, needs, values, and expectations of an individual. This would be influenced by individual background as well as expectations concerning personal capabilities, obstacles, effort, risk, and reward. Societal pressures and tax factors also come into play.

In individualistic cultures in free market economies (e.g., Canada, United Kingdom, United States, Australia), Maslow's "esteem" needs and "self-actualization" warrant attention, and there is comparison with what similar managers earn in comparable firms. Pay often includes performance bonuses in the form of cash, stock, or stock options. There might also be sign-on and retention bonuses and severance payouts (golden parachutes) for terminations caused by merger or acquisition. There can also be significant retirement benefits. Perquisites may also pertain (e.g., theater tickets, golf club memberships, flight time on the company jet). In some cases, though, just the prestige or the challenge of the job might be sufficient motivation.

By contrast, do you think an ideal managerial compensation package in a Confucian setting should look much different? Suppose that you (from a leading Western company) are contemplating such a plan for your new CEO (a local Chinese national) for your recently acquired assembly plant in Guangdong province, China.

What factors should influence your deliberation? Do you think that Nevis's Chinese need hierarchy (Table 6.12) is a more suitable guide (than Maslow's, or any other you know of) in structuring a reward package. Why or why not? Explain.

South Korea's *chaebol* business groups contributed much to its remarkable economic growth and development during the late 20th century. Some *chaebol* affiliates (e.g., within Samsung, LG, Hyundai and other groups) are now very visible abroad because of exports, foreign production, and ties with foreign firms. For some, nearly half of their shareholders are now non-Korean.

At home, Korea's guided-free-enterprise economic system (state-guided capitalism) along with close *chaebol* owner-family connections to government officials have brought favorable regulatory, financial, and other support and protection. Nowadays, however, traditional *chaebol* structure and practice are increasingly viewed as detrimental to economic progress. In that regard, a recent report by the Korea Fair Trade Commission (KFTC, 2008) noted that affiliates of *chaebols* through their "complex chain of cross-equity holding assumed a monopolistic or oligopolistic status or [have run] their business activities in more favorable position than small- and medium-sized companies in their market [and with] adverse effects that undermine fair competition" (p. 38). The commission is the nation's competition and consumer protection authority in matters of business collusion, abuse of market dominance, anticompetitive mergers and other interference with competition.

Some additional structural and operational concerns include disproportionate founding-family control (superproportional voting rights in relation to their diminished shareholdings, interlocking directorships between and among affiliates, high debt/equity ratios, intragroup debt guarantees, cross-subsidies and confusing accounting and reporting practices.

The KFTC has pressured for reduced cross-shareholding and lower-percent ownership when acquiring other (nonmember) local firms. It has also encouraged *chaebol* conversion to holding-company structures. In 2003, for instance, the LG Group launched a holding company (LG Corporation) for 34 of its 49 affiliates in a restructuring. The remaining 15 were mainly financial businesses or destined for spin-off from the group. The SK Group (nation's third-largest *chaebol*) was similarly restructured in 2007.

A holding company doesn't produce any goods or services itself but controls subsidiary companies through partial or complete ownership of their stock. The subsidiaries retain their corporate identities and management teams, but now have direct profit-and-loss accountability to the parent. Concurrently, it diminishes interlocking directorships and cross-shareholdings between affiliates.

Assignment: Investigate the extent to which one or more leading *chaebol* groups (or the several dozen or so altogether) have increased or diminished their presence in the South Korean economy during the past 10 years. Prominent groups include Samsung, LG, SK, Hanjin, Gumbo, Hanwa, Hyundai, Hyundai Motors, and Hyundai Heavy Industry. (Note: The Hyundai group was broken up into several groups in 2001.)

From a management point of view, what advantages and disadvantages derive from a holding company structure versus a traditional *chaebol* structure? Investigate and discuss.

If your non-Korean firm was contemplating a start-up, acquisition, or business alliance today in South Korea, to what extent might the *chaebol* system and its legacy influence your plan of action and prospects for success? Discuss.

Notes

1. According to Toynbee (1972) the six other major independent civilizations were the Sumero-Akkadian, Egyptiac, Aegean, Indus, Middle American, and Andean.

2. The term *Sinitic* (or *Sinic*) refers broadly to things Chinese or significantly influenced by Chinese civilization; Japan, too, has ancient Chinese roots but is discussed in the next chapter. Although Japanese, Korean, and Chinese cultures are all Confucian, each is distinctive; the Chinese script language characters (*hanzi*) are also used in Japanese and Korean language; however, the Koreans also use a phonetic alphabet (called *hangul,* introduced in the 15th century).

3. For Singapore, initially under Prime Minister Lee Kuan Yew (1959–1990) and then Goh Chok Tong. Even after 1990, Yew continued to exert influence behind the scenes as senior minister.

4. Two leading freedom rankings include the Heritage Foundation's annual global Index of Economic Freedom (http://www.heritage.org/Research/Features/Index/) and the annual Institute for Management Development *World Competitiveness Yearbook* (http://www02.imd.ch/wcc/).

5. Based on survey of 2,500 companies worldwide, published yearly in *strategy + business* magazine (Lucier, Wheeler, & Habbel, 2007).

6. Korean providers include Pusan National University (College of Business), Seoul National University (School of Management), Hongik University (School of Business Administration), University of Alsan (Department of Management), Hankuk University of Foreign Studies (College of Business and Economics), and Yonsei University (College of Business and Economics, Graduate School of Business Administration).

7. They include the University of Hong Kong (Department of Management Studies), Chinese University of Hong Kong (Faculty of Business Administration), Hong Kong University of Science and Technology (School of Business and Management), City University of Hong Kong (formerly Hong Kong Polytechnic) Department of Management, City Polytechnic of Hong Kong (Faculty of Business, Department of Business and Management), Hong Kong Baptist (School of Business, Department of Management), Lingnan College (Faculty of Business), Singapore's Nanyang Technological University (School of Accounting and Business), the National University of Singapore (School of Post-Graduate Management Studies), and Singapore Polytechnic (Department of Business Administration).

8. The schooling was at the Hanlin Academy, where entrants were admitted by competitive examination and the curriculum was based on the teachings and writings of Confucius and other Chinese sages.

9. In Western society, too, merchants long had lower social status than civil servants; there was not much postsecondary schooling for business in the United States until the emergence of larger corporations in the late 19th century.

10. Some participating European business schools include Bielefield University, Bocconi University, IESE, INSEAD, Université d'Aixe-Marseille, and London Business School.

11. In 2007, the numbers of companies listed on each major East Asian stock exchange (SE) were as follows: PRC (Shenzhen SE, 730 firms; Shanghai SE, 863 firms), with the Chinese government the dominant stockholder in most cases; Taiwan SE, 716 firms (2004); Singapore SE, 774 firms (2005); Korea SE, 1,787 firms; Hong Kong SE, 1,206 firms). By contrast, about 5,962 firms (including a few hundred foreign ones, some of them Chinese) were listed on the three leading U.S. stock exchanges in 2006 (NYSE, AME, Nasdaq). Information retrieved from the World Federation of Sock Exchanges (*Focus*, 2008, p. 43).

12. Many Chinese SOEs list a fraction of their shares on stock exchanges in both China and Hong Kong and sometimes abroad; the state also has minority equity holdings in a number of predominantly private Chinese firms.

13. Since 2007, the Chinese Ministry of Finance has required companies listed on the Shenzhen and Shanghai stock exchanges to adopt accounting and reporting guidelines consistent with established International Financial Reporting Standards. Progress has been slow.

14. For more detailed discussion of the *chaebol*, see Steers et al. (1989, pp. 46–48). Japan's pre–World War II *zaibatsu* conglomerates were controlled through holding companies that were dissolved after World War II. Their member firms then coalesced into *keiretsu* groups with cross-shareholdings.

References

Adler, N., Campbell, N., & Laurent, A. (1989). In search of appropriate methodology: From outside the People's Republic of China looking in. *Journal of International Business Studies, 20*(1), 61–74.

Agtmael, A. (2007). *The emerging markets century: How a new breed of world-class companies is overtaking the world.* New York: Free Press.

Aldrich, H., & Sakano, T. (1998). Unbroken ties: Comparing personal business networks crossnationally. In M. Fruin (Ed.), *Networks, markets, and the Pacific Rim: Studies in strategy* (pp. 32–52). Oxford, UK: Oxford University Press.

Area handbook for the People's Republic of China. (1972). Washington, DC: Government Printing Office.

Ball, R., Robin, A., & Wu, J. S. (2001). *Accounting standards in China. Beyond transition.* World Bank Group. Retrieved September 4, 2008, from http://www.worldbank.org/html/prddr/trans/octnovdec01/pgs19-20.htm

Boisot, M., & Child, J. (1996). From fiefs to clans and network capitalism: Explaining China's emerging economic order. *Administrative Science Quarterly, 41*(4), 600–628.

Briefing: Asia's skills shortages. (2007, August 18). *The Economist,* pp. 59–61.

Central Intelligence Agency. (2008). *The world factbook 2008.* Retrieved September 4, 2008, from https://www.cia.gov/library/publications/the-world-factbook

Chan, R. (2000). Overseas management style: Some reflections. In J. T. Li, A. Tsui, & E. Weldon (Eds.), *Management and organizations in Chinese context* (pp. 325–336). New York: St. Martin's Press.

Chen, M. (1995). *Asian management systems.* New York: Routledge.

Chen, Z., Guan, Y., & Ke, B. (2008). *Stock option compensation with Chinese characteristics: The case of Hong Kong–listed red chip firms.* Retrieved September 6, 2008, from http://ssrn.com/abstract=1249526

Child, J. (1994). *Management in China during the Age of Reform.* Cambridge, UK: Cambridge University Press.

The Chinese art of management. (1991, October 26). *The Economist,* p. 41.

Choe, S. (2000, October 1). Hyundai critics target management cliques. Associated Press wire.

Choy, C. (1987, May). History and managerial culture in Singapore. *Asia Pacific Journal of Management, 4*(3), 133–143.

Chung, K., & Lee, H. (Eds.). (1989). *Korean managerial dynamics.* New York: Praeger.

Cowley, A. (1991, November 16). Survey: Asia's emerging economies. *The Economist.*

Cultural revolution: Chinese accounting. (2007, January 13). *The Economist,* p. 63.

Dean, J. (2007, August 11–12). The forbidden city of Terry Gou. *Wall Street Journal,* p. 1.

The explorers map. (1998, February). Washington, DC: National Geographic Society, Historical Map.

Farh, J., & Cheng, B. (2000). A cultural analysis of paternalistic leadership in Chinese organizations. In A. Tsui, E. Weldon, & J. T. Li (Eds.), *Management and organizations in the Chinese context* (pp. 84–130). New York: Palgrave Macmillan.

Focus. (2008, August). No. 186. July 2008 statistics, p. 43. Retrieved September 4, 2008, from http://www.world-exchanges.org/WFE/showdoc.asp?document_id=4944&document=../publications/Focus808.pdf

The Fortune Global 500. (2007, July 23). *Fortune,* pp. 131–151.

Fruin, M. (Ed.). (1998). *Networks, markets, and the Pacific Rim: Studies in strategy.* Oxford, UK: Oxford University Press.

Fukuda, J. (1988). *Japanese management style transferred: The experience of East Asia.* London: Routledge.

Gomes, L. (1993, September 4). Chinese association members gather in San Jose. *San Jose Mercury News.*

Hagerty, B. (1997, April 10). Asian scramble. *Wall Street Journal,* p. R12.

Hall, E. (1959). *How cultures collide.* Garden City, NY: Doubleday.

Hall, E. (1976, July). How cultures collide. *Psychology Today, 10*(2), 66–74.

Hamilton, G., & Biggart, N. (1988). Market, culture, and authority: Comparative analysis of management and organization in the Far East. *Asian Journal of Sociology, 94*(Supplement), S52–S94.

Hattori, T. (1989). Japanese *zaibatsu* and Korean *chaebol.* In K. Chung & H. Lee (Eds.), *Korean managerial dynamics* (pp. 79–95). New York: Praeger.

Hayden, D. A. (1991, July 6). The art of managing Chinese ventures. *Asian Wall Street Journal Weekly.*

Hempel, P., & Chang, C. (2002). Reconciling traditional Chinese management with high-tech Taiwan. *Human Resource Management Journal, 12*(1), 77–95.

Henley, J., & Nyaw, M. (1986, November). Introducing market forces into managerial decision-making in Chinese industrial enterprises. *Journal of Management Studies, 23*(6), 635–656.

History of China. (1991, July). Washington, DC: National Geographic Society, Historical Map.

Hofstede, G. (1980). *Culture's consequences: International differences in work-related values.* Beverly Hills, CA: Sage.

Hofstede, G., & Bond, M. (1988). The Confucius connection: From cultural roots to economic growth. *Organizational Dynamics, 16*(4), 5–21.

Hsu, P. (1987, May). Patterns of work goal importance: A comparison of Singapore and Taiwanese managers. *Asia Pacific Journal of Management, 4*(3), 152–156.

Jacob, R. (2001, May 24). Corporate stars that squander their talent: Asian management. *Financial Times,* p. 14.

Javidan, M., & Carl, D. E. (2005, January). Leadership across cultures: A study of Canadian and Taiwanese executives. *Management International Review, 45*(1), 23–44.

Kahn, H. (1979). *World economic development: 1979 and beyond.* Boulder, CO: Westview.

Kan, Y., & KCTS/Seattle (Producers). (1992). *Doing business in Hong Kong,* [Videotape].

Kim, T., Oh, H., & Swaminathan, A. (2006). Framing interorganizational network change: A network inertia perspective. *Academy of Management Review, 31*(3), 704–720.

Kluth, A. (2001, April 7). In praise of rules. Asian business survey. *The Economist,* pp. 3–4.

Korea Fair Trade Commission. (2008). *2008 Annual Report, Republic of Korea.* Retrieved September 26, 2008, from http://www.ftc.go.kr/eng/

Kristof, N. (1991, August 18). Chinese relations. *New York Times Magazine,* p. 8.

Kyi, K. M. (1988, May). APMJ and comparative management in Asia. *Asia Pacific Journal of Management, 5*(3), 216–218.

Laaksonen, O. (1988). *Management in China: During and after Mao in enterprises, government and party.* Berlin: de Gruyter.

Leys, S. (1997). *The analects of Confucius: Translation and notes.* New York: W. W. Norton.

Li, C. (2005, September 20). Bridging China's MBA gap. *Wall Street Journal,* p. A15.

Lin, Y. (1966). *My country and my people.* Taipei, Taiwan: Mei Ya. (Original work published 1935)

Lucier, C., Wheeler, S., & Habbel, R. (2007, Summer). The era of the inclusive leader. *strategy+business, 47.* Retrieved August 22, 2008, from http://www.strategy-business.com/press/article/07205?pg=0

MacFarquhar, R. (1980, February 9). The post-Confucian challenge. *The Economist,* pp. 67–72.

Mallaby, S. (1995, June 3). South Korea: Quick, quick, quick. *The Economist,* p. S3.

Maruyama, M. (1984). Alternative concepts of management: Insights from Asia and Africa. *Asia Pacific Journal of Management, 1*(2), 100–111.

Maslow, A. (1954). *Motivation and personality.* New York: Harper & Row.

Miljus, R., & Moore, W. (1990, Winter). Economic reform and workplace conflict resolution in China. *Columbia Journal of World Business, 25*(4), 49–58.

Moskowitz, K. (1989). Ownership and management of Korean firms. In K. H. Chung & H. C. Lee (Eds.). *Korean managerial dynamics* (pp. 65–77). New York: Praeger.

Needham, J. (1954). *Science and civilization in China.* Cambridge, UK: Cambridge University Press.

Nevis, E. (1983, Spring). Cultural assumptions and productivity: The United States and China. *Sloan Management Review, 24*(3), 17–29.

Nisbett, R., Choi, I., Peng, K., & Norenzayan, A. (2001, April). Culture and systems of thought: Holistic versus analytic cognition. *Psychological Review, 108*(2), 291–310.

Open doors. (2008). International Institute of Education. Retrieved November 22, 2008, from http://opendoors.iienetwork.org/?p=131534

Pao-an, L. (1991). The social sources of capital investment in Taiwan's industrialization. In G. Hamilton (Ed.), *Business networks and economic development in East and Southeast Asia* (pp. 94–113). Hong Kong: Centre of Asian Studies.

PRC accounting standards convergence commentary: "Best or worst of times?" (2006, February 16). PricewaterhouseCoopers. Retrieved September 4, 2008, from http://www.pwc.com/extweb/ncpressrelease.nsf/docid/E7E3C547A9E9 F8E985257117005B62CB

Redding, S. G. (1990). *The spirit of Chinese capitalism.* Berlin: Walter de Gruyter.

Rigby, D., & Bilodeau, B. (2007a). Bain's global 2007 management tools and trends survey. *Strategy & Leadership, 35*(5), 9–16.

Rigby, D., & Bilodeau, B. (2007b). *Management tools and trends 2007.* Bain & Company. http://www.bain.com/management_tools/Management_Tools_and_Trends_ 2007.pdf

Sachs, S. (2001, July 22). Fujian, U.S.A.: A special report. Within Chinatown, a slice of another China. *New York Times,* p. 1.

Schlevogt, K. (2001). Asia-Pacific Web-mastery. *Asia Pacific Journal of Management, 18*(4), 556–560.

Schlevogt, K. (2002). *The art of Chinese management: Theory, evidence and applications.* New York: Oxford University Press.

Sin, G. (1987). The management of Chinese small-business enterprises in Malaysia. *Asia Pacific Journal of Management, 4*(3), 182–183.

Steers, R., Shin, Y., & Ungson, G. (1989). *The chaebol, Korea's new industrial might.* New York: Harper & Row.

The struggle of the champions: China's champions; China's big companies. (2005, January 8). *The Economist,* p. 58.

A survey of China. (2006, March 25). *The Economist,* p. 12.

Total worldwide remuneration 2005–2006. (2006, January 21). *The Economist,* p. 102.

Toynbee, A. (1972). *A study of history.* New York: Weathervane.

Tsui, A., Bian, Y., & Cheng, L. (Eds.). (2006). *China's domestic private firms: Multidisciplinary perspectives on management and performance.* Armonk, NY: M. E. Sharpe.

Tsui, A., Farh, J., & Xin, K. (2000). Guanxi in the Chinese context. In J. Li, A. Tsui, & E. Weldon (Eds.), *Management and organizations in the Chinese context* (pp. 224–242). New York: Macmillan.

Tu, I. (1991). Family enterprises in Taiwan. In G. Hamilton (Ed.), *Business networks and economic development in East and Southeast Asia* (pp. 122–123). Hong Kong: Centre of Asian Studies.

Tzu, S. (1983). *The art of war* (J. Clavell, Ed.). New York: Dell.

Uzzi, B. (1997, March). Social structure and competition in interfirm networks: The paradox of embeddedness. *Administrative Science Quarterly, 42*(1), 37–69.

Walder, A. (1984). Worker participation or ritual of power? Form and substance in the Chinese experience. In B. Wilpert & A. Sorge (Eds.), *International perspectives on organizational democracy* (pp. 541–558). London: Wiley.

Westwood, R. (1997). Harmony and patriarchy: The cultural basis for "paternalistic headship" among the overseas Chinese. *Organization Studies, 18*(3), 445–480.

Zhao, W., & Zhou, X. (2004, March–April). Chinese organizations in transition: Changing promotion patterns in the reform era. *Organization Science, 15*(2), 186–199.

Japanese Management 7
Tradition and Transition

> *Even a very cursory examination reveals that not only does Japan's managerial system differ from its counterparts in other highly industrialized nations, but in many of its aspects . . . [it] runs counter to what are considered sound principles of management in the Western world, particularly in the United States.*
>
> —Michael Yoshino (1968, p. ix)

Japan's high-growth era has passed, but there is sound reason to study its management patterns and practices. It remains the world's second largest economy,[1] and its premier companies compete well worldwide. Among them were 64 listed on the 2008 Fortune Global 500 (ranking by sales) and 39 on the FT Global 500 (2008, by market capitalization).[2] These and others influence lives and livelihoods (directly and indirectly, current and future) of many employees, partners, suppliers, creditors, investors, customers, rivals, regulators, and others throughout the world. All have much to gain from better understanding of one another's society and management patterns.

When riding high (before 1990), Japan's industrial policy and management practices were seen as the wave of the future. Today Japan's future rides on societal and managerial change.

Chapter Objectives

- To describe broadly the Japanese macroenvironment
- To note patterns in the personal backgrounds and career paths of CEOs
- To profile prevalent Japanese management and human resource practices
- To point out unique strengths, limitations, pressures, and problems of contemporary Japanese management
- To note social, economic, political, and other changes that are contributing to managerial change

The Japanese Macroenvironment

> In the garden outside my home in Japan, I grow the most appealing mix of
> plants and flowers I can—that is, given the kind of soil I have, the exposure,
> the light, the extremes of temperature. I do what the environment allows
> and encourages. . . . No green-thumbed expert has yet tried to convince me
> to lay out a bed for flora indigenous to desert, arctic tundra, or tropical rain
> forest. . . . They would not grow in Tokyo, and no one would expect them
> to. (Ohmae, 1989, p. 136)

Societal circumstance shapes management patterns and practices
in both obvious and subtle ways. This is certainly so for Japan, where
outsiders find an instinctively different culture, a unique government-
guided free enterprise economy, and many globally competitive firms.
See Figure 7.1 for a map of Japan.

CULTURAL TENDENCIES

Japanese culture draws from early Confucian roots (from China),
including a tendency for groupism, hierarchy, order, conformity, deference
to authority, emphasis on harmony, and reverence for education.

Group consciousness permeates all Japanese organizations (e.g.,
schools, businesses, government agencies). Japanese workers are more
inclined than Westerners to identify with their employer (e.g., to be a
"Mitsubishi man") than with their vocation (e.g., manager, mechanic,
engineer). Japanese journalist Nakazawa (1994) observed, "Perhaps com-
pany-hunting rather than job hunting most accurately describes the situ-
ation in Japan. What matters is not the job as such but the company for
which one works" (p. 21). For male employees in large companies, the
bond is usually career long. Groupism is also seen in the *keiretsu* business
networks and alliances.

There is an acute awareness of rank and hierarchy between organizations regardless of endeavor (e.g., universities, newspapers, sports teams,
corporations). In higher education, for instance, Tokyo and Kyoto universities are on top. In business, big companies have more status than small
ones, as H. Nakamura (1990) noted, "In Japanese society the thinking is
deep-rooted that large enterprises are excellent companies but that medium-
and small-size companies are inferior" (p. 11).

The sense of hierarchy in the workplace is reflected in surname suffixes
for addressing other employees (the *san-zuke* system). For instance,
Mr. Yamato (a mid-level manager) is addressed by his colleagues as
Yamato-*san;* he addresses his subordinate Mr. Koike as Koike-*kun;* he

Figure 7.1   Map of Japan

Demography of Japan

Population 127 million (2008, est.), not growing
High population density
High ethnic, racial, and cultural homogeneity
World's highest (and rising) median age
Highest (and rising) proportion of population over age 65

addresses his own boss by adding a job title (his department chief, Mr. Suzuki, is Suzuki-*bucho*) (Otsubo, 1986). At home, at school, and at work, younger people defer to higher-ups. Executives carefully scan one another's business cards for reference to title and rank.

Despite hierarchies, Japan has an egalitarian distribution of wealth and income (a pattern similar to Sweden and Norway). In 2003, for example, the ratio of average CEO pay to average worker pay was only 10.5 to 1, the lowest in the advanced industrial economies (Economic Policy Institute information cited in Burton & Weller, 2005).

Strong social pressure to conform, an intense desire to belong, and employer paternalism contribute to a view of one's employer as one's community (Abegglen, 2006) and source of self-identity (Inagami & Whittaker, 2005).

Japanese people are self-conscious about how they are seen by others and place high importance on personal honor and saving face. Social anthropologist Ruth Benedict (1946, pp. 222–224) observed that Japanese behavior was much shaped by avoidance of shame, whereas Westerners try to avoid guilt.

Japanese culture emphasizes harmony, compromise, and conciliation. Japanese people prefer to avoid confrontation when resolving disputes, and lawsuits are a face-losing course of action. In 2006, Japan had fewer lawyers per capita than any other developed nation. The following quote, which appeared in the first issue of *Fortune* magazine, reflects cultural attention to harmony:

> There are almost 50,000 passenger cars in Japan, of which 94% are American made. . . . Collisions are amicably settled. First there is much ceremony in the street. Then the driver of the larger car takes the blame, sends the driver of the smaller car apologies, flowers, fruit, money. ("Japan Meets the Auto," 1930)

Labor relations are harmonious. Unions (private sector) are organized by company rather than by industry, and they are seldom confrontational (at least since the 1950s).[3] Workers air their complaints and protests passively by picketing during lunch or after work hours or displaying symbolic armbands, hoping to embarrass (rather than cripple) the employer into concessions. Proportionately less time is lost to labor disputes than in other advanced industrial countries. (See Figure 2.1 in Chapter 2.)

The Japanese revere education, and teachers are highly respected and well paid. Parents, especially mothers, exhort children to excel academically so as to gain admission to high-ranked schools at each level of instruction. School days and school years are long (primary school students attend 225 days per year, compared with 180 days in the United States).

Consultant and entrepreneur Kenichi Ohmae (1982) sees Japan's educational system as instrumental in developing a strong work ethic and fostering cooperation:

> Japanese children . . . are taught to behave in ways that advance the public good, taught to harmonize with others, and taught to work lest they starve. Education begins so early, and these implicit values implanted so pervasively, that it is easy to miss the point that the work ethic is the direct result of education. (pp. 230–231)

Apart from their regular school day, many students enroll after hours in private tutorial schools (*gakushu juku*) to prepare for school entrance exams that shape their educational and occupational futures. Eventual admittance to a high-ranking university is key to career opportunities with a premier employer (a well-known large company or government agency). In corporate hiring, the applicant's university is usually more important than is academic performance or field of study.

These and other sociocultural tendencies are indicated in Table 7.1.

Although Japanese culture draws from early Chinese influence, it differs. For example, on Hofstede's cultural dimensions, there is a medium level of

Table 7.1   Prevalent Japanese Sociocultural Patterns and Tendencies

Predominantly Confucian sociocultural heritage.
Zen Buddhism and Shintoism are the main spiritual influences.[1]
Deference to authority, a strong urge to belong, and group loyalty and commitment permeate social, political, and economic institutions (e.g., schools, employers, communities, regions, government agencies, business groups).
Reverence for learning.
Strong work ethic.
Predominantly high-context culture, inclined toward tact and subtlety rather than toward directness in interpersonal communication; importance of interpersonal trust.
Flexible attitude toward time (but punctuality is valued in business dealings and appointments).
Sense of separateness from other cultures; distrust of outsiders.
Propensity for introspection and humility.

(Continued)

Table 7.1 (Continued)

Family and kinship ties are very important.

Importance of preserving honor and saving face; avoidance of shame.

Patience.

Perseverance.

Emphasis on harmony (*wa*) in human relations; in resolving disputes, a preference for conciliation and compromise rather than conflict and confrontation.

Eagerness to learn from and improve on successful ideas and practices of others and to adapt them to Japanese circumstance.

On Hofstede's cultural dimensions:
- Medium power distance (lower than in other Confucian settings but higher than in most Western ones)
- Medium collectivism (a group-oriented culture, but less so than the Chinese)
- High masculinity (aggressiveness and competitiveness are valued; women have long had subordinate social and occupational status)
- High uncertainty avoidance (preference for order, stability, continuity, risk aversion)
- Long-term time orientation

collectivism (compared with the higher collectivism of the Chinese). There is a higher masculine value orientation (i.e., more assertive, success driven, competitive) and higher uncertainty avoidance (preference for stability and continuity; less comfort with risk and change). Japanese are less likely than Westerners to change employers, a trait reinforced by the tendency of large companies to hire mostly at entry level and promote from within. A tradition of seniority-based pay lessens the incentive to leave an employer, lest one need to start all over again.

High risk aversion is reflected in high personal savings rates, early retirement age (historically around age 55–60 in most large companies but rising), limited public pension benefits, and underfunded corporate pensions. Moreover, long life expectancy and small family size contribute to financial anxiety about old age. Also, interest payments earned from personal savings are excluded from income tax.

Risk aversion in business was seen in the slowness to invest very heavily very early in the United States and Europe. Between 1950 and 1980, when U.S. and European firms spread aggressively onto one another's turf, Japanese investment went mainly to less developed countries. Only after 1980 did it move aggressively into the United States and Europe, spurred by a rising currency (the yen) that was slowing exports while making foreign assets more affordable. There was also threat of U.S. and European import restrictions.

The Japanese show high on Hofstede's masculine value dimension, reflected in the workaholism of its "salary men" and the presence of few women in upper management. Traditional career-long employment has been mainly for full-time male employees in large companies.

Figure 7.2 shows Linowes's synthesis of additional contrasts between Japanese and U.S. culture, reflecting the Japanese penchant for patience, harmony, and hierarchy and the U.S. preference for action, freedom, and equality.

THE ECONOMY

Japanese economic and industrial modernization gained momentum in the late 1800s after a long period of self-imposed isolation from the outside world. In a few decades, Japan became the world's first non-Western advanced industrial economy. Japan has relied extensively on a guided free enterprise economic system (coordinated market economy) with the following features:

- Significant government support for particular companies and industries judged to be vital for the future

- Pattern of alliance capitalism reflected in the *keiretsu* business groups and close ties between big business and government

- Job security for full-time male employees in large businesses (cost borne by customers through higher prices)

- Constraints on interest rates (burden on savers) that lowered the cost of debt capital, mainly from government (or government-backed) loans to corporations

Government Guidance[5]

Post–World War II indicative planning[6] by Japan's Ministry of International Trade and Industry (MITI; now the Ministry of Economy, Trade and Industry [METI] since 2001) brought substantial government encouragement and support for companies in line with the prevailing national economic vision. State assistance included trade protectionism, research and development subsidies, preferential purchasing, preferential lending, and information gathering. There has been occasional government support for declining industries (e.g., steel, shipbuilding) to ease transition to new fields of endeavor.

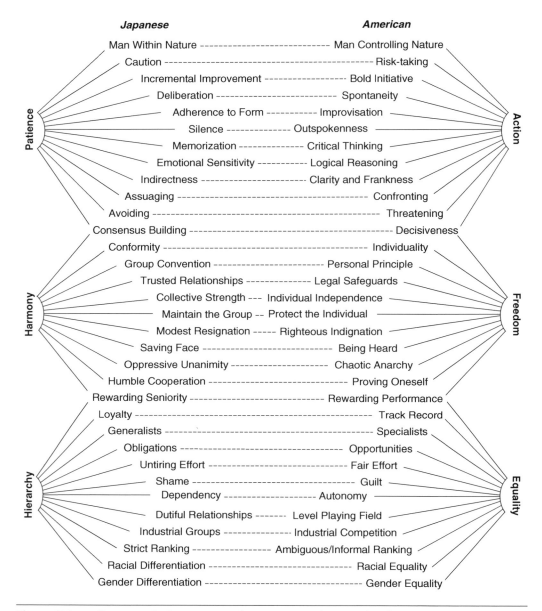

Figure 7.2   Contrasts in Japanese and American Values and Behavior

SOURCE: From R. Linowes, "The Japanese Manager's Traumatic Entry Into the United States: Understanding the American–Japanese Cultural Divide" (1993), *Academy of Management Executive,* 7(4), 24. Reprinted by permission.

Outsiders occasionally debate whether Japan's rapid post–World War II economic growth occurred because of or in spite of government guidance. For instance, early advances in microelectronics were attributed to the Very Large Scale Integration Program (1970s) in support of semiconductor research.[7] However, other efforts were less productive, such as the Fifth Generation mainframe computer project (advanced computer hardware) and backing for biotech, aerospace (commercial airliners, jet engines), computer software, engineering workstations, and advanced microprocessors (Zinsmeister, 1993). The corollary import protection also reduced choice and raised prices for consumers.

In effect, Japan gave rise a dual industrial system, some of it modern and efficient, able to compete well globally (e.g., Sony, Toyota, Canon) and the rest mainly local, expensive, and inefficient. The world hears much about the former and less about the latter. For example, Japan's food processing sector was reported to be 39% as productive as U.S. rivals (Postrel, 2004, p. C2). Its service sector (e.g., finance, transportation, communication) has been inefficient by world standards; so has agriculture (Bremner & Glasgall, 1997; "A Survey of Business in Japan," 1999). The outstanding successes have been in sectors where competition inside Japan was strongest (e.g., autos, consumer electronics) (see Kono, 1984; Ohmae, 1981; Porter, 1990).

These and other features of the Japanese economy are highlighted in Table 7.2.

Table 7.2   The Japanese Economy

Rapid economic growth after World War II (7% per year, on average, between 1951 and 1991); slow growth and stagnation after 1990.
A predominantly market-guided economy but with selective government guidance and assistance for targeted companies and industries; government planning has been indicative (suggestive) rather than directive; its protagonists have included the Finance Ministry (economic policy), Bank of Japan (credit and monetary policy), and Economic Planning Agency (financial forecasting); beneficiaries were firms in alignment with MITI economic vision (e.g., microelectronics); support has included loans, grants, subsidies, tax concessions, trade protectionism, temporary cartels, preferential regulation, information gathering, advice, consultation, exhortation, and occasional support for declining firms to ease the transition to new areas of endeavor.
Intense competition at home in industries that became the most successful in global markets (automobiles, consumer electronics, machine tools).
A producer-biased economy; less favorable to consumers (less choice; high prices), savers (low interest rates), homeowners (expensive housing), and small manufacturers.
For long time, a bank-dominated financial system, much of it government backed; belated development of equity markets; recent reform and consolidation of the banking system and lessening of government involvement.

(Continued)

Table 7.2 (Continued)

High personal savings rates, much of it on deposit with the government's Postal Savings Bank (now being privatized).
Notable cross-ownership of stock between companies, especially those within *keiretsu* business groups (now diminishing).
Inefficient (fragmented, highly regulated) agricultural and service sectors (e.g., telecom, retail distribution, financial services).
High personal income offset by low purchasing power (high-priced food, housing, and consumer goods).
Egalitarian distribution of wealth and income.
Low unemployment; much redundant employment, a burden borne mainly by large employers disinclined to lay off workers (with the cost passed on to consumers).
In recent times, growing number and proportion of part-time and contract workers.
Gradual transition to higher-wage, knowledge-intensive industries; some firms have moved some labor-intensive activity to lower-wage locations (Southeast Asia, China, Mexico).
Government employment, spending, and tax revenues were low in relation to gross domestic product between 1945 and the mid-1990s. Budget deficits were smaller (with occasional surpluses); since then, government spending has increased to stimulate the economy; government debt in proportion to gross domestic product recently highest among the advanced industrial countries.
A tradition of alliance capitalism, reflected in business enterprise networks (*keiretsu*) and cooperative relations between government and big business.
Many very small businesses.
Proportionately less inward and outward foreign direct investment than in other advanced industrial countries; also lower imports (in proportion to gross domestic product).

Alliance Capitalism

One long-standing feature of the Japanese economy has been its relational business alliances or networks known as *keiretsu*. These commonly include dozens (sometimes hundreds) of affiliated firms.

Imai (1990) described the *keiretsu* as "a family of independent companies free to conduct their business as they think best, yet bonded together by their collective ability to assist one another" (p. 17). Each group network involves "a [continuous] web of relationships ranging from tight to loose among companies working together..., a configuration...less tight than...an integrated corporation but tighter than...autonomous companies in a textbook free-market economy." The interrelationships include preferential purchasing (sourcing), cross-ownership of stock, and sharing of ideas, information, personnel, directorships, contacts, contracts, and capital.

Imai distinguished between *zaibatsu*-type and independent *keiretsu*, the former being descendants of large diversified pre–World War II *zaibatsu* groups, some dating back to the 19th century. Their holding company legal structures were banned by American occupation authorities after World War II, but remnant firms regrouped into *keiretsu* (the *zaibatsu*-type *keiretsu* are also called horizontal *keiretsu*).

By contrast, independent *keiretsu* (also called vertical *keiretsu*) are oriented around a large manufacturing or service company, with members bound by hierarchical buyer–supplier relationships.

Imai (1990, p. 18) identified five subtypes of vertical *keiretsu:*

• Groups containing companies in various fields separate from the parent organization that have grown into major, semiautonomous corporations and have put together their own networks of diverse affiliates and subsidiaries (e.g., Hitachi)

• Groups formed from a parent company, some of whose operating divisions have been set up as separate companies and have subsequently expanded within the same product area as the parent, acquiring subsidiaries and establishing networks of affiliated distributors and retailers (e.g., Matsushita)

• Groups in which the parent company has organized the subcontractors involved in the manufacturing process into a vertical, multilayered structure (e.g., Toyota)

• Groups led by companies that have granted independence to their regional manufacturing subsidiaries and expanded in new fields by spinning off satellite companies and fostering diverse affiliates (e.g., NEC)

• Groups of related firms united through the strong leadership of the parent company's founder or owner (e.g., the real estate and leisure companies held by Seibu Railway)

Scher (1997) more specifically applied the term *keiretsu* to groups of vertically affiliated companies (Imai's independent *keiretsu*) and *kigyo shudan* to the reconstituted *zaibatsu*. (See Figure 7.3 for his comparative configuration of both types.)

Prominent *kigyo shudan* (horizontal *keiretsu*) include the so-called Big Six, three of them centered around large banks (Fuji, Sanwa, and Dai-Ichi Kangyo banks) and three others more diversified (Mitsui,

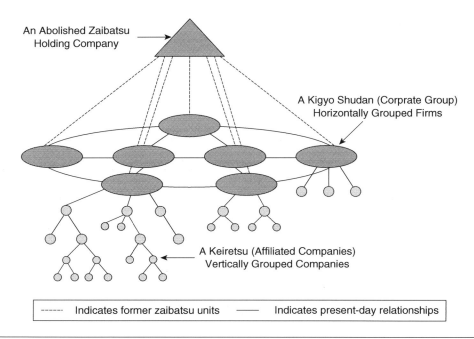

An Abolished Zaibatsu
Holding Company

A Kigyo Shudan (Corprate Group)
Horizontally Grouped Firms

A Keiretsu (Affiliated Companies)
Vertically Grouped Companies

------ Indicates former zaibatsu units   ——— Indicates present-day relationships

Figure 7.3   *Kigyo Shudan–Keiretsu* Power Relationships: A Three-Dimensional View

SOURCE: From M. J. Scher, *Japanese Interfirm Networks and Their Main Banks* (1997), p. 37, Figure 3.2. Reproduced by permission from Palgrave Macmillan.

Mitsubishi, and Sumitomo groups), which have large bank and trading company affiliates. In 2006, the Mitsui group had 30 companies in its core and several hundred others (at home and abroad) linked through supply, distribution, and other ties. These in turn had links with thousands of smaller subsidiaries, affiliated subcontractors, and others. Intragroup ties can involve varying degrees of coordination, consensus seeking, and cooperation between members, although some also compete with other members. Traditionally, Mitsubishi group activities have been coordinated by three core firms: Mitsubishi Bank, Mitsubishi Corporation (a general trading company), and Mitsubishi Heavy Industries. Mitsubishi's *kinyo-kai* (policymaking body for the group at large, also called the Friday Club) includes the presidents and chairs of 30 core companies. These managers meet informally for lunch on the second Friday of every month (Mitsubishi Web site, http://www.mitsubishi.com/e/group/about.html).

POLITICAL SYSTEM

Japan has a pluralistic democracy but one long dominated by one political party, the Liberal Democratic Party (LDP, formed in 1955). For all but brief interludes, the LDP has had a majority (or led a majority coalition) in the Japanese Diet (bicameral parliament) and thus been empowered to name the prime minister. The political powers of the prime minister and parliament have been weaker than in most countries, and the central government technocracy (professional administrative bureaucracy) has been stronger. "Government bureaucrat" is not a pejorative in Japan, and top students often aspire to civil service careers. Much national legislation is drafted by ministry technocrats rather than by legislators.[8]

Big business has been a longtime supporter of the LDP and has had considerable voice in economic policy deliberation councils.[9] These and other broad features of the Japanese government and political system are indicated in Table 7.3.

Table 7.3   Japanese Government and Politics

Pluralistic democracy; bicameral parliament (Diet) including an upper chamber (House of Councillors) and lower chamber (House of Representatives); the Diet chooses the head of state (prime minister).

Powers of the prime minister and parliament have been weaker than in other advanced industrial countries and the power of the central government bureaucracy (ministry technocrats) stronger.

Competent and influential civil service technocracy.

The LDP has dominated the Diet since 1955 (either alone or in coalition with other parties).

Elected legislators have had less influence over law and public policy than have senior civil servants.

Collaborative relationship between big business, key government ministries, and the LDP.

Big business participates on government policy committees and exerts political influence through its interindustry chambers and trade associations.

Weak government enforcement of antitrust rules.

Few independent political pressure groups (except for environmentalists); however, consumers are beginning to be heard.

About one fourth of the workforce is unionized; unions have been organized mainly by company rather than by industry or craft and have been mostly nonmilitant (except, on occasion, government employee unions); weak ties between unions and political parties.

The Japanese Manager

The homogeneity in Japanese society has led to uniformity in the personal backgrounds and career paths of senior managers in large companies. In the 1960s, Michael Yoshino's (1968) study of Japanese management noted that managers were "as a whole, quite homogeneous as to age, educational background, and work experience" (p. 91). In 1984, Toyohiro Kono reached the same conclusion, noting that "the typical Japanese manager . . . is a university graduate majoring in engineering or social science. He is likely to have joined a private company rather than a public organization, and not likely to have become an independent professional" (pp. 43–44).

Notable deviations from that pattern have included company founders (some now deceased), such as Akio Morita (Sony), Konosuke Matsushita (Matsushita), and Soichiro Honda (Honda), and immediate successors of founders.[10] Another exception is the *amakudari* ("descender from heaven"), a senior-level government official who after an extended civil service career becomes a corporate CEO or board director, often in a company or industry over which he had regulatory oversight.

Table 7.4 summarizes some prevailing tendencies in the backgrounds, career paths, and pay of senior managers in large Japanese companies.

Table 7.4   Background, Career Paths, and Pay of Senior (*Jomukai**-Level) Managers in Large Japanese Corporations

Job or career entry	Upon finishing university education. A notable exception is a "descender from heaven" (*amakudari*), a high-level government official who upon retiring from a civil service career becomes a senior corporate official (Colignon & Usui, 2003). Also, in some cases of company financial duress, a main bank creditor may orchestrate a mid- or late-career managerial replacement (Sheard, 1998).
Appointment to *jomukai* level	Usually after age 50.
Accession to CEO	At age 59, on average (vs. age 49–50 for U.S. and Western European counterparts) (Lucier, Schuyt, & Tse, 2005).[11]
Tenure	Career-long with one employer but just 6.3 years, on average, as CEO; turnover is high and tenure short because of advanced age upon appointment; most CEOs retire in office or become chairman (two thirds ascend to chairman); there are few forced (performance-based) departures.

Formal education	At least a bachelor's degree, often from a high-ranking national university; postgraduate degrees are common; academic backgrounds are most commonly in engineering and the social sciences.
Professional development	Rotation across tasks and departments, creating generalists with a broad perspective valued in upper management; mentoring of younger advisees (*kohai*) by a senior member (*senpai*).
Pace of promotion	Slow, gradual, in tandem with a cohort of peers until about age 40; thereafter, individual personal qualities, experience, ability, and achievement take precedence over age and seniority.
Key to advancement	Human relations skills (*jinmyaku* relations), strategic vision, and strategic decision-making ability (Suzuki, 1990); most CEOs have authority to pick successors, in consultation with other senior management.
Mobility	Low; it is unusual for a departing CEO to become CEO of another company.
Nationality	Almost exclusively Japanese; a few exceptions include firms that have substantial foreign ownership (e.g., Mazda, Nissan) or are very international (Sony).
Gender	Exclusively male.[12] Among advanced industrial countries, Japan has by far the lowest proportion of female senior officers in major corporations ("Helping Women Get to the Top," 2005).
Pay	Lower than in other advanced industrial nations (Table 7.5); has seldom included performance-based pay such as employer stock or stock options (some exceptions recently); semiannual salary bonuses are common, as are nonmonetary perquisites (e.g., golf club memberships).

*The term *jomukai* refers to "the managing directors' board" or "meeting of managing directors" (Otsubo, 1986; Shimizu, 1986). It typically includes company founders, board-level executives (e.g., company chairman [*kaicho*] and president [*shacho*], managing directors, and senior heads of functional departments [e.g., marketing, finance]).

Japanese Management Education

Given the Japanese reverence for education and relentless gauntlet of "examination hell" (perpetual school entrance examinations), large companies and government agencies recruit heavily at the more elite universities, where enrollees are already proven survivors.[13] In general, large

Table 7.5   Average Total CEO Compensation, 2005[a]

United States	$2,160,000
Switzerland	1,390,000
Germany	1,180,000
Mexico	1,000,000
Japan	540,000
India	290,000
China[b]	210,000

SOURCE: Figures from Towers Perrin, in "Real Pay" (2006, p. 102).

a. Figures rounded to the nearest US$10,000; companies with at least US$500 million in sales.

b. China figure excludes Hong Kong.

Japanese employers downplay job applicants' undergraduate academic specialization when recruiting and put more emphasis on their personal qualities (e.g., commitment, discipline).

It is noteworthy that many universities do not have business schools. Instead, business courses are offered in departments of economics and are often taught by part-time instructors. In the country's educational statistics, business enrollment is tabulated under "economics and commerce" and put in the social science category.

In 2006, about one in five undergraduate students specialized in "economics and commerce" (*Japan Statistical Yearbook 2008*, Table 22-16), a ratio very similar to that in the United States. However, the MBA degree has been much less common in Japan. Only one graduate student in 16 enrolls in "economics and commerce" (*Japan Statistical Yearbook 2008*, Table 22-18). In general, the MBA brings neither fast-track promotion nor higher pay (Kambayashi, Morita, & Okabe, 2008). By contrast, about one in four U.S. master's-level students study business, surpassed only by enrollment in teacher education.

Nevertheless, Japanese business education and MBA programs have been expanding. There were 45 graduate-level business schools in 2006 (Dvorak, 2006), up from just 8 in 1990 (compared with 850 graduate business master's programs in the United States). However, no Japanese provider, public or private, is ranked in the *Financial Times* annual rankings of top programs worldwide.[14]

Also, many Japanese employers provide formal and nonformal management education internally. A few (e.g., the Hitachi Institute of Management

Development and the Matsushita Institute of Government and Management) accommodate both internal and external students. Other business and management classes are sponsored by industry associations.

In academia, the Japan Society of Business Administration is the largest professional association and has ties with the International Federation of Scholarly Associations of Management (http://www.ifsam.org/Members/JSBA.doc/index.html). It publishes the *Journal of Business Management* (semiannual, in Japanese) and is also affiliated with the English-language *Asian Business & Management*.[15]

Japanese Management

Western management scholars have used the word *jungle* to describe the profusion of books and articles associated with management thought and theory (Koontz, 1961; Schollhammer, 1969). The same term has been applied to the English-language literature on Japanese management (Keys & Miller, 1984). The following section synthesizes some of it from the viewpoint of the management functions of planning, controlling, organizing, and directing. The content here is drawn from researchers, practitioners, journalists, and consultants. Emphasis is on general tendencies in large companies.

PLANNING

In regard to planning, the prototype large Japanese company historically has shown the following tendencies:

- Less formal, less detailed long-range planning than in similar U.S. and European firms
- More emphasis on direction taking and vision setting
- Extensive environmental scanning
- Less creative (more imitative) business strategy
- Less fixation on profits as a primary objective
- Consensus-based decision making

Less Formal Long-Range Planning

In the 1950s and 1960s, many large Japanese firms initiated formal long-range planning systems. Hayashi's 1978 study of planning in 19 Japanese multinational corporations noted less systematic formulation and monitoring of plans than in American firms. Toyohiro Kono's later study reported that "more than 70% of Japanese large corporations have had planning systems for years" (1984, pp. 274–276), which he described as similar to American ones but less sophisticated and refined. Kenichi Ohmae (1982), former longtime managing director in Japan for U.S. and global management consultancy McKinsey & Co., expressed a similar view:

> As a consultant I have the opportunity to work with many large Japanese companies. Among them are many companies whose success you would say must be the result of superb strategies. But when you look more closely you discover a paradox. They have no planning staffs, no elaborate, gold-plated strategic planning processes. (p. 2)

Vision Setting and Direction Taking

Ohmae (1982) noted that in Japan, "The whole organization [is] less planned, less rigid, but more vision- and mission-driven than . . . the Western organization" (pp. 224–225). Similar observations come from other consultants, executives, and researchers, Western and Japanese. For instance, Yang (1984) noted a disinclination for highly detailed formal long-range plans and more attention to vision setting, environmental scanning, and long-term thinking (see also "Mitsui's New Long-Term Management Vision," 1999). Terasawa (1974) judged that the Japanese firm had a superior "intuitive grasp of strategy" and put more emphasis on "direction taking," with less formality and detail in the planning process (p. 12). Kono (1992) noted a strong tendency for long-term "future visions" (pp. 37–39).

Although most Japanese firms do less formalized planning than their Western rivals, they do much long-term thinking and take a long-term perceptual horizon. Many also formulate very detailed short- and medium-term plans.

Environmental Scanning

Japanese business has been seen as more engaged than Western counterparts in environmental scanning and competitor intelligence, for which they commonly form special organizational units (Engle, 1987; Martin, 1991). A few employees in large companies have the sole function of meticulously scanning, reviewing, and analyzing foreign newspapers, newsletters, and industry trade publications for useful information.

Consultant Jan Herring of the Futures Group noted in 1991 that "only 3% of U.S. companies [had] specialized business/competitor intelligence systems . . . compared with 100% of Japanese corporations" (as quoted in Martin, 1991, p. 47). Also, some *keiretsu* groups draw from the intelligence gathering and information sharing capabilities of affiliate firms, especially those with an associated global general trading company (*sogo shosha*). Entities of the national government such as the METI, the Japanese External Trade Organization, and government commercial attachés abroad also collect and distribute competitor and market information on behalf of home-based firms. (The hunger for information is also reflected in Japanese newspaper circulation rates, which are much higher than in most other countries.)

Less Creative, More Imitative Strategy

American strategic planning expert Michael Porter (2000) judged that Japanese corporate success comes largely from continuous improvement in cost reduction and quality, flexible manufacturing, and reduction in time to market (see also Porter, 1996; Porter, Takeuchi, & Sakakibara, 2000). Their core business is often based on product imitation and less on unique enduring products or business strategies. Porter (2000, p. 20) concluded that "having a strategy is the exception in Japan rather than the rule" (he mentioned Honda, Shimano, and video game makers as exceptions) and saw this a major shortcoming:

> The missing link in Japanese management is strategy. Strategy requires establishing a unique position by creating a mix of value different from that of competitors. In Japan's personal computer industry, for example, imitation is rampant and no company has registered attractive financial returns. Contrast that with the success of Dell and Apple, the U.S. computer makers, each with a distinctive strategy. Advantages that come from best practice alone can be imitated away. Advantages that come from strategy are far more sustainable. (p. 20)

Japanese firms typically are less diversified than their Western rivals; when they do diversify, the route is spin-offs and alliances rather than takeovers and mergers. However, domestic merger activity has risen in recent years.

Less Fixation on Profits

Japanese companies seem less driven by near-term profit goals than their Western rivals. Profits aren't overlooked, but low profitability is accepted as long as other objectives are met (e.g., target market share, cash flow, supplier relationships, employee job security). In that regard, Abegglen (2006, p. 7) described Japanese companies as social organizations, communities of workers seeking to secure the future well-being of members of the community while meeting the requirements of effective economic performance. Large companies have shouldered the cost burden of the "tribe by the window" (*madogiwazoku*), that is, aging employees previously passed over for further promotion who become redundant but remain on the payroll until retirement.

For 1970–1991, Warburg Securities reported average pretax corporate return on equity for Japanese business to be 18.2% (compared with 24.5% for U.S. firms) ("Losing Its Way," 1993). Another source (Standage, 2007) noted recent average broad-based long-term posttax return on equity to be about 9% in Japan versus 14% to 17% in the United States and Europe. A similar profile was documented for 1973 through 2004 (Gwilym, Seaton, Suddason, & Thomas, 2005).

Consensus-Based Decision Making

An often-mentioned feature of traditional Japanese management is the *ringi* consensus-driven decision-making process.[16] This typically begins with a draft proposal (*ringi-sho*) preceded and followed by an exchange of information and opinion (a give-and-take process called *nemawashi*) between the people involved.[17] Participants receive and circulate the draft and associated documents, and when they reach agreement, they affix their personalized inked stamp (*hanko*), the Japanese equivalent of a signature.

The *ringi* process is integrative and iterative, aiming to enhance the quantity and quality of ideas and information and to help inform, clarify, and mobilize support so that implementation can proceed smoothly. On the other hand, it can be time-consuming and preclude quick change in direction.

However, not all managerial decisions are made consensually, and the degree of participation can depend on the type of decision and the knowledge and abilities of the participants. For example, *ringi* is not well suited for controversial decisions or for people who lack sufficient knowledge and experience to participate effectively (e.g., strategic decisions).

Some sources describe the *ringi* process as more top-down than bottom-up. According to the late Akio Morita (1986), the founder and longtime CEO of Sony,

> The concept of consensus is natural to the Japanese, but it does not necessarily mean that every decision comes out of a spontaneous group impulse. Gaining consensus in a Japanese company often means spending time preparing the groundwork for it, and very often the consensus is formed from the top down, not the bottom up, as some observers in Japan have written. While the idea may arise from middle management, for example, top management may accept it whole or revise it and seek approval and cooperation all down the line. (p. 198)

Yang (1984) argued that key executive factions (*jitsuryoku-sha* executives) dominate important decisions (e.g., long-range objectives and capital investment choices) without much participation from below. Kono

(1984) concluded that corporate strategy is decided at the top of the company and that operational and tactical decisions rely more on *ringi*. Misumi (1984) pointed out that important decisions are usually made consensually by senior executives, and then broader support is mobilized through *ringi* and *nemawashi,* in effect forging a consensual understanding rather than a true consensus-based decision.

Clark (1993) described the process in a similar vein:

> In reality, the planning occurs within a bureaucratic division, or ka. The director or a deputy director instructs and guides staff members as to the nature of the proposal and discusses any ideas he might have. The staffers then work together to develop the plan along these lines, usually with the deputy director. Once the division has developed a coordinated position, the director—if necessary—sells the proposal to other divisions and those at more senior levels. Agreement can of course take time, and re-drafts are possible, but the director's reputation rests on presenting a thorough, feasible and acceptable plan to divisional outsiders. . . . In the end, as the above explanation illustrates, the process resembles the typical Western pattern of decision making much more closely than the bottom-up tag leads us to believe. (p. 19)

Similarly, Howard and Teramoto (1981) defined *ringi* as the political process of arriving at an unofficial understanding before going forward.

CONTROL

Managerial control involves monitoring and correcting performance. Control can be broad (company-wide) or narrow (e.g., internal cost and budget controls, quality assurance, production scheduling, operating procedures, supervision). In well-established companies in advanced free market economies, the capital markets (especially equity markets) guide control on behalf of owners (individual and institutional shareholders). Subpar performance tends to depress share price, which in turn may lead to a change in managers, organizational restructuring, new alliances, or a merger, spin-off, or sale of the company (or even bankruptcy and liquidation). Historically, despite broad-based share ownership in Japan, equity markets have been a more passive instrument of control. Takeovers have been less common. Barriers include stable (not salable) cross-held shares within *keiretsu* groups. Until 1999, the law didn't allow buyouts involving exchange of one company's shares for another.

Hostile takeovers are almost unheard of and cause shame or embarrassment for the acquiree. The Japanese word for a takeover (*nottori*) is the same as that for a highjacking. Abbeglen and Stalk (1985) noted that the "sale of the company has about it the sense of buying and selling people, with implications of immorality and social irresponsibility." According to Nakamura (1990), "The Japanese company owner regards his company as something like a forest—a forest that he created. He wants to preserve this forest. To cut down the trees and sell them is unthinkable" (p. 11). Similarly, Kojima (1993) noted that "mergers and acquisitions sound somehow immoral, like buying a family" (p. 19). Nonetheless, the annual level of Japanese mergers and acquisitions has recently risen to 3% of gross domestic product, up from 0.4% in 1991 but well below the 10% numbers in the United States and Britain (Standage, 2007, p. 8).

Weaker-performing affiliates within *keiretsu* groups are sometimes reinforced by better-performing ones or by a main bank creditor. The bank can monitor performance and may also hold shares of debtors (now limited by law to 5% of shares), sit on their boards, and coordinate financial makeovers (Scher, 1997; Sheard, 1998).

Japanese company boards accept few independent (nonexecutive) directors, so there is no clear separation of execution (management) from supervision (governance). The board chair is often a current or former CEO of the company. Annual shareholder meetings are rarely occasion to challenge or criticize management.[18] Sterngold (1992) noted, "You think it can be a good thing when stockholders question management, but that is humiliation in Japan" (p. 1).

As mentioned previously, shareholder interests are secondary to other interests. In the words of Koichi Hori, president of consultancy BCG in Japan (quoted in Harney & Abrahams, 1998, p. 15), "Japanese companies have existed first for their employees, then the pensioners, third for business partners—suppliers and dealers, fourth for the main bank and fifth for the shareholders." These obligations decrease profitability and the market value of company shares.

Japanese companies show some noteworthy preemptive control practices.[19] One is the meticulous screening of prospective employees. Because hiring is intended to be for life (at least for the full-time male hires in large companies), staffing decisions must be judicious. Therefore, the senior human resource person in large firms is very important and often sits on the board of directors, an infrequent occurrence in the United States (Jacoby, 2005).

Other preemptive control measures include tight communication and integration with suppliers to ensure quality and timely delivery. One often-mentioned approach has been the Toyota *kanban* system (a just-in-time approach) for delivery of equipment, materials, components, and subassemblies from suppliers. Another is the attention to continual improvement (e.g., of process, product) expressed by the word *kaizen*. These and other control practices are described in Table 7.6.

Japanese automakers have shown speed and flexibility in introducing new car models by compressing development and retooling cycles (see Wheelright, 1981; Womack, Jones, & Roos, 1990). Coordination within automotive *keiretsu* (e.g., of Toyota, Honda, Nissan) strives for flexible integration of complex production systems. The leading firms have achieved manufacturing productivity rates and cost reductions among the

Table 7.6   Some Production Planning and Control Practices Pioneered by Leading Japanese Manufacturing Firms

Kanban	A just-in-time approach to procurement and inventory control pioneered by the Toyota Motor Corporation.
	Aims for delivery of supplies, parts, subassemblies, and materials just when needed (e.g., same day or even sooner).
	Reduces the cost of financing, storing, and handling inventory.
	Requires close communication and coordination with suppliers.
	The word *kanban* refers to a sign card used for signaling when inventory should be replenished.
Lean manufacturing	Streamlined flexible production that incorporates *kanban* and training and retraining of employees in multiple tasks.
	Conceived in the late 1940s and early 1950s by production engineer Taiichi Ohno of the Toyota Motor Corporation (see Womack, Jones, & Roos, 1990).
Total quality management or total quality control	Quality control is the responsibility of everyone, not just specialized quality inspectors.
	Individuals and teams are empowered to assess and respond quickly to problems.
	Monitoring can include statistical sampling, benchmarking, continual improvement (*kaizen*), and horizontal and vertical communication.
	Requires that everyone be attuned to objectives.
	Requires close communication between suppliers and customers.
Competitive benchmarking	Refers to comparing one's own practices, methods, and standards with the best found elsewhere (and not just in the same industry).
	The Toyota kanban system was inspired by the way U.S. supermarkets tracked and reordered inventory at the cash register by scanning barcodes.
Kaizen	Continual incremental improvement (e.g., of product design, production, people, quality, or any other endeavor).

highest in the world. One cost-reduction technique for auto manufacturing has been to determine a target market share and then compute a selling price expected to produce that share (Otsubo, 1986, p. 32). Cost efficiencies are then sought so as to make the price viable, in essence a price-driven (rather than cost-driven) system. Suppliers and subcontractors are pressured to reduce costs (Morita, 1992, p. 66).

ORGANIZING

The following are two organizational tendencies in large Japanese companies:

- Emphasis on hierarchy and centralization of authority
- Flexible integration and coordination of resources and effort

Hierarchy and Centralized Authority

In line with societal culture, Japanese enterprise attends to hierarchy and centralized authority. When expanding abroad, for example, firms have been less likely than American and European rivals to cede decision autonomy to their foreign subsidiaries and more apt to put a Japanese national (rather than a local national) in charge (Yoshino, 1976). Even these managers are closely controlled by central headquarters. Yoshimichi Yamashita (1991), then head of consultancy A.D. Little in Japan, concluded that "Japanese managers sent overseas are either unable or unwilling to act on their own" (p. A14). Another source reported frequent communication with headquarters, including urgent overnight commutes (*kamikaze* flights) back home to clarify decisions and actions with higher-ups ("Can Japan's Giants Cut the Apron Strings," 1990).

Hierarchies also permeate *keiretsu* groups, where key decisions come from a narrow core of higher-ranking member firms. When the fortunes of a core member falter, repercussions are commonly pushed to peripheral suppliers (e.g., through the transfer of redundant employees), and they are pressured to reduce costs.

Internal Corporate Management Hierarchy

In the prototype large Japanese business, Sheard (1998, p. 203) described the top management hierarchy to include the board chairman (*kaicho*), followed by the president (*shacho*), vice president (*fuku-shacho*), senior executive director (*senmu*), executive director (*jomu*), and managing director (*torishimariyaku*).

Otsubo (1986) observed that the English words *president* and *vice president* do not translate well into Japanese and that titles *chief executive officer* and *chief operating officer* are uncommon. The prevalent Japanese equivalents for CEO include "representative director and president," "representative director and chairman," and "representative director and senior managing director." "Chairman of the board" is often a symbolic honorary position for a semiretired president whose role is to represent the company to the broader public. In many cases, however, the chairman is also CEO. The company vice president is commonly called the senior managing director or executive director.[20] The term *director* in one's title also means one is a member of the board of directors, which in Japan consists mainly of insiders (with historically few independent directors).

Otsubo diagrammed the prototype large-firm hierarchy (Figure 7.4), including the chairman or president at the top, linked to a senior executive committee and the *jomukai* (weekly or bimonthly meeting of the managing directors).[21] The heads of the division (*honbu*), department (*bu*), section (*ka*), and subsection (*kakari*) follow.

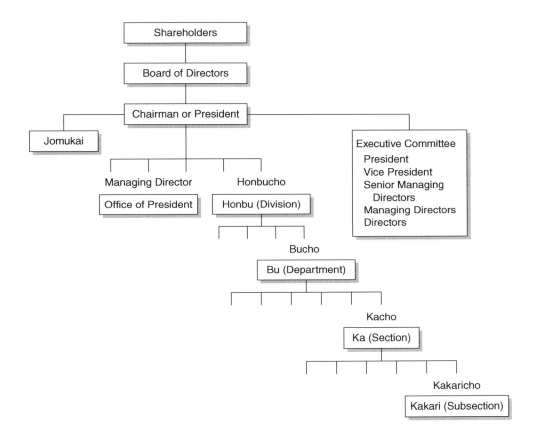

Figure 7.4   Model Strata of Japanese Corporations

SOURCE: From M. Otsubo, "A Guide to Japanese Business Practices" (1986), *California Management Review, 28*(3), p. 34. Reprinted by permission.

Flexible Integration and Coordination of Effort and Resources

An often-mentioned feature of Japanese business is flexibility in the structuring and organizing of work. In one sense, this is reflected in ambiguities in company organization charts. Consultant Kenichi Ohmae (1982) observed,

> Most Japanese corporations lack even a reasonable approximation of an organization chart. Honda . . . is obviously quite a flexible, strategy-oriented company, capable of making prompt and far-reaching decisions. Yet nobody knows how it is organized, except that it employs project teams very frequently. In most large corporations the managing director (jomu), enjoying a very great influence on operations, is not even shown in lined organization charts. . . . From the Western corporate point of view, such an arrangement would be confusing and unworkable. (p. 220)

Fruin (1992) notes flexibility in the permeable enterprise boundaries (e.g., in intergroup and intragroup networks) and calls the "process of acting interdependently to be the most outstanding and distinctive characteristic of the Japanese enterprise system" (pp. 9–10).

> While single firm groupings are not greatly diversified, inter-firm groupings typically are. . . . Given differences in . . . types of inter-firm networks, the nature of control, coordination, strategic intent, and action among them vary considerably. Yet the effect is the same: inter-firm networks connect the resources of dozens, hundreds, and even thousands of firms in order to compete in a world where size and scale of economic activity are paramount. Integration across organizations is a complement to differentiation and specialization among organizations. Inter-firm coordination provides a framework for tremendous breadth in activities even while individual firms remain highly focused in their pursuits. (Fruin, 1998, pp. 23–24)

Flexibility is also enhanced by job rotation and cross-training of employees, including within and across work units. Iwata (1982) noted the shared work responsibility and flexible coordination:

> An organization is comprised of various groups, the groups being sections, departments, bureaus, etc. In other words, each section or department is held responsible for accomplishing a certain group task.
>
> The distribution of work and responsibility within each section (or whatever unit) is determined by the manager of the unit, in accordance with the prevailing circumstances. This is adjusted quite flexibly depending on the total amount of work, distribution of ability within the work force and other factors. Even after the work is distributed and each person is notified of his share of the burden, he is expected to help out the others. . . . In other words, people are co-working under a very "loose" definition of "roles" keeping a flexible attitude towards various situations. (p. 68)

And Maruyama (1992) observed,

> A very common mistake American managers make in Japan is to organize the work by dividing the task and assigning [parts] to individuals. If you have five employees in your office in Japan, it is better to give the whole work to the group and let them figure out how to do it. (p. 89)

Ohmae (1982) added, "The whole organization looks organic and entre-preneurial, as opposed to mechanistic and bureaucratic" (pp. 224–225). Kono (1984) characterized internal corporate structure by comparing a stone-formed wall (Japanese structure) with a brick wall (American struc-ture). In the former, the stones (i.e., people, organizational units) are flex-ibly placed, without preordained positions, each complementing the other and together supporting the whole. By contrast, in a brick (American) wall, each brick has a more limited (specialized) location (p. 302).

Maruyama (1992) made a similar point using an architectural metaphor:

> European architecture was based on principles of unity by similarity and repetition, opposition, tension, and extension. Each space and each mass has a boundary, identity, and a permanently specialized function such as a dining room or a bedroom. . . . Similarly European and American manage-ment is based on principles of boundary, identity, specialization, opposi-tion, tension, and extension. . . . In contrast, in the traditional Japanese gardens . . . and houses, boundaries can be removed and space becomes a continuous flow, and each space is convertible. . . . The principles of conti-nuity and convertibility make job rotation quite natural and logical for Japanese people. (p. 89)

DIRECTING

Motivation

By international standards, most Japanese employees in large firms are highly motivated, diligent, and loyal. They work long and hard because layoffs are embarrassing and costly, given a seniority-based pay structure and risk of having to start over. Consequently, one's personal identity and financial security become linked to the survival of one's employer. As Noguchi (1994) noted,

> While an economics textbook might define the corporation as "an entity devoted to the accumulation of profit," the Japanese company is a social institution of a manifestly different character. . . . Contrary to what some may think, Japanese managers in no sense view their employees as mere cogs in the machine. Their basic aim is to ensure their workers' employment and improve their economic situation. Japanese workers, for their part, are less inclined than their Western counterparts to think in terms of "selling" their labor to the company. They derive their self-identity from the com-pany they work for and are more concerned with long-term promotion within the firm than with their short-term financial remuneration. As a result, they work tirelessly for the company. (p. 25)

Biggs (1982) judged that highly motivated "labor, not the art of management, is . . . key . . . to understanding [the Japanese]" and that employees "run like hell" in order to save face, to avoid shame, and to not disappoint their boss, coworkers, or family. The Japanese are less driven than Westerners by money alone and much less by praise (which is seldom forthcoming) from superiors. Kageyama (1989) noted that "Japanese rarely praise others because they are uncomfortable when others praise them. Praise is confused with flattery, and flattery is a cause of mistrust" (p. 15).

Sources suggest that the Japanese are more attuned to failure feedback than success feedback (Masumoto, 2004). Jeffrey Irish (1986), an American in his late 20s, found the absence of praise disappointing while employed at a large Japanese construction company in Tokyo:

> I think my most difficult adjustment problem has been dealing with the lack of encouragement and positive reinforcement. In the United States, my parents and my teachers always stressed my achievements and generally overlooked my mistakes. In my company in Japan, no matter how hard I try, I am only corrected and almost never complimented. (p. 38)

It is common for many Japanese to work for extra hours without additional pay. White-collar employees (salary men) often socialize on weekday evenings with colleagues and clients in restaurants and bars. There are also people who show up for work on their vacation days. Some newly unemployed people carefully hide their condition from neighbors by leaving home early in the morning as if going to work and then returning late in the day. Some employees work late to impress their neighbors, as reflected in the following quote:

> One night, an American securities firm manager stationed in his firm's Tokyo office worked late. On his way out, he encountered a Japanese employee still at his desk. "Why are you here?," the American asked. "Do you have some things to do?" The Japanese shook his head. "No, but if I go home early, the people in my block will think I am not a good worker." (Sullivan, 1992, p. 70)

Wage and salary schedules in large firms are tied more to seniority than to job title or productivity, especially during one's first 10–20 years of employment. Pay increments come yearly (the *nenko* system), much like in a civil service pay system. Thereafter, rewards can become more task or productivity based, but salaries are usually capped at about age 40–45 unless one ascends to higher management. The *nenko* system tends to reduce office politics to gain fast promotion and higher pay but can demotivate young employees. And there can be much political maneuvering for the most coveted work assignments and locations.

The promise of job security makes payroll costs burdensome during economic downturns. New hiring declines, but annual pay increments must continue, creating a top-heavy wage and salary structure. This can be alleviated by reducing the semiannual pay bonuses or using more part-time and temporary labor. (In the recent slow economic times, the proportion of temporary workers in the national workforce has risen substantially.)

Employers can reinforce employee motivation by attending to their well-being beyond the immediate work setting. In big firms, this holistic concern can include company-supplied housing, recreation facilities, child care services, home-buying assistance, personal savings programs, transportation, personal loans, consumer purchasing services, and even marital matchmaking. For example, the Mitsubishi Group and Fuyo Group companies have had marriage bureau (matchmaking) services, reflecting their concern that "if a worker stays a bachelor too long (into his early 30s), he becomes a problem; [therefore] it is the duty of the company to help with this" (Browning, 1985, p. 1).

Some firms (e.g., Matsushita and Nissan) even have employee cemeteries (Pollack, 1993). The nature and extent of such support practices can vary by company size, being more ample in larger firms. Even then, not all benefits are for everyone; for example, company-supplied housing is generally for young unmarried or newly married employees. Here, too, the economic slowdown has been reducing many privileges.

Leadership

In Japan, leaders are consensus builders, and there is little attraction to charismatic leadership. Yoshino (1968) noted that the ideal leader is not necessarily a strong person and that power can be tenuous (pp. 205–206). Hayashi (1986) pointed to the importance of fostering harmony through moral suasion, evenhandedness, modesty, kindness, and generosity. He described the ideal person as skillfully unassertive (p. 117). Shimizu (1986) concluded that the most admired leadership qualities are not personal initiative or decisiveness but rather moral strength, sensitivity, generosity, and broadmindedness; a good leader is moderate, fair, circumspect, and of even temperament (p. 33).

Ballon (1983) judged that "the Japanese image is . . . that of a leader inside the group . . . contributing to the direction in which the group is moving" (pp. 10–11). In general, Confucian culture emphasizes followership more than leadership, with people culturally conditioned to fit in, to conform, to sense their place in the order of things, and to act accordingly (Fallows, 1989, p. 117). Harmony is emphasized:

> As for consensus, if no action can be taken until everyone agrees on it, then no action will be taken. A consensual system inevitably gives the power of veto to one and all. And if action is in fact taken, the person who holds out longest will get his way. . . . Japanese do not like to stand out in a crowd. . . . This does wonders for wa (harmony), but it discourages risk taking. . . . And it does nothing to encourage leadership, the lack of which is so conspicuous. ("A Survey of Japan," 2002, p. 8)

Communication

As a rule, the Japanese are seldom outspoken or verbally direct, and are sometimes seen by Westerners as inarticulate communicators. Their communication style reflects their high-context culture, where messages are more often implicit and indirect, compared with the directness of low-context settings (Germanic, Nordic, and Anglo) (Hall, 1976). A message that is likely to disappoint its receiver is conveyed in a diplomatic and face-preserving way, with much of its meaning to be gained from context, unspoken words, manner of expression, and body language. A "yes" can mean "no" when one is "listening between the lines." These differences are reflected in the following observations:

> You cannot imagine a Japanese boss barking, "Yamata, clean up this god-damn mess." Rather, "It seems the floor might not be as clean as it once was" will prod Yamata's broom into a blur of motion. (Biggs, 1982, p. 44)

> Behavior which Americans consider trustworthy is often precisely that which the Japanese associate with shifty characters—and vice versa. To Americans, people who pause before replying to a question are probably dissembling. They expect a trustworthy person to respond directly. The Japanese distrust such fluency. They are impressed by somebody who gives careful thought to a question before making a reply. ("Go Along and Get Along," 1990, p. 76)

> In their conversations with each other—and more often than not in their conversations with foreigners—Japanese religiously shun explicit, carefully reasoned statements in favor of indirect and ambiguous ones basically designed not to communicate ideas but to feel out the other person's mood and attitudes. . . .
>
> Because of the . . . almost identical social and cultural conditioning of the Japanese people, it is often possible for one Japanese to determine the reaction of another to a particular situation simply by observing the second man's facial expressions, the length and timing of his silences and the ostensibly meaningless grunts he emits from time to time. (Christopher, 1983, pp. 42–43)

Kageyama (1989) noted the nonverbal communication:

> In Japanese culture silence is golden, and the real messages are often communicated subtly. Japanese value a listener who uses his perceptiveness to understand the speaker's meaning. From a small bit of information—perhaps from a simple gesture or the speaker's tone of voice—the Japanese listener gleans the whole meaning. The Japanese have learned from a very early age how to understand one another without direct verbal communication. (p. 15)

Christopher (1983) observed that most Japanese are comfortable with periods of silence (as opposed to the American compulsion to break silence with conversation):

At bottom, in fact, Japanese prefer whenever possible to avoid verbal communication entirely. Their language abounds in proverbs such as "Words are the root of all evil," and among themselves they rely to a remarkable degree on something called haragei—which can be translated as "visceral communication" or, less elegantly, as "belly language." (pp. 43–44)

Yoshino (1968) observed a well-developed sense of intuition among Japanese and skill at reading the boss' mind, which comes partly from physical proximity to the boss in open office areas, allowing people to be more aware of the boss's communications with others.

Kono (1984) noted less attention to written communications:

In the UK and in the USA written memos are used frequently, but in Japan oral communications are more often used. For individual-to-individual relations, a Japanese will communicate better with his colleagues and someone in authority will teach his subordinates. If he does not communicate with his colleagues well beforehand, he will be criticized during conferences. "Nemawashi" (lobbying or log rolling) is required before any group decision can be reached. (p. 304)

Chapter Summary

- Global interest in Japanese business and management followed from its rapid post–World War II economic growth and continuing commercial success of prominent Japanese companies.

- From a Western perspective, the economic, political, and cultural ambiance of Japan is unique.

- A Confucian heritage brings a tendency for groupism, order, hierarchy, harmony, social conformity, deference to authority, and reverence for education. The political system has been dominated by the Liberal Democratic Party. The powers of the prime minister and parliament have been weaker than in most other advanced industrial countries, and those of government technocrats and agencies are stronger.

- The predominantly free enterprise economy of Japan has been guided by the government through industrial policy support for targeted companies and industries. The system has long favored larger companies (and their employees) while disfavoring independent stockholders, consumers, savers, homeowners, and many smaller businesses.

- Senior Japanese managers in larger corporations are older, on average, than their Western peers and are more homogeneous in terms of

age, education, and career development. Career paths include transfer across tasks and departments, breeding generalists rather than
specialists. Pace of promotion is more gradual. Their advanced age
makes CEO tenure short. There is less performance-caused turnover
than in the West and much lower pay.

- Long-range planning is less formal than in the United States. There
  is extensive consensus-based decision making and environmental
  scanning and less concern about near-term profits. A significant con-
  straint on strategic decision making and action is job protection for
  core (mainly male) full-time employees.

- Firms typically are less diversified than their Western rivals; when they
  do diversify, they favor spin-offs and alliances rather than takeovers
  and mergers.

- Boards of directors are larger and bring in far fewer independent
  directors than do Western boards, so there is less separation between
  enterprise governance and operations. Shareholders are patient, and
  their interests are subordinated to employee interests. Annual shareholder meetings tend to be short and nonconfrontational. *Keiretsu*
  group member cross-holdings of stock block takeover attempts by
  outsiders. Historically, bank creditors have exercised control by monitoring debtor financial books, sitting on debtor boards of directors,
  and helping to orchestrate financial makeovers.

- Japanese businesses have popularized several production and quality
  control practices in leading manufacturers. For example, Toyota has
  attracted international attention for its just-in-time procurement
  systems, continual improvement, total quality control practices, and
  competitive benchmarking.

- Japanese companies rely heavily on hierarchy and centralized
  authority. Interfirm business networks (*keiretsu* and others) aim for
  flexible integration and coordination of resources and effort.

- In business, the ideal leader fosters harmony through personal modesty, moral suasion, calm temperament, and evenhandedness. As in
  all Confucian settings, followership is key to leadership, with people
  conditioned culturally to fit in, conform, and know their place in the
  social and organizational hierarchy. In general, Japanese are neither
  direct nor outspoken in their communication style.

- Japan has been experiencing economic, social, political, and other
  change that has begun to change traditional management and
  human resource practices. Consumer and quality-of-life issues have
  begun to emerge; younger people seem less motivated than their
  elders by job security and seniority-based pay.

Terms and Concepts

alliance capitalism
amakudari
competitive benchmarking
guided free enterprise system
indicative planning
industrial policy
kaizen
kanban
Keidanren

keiretsu
MITI (METI)
nemawashi
nenko
ringi; ringi-sho
total quality management
Type Z (Theory Z) company
wa
zaibatsu

Study Questions

1. Describe distinctive features of the social, cultural, economic, and political fabric of Japan.

2. Which traditional Japanese management practices, in your judgment, could be successfully adopted or adapted in other countries? See the list in Exercise 7.2 (Part II) and discuss.

3. Discuss some unique strengths and limitations of traditional Japanese-style management and labor practices.

Exercise 7.1

In 1991, the best-selling book *Theory Z* (1981), by William Ouchi, suggested that many U.S. firms might benefit from transition to a "Theory Z" management system that could blend features of traditional American (Type A) and Japanese (Type J) management (Table 7.7). Ouchi noted that several firms had already moved in that direction, mentioning General Motors, Ford, Chrysler, Hewlett-Packard, IBM, Intel, Rockwell International, and Texas Instruments.

Assignment: Investigate whether and to what degree any of the firms listed in Table 7.7 (or any others that you know of) have shown a Type Z profile.

Table 7.7　　Theory Z Management Profile

Type A Organization (American)	Type J Organization (Japanese)	Type Z Organization (modified American)
Short-term employment	Lifetime employment	Long-term employment
Individual decision making	Consensual decision making	Consensual decision making
Individual responsibility	Collective responsibility	Individual responsibility
Rapid evaluation, promotion	Slow evaluation, promotion	Slow evaluation, promotion
Explicit, formal control	Implicit, informal control with explicit formal measures	Implicit control with explicit formal measures
Specialized career paths	Nonspecialized career paths	Moderately specialized career paths
Segmented concern for employees	Holistic concern for employees	Holistic concern for employees

SOURCE: Adapted from W. Ouchi, *Theory Z* (1981), New York: Addison Wesley.

Exercise 7.2

Since 1990, Japan has experienced surprisingly slow economic growth, which followed the collapse of super-inflated stock market and real estate price bubbles. Circumstances contributed to a high volume of nonperforming bank loans, backed by overvalued (but later devalued) property and securities. Bank lending dropped off dramatically. Between 1989 and 2008, the economy grew by no more than 2% per year. By mid-2008, the Nikkei 300 stock index was still 60% below its all-time (1990) high. Banks' troubles were eased with government bailouts. Other recent worries include price deflation, high government debt, low consumer spending, and slow economic and political change.

Assignment: Part I

Investigate and report on the pace and depth of recent change in Japan. Your sources of information can include surveys, briefings, and reports from *The Economist* (Emmott, 2005; "Japan's Economy," 2006; Standage, 2007), or more recent ones if available. There is much coverage of Japan in major news publications such as the *Wall Street Journal*, *New York Times*, *Financial Times*, and *The Economist*.

Look for recent reporting on Web sites such as Nikkei Net Interactive (http://www.nni.nikkei.co.jp). See also *Nihon Keizai Shimbum* (*The Japanese Economic Journal*) and *Japanese Management Today*. Also, scan recent issues of *Asian Business Management*.

Some related books from the recent past include Inagami and Whittaker (2005), Jacoby (2005), Lincoln (2001), Lincoln and Gerlach (2004), and Tett (2003–2004).

Some examples of recent changes in Japan include the following:

1. Openness to imports and inward foreign direct investment has increased (but is still well below advanced industrial country averages).

2. Involvement of women in the workplace, including in nontraditional work roles, is increasing.

3. Protective and preferential business ties within *keiretsu* alliances are loosening up.

4. Banking privatizations and mergers and the end of interest rate ceilings on personal savings are reducing a long-running subsidy from ordinary savers to corporate borrowers. Also, the largest savings institution (the government's Postal Savings System) is being privatized gradually. A tightening of bank credit has contributed to more active stock and bond markets. Corporate debt/equity and debt/asset ratios have fallen. There is more transparency and rigor in financial reporting and in accounting and auditing practices.

5. Labor costs remain high, a consequence of slow population growth, an aging population, low immigration, and reluctance of firms to release redundant employees. Labor cost pressures have led to more outsourcing and some shift of more labor-intensive assembly operations (e.g., cameras, TVs, air conditioners) to Southeast Asia, China, and Mexico. Pressure to reduce costs at home has brought more reliance on part-time and contract labor.

6. Attention to shareholder value and higher dividend payout has increased (Morse & Moffett, 2007).

7. Consumer and lifestyle issues were expressed in the Maekawa Reports[22] of the mid-1980s and addressed further by the Hiraiwa Report, which recommended several dozen economic, legal, and regulatory reforms.[23] They included changing a Large Scale Retail Store Law that had long blocked the opening of new large stores and restricted their location, size, and business hours. Retailers now offer discount pricing. Product liability legislation has been introduced.[24] The growing number and proportion of elderly people are changing from net savers (as employees) to net spenders (as retirees), bringing more attention to consumer interests. The proportion of population over age 65 (already highest in the world) continues to rise.

Additional consumer pressures come from the increasing numbers of Japanese who study, travel, and work abroad, where the lower cost of living draws attention to high costs at home. The average Japanese family spends much more on food than its U.S. counterpart, and housing is more expensive and less spacious.

The Japanese government now aims to produce a lifestyle superpower. The Nippon Keidanren (a major business federation) vision document (Vision 2025) favors more quality-of-life goals, improved lifestyle choices, and more international openness (Nippon Keidanren, 2003).

Assignment: Part II

Discuss some potential near-term and longer-term implications (direct and indirect) of the aforementioned societal changes for the following traditional management and human resource practices:

Consensus-driven decision making

Lifetime employment; retirement at age 55–60

Low CEO pay

Seniority-bound compensation

Modest salary differences between managers and between managers and other employees

Semiannual or annual pay bonuses

Emphasis on entry-level recruiting and hiring

Continuous training

Slow promotion and evaluation

Deemphasis of organization charts and job titles

Open work environment; few isolated offices

Some menial labor for everyone

Company songs, uniforms, group physical exercises

Comprehensive concern for the employee, corporate paternalism, extensive company-sponsored support services for employees

Nonspecialized career paths, extensive rotation of people between tasks and departments

Unpaid overtime work

Fusion of work life and private life, much after-hours socializing with the boss and colleagues

Keiretsu enterprise networks

Aversion for hostile takeovers

Downplaying of profits as a primary business objective

Insider-dominated boards of directors

Precedence of employee interests (job security) over shareholder interests (dividend payout, share price gain)

Assignment: Part III

Investigate similarities and differences between the Japanese financial crisis of the 1990's and the worldwide one emerging in late 2008. What implications does the more recent crisis raise for management practice in Japan and abroad?

Notes

1. When adjusting gross domestic product for purchasing power, some sources put China second behind the United States (however, China has population 10 times that of Japan).

2. For a list of Japanese 50 largest firms by market value, see the Appendix at the end of this chapter; the most recent *Fortune* magazine and *Financial Times* newspaper rankings can be found, respectively, at http://www.fortune.com and http://www.ft.com.

3. There has been occasional labor confrontation involving government sector employees.

4. Buddhism emphasizes self-denial and correct thinking and living; its Zen branch pursues truth through introspection rather than through scripture. Shintoists believe in the divine forces of nature and in ancestor worship.

5. For a historical and conceptual contrast between Japan's guided free enterprise system and the U.S. economic system, see Vogel (1978).

6. Indicative planning encourages firms to move in a certain direction without dictating what they should do; firms haven't always followed government guidance.

7. See Johnson (1982) and Prestowitz (1988) for the view that Japanese government industrial policy was key to its economic transformation; for a contrary view, see "MITI's Identity Crisis" (1994) and Abegglen and Stalk (1985).

8. Unlike members of the U.S. Congress, Japanese legislators have few aides to gather information and help analyze or draft legislation (Schleshinger & Chandler, 1993).

9. Business political spokesgroups have included the 700-member Keidanren (Federation of Economic Organizations), Keizai Doyukai (Japanese Association of Corporate Executives), Nikkeiren (Japan Federation of Employers' Organizations), and Nihon Shoko Kaigisho (Japan Chamber of Commerce). The Nippon Keidanren was formed in May 2002 by combination of the Keidanren and Nikkeiren. In 2008, the joint membership included 1,351 companies (100 foreign owned), 129 industrial associations, and 47 regional employers' associations (Nippon Keidanren Web site at http://www .keidanren-usa.org).

10. Professor Ryuei Shimizu of Keio University identified four sources of senior managers: company founders; immediate successors of founders; internal, company-bred managers; and "descenders from heaven" (*amakudari*) (Shimizu, 1986, p. 2).

11. CEO age and turnover data (world's 2,500 largest based on market capitalization). See Lucier et al. (2005); Lucier, Schuyt, and Habbel (2006); Lucier, Wheeler, and Habbel (2007); Karlsson, Neilson, and Webster (2008).

12. In 1998, a woman, Eiko Kono, was named president of Recruit Corporation, a major publishing company (Guyon, 1998).

13. About one fourth of university students are enrolled in Japan's national universities (government funded). By contrast with most other countries, these public universities tend to have more prestige than do private ones.

14. FT Business Education (2005, 2006, 2007, 2008); these reports include worldwide business school rankings for different kinds of programs.

15. *Asian Business & Management* is published in association with the Euro-Asia Management Studies Association, Japan Academy of Labor and Management, Japan Society of Business Administration, and Association of Japanese Business Studies; see http://www.palgrave-journals.com/abm/index.html.

16. The word *ringi* combines the word *rin* (submitting a proposal to one's superior and receiving his approval) with *gi* (deliberation and decisions) (Yoshino, 1968, p. 254).

17. *Ringi* has been defined as the "political processes by which an unofficial understanding is reached before any official decision is made" (Misumi, 1984, p. 529). *Nemawashi* refers literally to a preparation process for the roots of plants before transplantation; in the *ringi* process *nemawashi* is a metaphor for preparing a consensus.

18. There are also *sokaiya* (shareholder meeting specialists), essentially provocateurs who acquire small holdings and then extort payment from management in exchange for a peaceful meeting.

19. See Morgan (1992) for a discussion of preemptive and remedial control practices in Japanese manufacturing firms.

20. Major U.S. companies often have many vice presidents, but the true one is generally called the executive vice president or senior vice president.

21. Ryuei Shimizu (1986, p. 208) translated the word *jomukai* as the "managing director's board" and called it "the highest executive organ of the president [and] the highest decision making body."

22. Refers to the April 1986 and April 1987 Maekawa Reports of the Advisory Group on Economic Structural Adjustment for International Harmony, chaired by Haruo Maekawa, former governor of the Bank of Japan.

23. The Hiraiwa Report came from the Advisory Group for Economic Restructuring (Economic Structural Reform), a high-profile panel that was led by Keidanren Chairman Gaishi Hiraiwa.

24. Lawyers estimate that since World War II, Japanese courts have accepted fewer product liability cases than U.S. courts handle in a single day.

References

Abegglen, J. (2006). *21st-century Japanese management.* New York: Palgrave Macmillan.

Abegglen, J., & Stalk, G. Jr. (1985). *Kaisha: The Japanese corporation.* New York: Basic Books.

Ballon, R. J. (1983). Non-Western work organizations. *Asia Pacific Journal of Management, 1*(1), 1–14.

Benedict, R. (1946). *The chrysanthemum and the sword: Patterns of Japanese culture.* Boston: Houghton Mifflin.

Biggs, B. (1982, May 17). The dangerous folly called Theory Z. *Fortune,* p. 41–46.

Bremner, B., & Glasgall, W. (1997, January 27). Two Japans: The gulf between corporate winners and losers is growing. *Business Week,* p. 24.

Browning, E. S. (1985, January 3). Postscript: Japan Inc. becomes a marriage broker. *Wall Street Journal,* p. 1.

Burton, J. A., & Weller, C. (2005, May). *Supersize this: How CEO pay took off while America's middle class struggled.* Center for American Progress. Retrieved September 9, 2008, from http://www.americanprogress.org/kf/ceo_pay_web_final.pdf

Can Japan's giants cut the apron strings. (1990, May 14). *Business Week,* pp. 105–106.

Christopher, R. (1983). *The Japanese mind.* New York: Linden Press/Simon & Schuster.

Clark, T. (1993, August). Decisions? Decisions. *Japan Update,* pp. 18–19.

Colignon, R. A., & Usui, C. (2003). *Amakudari: The hidden fabric of Japan's economy.* Ithaca, NY: Cornell University Press.

Dvorak, P. (2006, March 6). Shift in Japan: Executives who earned MBAs. *Wall Street Journal,* p. B1.

Emmott, B. (2005, October 8). The sun also rises. A survey of Japan. *The Economist.*

Engle, A. (1987). Number one in competitor intelligence. *Across the Board, 24*(12), 43–47.

Fallows, J. (1989). *More like us.* Boston: Houghton Mifflin.

Fruin, M. (1992). *The Japanese enterprise system.* Oxford, UK: Clarendon.

Fruin, M. (1998). *Networks, markets, and the Pacific Rim.* Oxford, UK: Oxford University Press.

FT Business Education. (2005, January 24, September 12; 2006, January 30, March 20, May 15, September 11, October 23; 2007, January 29, May 14, September 17, October 22; 2008, January 28). *Financial Times* special reports.

Go along and get along. (1990, November 24). *The Economist,* p. 76.

Guyon, J. (1998, October 12). The global glass ceiling and ten women who broke through it. *Fortune,* pp. 102–103.

Gwilym, O. A., Seaton, J., Suddason, K., & Thomas, S. (2005). *International evidence on payout ratio, returns, earnings and dividends* (Research Paper 2005-7). Aberystwyth: University of Wales School of Management & Business.

Hall, E. (1976, July). How cultures collide. *Psychology Today,* pp. 66–97.

Harney, A., & Abrahams, P. (1998, November 12). Death of the salaryman? *Financial Times,* p. 15.

Hayashi, K. (1978). Corporate planning practices and Japanese multinationals. *Academy of Management Journal, 21*(2), 211–226.

Hayashi, S. (1986). *Culture and management in Japan.* Tokyo: University of Tokyo Press.

Helping women get to the top. Special report: Women in business. (2005, July 23). *The Economist,* p. 11.

Howard, N., & Teramoto, Y. (1981). The really important difference between Japanese and Western management. *Management International Review, 21*(3), 19–30.

Imai, K. (1990). The legitimacy of Japan's corporate groups. *Economic Eye, 11*(3), 16–22.

Inagami, T., & Whittaker, D. H. (2005). *The new community firm: Employment, governance and management reform in Japan.* Cambridge, UK: Cambridge University Press.

Irish, J. (1986, June). A Yankee learns to bow. *New York Times Magazine,* p. 38.

Iwata, R. (1982). *Japanese-style management: Its foundations and prospects.* Tokyo: Asian Productivity Association.

Jacoby, S. (2005). *The embedded corporation: Corporate governance and employment relations in Japan and the United States.* Princeton, NJ: Princeton University Press.

Japan meets the auto. (1930, February). *Fortune.* Reproduced in *Fortune,* November 19, 1990, p. 214.

Japan's economy. Time to arise from the great slump. (2006, July 22). *The Economist,* pp. 65–67.

Japan statistical yearbook 2008. (2008). Statistics Bureau & Statistical Research and Training Institute, Ministry of Internal Affairs and Communications.

Johnson, C. (1982). *MITI and the Japanese miracle: The growth of industrial policy, 1925–1975.* Stanford, CA: Stanford University Press.

Kageyama, A. (1989, October). Cultural clues to Japanese management. *Asian Wall Street Journal Weekly,* p. 15.

Kambayashi, N., Morita, M., & Okobe, Y. (2008). *Management education in Japan.* Oxford, UK: Chandos.

Karlsson, P., Neilson, G., & Webster, J. (2008, Summer). CEO succession 2007: The performance paradox. *strategy + business.* Retrieved September 9, 2008, from http://www.strategy-business.com/press/freearticle/08208?pg=all

Keys, J., & Miller, T. (1984). The Japanese management theory jungle. *Academy of Management Review, 9*(2), 342–353.

Kojima, A. (1993, June). We, the company. *Japan Update,* p. 19.

Kono, T. (1984). *Strategy and structure of Japanese enterprises.* Armonk, NY: M. E. Sharpe.

Kono, T. (1992). *Long-range planning of Japanese corporations.* New York: Walter de Gruyter.

Koontz, H. (1961). The management theory jungle. *Journal of the Academy of Management, 4*(3), 174–178.

Lincoln, E. (2001). *Arthritic Japan: The slow pace of economic reform.* Washington, DC: Brookings Institution Press.

Lincoln, E., & Gerlach, M. (2004). *Japan's network economy: Structure, persistence, and change,* Cambridge: Cambridge University Press.

Linowes, R. (1993, November). The Japanese manager's traumatic entry into the United States: Understanding the American–Japanese cultural divide. *Academy of Management Executive, 7*(4), 24.

Losing its way. (1993, September 18). *The Economist,* p. 79.

Lucier, C., Schuyt, R., & Habbel, R. (2006, Summer). CEO succession 2005: The crest of the wave. *strategy + business, 43.* Retrieved September 9, 2008, from http://www.strategy-business.com/press/article/06210?pg=0

Lucier, C., Schuyt, R., & Tse, E. (2005, Summer). CEO succession 2004: The world's most prominent temp workers. *strategy + business, 39.* Retrieved September 9, 2008, from http://www.strategy-business.com/press/article/05204?pg=all

Lucier, C., Wheeler, S., & Habbel, R. (2007, Summer). CEO succession 2006: The era of the inclusive leader. *strategy + business,* special report. Retrieved September 9, 2008, from http://www.strategy-business.com/press/article/07205?pg=0

Martin, J. (1991, November). Still a distant second. *Across the Board,* pp. 42–47.

Maruyama, M. (1992). Changing dimensions in international business. *Academy of Management Executive, 6*(3), 88–96.

Masumoto, T. (2004). Learning to "do time" in Japan: A study of US interns in Japanese organizations. *International Journal of Cross Cultural Management, 4*(1), 9–27.

Misumi, J. (1984). Decision making in Japanese groups and organizations. In B. Wilpert & A. Sorge (Eds.), *International perspectives on organizational democracy* (pp. 5252–539). New York: Wiley.

MITI's identity crisis. (1994, January 22). *The Economist,* pp. 65–66.

Mitsui's new long-term management vision. (1999, November–December). *Mitsui in Action,* p. 3.

Morgan, M. S. (1992). Feedforward control for competitive advantage: The Japanese approach. *Journal of General Management, 17*(4), 41–52.

Morita, A. (with Reingold, E., & Shimomura, M.). (1986). *Made in Japan.* New York: E. P. Dutton.

Morita, A. (1992, March 9). Why Japan must change. *Fortune,* pp. 66–67.

Morse, A., & Moffett, S. (2007, February 23). Deal breaker: A landmark vote in Japan—shareholders just say no. *Wall Street Journal,* p. A.1

Nakamura, H. (1990, Spring). Interview. Chuken kigyo' play a significant role in Japan's economy. *Japan Update,* p. 11.

Nakazawa, T. (1994, August). Firm offers. The travails of job-seeking. *Japan Update,* pp. 20–21.

Nippon Keidanren (Japan Business Federation). (2003, January 1). *Japan 2005: Envisioning a vibrant, attractive nation in the twenty-first century.* Retrieved September 9, 2008, from http://www.keidanren.or.jp/english/policy/vision2025.pdf

Noguchi, Y. (1994, Autumn). Dismantle the 1940 setup to restructure the economy. *Economic Eye,* pp. 25–28.

Ohmae, K. (1981, January 26). Japan versus Japan: Only the strong survive. *Wall Street Journal.*

Ohmae, K. (1982). *The mind of the strategist: Business planning for competitive advantage.* New York: Penguin.

Ohmae, K. (1989). Planting for a global harvest. *Harvard Business Review, 17*(4), 136–145.

Otsubo, M. (1986). A guide to Japanese business practices. *California Management Review, 28*(3), 32–33.

Ouchi, W. (1981). *Theory Z.* New York: Addison Wesley.

Pollack, A. (1993, September 8). *Koyasan* journal: For Japan Inc., company rosters that never die. *New York Times,* p. A4.

Porter, M. (1990). *The competitive advantage of nations.* New York: Free Press.

Porter, M. (1996). What is strategy? *Harvard Business Review, 74*(6), 61–78.

Porter, M. (2000, July 5). Japan's twin demons. *Financial Times,* p. 20.

Porter, M., Takeuchi, H., & Sakakibara, M. (2000). *Can Japan compete?* New York: Basic Books.

Postrel, V. (2004, July 13). Economic scene: Why do certain countries prosper? *New York Times,* p. C2.

Prestowitz, C. (1988). *Trading places: How we allowed Japan to take the lead.* New York: Basic Books.

Real pay. (2006, January 21). *The Economist,* p. 102.

Scher, M. (1997). *Japanese interfirm networks and their main banks.* New York: Macmillan.

Schleshinger, J., & Chandler, C. (1993, June 25). While change roars through Japanese politics, real power lies in hands of bureaucrats. *Wall Street Journal,* p. A6.

Schollhammer, H. (1969). The comparative management theory jungle. *Academy of Management Journal, 12*(1), 81–97.

Sheard, P. (1998). Japanese corporate boards and the role of bank directors. In M. Fruin (Ed.), *Networks, markets and the Pacific Rim* (Ch. 10, pp. 200–232). Oxford: Oxford University Press.

Shimizu, R. (1986). *Top management in Japanese firms.* Tokyo: Chikura Shobo.

Standage, T. (2007, December 1). Going hybrid: A special report on business in Japan. *The Economist.* Retrieved September 22, 2008, from http://www.economist.com/specialreports/displayStory.cfm?story_id=10169956

Sterngold, J. (1992, December 6). Corporate Japan's unholy allies. *New York Times,* Sec. 3, p. 1.

Sullivan, J. (1992). Japanese management philosophies: From the vacuous to the brilliant. *California Management Review, 34*(2), 66–87.

A survey of business in Japan. (1999, November 27). *The Economist,* p. 5.

A survey of Japan. (2002, April 20). *The Economist,* pp. 3–6.

Suzuki, N. (1990). The world of the Japanese chief executive. *Management Decision, 28*(6), 45.

Terasawa, Y. (1974, May 12). Japanese style decision making. *New York Times,* p. 12.

Tett, G. (2003–2004). *Saving the sun: A Wall Street gamble to rescue Japan from its trillion-dollar meltdown.* New York: HarperCollins.

Vogel, E. (1978). Guided free enterprise in Japan. *Harvard Business Review, 56*(3), 161–170.

Wheelright, S. C. (1981). Japan: Where operations are really strategic. *Harvard Business Review, 59*(4), 67–74.

Womack, J., Jones, D., & Roos, D. (1990). *The machine that changed the world.* New York: Maxwell Macmillan.

Yamashita, Y. (1991, December 16). Managers journal: Japanese executives face life out of the nest. *Wall Street Journal,* p. A14.

Yang, C. Y. (1984). Demystifying Japanese management practices. *Harvard Business Review, 62*(6), 172–177.

Yoshino, M. (1968). *Japan's managerial system.* Cambridge, MA: MIT Press.

Yoshino, M. (1976). *Japan's multinational enterprises.* Cambridge, MA: Harvard University Press.

Zinsmeister, K. (1993, March 10). The great industrial policy hoax. *Wall Street Journal,* pp. 65–66.

Appendix

Largest Japanese Firms, Ranked by Market Value

Rank	Company	Market Value	Sector
1	Toyota Motor	$172.2 billion	Automobiles and parts
2	Mitsubishi UFJ Financial	93.8	Banks
3	Nintendo	72.4	Leisure goods
4	NTT DoCoMo	69.6	Mobile telecommunication
5	Nippon Telegraph & Telephone	68.0	Fixed line telecommunication
6	Canon	61.5	Technology hardware and equipment
7	Matsushita Electric Industrial	53.2	Leisure goods
8	Honda	52.4	Automobiles and parts
9	Mitsubishi	51.2	Support services
10	Sumitomo Mitsui Financial	51.0	Banks
11	Japan Tobacco	50.1	Tobacco
12	Taxeda Pharmaceutical	44.6	Pharmaceuticals and biotechnology
13	Mizuho Financial	41.8	Banks
14	Sony	40.1	Leisure goods
15	Nissan Motor	37.4	Automobiles and parts
16	Mitsui	36.9	Support services
17	Tokyo Electric Power	36.2	Electricity
18	Nippon Steel	34.5	Industrial metals and mining
19	Mitsubishi Estate	33.6	Real estate investment and services
20	East Japan Railway	33.3	Travel and leisure
21	Yahoo Japan	31.5	Software and computer services
22	Millea Holdings	29.7	Nonlife insurance
23	Nomura Holdings	29.4	Financial services
24	Denso	28.6	Automobiles and parts
25	Komatsu	27.7	Industrial engineering
26	KDDI	27.4	Mobile telecommunication
27	JFE Holdings	27.3	Industrial metals and mining
28	Inpex Holdings	26.3	Oil and gas producers
29	Seven & I Holding	24.0	Food and drug retailers
30	Kansai Electric Power	24.0	Electricity
31	Central Japan Railway	23.2	Travel and leisure

(Continued)

(Continued)

Rank	Company	Market Value	Sector
32	Fanuc	22.8	Industrial engineering
33	Shin Etsu Chemical	22.4	Chemicals
34	Daiichi Sankyo	21.7	Pharmaceuticals and biotechnology
35	Toshiba	21.7	General industrials
36	Astellas Pharma	20.1	Pharmaceuticals and biotechnology
37	Hitachi	20.0	Electronic and electrical equipment
38	Softbank	19.6	Mobile telecommunication
39	Chubu Electric Power	19.5	Electricity

SOURCE: Adapted from the Financial Times Global 500, 2008 (figures rounded to nearest $100 million). Retrieved September 16, 2008, from http://media.ft.com/cms/889d77f0-4142-11dd-9661-0000779fd2ac.pdf.

Management in Latin America

8

As a popular slogan in Latin America has it, the developing countries
are not underdeveloped, they are undermanaged.

—Peter Drucker (1973, pp. 13–14)

Management practice and performance deserve special attention in
late-emerging economies, where they are instrumental to social,
political, material, and other progress. Managers there face extra burdens
of interventionist states, underdeveloped infrastructure, rigid labor and
capital markets, and cultural resistance to change.

That profile describes Latin America, where long-term economic
growth has been slow compared with Confucian Asia. Nonetheless, the
region has made advances and has many dynamic small and medium-
size businesses and even some larger ones that compete globally.[1] These
include the world's leading maker of small passenger jet aircraft (Embraer,
Brazil), largest beef processor (JBS-Friboi, Brazil), leading iron ore company (Brazilian natural resource conglomerate Vale), largest corn flour
and tortilla maker (Gruma, Mexico), third-largest bread maker (Bimbo,
Mexico), third-biggest cement company (Cemex, Mexico), and first- and
third-largest copper companies (Chile's state-owned Codelco and private Grupo Mexico).[2]

This chapter explores the context and patterns of management practice
in Latin countries of the Western Hemisphere,[3] about which little has been
published in the management literature.

- To describe (broadly) Latin American society (polity, economy, and culture)
- To profile contemporary Latin American managers (senior managers in larger companies)
- To highlight prevalent management practices, problems, patterns, and performance in the region
- To note social, economic, and political change that has been contributing to managerial change

The Latin American Macroenvironment

Tables 8.1 and 8.2 identify some broad demographic, political, economic, educational, and cultural features of the Latin American macroenvironment.[4] Figures 8.1a and 8.1b show the areas discussed in this chapter.

CULTURE

Latin America reflects a mix of European, indigenous, African, and U.S. cultural influences. However, its mainstream values, attitudes, beliefs, and behavior draw much from long colonial ties to Europe's Iberian peninsula (Spain and Portugal).[5]

African heritage is seen mainly in Caribbean coastal and island nations and northeast Brazil, dating back to the slave trade era (c. 1550–1880). Most of the 30–35 million indigenous Americans are found in Mexico, Central America, and Andean South America. Caucasian populations dominate southern South America (Argentina, Uruguay, Chile, and southern Brazil), where the indigenous population was small and slave trade didn't reach. Notable Italian influence is seen in Argentina, Uruguay, and southern Brazil. For example, about 5 million Italian immigrants and their descendants live in São Paulo state, Brazil, including 3 million in the city of São Paulo. U.S. cultural influence is widespread but strongest in Mexico, Central America, and the Caribbean (from which now come about half of new U.S. immigrants).

On Hofstede's cultural dimensions, the region shows medium-to-high individualism, high masculinity, and high uncertainty avoidance. Latin society is hierarchical and elitist (high power distance), with status based on family background, occupation, education, and ethnicity. Salaried workers have much higher social status than wage workers, more so than in Europe and North America. Roman Catholicism is by

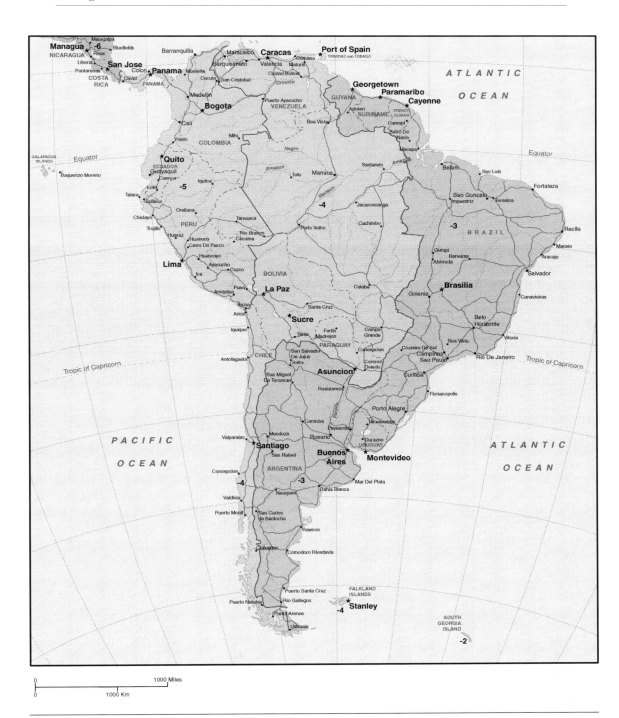

Figure 8.1a Map of South America

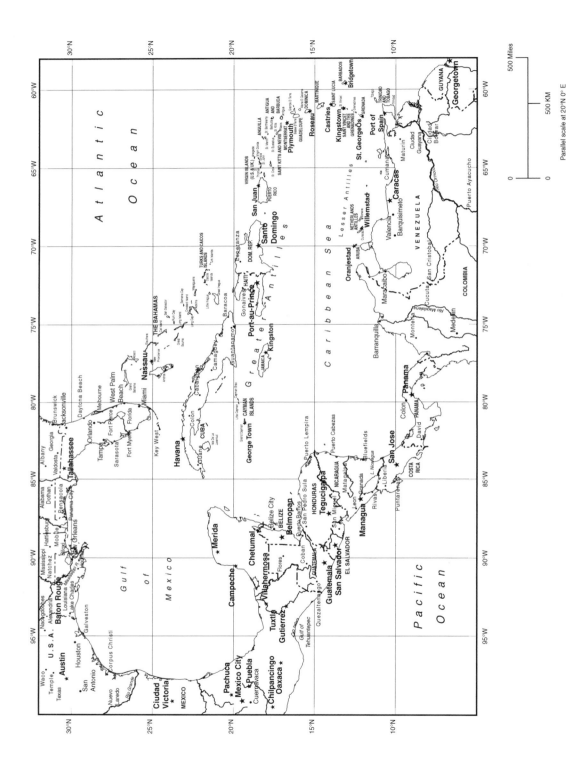

Figure 8.1b Map of Mexico (partial), Central America, and the Caribbean

Table 8.1   The Latin American Macroenvironment in the Early 21st Century

Demographic	Twenty nations; 557 million people (in 2007); more than half reside in Brazil and Mexico.
	Mixed ethnicity; substantial indigenous population (30–35 million) throughout Mexico, Central America, and Andean South America (mainly Bolivia, Peru, Ecuador); predominantly Caucasian in the far south (Argentina, Uruguay, Chile, southern Brazil); notable African heritage in the Caribbean basin and northeast Brazil.
	Young median age.
Political	After Spanish and Portuguese colonial rule, a long period of dominion by local elites.
	Ideological struggle after World War II between the political left (socialists, communists) and democrats; leftist ideology eroded after the collapse of the Soviet Union but with a recent revival in Venezuela, Bolivia, Nicaragua, and Ecuador. Cuba is socialist.
	All pluralistic democracies save for Cuba, but some tenuous.
	Weak legislatures.
	Uncertain legal and regulatory environment.
	Much government bureaucracy and red tape.
	Low labor union density; extensive government regulation of unionism and labor relations; labor rules inhibit new hiring and labor mobility.
Economic	Much inequality in household wealth and income.
	High unemployment and underemployment.
	Periodic financial panic and capital flight.
	Underdeveloped (but improving) institutional foundations for modern capitalism; thin equity and bond markets; undersized banking systems.
	Much tax evasion and off-the-books economic activity.
	Weak antitrust enforcement.
	Prominence of family-controlled business and business groups.
	Tradition of mixed economies (both private and state enterprise) but ever more private with passage of time.
	Free market economic reforms continue but remain incomplete; long-term trends (since 1990) have included the following: • Gradual sell-off of government-owned businesses to the private sector (although a few have been renationalized). • Greater exchange rate flexibility. • Reduced tariff and nontariff barriers to trade.

(Continued)

Table 8.1 (Continued)

Economic (continued)	• Improved tax enforcement. • Improved management of money supply growth has reduced inflation. • Decreasing restrictions on inward foreign private investment. Regional economic integration is progressing (intermittently). High dependence on raw material exports continues, but manufactured exports are growing.
Educational	Near universal primary and secondary education. Most public universities have open admissions and remain underfunded, understaffed, and much politicized. Limited but expanding higher education for business and management.
Cultural	High-context culture: • Importance of personal relationships and trust • Flexible attitude toward time On Hofstede's cultural dimensions, the following tendencies: • High power distance • High uncertainty avoidance • Medium to high individualism • High on masculine-associated values

far the dominant organized religion, but there has been a recent spread of Protestant evangelicals.

As befits a high-context culture, family relationships and personal connections are important for getting things done, and there is a flexible attitude toward time. Paternalism and personalism permeate family, social, and organizational life.

GOVERNMENT AND POLITICS

After gaining independence from Spain and Portugal in the early to mid-1800s, the region experienced long-term political instability and authoritarian government. Little headway was made toward democracy until late 20th century. In 1950, eight countries could be called democratic, but by the end of the century, all but Cuba were pluriparty democracies (some tenuous). Between 1945 and 2006, more than one third of the world's political transitions (change of head of state) were in Latin America (Santiso, 2006, pp. 50–51). The post–World War II era saw ideological struggle between proponents of state socialism and democratic pluralism. Despite Cuban socialism (since 1960) and brief socialist interludes in Chile (early 1970s) and Nicaragua (late 1980s), Marxist ideology and rhetoric waned after collapse of the Soviet Union and

Table 8.2   Latin American Nations by Population and Rank on the 2007–2008
U.N. Human Development Index (HDI)

	Population (millions)	HDI Ranking
Argentina	40.3	38
Bolivia	9.1	117
Brazil	190.0	70
Chile	16.3	40
Colombia	44.4	75
Costa Rica	4.1	48
Cuba	11.4	51
Dominican Republic	9.4	79
Ecuador	13.8	89
El Salvador	6.9	103
Guatemala	12.7	118
Haiti	8.7	146
Honduras	7.5	115
Mexico	109.0	52
Nicaragua	5.7	110
Panama	3.2	62
Paraguay	6.7	95
Peru	28.7	87
Uruguay	3.5	46
Venezuela	26.0	74
Total	557.4 million	

SOURCE: Central Intelligence Agency. (2007).

NOTE: The United Nations Human Development Index rates the world's countries on several dozen social and economic indicators; see http://hdr.undp.org/en/statistics/.

Eastern Europe (1990–1991). It has rekindled recently in Venezuela, Bolivia, Ecuador, and Nicaragua, but its future is uncertain.

Throughout the region, there is much government regulatory bureaucracy. Legal systems are politicized and vulnerable to corruption. For business, this brings added risk and uncertainty about contract enforcement, property rights, and dispute resolution.

Except in Argentina, labor unionism is not entrenched, and most union activity has been controlled by government. Most unrest has been among public employees (e.g., teachers and civil servants) and in state-owned enterprises (SOEs; e.g., mining and petroleum sectors) and a few large foreign firms (e.g., auto and auto part makers in Mexico and Brazil). In the main, the law has strongly protected job security (with severance penalties and long lead times required for layoffs), inhibiting aggressive hiring and labor mobility. A substantial proportion of the labor force is unemployed and underemployed.

ECONOMY

Though predominantly private, the region's economies have a mix of state-owned and private businesses. Since 1990, the number of SOEs has declined. In 2007, there were 40 SOEs among the region's 500 largest nonfinancial firms. Another 286 (of the 500) were local private owned, and 174 were foreign owned. Between 1999 and 2005, the number of local private firms in the 500 increased in proportion to SOEs and foreign ones (Table 8.3) but declined slightly in 2007.

SOEs dominate the petroleum sector (including the three largest companies in the region) and public utilities. (See Table 8.4.)

Table 8.3   The Largest 500 Firms in Latin America, by Ownership and Sales Revenue

	Number of Firms					Sales Revenues (US$ billion)			
	1999	2001	2003	2005	2007	1999	2001	2003	2005
Private local	267	272	270	297	286	260	332	360	624
Private foreign	198	182	181	161	174	243	270	271	351
State-owned	35	46	49	42	40	138	254	307	389
Total	500	500	500	500	500	641	856	938	1,364

SOURCE: Adapted and translated from "Las 500 por Propiedad," *AmericaEconomia,* July 14–August 17, p. 147, 2003; *AmericaEconomia,* July 4–31, p. 107, 2006; 2007 data from "Las Mayores Empresas de América Latina," *AmericaEconomia,* July 21, 2008, p. 110.

Table 8.4 Largest 25 Nonfinancial State-Owned Enterprises in Latin America, Ranked by Sales Revenue (billions of U.S. dollars, 2007, rounded to the nearest $100 million)

Company	Country	Sector	Sales
1 Petroleos Mexicanos (Pemex)	Mexico	Petroleum and gas	$103.9 billion
2 Petrobras	Brazil	Petroleum and gas	96.3
3 Petroleos de Venezuela (PDVSA)	Venezuela	Petroleum and gas	96.2
4 Pemex Refinación	Mexico	Petroleum and gas	43.5
5 Petrobras Distribuidora	Brazil	Petroleum and gas	20.7
6 Comisión Federal de Energía Eléctrica	Mexico	Electric power	20.7
7 Pemex Gas y Petroquímica Básica	Mexico	Petrochemical	20.5
8 Codelco	Chile	Mining	17.0
9 Eletrobrás	Brazil	Electric power	12.7
10 Ecopetrol	Colombia	Petroleum and gas	10.9
11 Enap	Chile	Petroleum and gas	9.0
12 Petroecuador	Ecuador	Petroleum and gas	7.7
13 Pemex Petroquímica	Mexico	Petrochemical	5.3
14 Correios e Telégrafos	Brazil	General services	5.3
15 Compañía Luz y Fuerza del Centro	Mexico	Electric power	4.3
16 Sabesp	Brazil	Utilities	3.4
17 Petroperú	Peru	Petroleum and gas	3.2
18 Pequiven	Venezuela	Petrochemical	3.1
19 Copel	Brazil	Electric power	3.0
20 Furnas	Brazil	Electric power	2.9

(Continued)

Table 8.4 (Continued)

Company	Country	Sector	Sales
21 Empresas Públicas de Medellín	Colombia	Public utilities	2.7
22 Eletronorte	Brazil	Electric power	2.6
23 Aeropuertos y Servicios Auxiliares	Mexico	General services	2.5
24 Recope	Costa Rica	Petroleum and gas	2.2
25 Transpetro	Brazil	Transport and logistics	1.9

SOURCE: Excerpted, adapted, and translated from "Las Mayores Empresas de América Latina," *AmericaEconomia,* July 21, 2008, p. 110.

Table 8.5   The Largest Nonfinancial Firms in Latin America, Number by Country, 1999–2007

	1999	2000	2001	2002	2003	2004	2005	2006	2007
Brazil	220	192	165	137	195	203	204	207	210
Mexico	132	181	217	241	170	154	138	111	134
Chile	32	34	35	45	48	48	55	63	54
Argentina	76	54	43	24	25	32	35	41	35
Colombia	23	19	21	25	18	28	30	35	31
Peru	6	8	8	7	8	11	12	18	15
Venezuela	7	8	6	10	9	11	11	12	7

SOURCE: Excerpted, adapted, and translated from "Las Mayores Empresas de América Latina," *AmericaEconomia,* July 21, 2008, p. 110.

The region's largest 500 firms (by sales) all showed more than US$800 million in sales in 2007; 437 surpassed US$1 billion. Brazilian and Mexican firms dominated the group (Table 8.5). Of 34 firms with at least $10 billion in sales in 2007, 15 were Brazilian and 12 were Mexican. Proportional to population, Chile was most represented in the 500 (54 firms); Argentine numbers fell from 76 to 35 (due largely to an abrupt currency devaluation in 2001 that shrunk sales by two thirds when expressed in U.S. dollars).

Table 8.6 identifies the 50 largest nonfinancial firms under private local ownership. One prevalent feature, historically, has been their family control. Leading family surnames, where available, are indicated in the right-hand column of the table.

Table 8.6   50 Largest Local Private Nonfinancial Companies (by sales) in Latin America (billions of U.S. dollars, 2006, rounded to the nearest $100 million)

Company	Country	Sector	Sales	Family Surname
1 América Móvil	Mexico	Telecom	$21.7 billion	Slim
2 Cia. Vale Do Rio Doce (now Vale)	Brazil	Mining	21.2	Privatized state firm
3 Cemex	Mexico	Cement	18.2	Zambrano
4 Telmex	Mexico	Telecom	16.2	Slim
5 Techint	Argentina	Holding	15.9	—
6 Grupo Votorantim	Brazil	Holding	13.6	Ermírio de Moraes
7 Empresas Petroleo Ipiranga	Brazil	Petroleum and gas	13.5	—
8 Dist. de Prod. de Petróleo Ipiranga	Brazil	Petroleum and gas	12.0	—
9 FEMSA	Mexico	Beverages	11.7	Garza Sada
10 Gerdau	Brazil	Metallurgical	11.0	Gerdau
11 Cia. Brasileira de Petroleo Ipiranga	Brazil	Petroleum and gas	10.4	—
12 Telcel	Mexico	Telecom	10.1	Slim
13 Odebrecht	Brazil	Holding	9.5	Odebrecht
14 Grupo Carso	Mexico	Holding	8.5	Slim
15 Empresas Copec	Chile	Holding	8.3	—
16 Telemar Participações	Brazil	Telecom	8.1	Privatized state firm
17 Tenaris	Argentina	Metallurgical	7.7	—
18 Grupo Alfa	Mexico	Holding	7.1	Garza Sada
19 Grupo México	Mexico	Mining	6.6	Larrea
20 Ternium	Argentina	Metallurgical	6.6	—

(Continued)

Table 8.6 (Continued)

Company	Country	Sector	Sales	Family Surname
21 CBD Grupo Pão de Açúcar	Brazil	Retail	6.5	dos Santos Diniz
22 Braskem	Brazil	Petrochemical	6.1	Odebrecht & Mariani
23 Grupo Bimbo	Mexico	Foods	5.9	Servitje
24 CENCOSUD	Chile	Retail	5.9	Paulmann
25 Usiminas	Brazil	Metallurgical	5.8	Privatized state firm
26 Grupo Bal	Mexico	Holding	5.5	—
27 Southern Peru Copper	Peru	Mining	5.5	Larrea (Mexico)
28 Casas Bahia	Brazil	Retail	5.4	Klein
29 Organización Soriana	Mexico	Retail	5.4	Martin
30 Coca-Cola Femsa	Mexico	Beverages	5.3	Garza Sada
31 Grupo Modelo	Mexico	Beverages	5.3	Fernandez
32 Grupo Salinas	Mexico	Holding	5.0	Salinas
33 Gerdau Açominas	Brazil	Metallurgical	4.5	Gerdau
34 Falabella	Chile	Retail	4.4	Solari
35 CSN	Brazil	Metallurgical	4.2	Steinbruch
36 Grupo Com. Mexicana	Mexico	Retail	4.2	—
37 CPFL Energia	Brazil	Electric power	4.2	Ermírio de Moraes
38 Claro	Brazil	Telecom	3.9	—
39 Embraer	Brazil	Aerospace	3.9	Privatized state firm
40 Grupo Camargo Correa	Brazil	Holding	3.9	—

Company	Country	Sector	Sales	Family Surname
41 Antofagasta PLC	Chile	Mining	3.9	—
42 Sudamericana de Vapores	Chile	Transport and logistics	3.8	Claro
43 Cemex Mexico	Mexico	Cement	3.6	Zambrano
44 Liverpool	Mexico	Retail	3.6	—
45 Alpek	Mexico	Metallurgical	3.5	Garza Sada
46 Grupo Televisa	Mexico	Media	3.5	—
47 US Commercial	Mexico	Retail	3.5	Slim
48 Grupo Imsa (Acero)	Mexico	Metallurgical	3.5	Clariond
49 Industrias Peñoles	Mexico	Mining	3.4	—
50 TAM	Brazil	Mining and logistics	3.4	—

SOURCE: Excerpted, adapted, and translated from "Las Mayores por Propiedad," *AmericaEconomia,* July 9, 2007, p. 134; family surname ties were tracked from the corporate history and investor relations links on individual company Web pages.

NOTE: Prominent family surname ties are indicated at right, if available.

Table 8.7 lists the largest 50 foreign-owned private firms in the region. U.S. companies dominate, but there is also notable European presence.

Over the years, Latin America has depended greatly on agricultural and raw material exports, recently spurred by Chinese purchases. Historically, manufacturing was slow to emerge. Reasons included chronic economic and political instability, high inflation, persistent currency devaluation, and bouts of capital flight. A significant push into manufacturing by both local and foreign-owned firms came after World War II, sustained by an import substitution model of industrialization, that is, trade barriers imposed to protect local production. Longer-term consequences of that policy came to include weakened competitiveness and slow economic and industrial

Table 8.7 50 Largest Foreign-Owned Nonfinancial Businesses in Latin America, Ranked by Sales (billions of U.S. dollars, 2006, rounded to the nearest $100 million)

Company	Country	Sector	Sales	Headquarters Country
1 Wal-Mart de México	Mexico	Retail	$18.4 billion	U.S.
2 General Motors (México)	Mexico	Automotive	15.2	U.S.
3 Daimler Chrysler	Mexico	Automotive	9.9	Germany and U.S.
4 Telefónica	Brazil	Telecom	9.5	Spain
5 Escondida	Chile	Mining	8.4	Australia
6 YPF	Argentina	Petroleum and gas	8.3	Spain
7 Ambev	Brazil	Beverages	8.2	Belgium
8 Shell	Brazil	Petroleum and gas	8.2	U.K. and Netherlands
9 Volkswagen (Brazil)	Brazil	Automotive	8.1	Germany
10 Volkswagen (México)	Mexico	Automotive	7.9	Germany
11 Enersis	Chile	Electric power	7.3	Spain
12 Telesp	Brazil	Telecom	6.8	Spain
13 Arcelor	Brazil	Metallurgical	6.6	Luxembourg
14 Wal-Mart (Brazil)	Brazil	Retail	6.1	U.S.
15 General Motors	Brazil	Automotive	6.0	U.S.
16 Bodega Aurrerá	Mexico	Retail	5.9	U.S.
17 Fiat Automóveis	Brazil	Automotive	5.8	Italy
18 Chevron	Brazil	Petroleum and gas	5.7	U.S.
19 Cargill	Brazil	Agroindustrial	5.7	U.S.
20 Bunge Alimentos	Brazil	Agroindustrial	5.6	U.S.

Company	Country	Sector	Sales	Headquarters Country
21 Vivo	Brazil	Telecom	5.1	Spain and Portugal
22 Ford	Brazil	Automotive	5.1	U.S.
23 Carrefour	Brazil	Retail	5.1	France
24 Sam's Club	Mexico	Retail	5.0	U.S.
25 Wal-Mart Supercenter	Mexico	Retail	5.0	U.S.
26 Brasil Telecom	Brazil	Telecom	4.8	U.S.
27 TIM Participações	Brazil	Telecom	4.7	Italy
28 The Coca-Cola Company	Mexico	Beverages	4.7	U.S.
29 CEMIG	Brazil	Electric power	4.5	U.S.
30 Daimler Chrysler	Brazil	Automotive	4.5	Germany
31 Ford	Mexico	Automotive	4.4	U.S.
32 Esso (Brazil)	Brazil	Petroleum and gas	4.3	U.S.
33 Eletropaulo	Brazil	Electric power	3.9	U.S.
34 Embratel	Brazil	Telecom	3.8	U.S. (Worldcom)
35 Petrobras Energía	Argentina	Petroleum and gas	3.8	Brazil
36 Belgo Siderurgia	Brazil	Metallurgical	3.8	Belgium
37 PepsiCola Mexicana	Mexico	Beverages	3.2	U.S.
38 Collahuasi	Chile	Mining	3.2	International consortium
39 Caterpillar	Brazil	Machinery and equipment	3.1	U.S.
40 General Electric	Mexico	Electronics	3.0	U.S.

(Continued)

Table 8.7 (Continued)

Company	Country	Sector	Sales	Headquarters Country
41 Nestlé	Brazil	Food	2.9	Switzerland
42 CST	Brazil	Metallurgical	2.9	Luxembourg
43 BCP	Brazil	Telecom	2.9	—
44 Telefónica	Argentina	Telecom	2.9	Spain
45 Minería Antamina	Peru	Mining	2.8	International consortium
46 Grupo Bavaria	Colombia	Beverages	2.8	U.S.
47 Movistar	Venezuela	Telecom	2.7	Spain
48 Neoenergía	Brazil	Electric power	2.7	—
49 Telesp Celular	Brazil	Telecom	2.7	Portugal
50 Light	Brazil	Electric power	2.5	—

SOURCE: Excerpted, adapted, and translated from "Las Mayores por Propiedad," *AmericaEconomia,* July 9, 2007, p. 134.

NOTE: Headquarters country listed, where available.

growth relative to leading emerging nations. (See Figure 8.2, in which the tallest bars show the higher growth rates of East Asia and Pacific region.)

The slow growth brought new thinking and economic policy reforms in the 1990s, including less government ownership and regulation, more exchange rate flexibility, and reduced trade barriers. However, no regional nation except Chile yet scores high on global indices of economic freedom. In the 2008 Heritage Foundation/Wall Street Journal Index of Economic Freedom, Chile ranked number 8 among 162 countries (http://www. heritage.org/research/features/index/countries.cfm; see also O'Grady, 2008), followed in Latin America by El Salvador at number 33 and Mexico at number 44. The 2007–2008 Global Competitive Index of the World Economic Forum (131 countries) listed Chile at number 26, followed in the region by Mexico (number 52) and Panama (number 59), and the others well lower (http://www.weforum.org/en/initiatives/gcp/Global%20 Competitiveness%20Report/index.htm).

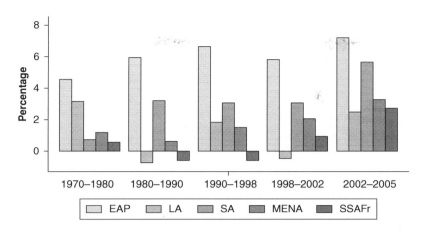

Figure 8.2   Growth in Gross Domestic Product per Capita in
Developing Country Regions, 1970–2005

SOURCE: Zettelmeyer (2006, p. 5).

EAP: East Asia & Pacific

LA: Latin America

SA: South Asia

MENA: Middle East and North Africa

SSAfr: Sub-Saharan Africa

There continue to be problems of local monopoly and oligopoly business structures in key sectors. In Mexico, for instance, this occurs in telecommunication, petroleum (state monopoly), cement, corn flour, television broadcasting, aviation, and retail banking (Castañeda, 2007; Perez Motta, 2007). Here and elsewhere, "political entrepreneurs" gain advantages (e.g., import protection, preferential loans, government business contracts, tax concessions, regulatory exemptions) that reduce competition (de Soto, 1989; Roberts & Araujo, 1997), to the disadvantage of consumers. Antitrust enforcement has been weak.

Banking and capital markets have been undersized relative to gross domestic product. Personal savings rates are low. Not many companies go public (however, in 2007, Brazil had a record number of initial public offerings). Throughout the region, the volume of capital investment and bank lending is below world averages (relative to gross domestic product). The regional physical infrastructure (transportation, communication, energy) has many shortcomings. Regional economic integration has advanced slowly and unevenly (e.g., in the Mercosur and Ancom customs unions of South America, in the Central American Common Market [still just a customs union despite the name], and through bilateral trade agreements).

The Latin American CEO

Information about Latin American CEOs has been scant. Because so few firms go public, few are obliged to disclose much internal information. And there has been little academic research on Latin American business and management, leading one historian to conclude that "arguably, business people are the most understudied group in modern Latin America" and that "the absence of serious studies of the history of business in Latin America is striking" (Eakin, 2000, p. 156). Also, the region's business schools have not been oriented toward research.

Consequently, the CEO profile presented here is selective, focusing mainly on well-established companies, that is, ones found in popular rankings of larger firms (e.g., on *Financial Times, Latin Trade,* and *América-Economía* rankings), which get the most attention in the local and international press. Many of these companies pursue foreign funding and list their shares on both local and foreign stock exchanges (e.g., in New York, London, Madrid) and must disclose considerable information. Also, corporate governance and investor information on their Web sites commonly includes a brief company history and list of names (and sometimes personal backgrounds) of senior executives and board directors. (See Table 8.8 for top management titles in English, Spanish, and Portuguese.)

Table 8.8   Top Management Titles in Three Languages

English	Spanish	Portuguese
Management	*Gerencia* *Gestión*	*Gerencia* *Gestão*
Manager	*Gerente*	*Gerente*
CEO Chief executive officer President	*Director executivo gerente* *Director gerente* *Director general* *Presidente*	*Diretor gerente* *Diretor geral* *Presidente*
Corporate governance	*Gobernanza corporativa*	*Governança corporativa*
Board of directors	*Consejo de administración*	*Conselho de administração*
Chairman (of the board of directors)	*Presidente del consejo de administración*	*Presidente do conselho de administração*
Business administration	*Administración de empresa*	*Administração de empresa*

There is also some information from consultancies. For example, human resource consultancy Towers Perrin annually reports CEO pay for Argentina, Brazil, Mexico, and Venezuela. Also, leading local business magazines have coverage of leading companies.

In the early 20th century, when Latin America began to industrialize, the pioneers were often immigrants or their immediate descendants (Cardoso, 1967; Strassmann, 1964). Although that pattern also holds in other settings (including the United States), it was particularly strong in Latin America. Sociologist Seymour Lipset (1967, pp. 24–25) cited corroborating evidence in the following quotations:

> Among the 32 outstanding business leaders in Mexico, 14 reported a foreign paternal grandfather (Vernon, 1963).

> Analysis of the backgrounds of 286 "prestigious" entrepreneurs, taken from the Argentine Who's Who, indicates that 45.5% were foreign born (Imaz, 1964).

> Data from a survey of heads of 46 out of the 113 industrial establishments in Santiago, Chile, which employ more than 100 workers indicate that 76% of them are immigrants or the children of immigrants (Higgins, 1963).

Bresser-Pereira (1964) noted that 84% of industrial pioneers in early 20th-century São Paulo (city and state of São Paulo, Brazil's industrial epicenter) were either immigrants or their immediate descendants (see also Bresser-Pereira, 1974). In those days, entrepreneurship was an open path for outsiders (immigrants and others) to gain financial security and social status beyond routes dominated by local elites. The latter were more likely to be in landholding, the military, or public office.

Brandenburg (1964) noted that the earliest industrial firms in Latin America were neither large nor technologically complex. They produced mainly consumer goods (e.g., textiles, clothing, processed foods, beverages). Also, the professional ability of entrepreneur–owner–managers wasn't as critical for survival then. More important were their entrepreneurial instincts, personal and political skills, and business and political connections. Some reasons included fewer competitors and more protected markets. Founders' children commonly took over when parents aged. Much nepotism still prevails in the region, though it is gradually declining.

Over time, by choice and by chance, many family businesses evolved into business groups, a pattern that reduced their vulnerability to business cycles and created additional career paths for relatives and acquaintances. Brandenburg (1964) described the pattern:

> The purpose of the enterprise was primarily to provide income for maintaining and improving the status, influence, and living standards of the family or small group of associates owning the business. . . . Management positions and responsibilities were usually reserved for members of the family. Little, if any, effort was made to train and promote non-related

employees to managerial levels within the enterprise, nor was much responsibility delegated to outsiders who might achieve supervisory positions. Younger members of the family qualified for future responsibilities by learning the business from within and not by obtaining managerial and technical training at modern universities or professional schools. (p. 6)

Derossi's (1971) study of familism and family enterprise in Mexico noted that an overwhelming majority of the firms (336-firm sample) were family owned. That pattern continues today but to a lesser degree (some leading family surnames were listed previously in Table 8.6) as time passes.

In general, when companies grow and mature, they need managerial talent beyond what ownership families can provide (cf. Brandenburg, 1962; Davis, 1968). Thus, nepotism diminishes gradually. Also, the entrepreneurial zeal of second- or third-generation family members often erodes as some pursue other career interests. Other pressures contribute to increased professionalism in management, including the taking public of some firms by their owners (and hence separation of ownership and control), more foreign sourcing and sales, and more alliances with foreign firms both at home and abroad. Also, a more integrated global economy brings stronger competitive pressures.

The demand for professional managers has brought increased interest in higher education oriented toward business and management.

HIGHER EDUCATION FOR BUSINESS AND MANAGEMENT

Formal higher education for business careers emerged slowly in Latin America. Its universities long downplayed applied disciplines such as business and engineering while attending more to law, medicine, and the social sciences. Economics and accounting (rather than management and business administration) were the focus for students pursuing business careers. In addition, the region's public universities have been constrained by heavy reliance on part-time instructors, low instructor pay, open admissions, overcrowding, and rigid administration.

These shortcomings induce many ambitious and affluent students to study abroad, especially in the United States and Europe. A U.S. or Western European master's degree in business has prestige locally. Also, study abroad can enhance English language skills, vital in a world where English has become the main language of global business.[6] At the MBA level, both North American and Spanish business schools recruit actively in Latin America, and many have joint degree programs with Latin American counterparts.

Latin American enrollment in business education has been expanding. In Brazil, for instance, about 14% of undergraduate university students now enter business studies (Wood, 2002), and there are accreditation standards for providers. In Mexico, too, enrollment has grown (Gomez, 2006). In 2007, a Mexican accreditation council for accounting and business studies (Council for the Accreditation of Accounting and Administration Studies) was active (http://www.caceca.org/Introduccion.htm).

A survey of 550 Latin American business executives in several countries asked respondents, "In which Latin American country(ies) other than your own would you select or recommend an MBA program?" Chile drew the highest response rate (59%), followed by Mexico (51%) and Brazil (32%) (AméricaEconomía Intelligence, 2002). Chile also had 3 of the top 8 ranked providers (and 11 of the top 49) in the 2008 *AméricaEconomía* magazine annual ranking of regional MBA programs (Table 8.9). In 2008, it also had the most institutional memberships (17) in the Latin American Council of Business Schools (http://www.cladea.org), followed by Colombia (14 members) and Brazil and Mexico (9 each).

Overall, private providers (universities, foundations, and technical institutes) have been more proactive in business education than have state-funded ones. Individual businesses, business spokesgroups, trade associations, and chambers of commerce are also initiators. For instance, the Brazilian Capital Markets Institute (IBMEC) created IBMEC Educacional (now IBMEC São Paulo), whose MBA program later moved to a private foundation. The Instituto Panamericano de Alta Dirección de Empresa (IPADE) is a high-level Mexican business school begun in 1967 with support from business leaders and later annexed to private Panamerican University. It now has permanent instructional sites in Mexico City, Monterrey, and Guadalajara and temporary ones in other cities. Mexico's DUXX Graduate School was started in 1993 with support from Monterrey businessman Alfonzo Garza Romo.

Monterrey is also home to the Escuela de Graduados en Administración y Dirección de Empresas (EGADE), a private provider affiliated with ITESM (Monterrey Technological Institute of Advanced Studies, "Mexico's MIT") and has branch operations in other cities. Mexican business magazine *Expansión* reported that EGADE and IPADE had educated about half of senior executives in large Mexican companies (reported in Authers & Silver, 2002, p. 5). Another survey (*Inversionista* magazine) reported that 40 CEOs from among Mexico's 250 largest companies attended one of those two schools (reported in Authers & Silver, 2002, p. 5).

Brazil's best-known provider has been the Getulio Vargas Foundation School of Business Administration (Escola de Administração de Empresas de São Paulo da Fundação Getulio Vargas [FGV-EAESP]), a private school begun in 1954 with support from Michigan State University. The foundation also supports the Brazilian School of Public and Business

Administration (FGV/EBAPE) in Rio de Janeiro. Other leading Brazilian providers include FIA-USP (Fundação Instituto de Administração of the University of Sao Paulo) and COPPEAD-UFRJ (Federal University of Rio de Janeiro).

In 2008, ITAM (Instituto Tecnológico Autónomo de Mexico) was the number 1 ranked MBA program in Latin America (*AméricaEconomía* magazine ranking). Number 2 was INCAE (Central American Institute of Business Administration), which had been number 1 the previous year.[7] INCAE has functioned since 1964, initially in Nicaragua with assistance from the business community, governments (U.S. and Central American), and the Harvard Business School. It is now based in Costa Rica and draws more than half of its faculty from business schools in the United States, Canada, and Europe; it pays them well and encourages research (not usual in Latin America) in tandem with teaching obligations.

See Table 8.9 for the 2008 *AméricaEconomía* magazine ranking of business schools. Most of those institutions meet accreditation standards of one or more leading international accreditors, such as the Association to Advance Collegiate Schools of Business (United States), the European Quality Improvement System, the Association of MBAs (United Kingdom), and the Southern Association of Colleges and Schools (United States).

Efforts to professionalize management education in the region have included a professional academic association, the Ibero-American Academy of Management, founded in 1997, with members drawn mainly from the Americas, Spain, and Portugal, and others with an interest in the region. That group has ties to the International Federation of Scholarly Associations of Management, the Academy of Management, and Global Foundation for Management Education. There are also professional associations at the country level, such as in Chile (Academia Chilena de Administración y Economía de Empresas) and Brazil (Academia Brasileira de Ciencia de Administração), and also some academic journals.[8]

EDUCATIONAL BACKGROUND OF LATIN AMERICAN CEOs

The region's CEOs are well educated, with degrees in diverse disciplines. Table 8.10 shows findings of a survey of senior executives in small, medium, and large businesses in five countries. It indicates that the larger the company, the more well educated is the CEO, a pattern that has prevailed also in the United States ("Corporate Elite," 1992, 1993). In larger firms in the *AméricaEconomía* survey, 94% of CEOs had earned a university degree; half had a postgraduate degree (master's or doctorate), numbers comparable to the U.S. "Corporate Elite."

Table 8.9 Leading MBA Programs in Latin America, *AméricaEconomía* Ranking, 2008

Program	Country	No. of Full-Time Professors	Percentage PhD Qualified
1 ITAM (Instituto Tecnológico Autónomo de Mexico)	Mexico	65	86.2
2 INCAE	Costa Rica	44	90.9
3 Universidad Adolfo Ibañez	Chile	50	72.0
4 PUC (Pontificia Universidad Católica) de Chile	Chile	30	60.0
5 Universidad de Los Andes	Colombia	36	80.6
6 EGADE, Tec de Monterrey, Campus Monterrey	Mexico	44	95.5
7 Instituto de Estudios Sup. de Administración	Venezuela	36	75.0
8 Universidad de Chile (Depto. Ingenieria Industrial)	Chile	51	85.5
9 Fundação Getulio Vargas FGV–EAESP (São Paulo)	Brazil	49	100.0
10 IAE (Universidad Austral)	Argentina	50	66.0
11 Universidad Torcuato di Tella	Argentina	22	81.8
12 Universidad del Desarrollo	Chile	21	57.1
13 CENTRUM, Pontificia Universidad Católica del Peru	Peru	48	83.3
14 Fundação Instituto de Administração–Universida de de São Paulo (FIA-USP)	Brazil	66	100.0
15 Universidad Técnica Federico Santa Maria	Chile	34	100.0
16 EGADE, Campus Zona Centro	Mexico	36	97.2
17 IPADE (Instituto Panamericano de Alta Dirección de Empresas	Mexico	64	32.8

(Continued)

Table 8.9 (Continued)

Program	Country	No. of Full-Time Professors	Percentage PhD Qualified
18 Universidad de San Andrés	Argentina	25	76.0
19 ESAN (Escuela de Admin. de Negocios Para Graduados)	Peru	36	58.3
20 EGADE, Campus Zona Metropolitana	Mexico	40	87.5

SOURCE: Condensed and adapted; 49 schools were included in the ranking, in "Especial: Escuelas de Negocios 2008," *AmericaEconomia,* July 25, 2008, pp. 22–23; for the criteria used in the ranking, see "Metodología ranking MBA 2008," available at http://beta.americaeconomia.com/rankings/111956-Metodologia-ranking-MBA-2008.note.aspx.

Table 8.10   Educational Background of Higher-Level Managers in Five Latin American Countries (Brazil, Mexico, Venezuela, Chile, Argentina), 1998

	Technical or Other	University	Postgraduate
Small firms	27%	45%	28%
Medium-size firms	19%	38%	43%
Large firms	6%	44%	50%

SOURCE: Data from nonrandom samples of 100 executives in each of five countries; see "Informe Especial," *AmericaEconomia,* October 22, 1998, p. 74. The data do not distinguish between Latin American nationals working in local private and government firms and ones employed locally in foreign-owned firms.

GENDER

Latin American CEOs are nearly exclusively male except for the occasional widow, sister, daughter, or niece of a family patriarch. There are few female board directors. *Latin Trade* magazine reported in 2005 that 64 of the region's 100 largest publicly traded companies had not one female director and that women accounted for just 5% of all directors (and these were usually family members of owners).

CEO MOBILITY

By global standards, CEO mobility between employers has been low. In that regard, consultancy Booz Allen Hamilton's annual survey of CEO turnover (world's 2,500 largest publicly traded companies) doesn't even categorize Latin America separately but rather puts its figures into a residual "other" category. One reason for low turnover is the small number of large publicly traded companies. Another is that company founders, or family members, dominate management and are generally disinclined to bring in outsiders.

There are also few independent directors, and there is not much tradition of stockholder activism, and hence less pressure to displace incumbent managers. Even in firms that go public, the family commonly retains a controlling block of stock.

Low executive turnover is also reflected in low professional search activity. According to the Association of Executive Search Consultants, the Central and South America region accounted for just 7% of the global retained executive search market in 2007 (compared with 42%, 35%, and 16%, respectively, for North America, Europe, and Asia/Pacific) (Association of Executive Search Consultants, 2007).

However, there are signs of increasing search activity. Pressure comes partly from growing competition and increased investment abroad by prominent Latin firms. Their expansion requires more managers than the ownership family can provide. The preferred candidates have a track record in other companies. Additional demand for talent comes from increased U.S. and European investment in the region. All this has spurred more interest in higher education in business and management and has put upward pressure on CEO pay. It is also influencing the composition of that pay.

PAY

CEO pay in Mexico and Brazil is nearly as high as in Western Europe but lower than in the United States. Argentine and Venezuelan CEOs earned about half as much as those in Mexico and Brazil. (The Towers Perrin Latin American numbers do not distinguish between pay by local and foreign-owned firms.) Average CEO pay in the region as a multiple of average workers' pay has been reported to be at least as high as in the United States.

Towers Perrin also observed that foreign investors have been introducing long-term incentive pay, including stock options, restricted stock, and performance shares. Although these are less common in Latin America than in the United States and Europe, they are more common than in Japan and India (Tables 8.11 and 8.12).

The following sections reflect on the management process (management functions) in Latin America, starting with planning.

Table 8.11   Mean CEO Pay, With Percentage Breakdown by Pay Component, 2005

	Total Pay (US$ million)	Basic Compensation	Variable Pay	Benefits	Perquisites
Mexico	1.00	48%	40%	7%	5%
Brazil	0.80	35	36	22	7
Venezuela	0.47	39	38	13	10
Argentina	0.40	43	31	14	12
India	0.29	45	14	8	33
Japan	0.54	56	22	15	7
United States	2.16	27	62	6	5
Canada	1.07	38	51	9	2
United Kingdom	1.20	43	35	19	3
France	1.20	40	41	19	0
Germany	1.18	37	52	11	0
Italy	1.10	41	35	21	3

SOURCE: Data from human resource consultancy Towers Perrin; some of the pay totals are approximate (from bar charts) in "Executive Pay" (2006, p. 102), and some are actual numbers in "Are CEOs Worth Their Weight in Gold?" (2006, p. A7).

The percentage figures are from "Managing Global Pay and Benefits" (2005, p. 24); all figures are for firms with at least $500 million in annual sales.

NOTE: *Variable pay* refers to bonuses tied to individual performance and long-term incentives (stock options, stock grants, and similar awards).

An abrupt devaluation of the Argentine peso in 2001 reduced Argentine CEO salaries, when expressed in U.S. dollars, to one third of their previous level; however, the purchasing power of those salaries inside Argentina didn't change much.

Table 8.12 Estimated Percentage of Companies Offering Long-Term Incentive Awards (excludes cash awards; includes stock options, restricted stock, and performance shares)

	2001	2005 (estimated)
Argentina	40%	60%
Brazil	40	65
Mexico	15	55
China (Shanghai)	20	35
South Korea	15	25
Japan	15	35
India	10	20
United States	100	95
United Kingdom	100	95
Spain	50	70
France	90	95
Germany	60	85
Italy	50	85

SOURCE: "Equity Incentives Around the World" (2005, p. 4).

Latin American Management

PLANNING

In business, planning determines where a company should be headed and for what reasons, by which paths, by when, and by whom. Whether done formally or informally, it is a rational way to deal with change in organizations and their environments. Business planning is influenced by organizational context, such as size. For example, small firms operating in isolated or protected home markets (common, historically, in Latin America) tend to do less formal planning, and less of it long term, than do large firms serving bigger and more open markets.

In Latin culture, there is a historical tendency to procrastinate, and people sometimes are more inclined than their peers in North America, northern Europe, and Japan to work to live rather than live to work, and to survive day by day. Political and economic uncertainty also force this focus to be more near term. Brazilian professor de Almeida Prado (2002) observed, "It is our tendency as Brazilians to persevere with an adequate but minimum level of effort in pursuing objectives. . . . You could say that the Brazilian doesn't plan or pursue optimal use of available resources; rather we are drawn to short-term rewards" (p. 12).

In regard to corporate strategy, Collins, Holzmann, and Mendoza (1997) judged that Latin American firms have more often been defenders (defending established product niches and pursuing cost efficiencies) rather than "analyzers/prospectors" pursuing new products or technologies. Defenders, they suggested, are less likely than "analyzers/prospectors" to do formal long-range planning. The Brazilian government's Institute for Applied Economic Research (Instituto de Pesquisa Economica Aplicada) reported that of 72,000 industrial enterprises, only 1,200 competed by differentiating their products ("A Special Report on Brazil," 2007).

Throughout Latin America, government intrusion can complicate corporate planning and action in both private and state-owned business. This is especially so in large state-owned firms such as Petroleos Mexicanos (Pemex) and Petroleos de Venezuela (PDVSA), where most earnings go directly to the government treasury. In these and other state firms, political pressures, labor unions, and the law often hinder efforts to spur productivity (e.g., laying off employees). Firms struggle to balance long-term objectives (efficiency, competitiveness) with near-term political pressures (political patronage, politically driven social spending, job protection). Their CEOs and directors are often political appointees displaced by change in public administration. In Mexico, for instance, Pemex's 11-member board of directors recently had 6 presidential appointees, including its chairman, and 5 labor union representatives. In Venezuela in 2008, the CEO of PDVSA, Rafael Ramirez, was also the nation's energy minister.

Private enterprise also faces significant government intrusion. In Argentina, for instance, the government has pressured individual businesses to curtail price increases and limit exports (e.g., of food products, including beef) to fight inflation. In the Argentine telephone and electricity sectors, price controls have slowed providers' plans to expand capacity and led to divestment by Spanish and French firms. The government-suppressed prices, in turn, have boosted usage, putting even more pressure on current capacity.

Throughout the region, political risk, regulatory change, and infrastructural shortcomings (e.g., transportation bottlenecks, inefficient public services, energy shortages) force more flexibility in planning, more frequent adjustments of plans, and more contingency planning, and make long-term planning difficult.

This has contributed to and reinforced a tradition of flexibility and improvisation in planning and action. For example, Brazilians popularly acknowledge and depend on the *jeitinho,* an inventive way to deal with forces and factors (e.g., bureaucracy, laws, norms, taxes, rules) that impede action (Amado & Brasil, 1991; de Almeida Prado, 2005). In essence, by hook or by crook, through creative legal, quasilegal, and illegal means, obstacles can be overcome and benefits gained.

This is certainly seen in the large informal part of the economy that operates in tandem with the official one (to circumvent taxes, labor law, and other regulations). This includes manufacturers who outsource some of their assembly work off the books to private households and small businesspersons and entrepreneurs not formally registered for social security tax contributions (de Soto, 1989; Ghersi, 1997).

Today, more intense business competition, spurred by regional economic integration and globalization, is forcing prominent Latin American companies to formalize more of their planning. So concluded a study (Trevino, 1998) in which Mexican executives reported changes in their planning practices after Mexican accession to the General Agreement on Tariffs and Trade in the mid-1980s. Until then, local firms were protected by trade barriers. Planning was more short term, but this changed gradually with the erosion of trade barriers. Trevino (1998, p. 79) observed that "on many dimensions of planning, strategy, structure, and decision processes, Mexican managers . . . responded . . . much like other global managers in more advanced countries." In so doing, they initiated more formal planning, more systematic monitoring of the business environment, and more industry and competitive analyses than previously. Those tendencies likely intensified after Mexican accession to the North American Free Trade Agreement in 1994.

Today, CEOs in leading Latin American firms are generally attuned to management practices abroad (including more sophisticated planning practices). Many are allied with foreign firms. A significant number are multinational companies in their own right ("Especial Multilatinas," 2008; Krauss, 2007; Martinez, De Souza, & Liu, 2003). Moreover, the spread of management consultancies in the region has contributed to more formal planning (Wood, 2002). This is reflected in consultancy Bain & Company's annual "Management Tools" survey of global executives (cross-section of large, medium, and small firms in diverse businesses worldwide). The Bain 2007 survey queried 1,220 executives (10% from Latin America) about their use of 25 popular management tools, including several associated with formal planning. On four of the six listed in Table 8.13, Latin American numbers were comparable to those for North America and Europe.

Table 8.13   Use of Corporate Planning Tools (Techniques)

	North America	Europe	Asia	Latin America
Strategic planning	90%	90%	85%	91%
Mission and vision statements	83	76	76	79
Strategic alliances	75	66	66	56
Scenario and contingency planning	72	74	64	72
Core competencies	81	80	79	63
Growth strategies	67	65	61	73

SOURCE: Adapted from Rigby and Bilodeau (2007).

Strategic planning: The comprehensive process of determining what a business should become and how to allocate scarce resources to get there.

Mission and vision statements: Codified definitions of a company's business, objectives, approach, and desired future position.

Strategic alliances: Creation of agreements between firms in which each commits resources to achieve a common set of objectives.

Scenario and contingency planning: The raising and testing of various "what-if" scenarios.

Core competencies: Identification and investment in special skills or technologies that create unique customer value.

Growth strategies: Identification and direction of resources toward opportunities for profitable growth.

CONTROL

The management process of control is concerned with monitoring performance and ensuring accountability to stakeholders, including owners, employees, communities, suppliers, creditors, and the government. In a broad sense, this is the realm of corporate governance and profitability. More narrowly, it involves day-by-day monitoring of operations (e.g., feedback, supervision, quality control) and making adjustments, as needed, to operations and plans.

Except for a few settings (e.g., the United States, United Kingdom, Canada, Ireland, Australia, Japan), prominent private businesses and business groups around the world remain largely family controlled, even for firms that go public (LaPorta, Lopez-de-Silanes, & Schleifer, 1999). This applies particularly in Latin America, where equity markets have been small and there are fewer independent shareholders. Table 8.14 indicates the extent of family ownership in major corporate groups in several countries (including seven in Latin America).

Table 8.14   Extent of Family Control in the 10 Largest Private Conglomerates, by
             Country

Argentina	85.2%
Brazil	91.3
Chile	100.0
Colombia	85.2
Mexico	100.0
Peru	100.0
Venezuela	100.0
United Kingdom	15.9
Ireland	27.9
United States	18.8
Netherlands	19.8
Japan	0.0
Singapore	15.8
Hong Kong	42.7
Philippines	100.0
France	38.2
Italy	67.1
Spain	46.8
Portugal	96.0

SOURCE: Based on Dun & Bradstreet data for publicly held corporations, reported in Fogel (2006, p. 608, Table 1).

Family control can continue even when the family holds a small proportion of company stock if the other shareholders are dispersed portfolio investors not interested in a voice in management. Control can also continue through complex ownership pyramids and cross-shareholdings. Family owners often own "preference shares" that carry superproportional voting rights. In Fomento Económico Mexicano, S.A. (a Mexican beverage company), for example, two families (Garza and Fernandez) have controlled more than half of the voting rights while owning less than 30% of the stock (Mandel-Campbell, 2001). In Televisa (a Mexican media company), three fourths of shares were widely held but had less than half of the voting rights. In some firms, nonfamily investors are limited to nonvoting and restricted stock.

In the prototype private Latin American business or business group, a family patriarch (CEO or board chairman) commonly oversees operations. Boards of directors are often stacked with relatives and acquaintances disinclined to challenge managerial decisions or actions. In the controlling family, continuity of management takes priority over optimal financial results, hence the reluctance (except in a crisis) to hire a professional non-family manager or to form independent boards.

In Latin America, there is little tradition of shareholder activism. Less than 5% of the population owns stock, either individually or through investment pensions or mutual funds. By contrast, more than one half of U.S. citizens and many Western Europeans directly or indirectly own company stock.

Effective external and internal corporate control requires reliable, timely, clear reporting. In Latin America, the interpretation of financial reports can be problematic because of irregular reporting practices and ambiguous accounting standards. These are set locally, not harmonized regionally or with the International Financial Reporting Standards of the International Accounting Standards Board.

Standard & Poor's regularly ranks the region low in terms of finance and accounting transparency and disclosure (Table 8.15). Also, Latin America scores low on the PricewaterhouseCoopers opacity index.

In the past, analysis of Latin American financial reports has been complicated by high price inflation and currency (exchange rate) devaluations (Blake, Wraith, & Amat, 1998). Fortunately, in many countries, inflation rates have diminished, but they continue to be troublesome in others (e.g., Argentina and Venezuela).

Hazy and incomplete financial disclosure contributes to the small equity markets, low investor confidence, and low share turnover. For these and other reasons, stock markets have not been an active instrument of corporate control (not used much to effect takeovers, buyouts, mergers, or CEO departures).

The more prominent private Latin American firms also list their shares on U.S. and European stock exchanges (Table 8.16). Brazil's Vale (formerly CVRD), for instance, is listed in New York, London, and Madrid, where the accounting and financial disclosure standards and requirements are high. In 2007, 86 Latin America firms were listed on the New York Stock Exchange, and these were mainly from four countries: Brazil (35 firms), Mexico (16), Chile (17), and Argentina (11).

Table 8.15   Transparency and Disclosure Scores* for Emerging Markets

	Number of Companies	Average Transparency and Disclosure Score
Asia	200	43
Latin America		
Argentina	9	29
Brazil	30	32
Chile	19	32
Mexico	15	24
Brazil	7	22
Eastern Europe, Middle East	53	36
South Africa	21	55

SOURCE: This table is a condensed and adapted version of a chart in Patel, Balic, and Bwakira (2002, p. 12). See also Patel and Dallas (2002).

NOTE: The figures came from Dun & Bradstreet and were based on corporate disclosure in more than 1,200 companies worldwide, including 80 from Latin America. Respondents were asked 98 questions about ownership structure, financial transparency, and board and management structure and processes. The report included reviews of company annual reports, 10K and proxy statements, and voluntary disclosures beyond what the law required; it didn't look at company Web sites. The higher the score, the more open and comprehensive is financial reporting.

ORGANIZING

There has been no systematic tracking of Latin American organization patterns and structures comparable to that for Western European and U.S. enterprise, or for the Japanese *keiretsu* and Korean *chaebol*. However, two patterns are apparent in the region, both common to emerging economies. One is the small size of private sector businesses and the other is extensive corporate groupism (family-controlled conglomerates of mainly small and medium-size businesses).

Small Size

Like those in Latin Europe (e.g., Italy, Portugal, Spain), Latin American businesses (especially manufacturers) have been small by comparison with peers elsewhere. In that regard, the 2008 Fortune Global 500 (ranking by

Table 8.16   Stock Exchange Listings, by Country, c. 2007

	Local Stock Exchange	Number of Locally Listed Companies
Brazil	Bolsa de Valores do São Paulo	495
Mexico	Bolsa Mexicana de Valores	150
Chile	Bolsa de Comercio de Santiago	245
Argentina	Bolsa de Comercio de Buenos Aires	100
Colombia	Bolsa de Valores de Colombia	98
Peru	Bolsa de Valores de Lima	93
London	London Stock Exchange	3,091
Tokyo	Tokyo Stock Exchange	2,351
United States	American Stock Exchange	595
	NASDAQ	3,164
	NYSE	2,270

SOURCE: From World Federation of Exchanges (2007).

sales) listed just 10 private firms from the region. Five were Mexican, including state-owned Pemex (petroleum) and CFE (electric power), plus telecom providers America Movil and Carso Global Telecom and cement multinational Cemex. Another five were Brazilian, including state-owned Petrobras (petroleum) plus mining giant CVRD (now called Vale) and three financial institutions (Banco do Brasil, Banco Bradesco, and Itaúsa Investments). Cemex was the only manufacturer among the 10. Vale is a former SOE.

The 2008 *Financial Times* Global 500 (ranking by market value of company shares) had 17 private Latin American entries, including 4 from Mexico, 11 from Brazil, and one each from Argentina and Chile.

A study of largest local Latin American nonfinancial firms found their size to be about half that of most other countries, based on their assets in relation to gross domestic product (Herrera & Lora, 2005). Only Chile was close to the international norm. The average number of employees in these firms was about one third that of other developing countries (in proportion to the national working-age population). That study and others attributed the smaller size to fragmented and protected home markets, underdeveloped infrastructure, undersized capital markets, and too few experienced managers. Cultural factors also pertain. As in Latin Europe, long-standing family owners have been reluctant to rapidly increase the size of their businesses, preferring family control and continuity. Growth commonly entails significant external capital and dilution of control and brings more outsiders into management and onto boards of directors.

However, economic change (including globalization) is bringing substantial growth in some Latin American firms, with many induced to integrate and coordinate domestic and international operations. These firms no longer rely on the simpler business function–oriented organization structures historically found in smaller firms but rather use divisional structures (product or geographic area divisions).

Groupism

The other feature of private Latin American business is pervasive groupism (family-based conglomerates of small and medium-size firms). Some are quite diversified, and others are more focused on a single business sector. Groups arose not so much from a desire to spread business risk (a corollary benefit) or from strong government pressure or guidance but rather from favorable business circumstances and the need to put extra cash flow somewhere productive in view of the thin, illiquid, and underdeveloped local capital markets.

New business opportunities arose from preferential government regulations, personal connections, and alliances with foreign firms. In effect, many families developed the capability for new business entry, a catalyst to modernization (Guillen, 2000; Leff, 1978). This also produced more managerial employment for kin.

Most Latin American business groups continue to be closely tied to founder families. An unusually large group is the Slim family business empire (Carlos Slim-Helu, Mexico), engaged in telecom, hotel, retail, media, financial service, and industrial ventures both inside and beyond Mexico (Meta, 2007). Its two largest members (América Movil and Grupo Carso Telecom) were listed on the 2008 Fortune Global 500. Five Slim enterprises were listed in Table 8.6. One of them (Grupo Carso) is itself a diversified holding company. Other Slim family capital is invested beyond the group (e.g., in Televisa). Televisa (Azcárraga family) is engaged in broadcast media and programming, film, live entertainment, publishing, and Internet services. Grupo Alfa is one of several linked to long-standing Monterey entrepreneurial clans (Garza, Sada, and others) and engaged in petrochemicals, metallurgy, refrigerated foods, auto parts, and telecommunication. The Salinas Group is active in media, telecom, auto parts, financial services, and retail (appliances and consumer electronics). The Senderos family is linked to Grupo Kuo (formerly Desc), involved in auto parts, chemicals, consumer goods, and foods. There are many others.

In Brazil, business groupism is extensive. For example, the Votorantim group (Emirio de Moraes family) is engaged in financial services, building materials, food products, pulp and paper, metals, chemicals, and agribusiness. The Itausa Group (Egydio and Setubal family) is involved mainly in financial services but also in real estate, building products, chemicals, electronics, and information technology. Grupo Camargo Correa (Camargo family) is engaged in construction, engineering, steel, textiles, footwear, electronics, and other pursuits.

Elsewhere in the hemisphere, such as in Colombia (Antioquia province), the Grupo Empresarial Antioqueño binds three diversified groups and 125 businesses engaged in financial services, food products, cement, and other ventures. In Chile, the Luksic family group is involved in banking, beverages, foods, mining, and other industries.

Regional and global competitive forces have been eroding the more diversified groups, as also happened in the United States and Western Europe, where few family-run conglomerates remain. In Brazil, between 1994 and 1998 the number of family-controlled groups among the largest 300 local private firms decreased from 287 to 265 ("Generation Game," 1999). The trend there has been toward more focus, effected gradually through sell-offs, mergers, acquisitions, and spin-offs.

DIRECTING

The managerial function of directing involves leadership, communication, and motivation and is much influenced by culture. Here, Latin American and Latin European countries share some commonalities. Both show a similar profile on Hofstede's cultural dimensions (Table 8.17).

Historically, the prevailing leadership style in Latin society has been benevolent authoritarian and patriarchal. A family patriarch runs the business in paternal fashion. It is not unusual for an owner or boss to take protective personal interest in the work life and private life of key subordinates. Subordinates' loyalty to the boss (or owner) is commonly stronger than to firms. Personalized face-to-face communications are more important than impersonal written reports and memos. There tends to be a flexible view of time (common in high-context settings). Interpersonal communication is more often implicit and indirect than in low-context cultures. At work, evaluation of subordinate performance is best done tactfully rather than bluntly. Personal relationships, trust, and rapport generally take precedence over procedures and formalities.

Jaeger (1986) and Bourgeois and Boltvinik (1981) suggested that the high power distance in Latin culture is not conducive to much employee participation in decision making or extensive delegation of authority to subordinates. Forms of employer–employee involvement sometimes used in low-context cultures, such as bottom-up evaluation of superiors by subordinates, employee decision sharing, and planned organization development interventions can be more problematic in Latin settings (Bourgeois & Boltvinik, 1981; Jaeger, 1986).

Table 8.17 contrasts some cultural values favorable to behavioral interventions with some conflicting Latin value patterns.

In interpreting human behavior, sociologist Talcott Parsons (1977) conceptualized several contrasting pairs of "pattern variables" that orient human

Table 8.17   Organization Development Values and Latin American Cultural Values

Values Favorable to Productive Organization Development Interventions	Latin American Values
Low-to-Medium Individualism Contributes to consensus building and stronger orientation toward group goals and interests.	**Medium-to-High Individualism** If high, self-interest can take precedence over group interests.
Low Masculinity Conducive to group solidarity and decision sharing.	**High Masculinity** Conducive to a directive, authoritarian leadership style rather than a participative one.
Low Power Distance Contributes to stronger sense of equality and participation.	**High Power Distance** Likely to impede participation and social interaction in organizational hierarchies
Low Uncertainty Avoidance Increases acceptance of change.	**High Uncertainty Avoidance** Inhibits acceptance of new ideas and change.

SOURCE: This schema draws from ideas and views expressed by Jaeger (1986), Bourgeois and Boltvinik (1981), and Hofstede (1984).

mind-sets and social interaction. Two Parsonian value pairs that are pertinent here are universalism versus particularism and achievement orientation versus ascription. These are relevant, for example, in hiring and promotion and also in leadership, followership, and motivation.

Where universalistic values prevail, more emphasis is placed on merit in hiring and promotion, that is, on proven competence based on impartial standards and norms. Society is more achievement oriented. Self-worth, image, and identity are based more on career path and performance. By contrast, where particularist tendencies prevail, individuals succeed or prosper (e.g., are hired, promoted, and compensated) based more on who they are related to or personally connected to (family and other preferential connections).

Individuals in universalistic, achievement-oriented cultures are more likely to be self-motivated. There is generally more extensive delegation of authority and more individual initiative and leadership. By contrast, in more traditional (particularistic, ascriptive) societies (Latin America, historically), motivation is more influenced by interpersonal ties and obligations to an owner or boss than by those to the collective (i.e., the company), and there is a stronger tendency for passive followership. Leaders tend to hoard authority rather than delegate or decentralize it to others, and there is less expectation and acceptance of delegated authority by subordinates.

Chapter Summary

- Latin nations of the Western Hemisphere have been much overlooked from a managerial perspective. Despite economic advances and some globally competitive businesses, overall economic and social progress has been slow compared with that in East Asia.

- From a cultural perspective, Latin society has had cultural, linguistic, and demographic ties to Iberian Europe. The culture is high context; that is, relationships and personal connections are important for getting things done, and there is a flexible view of time.

- Politically, democracies prevail, but political uncertainty, regulatory ambiguity, and excessive government intrusion in economic life persist. Economies have a mix of private and state enterprises, but the private sector is large and has gained ground in recent years. However, the region's biggest firms are state owned (mainly in natural resource extraction and electric power generation).

- Fuller economic freedom has been elusive, and markets for human, physical, and financial resources are constrained. Banking and capital markets are underdeveloped, and there are shortcomings in education and physical infrastructure.

- Historically, immigrants and their immediate descendants pioneered industrial development in the region. Their businesses commonly evolved into family-controlled business groups that have dominated the economic landscape, but decreasingly so as time passes.

- CEOs of the largest companies are well educated. There are few female corporate officers and directors. CEO mobility between firms is low. Local and international business competition and cooperation have been eroding family-based management, and there is an increasing emergence of professional managers. This, in turn, has brought more attention to higher education for business and management. It has also contributed to rising CEO pay and increasing incidence of incentive pay. CEO pay is lower than in advanced industrial countries (except in Mexico and Brazil, where it is near Western European levels).

- The smaller size of Latin American businesses, political and economic uncertainty, and government intrusion make formal corporate planning problematic. Circumstances are conducive to improvisation, frequent adjustments of plans, and contingency planning. However, there is evidence that competition spurred by regional economic integration and globalization is forcing change.

- Prominent businesses and business groups remain family controlled, even ones that go public. Corporate shareholdings are concentrated.

Boards of directors are staffed mainly with relatives, friends, and others not much inclined to challenge management decision or actions. Continuity of family control has often had higher priority than optimal financial efficiency.

- Economic volatility (business cycles, price inflation, and currency fluctuations) has complicated financial and accounting reporting; accounting standards aren't harmonized with international standards. For these and other reasons, stock markets have been a weaker instrument of corporate control (e.g., fewer takeovers, buyouts, or mergers involving exchange of stock). However, many prominent Latin firms list their shares abroad, where accounting and reporting standards are more rigorous, to facilitate new external capital and alliances.

- The modest size and narrow product lines of most private Latin American businesses are conducive to simpler corporate structures focused on business functions. However, a few firms have aggressively expanded business across and beyond the region. They face choices about how best to integrate and coordinate their domestic and international operations.

- In Latin society, leadership has been traditionally authoritarian (benevolent authoritarian), personal, and paternalistic. Cultural acceptance of social inequality (high power distance) is conducive to centralized authority and more limited delegation of decision-making authority to subordinates.

Terms and Concepts

family capitalism
free market economic reforms
gerente
high-context culture
jeitinho
Latin America

mixed economy
nepotism
particularism
personalism
transparency and disclosure index

Study Questions

1. What is distinctive about the economic and political context in Latin America, and what implications does this raise for successfully managing a business there?

2. Describe the prominent traits and tendencies in Latin American culture from the perspective of Edward Hall (high-context vs. low-context

culture) and Geert Hofstede (dimensions of culture). What implications do these raise in regard to the management function of directing (leadership, communication, and motivation)?

Exercise 8.1

Pick a private Latin American family corporate group whose CEO is from that family (it could be from a list in this chapter). To what extent and at what level are other family members involved in managing or advising the company?

Develop a personal profile of two or more of those family members with respect to their age, educational background, gender, and work experience. You could check the company's Web page (many Latin American company Web sites are bilingual) and scan for coverage in the business press.

Exercise 8.2

Investigate an academic degree program (bachelor's or master's level) in a Latin American business school and describe how it is different from your own or another with which you are familiar.

Notes

1. See "100 Competitivas de America Latina" (2006), an annual ranking of 100 internationally competitive Latin American firms based on their last 3-year return on assets relative to that of their business sector; also, 8 Latin American firms are listed in a ranking of "top 25 world class emerging multinationals," in van Agtmael (2007).

2. The 2007 Fortune Global 500 (ranking by sales) 10 Latin American firms, including 5 from Mexico (state-owned Pemex and CFE and private America Movil, Cemex, and Carso Global Telecom) and 5 from Brazil (state-owned Petrobras; private banks Banco Bradesco, Itaúsa-Investimentos Itaú, and Banco do Brasil; and CVRD, now called Vale). The 2006 Financial Times Global 500 (ranking by market value of company shares) listed 4 Mexican firms (America Movil, Cemex, Wal-Mart de Mexico, and Telmex), 6 from Brazil (Petrobras, Vale, Bradesco, Itausa, Ambev, Banco Brasil), and Argentine steel maker Tenaris.

3. *Latin America* refers to Western Hemisphere nations with languages derived largely from Latin (language of early Rome) including Spanish (18 nations), Portuguese (Brazil), and French (Haiti).

4. See also the latest *Regional economic outlook: Western Hemisphere* by the International Monetary Fund; see also recent country and region surveys from *The Economist* and *Financial Times*.

5. Haiti is the region's lone nation state with French heritage.

6. In 2007–2008, about 12% of 623,805 non-U.S. students enrolled in U.S. higher education were from Latin America, led by Mexico (14,837), Brazil (7,578), and

Colombia (6,662). About one fifth of foreign students in the United States enroll in business studies, and about one half of these students are enrolled in MBA or doctoral programs (*Open Doors*, 2007).

7. *Latin Trade* magazine also publishes an annual rating of regional business schools; its version includes several U.S. institutions that give attention to Latin America in their academic programs.

8. Brazilian academic journals on management include *Revista de Administração, Revista de Administração Contemporânea, Revista de Administração de Empresas, Revista Latinoamericano de Administración, Revista Ciência Empresarial, Revista Brasileira de Administração,* and *Revista Nacional Angrad*.

References

100 competitivas de America Latina [100 competitive corporations in Latin America]. (2006, April 14–May 4). *AméricaEconomía*, p. 322.

Amado, G., & Brasil, H. (1991). Organizational behaviors and cultural context: The Brazilian "jeitinho." *International Studies of Management and Organization, 21*(3), 38–61.

AméricaEconomía Intelligence. (2002, August 23). Más que mil palabras. *AméricaEconomía*, p. 46.

Are CEOs worth their weight in gold? (2006, January 21). *Wall Street Journal*, p. A7.

Association of Executive Search Consultants. (2007). *Executive search industry revenues continue to rise despite the drop in financial markets.* Retrieved September 11, 2008, from http://www.aesc.org/article/pressrelease2007111301/

Authers, J., & Silver, S. (2002, May 28). Profile EGADE and IPADE; sights set on foreign students. *Financial Times*, p. 5.

Blake, J., Wraith, P., & Amat, O. (1998, April 1). Management accounting in Latin America. *Management Accounting, 76*(4), 56.

Bourgeois, L. III, & Boltvinik, M. (1981, Spring). OD in crosscultural settings: Latin America. *California Management Review, 23*(3), 75–81.

Brandenburg, F. (1962, Winter). The case of Mexico: A contribution to the theory of entrepreneurship and economic development. *Inter-American Economic Affairs, 16*(1), 3–23.

Brandenburg, F. (1964). *The development of Latin American private enterprise.* Washington, DC: National Planning Association.

Bresser-Pereira, L. (1964, June). Brazil: Ethnic and social origins of the industrial entrepreneurs. *Revista de Administração de Empresas, 4*(11), 83–103.

Bresser-Pereira, L. (1974). *Empresários e administradores no Brasil* [Businessmen and managers in Brazil]. São Paulo: Editora Brasiliense.

Cardoso, F. (1967). *The industrial elite.* In S. Lipset & A. Solari (Eds.), *Elites in Latin America* (pp. 94–114). Oxford: Oxford University Press.

Castañeda, J. (2007, February 5). Mexico needs to be freed from unhealthy monopoly. *Financial Times*, p. 13.

Central Intelligence Agency. (2007). *The world factbook 2007.* Retrieved September 11, 2008, from https://www.cia.gov/library/publications/the-world-factbook/index.html

Collins, F., Holzmann, G., & Mendoza, R. (1997). Strategy, budgeting, and crisis in Latin America. *Accounting, Organizations and Society, 22*(7), 669–689.

Corporate elite. (1992, October 12). *BusinessWeek,* pp. 119–146.

Corporate elite. (1993, October 11). *BusinessWeek,* pp. 64–109.

Davis, S. (1968, December). Entrepreneurial succession. *Administrative Science Quarterly, 3,* 402–416.

de Almeida Prado, M. C. (2005). *"Jeitinho" e cultura organizacional brasileira: Ultrapassando a abordagem de integração* ["Jeitinho" and Brazilian organizational culture]. GVpesquisa, FGV EAESP, Relatório 25/2005. Retrieved September 11, 2008, from http://www.eaesp.fgvsp.br/Interna.aspx?PagId= DLMJMMTJ&ID=337

Derossi, F. (1971). *The Mexican entrepreneur.* Paris: OECD Development Centre.

de Soto, H. (1989). *The other path: The invisible revolution in the third world.* New York: Harper & Row.

Drucker, P. (1973). *Management tasks, responsibilities, practices.* New York: Harper & Row.

Eakin, M. (2000). [Untitled review]. *The Americas, 57*(1), 156–157.

Equity incentives around the world. (2005). Towers Perrin HR Services. Retrieved July 1, 2005, from http://www/towersperrrin.com.

Especial: Escuelas de negocios 2008 [Special: Business schools]. (2008, August 25). Ranking Latinoamericano. *AméricaEconomía,* pp. 22–23.

Especial: Multilatinas [Special: Multinationals]. (2008, April 1). *AméricaEconomía,* pp. 26–36.

Executive pay. (2006, January 21). *The Economist,* p. 102.

Financial Times Global 500. (2008). *Financial Times.* Retrieved September 11, 2008, from http://media.ft.com/cms/8ebb955e-4142-11dd-9661-0000779fd2ac.pdf

Fogel, K. (2006). Oligarchic family control and the quality of government. *Journal of International Business Studies, 37*(5), 603–623.

Fortune Global 500. (2008, July 21). *Fortune,* pp. 165–182.

Generation game. (1999, June). *Latin Finance, 108,* 20–22.

Ghersi, E. (1997, Spring). The informal economy in Latin America. *The Cato Journal, 17*(1), 99.

Gomez, J. A. (2006). Mexico. In *A global guide to management education 2006* (pp. 127–131). Global Foundation for Management Education. Retrieved September 11, 2008, from http://www.gfme.org/

Guillen, M. (2000). Business groups in emerging economies: A resource-based view. *Academy of Management Journal, 43*(3), 362–380.

Herrera, A. M., & Lora, E. (2005, July 7). Why so small? Explaining the size of firms in Latin America. *The World Economy, 28,* 1005–1028.

Hofstede, G. (1984). *Culture's consequences: International differences in work-related value* (Abridged ed.). Beverly Hills, CA: Sage.

Informe especial: Gestión empresarial en América Latina 1998 [Special report: Corporate management in Latin America]. (1998, October 22). *AméricaEconomía,* p. 74.

Jaeger, A. (1986). Organization development and national culture: Where is the fit? *Academy of Management Review, 11*(1), 178–190.

Krauss, C. (2007, May 2). New accents in the U.S. economy: Latin American companies make gains north of the border. *New York Times,* p. C1.

La Porta, R., Lopez-de-Silanes, F., & Schleifer, A. (1999). Corporate ownership around the world. *Journal of Finance, 54*(2), 471–517.

Las 500 por país [The 500 by country]. (2007, July 9). *AméricaEconomía,* p. 64.

Las 500 por propiedad [The 500 by ownership]. (2003, July 14–August 17). *AméricaEconomía,* p. 147.

Las 500 por propiedad [The 500 by ownership]. (2006, July 4–31). *AméricaEconomía,* p. 107.

Las mayores empresas de América Latina [The largest companies in Latin America]. (2008, July 21). *AméricaEconomía,* p. 110.

Las mayores por país [The largest firms by country]. (2003, July 4–31). *AméricaEconomía,* p. 110.

Las mayores por país [The largest firms by country]. (2006, July 14–August 17). *AméricaEconomía,* p. 172.

Las mayores por propiedad [The largest by ownership]. (2007, July 9). *AméricaEconomía,* p. 134.

Leff, N. (1978). Industrial organization and entrepreneurship in developing countries: The economic groups. *Economic Development and Cultural Change, 26,* 661–675.

Lipset, S. (1967). Values, education, and entrepreneurship. In S. Lipset & A. Solari (Eds.), *Elites in Latin America* (pp. 24–25). Oxford, UK: Oxford University Press.

Managing global pay and benefits. (2005). Towers Perrin HR Services. Retrieved January 11, 2006, from http://www.towersperrin.com

Mandel-Campbell, A. (2001, July 3). A corporate revolution in Mexico. *Financial Times,* p. 15.

Martinez, A., De Souza, I., & Liu, F. (2003, Fall). Multinationals vs. multilatinas: Latin America's great race. *strategy + business, 32.* Retrieved September 12, 2008, from http://www.strategy-business.com/press/article/03307?pg=0

Meta, S. (2007, August 20). Carlos Slim: The richest man in the world. *Fortune,* pp. 23–29.

O'Grady, M. A. (2008, January 15). The real key to development. *Wall Street Journal,* p. A10.

Open doors. (2008). International Institute for Education. Retrieved November 22, 2008, from http://opendoors.iienetwork.org/?p=131534

Parsons, T. (1977). *Social systems and the evolution of action theory.* New York: Free Press.

Patel, S., Balic, A., & Bwakira, L. (2002, May). *Measuring T&D at firm-level in emerging markets.* New York: Standard & Poor's.

Patel, S. A., & Dallas, G. (2002, October 16). *Transparency and disclosure: Overview of methodology and study results—United States.* New York: Standard & Poor's. http://www.theiia.org/chapters/pubdocs/86/S&P.pdf

Perez Motta, E. (2007, May 9). A commitment to markets is needed. *Financial Times,* p. 6.

Rigby, D., & Bilodeau, B. (2007). *Management tools and trends 2007.* Bain & Company. Retrieved September 12, 2008, from http://www.bain.com/management_tools/Management_Tools_and_Trends_2007.pdf

Roberts, P., & Araujo, K. (1997). *The capitalist revolution in Latin America.* New York: Oxford University Press.

Santiso, J. (2006). *Latin America's political economy of the possible: Beyond good revolutionaries and free-marketeers.* Boston: MIT Press.

A special report on Brazil. (2007, April 14). *The Economist,* p. 10.

Strassmann, P. W. (1964). The industrialist. In J. Johnson (Ed.), *Continuity and change in Latin America* (pp. 161–185). Stanford, CA: Stanford University Press.

Trevino, L. (1998, May–June). Strategic responses of Mexican managers to economic reform. *Business Horizons, 41*(3), 73–80.

van Agtmael, A. (2007). *The emerging markets century: How a new breed of world class companies is overtaking the world.* New York: Free Press.

Wood, T. Jr. (2002). *Pop-management: MBAs no Brasil.* Fundação Getulio Vargas, Escola de Administração de Empresas de São Paulo. Retrieved September 12, 2008, from http://www.eaesp.fgvsp.br/Interna.aspx?PagId=DLMJMMTJ&ID=243

World Federation of Exchanges. (2007). *Annual report.* Retrieved September 12, 2008, from http://www.world-exchanges.org/WFE/home.Asp?nav=ns6

Zettelmeyer, J. (2006). *Growth and reforms in Latin America: A survey of facts and arguments.* International Monetary Fund working paper no. 06/210, from IMF World Economic Outlook database. Washington, DC: IMF.

Yesterday, Today, and Tomorrow 9

> *Somerset Maugham once remarked that to know one foreign country, it is necessary to know at least one other. This literary observation would seem to apply also to students of management . . . for in [this field] much interest is being elicited by what is happening abroad—particularly in comparative perspective.*
>
> —Jean Boddewyn (1969, Preface)

This book is about management, that is, getting things done through and with people in organized groups. Management purpose and process are universal, that is, applicable in all groups, business and non-business, small and large, local, national, regional, and global. However, management practice is situational, influenced by circumstances unique to each organization. In a business, that includes its size, accessible resources, competencies, experience, strengths, and limitations. These are continually influenced by management decision and action and by external forces, such as competition, economic and political currents, and social, demographic, technological, cultural, and educational change. A notable feature of this book is the coverage of cultural, economic, and political context (current and historical) in different settings.

By nature, management is a broad and interdisciplinary subject. For that reason, the content here has been selective, influenced by available research, writing, reporting, and opinion from which to synthesize discussion and conclusions. The focus has been mainly on bigger-scale business. Nonetheless, smaller business was included in the coverage of private Chinese enterprise (Chapter 6), Latin American family capitalism (Chapter 8), and examples of cooperative and communal enterprise (Chapter 5).

Whether in Europe, the Americas, Asia, or beyond, effective management requires astute judgment along with pertinent social and other skills, mind-sets, personal qualities, and experience. These coalesce throughout life from all social, intellectual, occupational, leisure, and other endeavor, including formal education.

Geared for higher education, this book brings a comparative perspective, attending to similarities and differences in management practice, performance, and environment in different settings. By learning about others, we can better understand ourselves and ascertain what can be adopted or adapted from others. It can also enhance engagement, cooperation, and competition with others.

The framework for this book has been the management process (broadly, the management functions of planning, controlling, organizing, directing, and staffing), a common orientation in most introductory management textbooks. However, few textbooks include much coverage of other nations and regions. One challenge has been to find conceptually equivalent treatment of similar themes in different settings. For some, there has not been much published information about contemporary managers and management. That applies certainly to Eastern Europe, Russia, Southeast Asia, India, and Africa and the Islamic world. For China, there is much yet to be investigated and reported about managerial developments there. By contrast, there is much more material for North America, Western Europe, and Japan. Even here, though, there is disparity in the nature, quality, availability, and comparability of information.

Exercise 9.1

Develop a brief bibliography of recently published books and articles focusing on managers and management in Russia, non-EU Europe, India, Africa, or the Middle East. From the titles and accessible abstracts, briefly describe what you find in terms of topics covered.

Note: Do not look for coverage about doing business in the country or region but rather about managers (including personal backgrounds) and issues, practices, and problems associated with planning, control, organizing, and directing of organizations.

Exercise 9.2

Beyond Western nations, management is less often viewed as an academic and professional discipline. That will change, though, with increasing mobility of people, goods, services, and information across national borders (globalization). All companies, domestic and cross-national, must deal sooner or later (directly or indirectly) with global context.

In the business press and other forums, the terms *international, multinational,* and *global* are often used interchangeably. Here, some distinctions are in order. For example, the term *international* can be applied to any enterprise with any cross-border business, ranging from modest sales and sourcing up to extensive foreign direct investment, licensing, and other involvement.

The term *multinational* applies if a significant proportion of a company's sales, earnings, assets, and employees are located outside its home country and it is active in several countries.

If proportions are high and widely dispersed, the company could be called *global*. However, few companies are yet truly global. In that regard, Rugman (2005) investigated the internationalness of a large sample (365+) of Fortune 500 companies. He categorized as global those with 20% or more of their sales revenue from each of three world regions (America, Europe, and Asia) but with no single region accounting for more than 50%. By that definition, he found only nine global firms.

A truly *global* company would be free of any strong national bias in terms of its investors, directors, senior managers, business strategies, and operations.

Assignment: Investigate a small number of companies located at or near the top of any national or international ranking of large companies. As best you can, determine the extent to which each is free from strong national bias.

Much relevant information can be found on individual company Web sites (including annual reports, company histories, and profiles of senior executives and directors).

Also,

1. Suggest some additional criteria with which to classify a company as global.

2. Identify societal forces that facilitate and restrain globalization.

3. In your opinion, to what degree, and how quickly, will business globalize during your lifetime?

4. Do you think management environment and practice around the world will converge over time? Discuss.

Exercise 9.3

Another take on globalization is at the individual level, that is, the degree to which individuals are free from national, regional, or cultural bias in terms of their mind-sets, competencies, and experience.

Assignment: Draft a list of specific criteria that could describe a globalized individual. In your opinion, do many individuals meet your criteria?

As was previously noted, this book includes considerable historical context. A sense of the past can bring useful perspective for present and future decisions and actions. For example, much insight can be gained from former Soviet socialist management context and practice (described in Chapter 4). An often-cited dictum applies here: Those who cannot remember the past are condemned to repeat its mistakes. The lessons of socialist management didn't end with the collapse of socialist economies. Their legacy continues to influence management mind-set and performance today in Russia and other former socialist states in transition toward more open economies (e.g., former Eastern Europe, China, Vietnam) (Puffer, Shekshnia, & McCarthy, 2005). Also, socialist-like context can show up even in advanced capitalist economies (e.g., United States, Western Europe) in any group without competition, autonomous goals, or valid and reliable performance criteria. It can occur in any cost center, that is, any group without autonomous profit and loss accountability. It applies to monopolies, nonprofit organizations, and most government enterprise and programs (e.g., public education, medical insurance, the military). These organizations show similarities with former socialist enterprise, including information omission or distortion, resource rationing, motivational shortcomings, and other problems requiring compensatory managerial (or contextual) adjustment.

In Russia itself, historical repercussions loom large (Exercise 9.4).

Exercise 9.4

In view of Russia's recent export growth (predominantly raw materials) and notable inward foreign investment, many economists see it on the verge of significant long-term economic growth. Political stability has also improved (although no mature democracy will emerge there soon).

In view of Russia's low labor costs and well-educated labor force, you, a Western CEO, have teamed up with an experienced Russian national to comanage a venture there to manufacture consumer goods for the internal market and Eastern Europe.

A veteran management consultant informs you that remnants of Soviet-era mind-set, practice, and style could complicate the management of the venture. What might this consultant have in mind? Discuss.

Historical context also permeates Chapters 2 and 3. The United States and Western Europe gave rise to most of the world's most successful economies and companies. European sociopolitical heritage contributed to a more egalitarian model of capitalism (welfare state capitalism; social market economy) oriented toward job and income protection and modest equalization of wealth and income through taxation and state social spending. This brought more state-owned enterprise (now much diminished) and more government intrusion in managerial autonomy (e.g., more oversight of acquisitions, mergers, and plant closures). It brought more mandatory consultation with labor interests (works councils, labor–management committees, and sometimes employee directors).

Despite these and other differences, both regions have many similarities, including their extensive economic and political freedom, emphasis on private initiative, independent media, mature legal systems, and well developed transportation, communication, and public service infrastructure. Both have seen gradual erosion of family ownership and control in bigger business and spread of professional management (separation of ownership from control).

Over the years, Western Europe has moved gradually toward the managerial and financial capitalism of the United States. One indication is declining blockholdership of shares (that is, ever more dispersed ownership). Europe now depends more than before on equity markets as an instrument of control, that is, to effect acquisitions, divestments, and mergers. Merger and buyout volume is now similar to that of the United States. Equity buyout and venture capital investment have risen. As was noted in Chapter 3, Western European CEO turnover is now at U.S. levels, much of it performance driven. Foreign influence in European stock and bond markets has grown (for example, more than one third of French corporate equity is now foreign owned). This has brought more attention to "shareholder value." A contributing factor has been regional economic integration (the European Union), which has brought more intense competition and gradual harmonization of business law, capital markets, and accounting and auditing practices.

Conversely, U.S. managers have been influenced by European context, thinking, and practice. For instance, Europeans more often separate the positions of CEO and chair of corporate boards of directors, an idea gaining greater attention in the U.S.

Exercise 9.5

It is less common (in custom and in law) in Western European public corporations (relative to ones in North America, East Asia, and Latin America) for the CEO (or a former one) to also chair a firm's board of directors. Discuss advantages and disadvantages of such a separation. In your judgment, would your list apply equally well in North America, the Far East, and Latin America? Explain.

Europeans have been less oriented toward the short-term financial reporting cycles of the United States and the frequent feedback U.S. firms provide stock analysts and investors about near-term earning projections. Change in those practices is being discussed in the United States. Also, the internationalness of European managers and business schools has pressured U.S. business schools to increase their proportion of international students and faculty and to internationalize their course and program content. European influence is also seen in discussion about high CEO pay (Exercise 9.6).

Exercise 9.6

As described in Chapters 3 and 4, American CEO pay has been substantially higher than in Europe. This sometimes creates a dilemma when a European firm buys or merges with a U.S. one. For example, in the 1998 Daimler-Benz acquisition of Chrysler, several senior Chrysler vice presidents (U.S. nationals on a U.S. pay scale) were being paid much more than their new German expatriate colleagues assigned to the United States and even more than the Daimler CEO in Germany.[1]

The intercontinental pay differences haven't been mainly in base salary but rather in supplemental pay (e.g., sign-on and retention bonuses, performance pay, and severance payouts). However, the incidence and size of incentive pay have been rising in Europe.

The European public and its media regularly criticize high executive pay and on occasion have forced pay givebacks by some managers. A few governments levy extra high taxes on extra-high salaries; some constrain the size of severance payouts (golden parachutes) for managers displaced by mergers and acquisitions.

Analogous concern about high compensation has emerged in the United States, especially when executive compensation hasn't correlated strongly with corporate performance (Colvin, 2008; "Hail, Shareholder," 2007; Morgenson, 2007). U.S. securities market regulators now require more detailed individual pay disclosure, and some stockholder groups more closely monitor and influence board-approved pay packages.

Questions:

1. In your view, why has there been a transatlantic pay gap for CEOs of large corporations?

2. Investigate whether the gap has shrunk or widened over time.

3. Does it, or should it, raise public social, ethical, or other concerns?

4. To what extent should government intervene in monitoring and regulating CEO pay?

European egalitarian values also show up in incidence of management by democracy (Chapter 5). This refers to bottom-up decision making and approval, review, and supervision of managerial appointments, decisions, and actions by rank-and-file employees. It is sometimes seen as the wave of the future. Its concept and practice have been compatible, historically, with both socialist and capitalist economic systems. As described in

Chapter 5, it was tried for several years in the former Yugoslavia before it split up into separate nations after 1990. Its purest form, conceptually, is in small communal enterprises. It has also been tried in cooperatives in diverse settings. It can occur in startups and professional partnerships (e.g., accounting, consulting, and law partnerships). Cooperative farming continues on a large scale in contemporary Russia.

Historically, its implementation has been problematic. In business, bottom-up control is seldom as successful as conventional organizational hierarchies when judged solely on economic grounds. And the degree of democracy is often weaker than anticipated, with not all people willing or able to participate actively.

Nonetheless, certain conditions can facilitate success, such as small organization size, selective membership, a stable macroenvironment, and strong personal and cultural bonds between members.

Exercise 9.7

In broadly owned professionally managed companies, the CEO typically is empowered to serve stockholder interests. Boards of directors are stewards of those and other stakeholder interests.

Directorship appointments can be influenced by law, company bylaws, and custom. Directors are often nominated by the CEO or by current directors. Stockholders seldom have much direct say in the matter.

Some sources propose that some or all board directors should be democratically elected from among competing candidates by majority vote of all shareholders (one share, one vote).

Question: What advantages and disadvantages do you see in adopting an electoral approach to selecting or removing board members?

Exercise 9.8

Many public universities (and some private ones) are controlled democratically by their faculty (professors, through a committee system) in tandem with hired professional administrators (e.g., presidents, provosts, vice presidents, deans). For example, senior administrative candidates are screened and recommended by faculty-led search committees. (These committees are often elected but are sometimes appointed.) Trustee, alumni, and community advisory boards may also have a voice in the process. The faculty periodically evaluate incumbent administrators' performance.

Full-time faculty are often regularly involved in choosing their department chairs and in the hiring, development, promotion, and retention of full-time colleagues. They also develop curricula and set academic standards. However, they rarely have much say in major financial decisions such as institutional budgets, student fee setting, and faculty and staff salaries. Other stakeholders such as administrative support staff, part-time instructors, and students generally have limited voice.

Assignment: Investigate and describe the extent of administrative democracy at your school (or one you are familiar with, or curious about, in any country).

Question: To what extent could or should stakeholders (e.g., students, faculty, administrators, support staff, community, public officials) have significant voice in academic, administrative, or other affairs? Discuss.

In recent decades much management interest has been directed toward East Asia (covered in Chapters 6 and 7). The earliest and most intense focus was on Japan because of its rapid recovery from World War II and pathbreaking firms in its leading industries (autos, consumer electronics). In 2008, 64 Japanese firms were listed on the *Fortune* magazine Global 500, more than in the rest of Asia combined.

In the 1980s, many outsiders saw a Japanese economy and management system worthy of emulation (Vogel, 1979). Interest led to many related books and articles (Keys & Miller, 1984).

Japan has had a government-guided free enterprise economy offering preferential support periodically to certain companies and industries, a pattern much repeated by South Korea and China. As described in Chapter 7, another prominent feature has been its business group alliances (*keiretsu*), with member firms relationally bound through cross-shareholding, preferential purchasing, information sharing, and other mutual support (convoy capitalism). The South Korean *chaebol* groups and Chinese government-supported "national champions" were inspired by the *keiretsu* (some differences between the *keiretsu* and *chaebol* were noted in Chapter 6).

When the Japanese economy faltered after the collapse of its stock and real estate price bubbles, an extended period of stagnation followed (after 1990). In retrospect, the Japanese economic, business, and management systems contributed to the stagnation and delayed recovery. For example, important economic stakeholders were long disadvantaged. The emphasis was on preserving job security. Shareholder interests were secondary. Persistent trade and investment protectionism raised prices for consumers. Whatever outside shareholders could reap from capital gains (share price appreciation) was lost when the stock market collapsed and didn't recover. (In late 2008, the Nikkei 225 share price index was still 50% below its 1989 all-time high.) Government-controlled banks long capped depository interest rates, to the detriment of savers. Relational ties between borrowers and lenders overlooked credit risk, contributing to a high proportion of non-performing loans. The stock and real estate market collapse eroded the collateral that was backing the loans. A government bailout of lenders pushed the burden onto taxpayers. High government spending intended to perk up the economy contributed to a high level of government debt.

Exercise 9.9

As this book was in its final stages (late 2008), the United States and much of the world were experiencing a financial crisis that some see as similar to the one that plagued Japan. Circumstances included deflation of real estate price bubbles, excessive nonperforming loans, liquidity problems in many financial institutions, falling stock price indices, and widespread financial uncertainty. This brought bankruptcies (e.g., Lehman Brothers investment bank), government-guided workouts and rescues (e.g., the purchase and merger of Countrywide Bank and Merrill-Lynch by the Bank of America), temporary government takeovers (e.g., of U.S. mortgage guarantors Fannie Mae and Freddie Mac), and government (taxpayer-funded) funding for private companies judged to be too large and too important to fail (e.g., AIG insurance group).

Question: What has evolved (both locally and globally) in regard to the aforementioned crisis? In reflecting on the societal macroenvironment and on the corporate managerial tendencies and traditions in both the United States (Chapter 2) and Japan (Chapter 7), do you think the West will weather the financial storm any better than did Japan? Discuss.

Exercise 9.10

Lars-Olaf Anderson, a Swede, and his long-standing Japanese colleague Miya (Nakamura) Michel have been successfully teamed up in Europe for years as executive search consultants, helping firms find senior and midlevel managers for positions in the European Union, the United States, and Canada. This dynamic duo first met in graduate school (an MBA program in France) and later founded the boutique executive search firm Nakamura–Anderson in London, where both currently reside with their spouses.

Miya's husband is French, and Lars-Olaf's wife is British. Miya has two university-age daughters, one studying Japanese in Japan (living there with relatives) and the other a theater arts student in Quebec. Lars-Olaf's son has entered an East Asia study program in Hawaii.

Nakamura–Anderson's services are typically compensated by a client fee equal to one third of each placement's first-year cash compensation. Part of the fee is paid in advance, before starting a search.

Now facing intense search competition in Europe, the firm is looking for new horizons. In that regard, a German exporter of advanced endoscopic surgical systems recently approached them about an urgent need for a CEO in Japan. Miya and Lars-Olaf have agreed to test the waters with a preliminary search while exploring and developing contacts there. They know that Japan has been one of the least international countries in terms of cultural diversity, imports, and immigrant and temporary visas and work permits.

Also, traditional Japanese management and recruitment practices make executive search seem daunting. The Association of Executive Search Consultants reported last year that the Asia-Pacific region (including Japan) accounted for less than 20% of member firm searches (compared with 70% for North America and Europe).

Nonetheless, economic and cultural change in Japan may well improve their chances for success. They hope to find more midcareer job changers who now have no hope for career-long employment with their current employers. They note that big U.S. search firms Korn/Ferry and Heidrick & Struggles already have a presence there.

Questions:

1. In view of Japan's managerial traditions and from what you have heard and read about recent change there, how do you assess Nakamura–Anderson's prospects for success for their German client and others?

2. If they proceed, how should they go about finding candidates?

3. Should they limit their search to Japanese nationals?

4. To what extent might candidate age, gender, and national origin influence candidate selection and recruitment?

5. In what ways might they need to modify their search practices for the Japanese market? Explain.

Apart from Japan, much world attention has also been directed toward other Confucian zone economies (South Korea, Taiwan, Singapore, Hong Kong, and China).

Hong Kong and Singapore are affluent microeconomies, with much success based on their economic freedom, a stable legal environment, a competent labor force, and a strong work ethic. Both have regularly ranked at or near the top of world indices of economic freedom and business competitiveness.

Like Japan, South Korea has had a government-guided free enterprise system, including a similar-style trade and investment protectionism and preferential support for certain businesses (including *chaebol*). However, economists question whether the Japanese and South Korean economic progress occurred because of or in spite of government guidance, protection, and support. It is also noteworthy that in both settings, enterprise groupism and economic isolationism are now viewed as detrimental to long-term competitiveness. The South Korean government has curtailed preferential support for *chaebol* enterprises and pressured them to reduce intragroup loan guarantees and cross-shareholdings. In the Japanese *keiretsu* groups, too, relational ties and cross-shareholdings have been eroding.

China has been attracting much attention in its transition toward greater economic freedom. As noted in Chapter 6, it has a mixed economy (state-owned, cooperative–communal, and private enterprise). Most of its biggest firms are state owned remnants from the state socialist era. However, its private sector has grown dramatically and so has inward private foreign investment.

The Chinese government has also been intervening in the economy to foster "national champions" it hopes will succeed globally. Some candidates include so-called red-chip enterprises, some in the mold of *keiretsu* and *chaebol*. The red chips are government-controlled firms incorporated in Hong Kong or abroad (e.g., in the United States, Singapore) but with most of their business activity on the mainland (De Trenck, Cartledge, Daswani, Katz, & Sakmar, 1998). Some examples include the China International Trust and Investment Company (now called the CITIC Group), Guangdong Enterprises, and Beijing Enterprises Holdings.

Exercise 9.11

From the list of Chinese "national champion" companies listed in Table 6.8 (Chapter 6) or that of Hong Kong–registered red chip corporations (http://en .wikipedia.org/wiki/Hang_Seng_China-Affiliated_Corporations_Index), compare the personal managerial backgrounds of any two company CEOs. From their corporate Web sites and other Web resources, investigate their age, education, gender, tenure, pay, experience, and any apparent criteria by which they attained their position.

Question: In what significant ways do their personal backgrounds differ from those of CEOs of large firms in your home region or country?

As noted in Chapter 6, it has not been usual, historically, for private sector Chinese to create and manage large vertically integrated companies comparable to titans found in Japan, South Korea, and the West. Despite size handicaps, some small and medium-size ones (e.g., in Taiwan, in Hong Kong, and on the mainland) can attain virtual large size through extensive business networking. This has been evident in Taiwanese shoe and electronics contract manufacturers that operate throughout East Asia. Drawing from widespread personal connections, they tap the capabilities and resources of many businesses. Their ties are viewed as more intense and more flexible than the traditional arm's-length contractual ties and alliances between Western firms.

In Western academic circles, there is ongoing debate about whether such network structures are a unique organizational innovation, a prototype to emulate or adapt elsewhere. Interest has contributed to a subset of organization and management theory called network theory (Borgatti & Foster, 2003). However, the countervailing view is that the ethnic Chinese business networks are unique to a particular time, place, and context in which technology and markets move very quickly (Borgatti, 2001).

Exercise 9.12

Suggested examples of network organizations include Taiwan-based electronic contract manufacturers such as Hon Hai Precision Industry, Acer, Quanta, and others engaged in computer and communications equipment and related peripherals, subassembly, and components. Another, Yue Yuen Industrial, has focused on footwear and textiles. These compete on the basis of high-quality, effective supply chain logistics and fast turnaround times, through extensive and flexible supplier networks.

Assignment: Discuss the extent to which you think private Chinese-style network organization structures have promise for adoption beyond East Asia.

Latin America (covered in Chapter 8) has been a much-overlooked region in terms of its business and management patterns and traditions. Its commercial and industrial history has focused on family-controlled firms and business groups (family capitalism). Many small and medium-size firms there were founded by European immigrants or their immediate descendants and continue to be run by family members.

Managers in the region face contextual constraints common to emerging economies, including underdeveloped infrastructure (e.g., transportation, communication, energy), lagging educational systems, and excessive (and often incompetent) government intrusion in business.

Undercurrents of nationalism, populism, and anticapitalist ideology impede fuller economic freedom. The region has lagged most of Confucian Asia in terms of economic development. Nonetheless, there has been significant progress in places such as Chile, southern Brazil, and northern Mexico. And there are many competitive Latin American multinational enterprises and cross-national business alliances. In a recent selection of the top 25 world-class multinationals from emerging economies (van Agtmael, 2007), 10 hailed from Latin America (compared with 9 from Taiwan, South Korea, and China combined and 3 from India). There has also been deepening of Latin American banking and capital markets, notably in Brazil and Mexico. As occurred previously in the United States and Western Europe, family-based capitalism has been yielding, albeit slowly, to managerial and financial capitalism.

Exercise 9.13

You are the senior vice president for human resources in a Dutch consumer goods company that is strongly considering a woman to head its Argentine subsidiary (a 3-year assignment in Buenos Aires). Her name is Nora Kurtin Bejar, age 42, originally from Argentina but now residing in Madrid, Spain. Her predecessor in the Argentine position was a highly successful local man of Italian background who has been promoted to headquarters in Amsterdam.

There are few female CEOs in Latin America, and many are often relatives of founder–owners. You have concluded that Nora is a worthy candidate. She holds a bachelor's degree in business administration from St. Louis University (United States) and an MBA from Madrid's Instituto de Empresa, a leading private European business school.

Nora's husband, Agustín, is employed by Deutsch Telecom (a German firm) in Spain. They have two young children, ages 5 and 7. The pair are willing to move temporarily to Argentina (her parents and other relatives live in Buenos Aires), and Deutsch Telecom has agreed to transfer Agustín to help consolidate some operations in Argentina and Brazil.

After earning her MBA, Nora worked for 3 years in strategic planning in Europe for French food and facility management service firm Sodexho, followed by 6 years with Johnson & Johnson (U.S. subsidiary in Spain), where she ascended to vice president.

Upon hearing that Latin America has a predominantly male-dominated business culture and few senior female executives, your CEO is hesitant to make the choice and has asked for your impartial analysis. What arguments, pro and con, can you make for naming Nora to the position?

Note

1. Daimler and Chrysler parted ways in 2007.

References

Boddewyn, J. (1969). *Comparative management and marketing.* Glenview, IL: Scott, Foresman.

Borgatti, S. (2001). *Virtual/network organizations.* Retrieved September 19, 2008, from http://analytictech.com/mb021/virtual.htm

Borgatti, S., & Foster, P. (2003). The network paradigm in organizational research: A review and typology. *Journal of Management, 29*(6), 991–1013.

Colvin, G. (2008, April 28). Rewarding failure. *Fortune,* p. 22.

De Trenck, C., Cartledge, S., Daswani, A., Katz, C., & Sakmar, D. (1998). *Red chips and the globalization of China's enterprises.* Hong Kong: Asia 2000 Ltd.

Hail, shareholder. (2007, June 2). *The Economist,* pp. 65–66.

Keys, J., & Miller, T. (1984). The Japanese management theory jungle. *Academy of Management Review, 9*(2), 342–353.

Morgenson, G. (2007, June 17). Hear ye, hear ye: Corralling executive pay. *New York Times,* Sec. 3, p. 1.

Puffer, S., Shekshnia, S., & McCarthy, D. (2005). *Corporate governance in Russia.* Cheltenham, UK: Edward Elgar.

Rugman, A. (2005). *The regional multinationals, MNEs and "global" strategic management.* Cambridge, UK: Cambridge University Press.

van Agtmael, A. (2007). *The emerging markets century: How a new breed of world-class companies is overtaking the world.* New York: The Free Press.

Vogel, E. (1979). *Japan as number one: Lessons for America.* Cambridge, MA: Harvard University Press.

Index

About the Author

Ralph B. Edfelt is Emeritus Professor of Management and International Business at San Jose State University, in California's Silicon Valley, a pioneer in its international business studies program (since 1976). His teaching assignments have included International Business, International & Comparative Management, and Business Strategy. Professional affiliations include the Academy of International Business and Academy of Management. His published articles have appeared in *Long Range Planning*, *Comparative Education Review*, *California Management Review*, *The Information Society*, and other publications.

Born to Swedish immigrant parents in Washington State, his undergraduate study was at the University of Washington (BA, Geography, 1963). He holds an MA in Latin American Studies (1968) and a PhD in Management (1975) from the University of California, Los Angeles.

Dr. Edfelt has several years' life experience in Latin America, including study at Mexico's National Autonomous University (UNAM), master's thesis research in Venezuela, and a year of doctoral research in Brazil. He served 2 years in the U.S. Peace Corps in Venezuela, followed by Viet-Nam-era military service in Panama, where linked to the Inter-American Geodetic Survey (Natural Resources Division). His spouse is from Argentina.

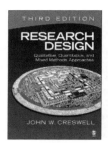

Made in the USA
Monee, IL
15 March 2020